A CENTURY OF TRIUMPH
THE HISTORY OF AVIATION

CHRISTOPHER CHANT

ILLUSTRATIONS BY JOHN BATCHELOR

THE FREE PRESS

NEW YORK   LONDON   TORONTO   SYDNEY   SINGAPORE

*f*P

THE FREE PRESS

A Division of Simon & Schuster, Inc.

1230 Avenue of the Americas

New York, NY 10020

For information about special discounts for bulk purchases,

please contact Simon & Schuster Special Sales:

1-800-456-6798 or business@simonandschuster.com

Design by Vertigo Design, NYC

Manufactured in the United States of America

10 9 8 7 6 5 4 3 2 1

Library of Congress Cataloging-in-Publication Data

Chant, Christopher.

A century of triumph: the history of aviation / Christopher Chant; illustrations by John Batchelor.

p. cm.

Includes index.

1. Aeronautics—History. I. Title.

TL515 .C38323 2002

629.13'09—dc21   2002073944

ISBN 0-7432-3479-0

CONTENTS

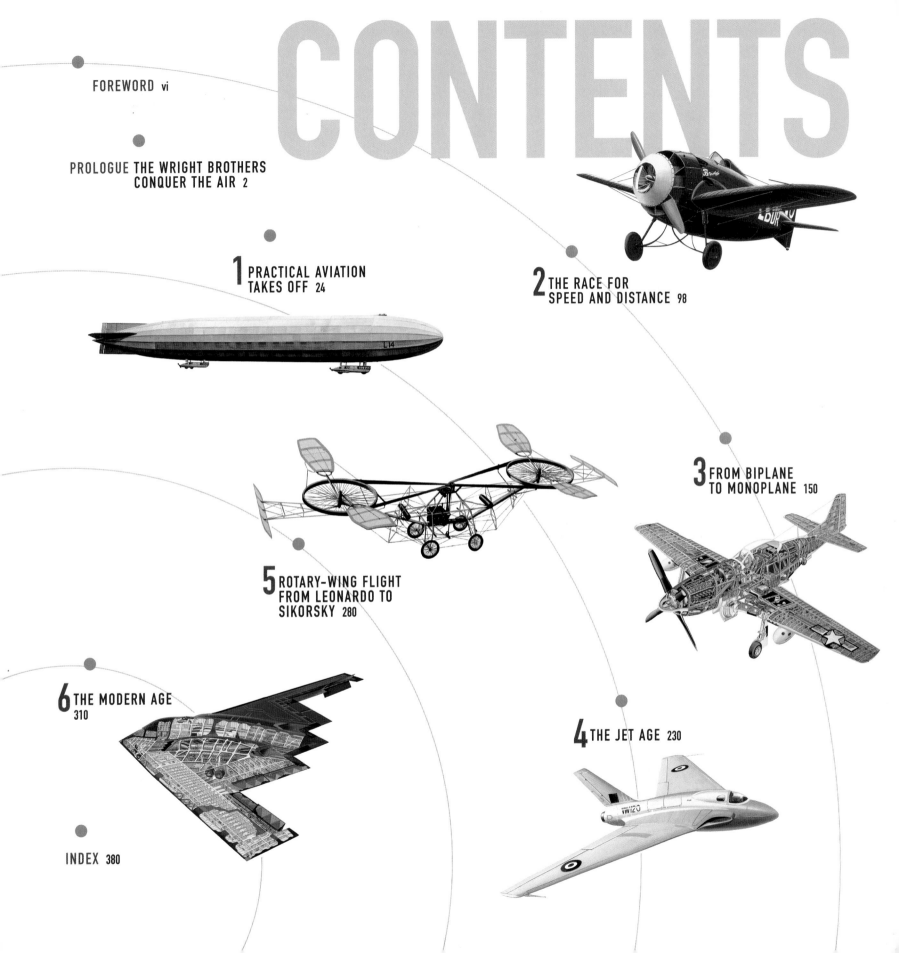

FOREWORD:
GREAT MOMENTS IN AVIATION HISTORY

A LOOK BACK AT THE CREATION OF THE VOYAGER:
SMALL TEAM, GIANT CHALLENGE

BY BURT RUTAN

Since 1972, when I left my government job testing U.S. Air Force aircraft, I have had the privilege to work with small groups in a true entrepreneurial environment to develop and test over thirty new aircraft types. Of these, the *Voyager* was the most rewarding because the goal of a globe-circling, nonrefueled craft was so challenging, and because the six-member development team (during the initial phase) was free to make its own rules. We had to develop an aircraft that could double the world's distance record, and we had very limited resources. Our original plan was to obtain funding from a major sponsor and to contract out much of the aircraft's fabrication. When we failed to find a sponsor, we decided to structure a two-phase development program. The first phase—managed by Rutan Aircraft Factory, my homebuilt aircraft company—developed the basic *Voyager* design and got the prototype into initial flight test. The phase-one team was only a few people, including the flight crew; they worked quickly and in secrecy. The second phase—managed by my brother's company, Voyager Aircraft Inc.—was responsible for getting the aircraft equipped for long-range flight, testing the refined systems, and flying the record-setting distances. This team, including volunteers, was larger and addressed the many complex disciplines of navigation (in a pre-Global Positioning Satellite era), world communication, and weather planning. Both phases were financially possible only because manufacturers and material suppliers eagerly agreed to donate their products.

For me as a designer, the most rewarding aspect of the *Voyager* program was the difficult technical challenge. I knew the required range was possible, but it was achievable only by applying our very best efforts. The range of an aircraft is determined by three basic criteria: its propulsion efficiency, its weight, and its aerodynamic efficiency. I had to make major improvements in one or more of these areas in order to build an aircraft that could fly more than twice as far as any previous flight.

To maximize propulsion efficiency I used engine staging: After the first several days of the trip one engine was shut down so the remaining engine could then operate at a higher, more efficient power setting. The primary reason we were able to double the old distance record related to our success in weight control. By using a new, unusual configuration, we could place a large amount of fuel at the fuselage and two large booms at 30 percent of the distance out to the wingtips. A very light main wing and canard wing provided just the amount of structural support for this large fuel mass. Having two lightweight wings to support the fuel-laden booms was *Voyager*'s secret to success. The fuel comprised 73 percent of the craft's total takeoff weight. This phenomenal weight performance was the main reason we were able to achieve a range in excess of 13,000 statute miles.

The risks we took for *Voyager*'s launch on the early morning of December 14, 1986, were high indeed. The aircraft, loaded to a gross weight of 9,700 pounds, was 15 percent heavier than it had ever been in midair. This new weight would nearly double the runway required at the heaviest flight before this one. The structural dynamics were expected to be very bad, maybe even uncontrollable. An earlier trip had left the crew exhausted from flying the *Voyager* in turbulence for only a few hours. Now they were to head off over the Pacific with its equatorial storms, not to land again for more than nine days. In its 2½-year test program of sixty-four flights totaling 340 hours the *Voyager* had experienced many systems failures. Several of these resulted in an inability to maintain altitude and an emergency landing. The flight plan of the world route was for 225 hours, the vast majority of it over oceans. Most of the time they would be positioned many hours from the nearest airport.

Looking back now at these risks, it is easy to conclude that we should not have attempted the flight. However, in late 1986, we were filled with adrenaline even though exhausted after a five-year research and development program. We were thinking of little else except the chance to reach the goal. Today, as I recall our activities from the concept layout in 1981 to the world flight in late 1986, the hard part was not the design, but the details of building and testing a large, complex aircraft. The job proved to be much more difficult than any of us predicted. Much of that five-year effort involved long hours of hard work from a small group with modest resources. The excitement of someday achieving a historically significant aviation milestone was what motivated the team. Our close-knit group operated in an environment that allowed us to revise the ground rules and quickly decide to accept a new risk. This, more than any other factor, helped us to achieve new heights and is the reason that significant new breakthroughs are rarely seen in typical research and development programs.

ONE MAN'S BEING THERE

BY EUGENE A. CERNAN

When one departs his home in Earth orbit and leaves behind the safety and comfort of his own planet, things suddenly become "different." The horizon, once slightly curved, now closes around and upon itself, evoking a strange, yet familiar sight. No longer are you speeding over oceans and continents in a matter of moments, but now find yourself peering across their entirety. Those magnificently beautiful sunrises and sunsets which once occurred each ninety minutes during your traverse around our world are somehow "happening" before your very eyes. All this while heading out at 25,000 mph for a rendezvous somewhere in space with another body in our universe—someplace we have chosen to call the Moon. As Earth grows smaller—quickly at first, then more slowly as we approach our destination a quarter million miles from home—it continues to revolve mysteriously yet majestically through the heavens with logic and purpose, reinforcing a belief that "it is just too beautiful to have happened by accident." The landing on the Moon, orchestrated within this now almost natural environment, was perhaps the most demanding dozen minutes of my lifetime. The Valley of Taurus Littrow, our home, our Camelot for the next three days, was carved out of rugged lunar terrain, surrounded on three sides by mountains reaching higher than the Grand Canyon is deep. Those first steps, although taken by others, were now for me a challenge not to be denied. A fantasy? Perhaps. Even thirty years later, I must admit it is sometimes difficult to accept such an event. But then, looking over my shoulder, there was the Earth—hovering with all its warmth and beauty low on the horizon just above that mountain in the southwestern sky of our Moon—my only identity with reality from a place where "reality itself was almost like a dream."

This moment in history of "one man's being there" is now the legacy of a nation—a rare privilege I'm proud to share with you.

A CENTURY OF TRIUMPH
THE HISTORY OF AVIATION

PROLOGUE
THE WRIGHT BROTHERS
CONQUER THE AIR

The first man to reach a full understanding of the forces working on an airplane in flight was Sir George Cayley, who committed his concept to posterity in the form of a 1799 engraving on a silver disc.

Man is a dreaming animal, the only one to possess imagination. This defining capability has been of paramount importance in his evolution into a tool-user and an artist. Sometimes, human creativity produces artifacts that are both useful *and* attractive. There are many machines that possess a functional beauty, that work well because they look right, and vice versa. Aircraft may be the most beautiful and useful of all.

The desire for flight is probably one of the oldest in human experience, and yet it has been among the most recent to be achieved. From his earliest days man looked up into the sky and envied the bird, and until very recent times bird flight has been featured strongly in folklore and the arts. So it is hardly surprising that man has long sought to rival the flight of birds. At first, he did so quite literally, with ornithoptering, or flapping wings in flying machines.

The experimenters were a strange mix: Some of them, such as the great Leonardo da Vinci, were visionaries, others were eccentrics or even fanatics. These pioneers pursued false leads with an enthusiasm that was often fatal, and the public almost always, and with strong justification, dubbed them madmen. Only in 1783 did man finally manage to leave the ground for the first time in the hot-air balloon built in France by the Montgolfier brothers. Shortly after this Sir George Cayley, an eccentric and underestimated British pioneer, formulated the problem of heavier-than-air flight on a scientific basis and evolved the basic layout of the machine that would overcome it. Though few said so at the time, success was inevitable once the internal combustion engine had been developed during the last quarter of the nineteenth century, and indeed the Wright brothers marked the start of a glorious new era in December 1903.

It is with the age of aviation brought about by the genius of the Wright brothers that this book is concerned. But this is less an account of aircraft than a story of the relationship of people and their flying machines. There are few people in the developed world who have not been affected by powered flight. Some have also been the victims of aircraft, especially in World War II, and in the fear of annihilation by nuclear weapons that can be delivered, among other means, by strategic bombers. Most have primarily benefited from air travel as a crucial component of economic life.

But there are other aspects of aviation that are closer to man's original inspiration for flight: a desire to emulate the birds for no reason other than for the joy and the delight of it. Just as interesting as the "hard" relationship of economic dependence is the "soft" relationship of sport flying, gliding, aerobatics, and racing, usually in aircraft designed, built, or extensively modified by their pilots or by small organizations.

This book tells the stories of civil, military, and private aviation, touching on such heroes and heroines as Manfred von Richthofen, Charles Lindbergh, Amy Johnson, and Amelia Earhart, and the attraction to the drama of events such as the first great aviation meeting at Reims in France during 1909, the MacRobertson air race from the United Kingdom to Australia in 1934, the great seaplane races between France, Italy, the United Kingdom, and the United States for the Schneider Trophy in the 1920s, and the National Air Races that attained massive popularity in the United States during the 1920s and 1930s before making a strong comeback in the public mind over more recent years.

The story of aviation is a history of the relationship between man and airplane in its technical, social, political, economic, and emotional aspects. It is a story not so much of what men and their flying machines have done, but of why they have done it and why they have been able to do so. It is a history of motive as well as of deed. The history of powered flight during the century since 1903 is in many respects a reflection of the best and worst of our civilization.

KITTY HAWK AND BEFORE

The first successful flight in a heavier-than-air machine was the first of four made by the Wright brothers, Orville and Wilbur, on December 17, 1903. These four flights marked the start of practical aviation. They were also the culmination of efforts over the previous century, so the work of earlier pioneers, some of them realists and others mere dreamers, should not be discounted.

It was only after four years of experimental work with gliders that the Wright brothers were finally ready with their first powered heavier-than-air craft, which was a machine driven by a 12-hp (8.9-kW) engine they themselves had designed and an assistant built. The Flyer was crated for transport from the Wright establishment in Dayton, Ohio, to the Kill Devil Hills, North Carolina, where the machine was reassembled in December 1903. The brothers chose this site not for its remote location, although they were certainly concerned to keep the details of their machine secret until they were in a position to exploit its commercial potential, but for its moderately strong and steady wind, which had greatly aided the brothers' gliding experiments in previous years.

It was Wilbur who made the first attempt at a powered flight on December 14, but the flight was unsuccessful when coarse movement of the elevator control sent the Flyer into the sand as it left its takeoff trolley. The brothers' team completed repairs over the following days, and on December 17 the brothers were once again ready to continue. After five local witnesses had arrived, Orville took his place prone on the lower wing of the Flyer, opened the engine's throttle, and signaled for the machine to be released. The Flyer gathered speed down the 60-ft (18-m) rail that had been laid into the wind and, as it reached its flying speed of about 25 mph (40 km/h), lifted off the trolley and entered wing-borne flight. Twelve seconds later the Flyer touched down after flying about 120 ft (150 m) through the air. The time was shortly after 10:35 in the morning. During the next 90 minutes, the brothers achieved three more flights. The last of them was made with Wilbur at the controls, and was the most successful flight of the day, the Flyer covering more than 852 ft (800 m) in the air during 59 seconds.

The Wright brothers thus became the first men anywhere in the world to fly a heavier-than-air craft able to satisfy the four primary criteria for successful powered flight: the ability to take off from level ground, travel through the air under its own power, be effectively controlled during its flight in all three dimensions, and land at a spot not significantly lower than the takeoff point.

The day's historic events were reported to the press, but amazingly this turning point in history received little coverage, and in general was ignored. Without any fuss, the Wrights then disassembled the Flyer and transported it back to Dayton, where they set about the construction of a new machine that incorporated the lessons learned in North Carolina with the Flyer, or Flyer I as it is now generally known.

The Wrights were the first men to fly successfully under power, but others had flown without it. Cayley, for instance, had arrived at a neat summary of the factors controlling flight just over 100 years earlier. In 1799 he had defined his theory about the forces acting on a body in flight and inscribed the resulting diagram on a silver disc. On the other side of the disc was a simple drawing of a glider containing all the elements necessary for flight. Cayley continued to work on the idea of flight at intervals during the next 50 years before building a full-scale model in 1849. The control surfaces had to be fixed before flight, but several short glides were made with the machine in ballast before Cayley decided that he had progressed sufficiently for an experiment with a live passenger, the son of a worker from his estate near Scarborough in the county of Yorkshire. Although he was only a passenger, the unknown boy has the distinction of being the first person to fly in a heavier-than-air machine. Cayley continued with his design work, and in 1853 produced an improved glider in which his coachman was launched across a small valley on the estate. Cayley worked on the theory of flight until 1855.

Cayley might have achieved considerably more if an adequate power source had been available to him. Cayley did experiment with various types of engines, but none of these proved successful. This lack of an adequate powerplant also affected the work of other pioneers for the next quarter century until a German, Nikolaus A. Otto, perfected his four-stroke internal combustion engine. The pioneers of flight had to wait nearly another 25 years before engine technology could provide a powerplant with the right power/weight ratio.

The drawing boards of these men were littered with a multitude of designs notable for their widely differing practicality and safety. Some designs were translated into hardware: a minority saw the light of day as gliders, but the majority appeared as powered, unmanned machines with their creators' hopes pinned on an assortment of gas, steam, or even gunpowder engines.

One of the earliest of these pioneers was a Frenchman, Félix du Temple, who in 1857 made his first successful powered model airplane, and in about the same year built a full-sized monoplane with which the designer tinkered until 1874. The du Temple monoplane, with a swept-forward wing, became the first powered airplane to take off, although this may be overstating the case: The airplane careered down and then off a ramp, but was incapable of sustained flight and came down almost immediately after its launch.

Some 16 years later, in 1890, the Eole, designed by Clément Ader, another Frenchman, became the world's first airplane to take off from level ground. This was a genuinely unusual machine configured something like a bat, with a fuselage-mounted 20-hp (14.9-kW) steam engine driving a large tractor propeller. The machine took off and moved some 160 ft (50 m) through the air on October 9, 1890, but this can in no way be considered a true flight, as the Eole lacked any type of control surface and was incapable of sustained flight. Even so, Ader was highly encouraged by his "success."

While it had been Cayley who had first developed the theory of lift through the use of cambered wing surfaces, it was to be almost 100 years before Horatio Phillips, another Briton and the world's first great aerodynamicist, patented his theory of lift based on different degrees of camber between the upper and lower surfaces of the wing section. The idea was that if the curvature of the upper surface of a wing is greater than that of its lower surface, the air flows over the upper surface at a greater velocity and thus declines in pressure relative to the air flowing across the lower surface. An upward force, generally known as "lift," is thereby generated as the higher pressure under the wing seeks to equalize the pressure differential with the lower-pressure air above the wing. His first patent was granted in 1884, and in 1891 Phillips made and flew a large multiplane model whose cellule of superimposed and very narrow-chord wings resembled a Venetian blind. Phillips's thinking and practical experiments were of great importance to all later aircraft pioneers, for this far-sighted Englishman had paved the way into the future by creating a theory of true aerodynamic lift in place of the planing lift used in kites and earlier powered aircraft.

Over the years much has been claimed at times for the huge "flying machine" built in 1894 by Hiram Maxim, better known as the inventor of the first true machine gun. In reality little can be said for Maxim's biplane machine, which was monumentally costly and was really a test rig for the investigation of lift. Powered by two 180-hp (134-kW) steam engines each driving a propeller with a diameter of almost 18 ft (5.49 m), the test rig ran on a two-rail track and was prevented from rising more than a few inches by wooden guard rails. During the course of a test run in July 1894 the machine produced enough lift to rise from its supporting track and break through the guardrails. It then crashed, as there was no means of controlling the machine in the air. Maxim abandoned his efforts, but later attempted to secure another place in history for himself by making extravagant claims for his rig.

In 1897 Ader produced the Avion III as his third full-sized machine after abandoning his Avion II while still incomplete in 1892. The Avion III was similar to the Eole in basic layout, but was powered by two 20-hp (14.9-kW) steam engines driving two counter-rotating propellers. As with the earliest Ader machines, the Avion III had no adequate provision for control in the air, but this was not a problem, as on both the occasions on which it was tested the Avion III refused to leave the ground. Nevertheless, claims for Ader to be considered the first man to fly have been made at various times since the beginning of the century.

OTTO LILIENTHAL AND THE GLIDER

Realizing that there was no immediate prospect of an engine offering a power/weight ratio adequate for success, more practically minded pioneers saw that gliding flight, in which the pull of gravity replaces the thrust of the propeller, offered the opportunity for more limited but real advance. Chief among these exponents of gliding was Otto Lilienthal, the great German pioneer. Lilienthal was happy to advance by a process of slow evolutionary steps, and therefore did not seek to launch anything into the air until he had fully considered its capabilities. In common with many other pioneers, Lilienthal possessed a fascination with the flight of birds but, unlike many of these others, did not believe that the answer to human flight lay in a slavish imitation of them. Lilienthal instead established the basic principles of bird flight and then applied the principles to a structure that was mechanically adequate to the forces that would be exerted on it. In 1889 Lilienthal published his findings in a book entitled *Der Vogelflug als Grundlage der Fliegekunst (Bird Flight as the Basis of Aviation)*, which soon became one of the "bibles" of subsequent pioneers.

Lilienthal built his first successful glider in 1891, and by 1894 had developed the standard monoplane glider that proved highly successful and appeared in so many photographs of the period. Lilienthal's gliders were not without their faults and limitations, but they proved that heavier-than-air flight was indeed possible. This did much to increase a general enthusiasm for flight and also encouraged other pioneers.

Lilienthal's control system was based on the movement of the glider's center of gravity rather than of control surfaces. This was inevitable as a result of the light weight and flimsy structures of Lilienthal's machines, which could not easily have been made to incorporate moving surfaces and their controlling cables. The pilot hung with his upper chest in a gap between the wings so that his lower torso and legs could swing anywhere in the hemisphere below him: He moved them in the direction he wished his craft to go, the movement of the center of gravity in that direction effecting the change. This system obviated the need for landing gear, as the pilot merely ran down his chosen slope until he had reached flying speed and lifted off; landing was simply effected by touching down onto his feet.

Lilienthal went off at a tangent in 1896 when he started to experiment with ornithoptering (flapping) wings powered by a small gas engine. There is every reason to expect that he would soon have switched to a more practical form of propulsion, but on August 9, 1896, Lilienthal stalled during a flight, crashed, and died in hospital the follow-

OTTO LILIENTHAL AND THE GLIDER

OTTO LILIENTHAL (1848–96) The significance of Otto Lilienthal in the development of
heavier-than-air flight has been neatly summarized in the sentence "If Cayley is aviation's grandfather, Otto Lilienthal is its uncle." Lilienthal was born on May 23, 1848, in
Anklam, Prussia (now Germany). After graduating from the trade school at Potsdam
and the Berlin Trade Academy, he began to experiment with model gliders of the
ornithoptering and fixed-wing varieties. His book *Der Vogelflug als Grundlage der
Fliegekunst* and his essays on flying machines soon came to be recognized as some of the
most important basic works on flight. The Wright brothers made it abundantly clear

The first man to fly
successfully in a
heavier-than-air
plane was the
German Otto
Lilienthal, captured
by the camera in
1894 as he pilots
one of his "standard"
type of hang gliders
after launching
himself and his
machine from the
top of an artificial
mound.

that Lilienthal was a seminal source of inspiration for their efforts. Certainly the brothers' early thinking about the problem of flight was derived largely from Lilienthal's concepts and experience.

Up to 1881, efforts to create heavier-than-air flying machines had been spasmodic, but Lilienthal changed that by turning aviation from a subject on the fringes of respectable thinking to one worthy of reputable researchers. Lilienthal was the first to engage in practical, rather than far-fetched, experiments. In a mere five years of active work in the 1890s, Lilienthal created no fewer than 18 different glider types, 15 of them monoplanes and the other three biplanes. Each was a hang glider, controlled by the movement of the pilot's weight rather than activation of any moving control surfaces.

The writer Sir Charles Gibbs-Smith once classified the pioneers of aviation into "chauffeurs of the air" and "airmen." The former conceived of piloting an airplane as nothing more than the management of a road vehicle, with emphasis on power rather than lift and control, while the latter understood that movement through air was a fluid task requiring an altogether different and more intuitive approach in piloting skills. Lilienthal was most decidedly an "airman."

His No. 1 Glider was a tailless contraption comprising little more than a pair of wings. He tested this glider by jumping off a board, and it was wholly unsuccessful. His first successful type was the No. 3 Glider monoplane of 1891, and the rate of Lilienthal's progress accelerated after he had built an artificial mound, in Lichterfelde outside Berlin, from which he could take off regardless of the wind direction. Lilienthal also used the Gollenberg hill near Stölln and other natural features for the higher takeoff points that opened the way to longer glides.

Lilienthal's Glider No. 11 of 1894, the Normal-Segelapparat (standard glider), made his name and spurred the creation of at least eight copies. The Glider No. 11 was a monoplane with a wing of 139.94 sq ft (13 m^2), and it worked well. However, it was on this glider that Lilienthal suffered the accident that led to his death: After taking off from the Gollenberg, the glider was brought to a halt by a gust, the starboard wing then dropped, and the glider sideslipped into the ground from a height of some 50 ft (15 m). On the following day, August 10, 1896, the great German pioneer died of his injuries at the Bergmann Clinic in Berlin.

Lilienthal is remembered for two of aviation's greatest quotations: "To invent an aeroplane is nothing. To build one is something. But to fly is everything," and "Sacrifices must be made."

ing day. Although Lilienthal was not always on the right track, he was vitally important in the history of flight: He was the first man to fly in a controllable airplane. From his time onward the need for the effective means of controlling an airplane in the air was clear. Earlier pioneers had ignored the problem, imagining perhaps that the airplane would somehow fly and control itself once it had risen into the air.

Lilienthal's greatness may be gauged from the spate of imitators he inspired, principally in the United Kingdom and United States. Percy Pilcher, a Scotsman, built the sturdy and practical Hawk, which had landing gear and could be towed off the ground, but this machine was still controlled in the Lilienthal "hang glider" fashion. Pilcher's death after a gliding accident in 1899 was a great blow to the development of British aviation, as serious experimentation came to an end for nearly 10 years. In the United States Lilienthal's imitators included Octave Chanute and Augustus M. Herring, the latter cooperating with Chanute in the design process and then doing most of the flying since Chanute was too old for the task. The two men produced a few relatively successful types in 1896 and 1897, but Chanute's real importance was as a propagandist of flight. Realizing that he was too old to contribute anything but ideas to the cause, he concentrated on the help and encouragement of younger and more dynamic designers, including the Wright brothers. Chanute did, however, improve upon the structural concept of the basic Lilienthal hang glider by introducing the braced biplane formula, with its wing divided into bays by struts and diagonal bracing wires to create a stronger and more rigid cellule.

Similar progress in structures and aerodynamics was also being made at the same time by an Australian, Lawrence Hargrave, who invented the box kite in 1893. This type of flying toy gained considerable popularity in Europe and the United States during the late 1890s, and its basic shape was soon to be copied in a number of European aircraft, notably the Voisin and Farman types.

UPSTAIRS IN A BICYCLE SHOP

It is at this point that Orville and Wilbur Wright come onto the aviation stage as Chanute's ablest students. Determined and serious, and possessing both analytical and constructive imagination, the brothers were members of a tight-knit family in Dayton, Ohio. Wilbur and Orville were the Wrights' third and fourth sons respectively, and in addition to two older brothers had a younger sister. As young men they joined forces with a friend to start a weekly newspaper, the *West Side News,* their tasks including printing on a press that Orville and Wilbur built at the ages of 18 and 22 years respectively. In 1890 the three moved into a more ambitious project, *The Evening Item,* but this lasted for only four months before competition with the more securely established Dayton dailies forced them out of business.

At this time the new "safety" bicycle, with two equal-size wheels instead of one large and one small wheel, was gaining rapidly in popularity. The brothers applied their engineering skills after gaining experience selling bicycles. At first they repaired damaged machines, and later they constructed and sold their own "Wright Special." Its success meant that the brothers had a secure, steady income as well as access to their own light engineering facilities. The brothers' work with bicycles was also important in giving them a keen appreciation of the importance of light weight in combination with strength in transportation, and furthermore it taught them much about balance and control.

The brothers had become interested in flight while they were still young after their father, the local bishop of the United Brethren Church, gave them a toy helicopter powered by a rubber band. Orville and Wilbur built successful replicas of the model, but failed in their efforts to fly a scaled-up model. After several failures they abandoned the idea and, over the next few years, limited their interest in flight to the soaring of birds. News of Lilienthal's death rekindled their interest, and the two decided to work toward the creation of a heavier-than-air flying machine. It was not in the nature of the brothers to rush into a subject of which they knew very little, so Orville and Wilbur started by reading all that they could obtain, but accepted as fact only what they were able to verify themselves either by experiment or by direct observation of birds.

Right from the beginning, the Wright brothers saw that the current problem of flight was not how to get into the air in aerodynamic terms, a process already established by men such as Lilienthal and Chanute, and also in propulsion terms, as engineers were now producing more effective gasoline engines. The brothers appreciated that the real problem in fact lay with the control of the airplane after it had taken off. Control in pitch around the lateral axis was simple, for it required only a "horizontal rudder," now known as the elevator, which could be mounted in front of the wing cellule or alternatively behind it. A vertical rudder, too, could control yaw around the vertical axis. But the problem of control in roll around the longitudinal axis was more problematical. Lilienthal had been experimenting with controlled wing warping, in which the trailing edges of the wing could be twisted differentially so that the wing with its trailing edge depressed produced more lift than the other wing with its trailing edge lifted. The resulting differences in lift would roll the airplane toward the side with the lifted trailing edge, thus giving a measure of control. But Lilienthal had not seen that this concept of wing warping was attended by its own particular problems: the wing with the better lift would also generate more drag, and would tend to slew the airplane round in yaw once the warping was applied.

From their observation of the flight of buzzards, the Wright brothers made the same discovery of the effects of differential warping of the tips of the wing, and in 1899 decided to apply the same principle to their emerging concept for an airplane. After working out the means by which their machine could be controlled in all three dimensions, the brothers decided that the time was ripe for a practical start through the building of a biplane kite-glider model to test the wing warping. This first kite-glider spanned 5 ft (1.52 m), and was ready for test in August 1899. The kite-glider was related in structural terms to Chanute's biplane glider, possessed a fixed tailplane for longitudinal stability, and was controlled by means of four lines. The kite-glider was very successful, the wing warping in particular producing good lateral control.

The Wrights' next logical step was the construction of a small man-carrying glider, and this first No. 1 Glider was ready for testing in the fall of 1900. In configuration the No. 1 Glider was similar to the kite-glider, but was larger with a span of 17 ft (5.18 m), and the elevator was located forward of the wings as the Wrights believed that this would make for faster and more effective pitch control. This monoplane forward elevator had no fixed element, and there were no vertical surfaces, either fixed or moving.

The Wrights selected Kitty Hawk, North Carolina, for the tests of their new machine because there were strong, steady winds there for most of the year, and because the sand of this coastal area would soften any hard landing and thereby reduce the chances of damage.

Tests soon showed that the No. 1 Glider lacked adequate lifting area to support the weight of a man unless the wind was blowing quite strongly. As a result, the No. 1 Glider was generally flown as a kite-glider, its success in this form revealing that the brothers were working along the right basic lines. This No. 1 Glider was also tested with dihedral wings—with the tips higher than the roots. This was meant to provide a measure of inherent lateral stability, but it made control so difficult in the strong breezes of Kitty Hawk that the brothers abandoned the idea almost entirely. Indeed, they went to the opposite extreme of making their machines inherently unstable by giving the wings anhedral, so that the wing tips were lower than the roots.

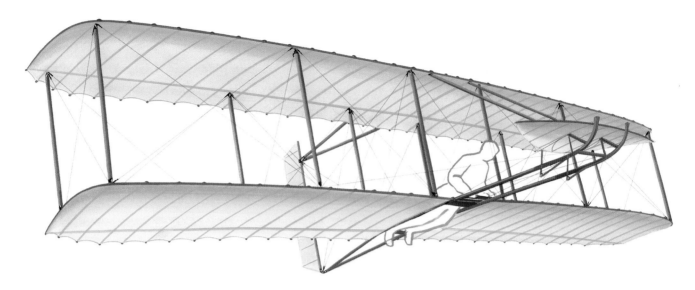

Proceeding with their customary evolutionary care, the brothers built their No. 2 Glider in 1901. The new glider was conceptually similar to the No. 1 Glider, but had a wing cellule increased in span to 22 ft (6.71 m) for the additional lifting area that would make it feasible to undertake manned flights. The wing was again anhedraled, and to improve lateral control a new warping mechanism was introduced: This was based on a moving cradle for the prone pilot's hips so that when he swung his torso to the right or left the wires attached to the cradle operated the warping mechanism.

Flown over the Kill Devil Hills south of Kitty Hawk, the No. 2 Glider was only moderately successful, and the Wrights realized that there was still something, or rather two things, wrong with their design. Up to this point the only data they had not independently verified for themselves were those in Chanute's writings, but the No. 2 Glider's tests revealed that Chanute, working on the basis of Lilienthal's thinking, had opted for too great a degree of camber for the wing section. The Wrights therefore constructed a small wind tunnel, thought to have been the first ever built, and during the winter of 1901–02 undertook experiments to validate or correct the figures they had inherited from Lilienthal and Chanute. The other problem was that of the slewing of the glider when the wing-warping mechanism was used. The Wright brothers tried to solve this problem by adding a fixed double fin at the rear of booms extending from the trailing edges of the wings: This, the brothers hoped, would provide a measure of weather-cock stability and so check the glider's tendency to turn toward the side of the positively warped wing.

The No. 3 Glider of 1902 proved that the Wright brothers were on the right track in their quest for fully controllable flight. All that they now needed for powered and sustained flight were greater lifting area and a powerplant based on an engine offering a good power/weight ratio.

Tests with the No. 3 Glider in September 1902 showed that the introduction of the fixed vertical tail surfaces actually worsened matters: Once the slewing motion had started, the tendency of the airplane to sideslip as a result of the banking caused the fins to act as a lever aiding the slewing movement. The brothers swiftly and accurately analyzed the problem, and as a result turned the No. 3 Glider into what historians now call the No. 3 Glider (Modified), with the fixed double fins replaced with a single moving rudder. The control wires for this rudder were fixed to the warp cradle so that when, for instance, left bank was applied the rudder moved automatically to the left to counteract any tendency for the machine to slew to the right. First flown in October 1902, the No. 3 Glider (Modified) was very successful. This was the basis of their great achievement, once the glider had been turned into a powered airplane by the addition of propulsion.

The Wright brothers used the winter of 1902–03 to manufacture their first powered airplane. Their main problem was to establish the nature and disposition of the powerplant. They decided on a pusher arrangement with a pair of pusher propellers driven from a single engine by means of chain drives, one of them crossed so that the propellers rotated in opposite directions and therefore each canceled out the torque reaction of the other. It was also decided that the pilot would lie slightly to the left of the centerline with the engine offset marginally to the right so that these two weights would balance each other.

As they had with nearly every component of their gliders, the brothers decided that they would have to make their own engine and propellers as there were no suitable units available for purchase. Derived with the aid of data from the brothers' wind tunnel, the two-blade propellers were efficient to a degree that was not equaled by other propellers for another six years, and the engine was an ingenious, light, but robust four-cylinder unit, which delivered 12 hp (8.9 kW) for a weight of 179 lb (81.4 kg).

The Flyer was somewhat larger than the gliders, with a span of 40 ft 4 in (12.29 m), which was 8 ft 3 in (2.51 m) greater than that of the No. 3 Glider. To take advantage of their improved efficiency at lower speeds, the propellers were geared down from the engine, and to avoid unnecessary complication and weight, the landing gear was based on a side-by-side pair of skids without wheels. This landing gear posed problems of its own, and demanded that a special takeoff technique be created. The brothers used a 60-ft (18.39-m) grooved wooden rail to carry a light wheeled trolley. The airplane rested on this trolley and was restrained by a tethering rope until the engine had been run up to full power, only then being released to allow the Flyer-carrying trolley to accelerate along the rail until the Flyer had reached flying speed and lifted into the air.

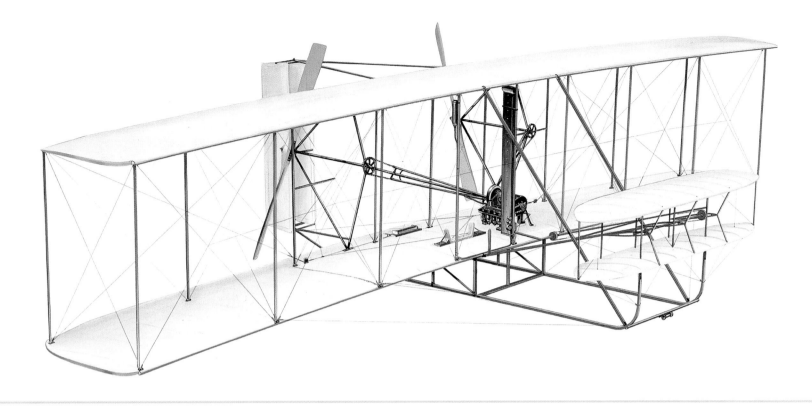

ABOVE With the Wright brothers' Flyer of 1903 powered flight in a heavier-than-air craft finally became a reality. The Flyer opened the way to the era of practical aviation, as it was capable of sustained and controlled flight after taking off under its own power.

BELOW The key to the Wright brothers' initial success was the combination of an airframe that was notably advanced for its time with an engine that also pushed the boundaries of current thinking. The Wright engine was a four-cylinder unit of the air-cooled type and was notable for its high power/weight ratio by the standards of the time.

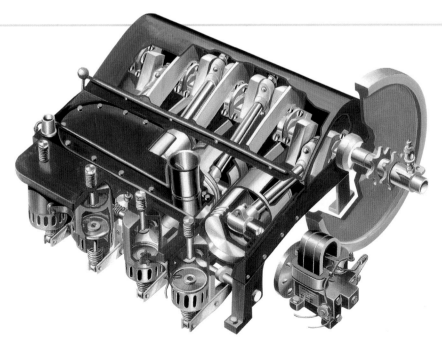

Detractors of the Wrights have often claimed that the brothers did not succeed in making a powered, sustained flight in 1903 because they used an accelerating device to catapult the Flyer into the air. This was not so: It was not until 1904 that the Wrights introduced their accelerator device, and then it served only as a refinement and not as an essential component of launching.

The Wrights took the Flyer to Kill Devil Hills in December 1903. After refreshing their piloting skills on a glider, on December 17 the brothers made the world's first powered, sustained, and controlled flights as they took off from level ground, climbed, and then descended to ground no lower than that from which they had taken off.

Having gained no public acclamation for this feat, Orville and Wilbur Wright returned to Dayton to refine their plans. Clearly the most important matter was to improve the airplane and its engine, for the combination had only just been capable of flight. In the winter of 1903–04, therefore, the brothers built a new airplane almost identical with the Flyer, but with wings of reduced camber. A new engine was also built, and this delivered an additional 4 hp (3 kW) of very useful power.

The Wright brothers fully realized the commercial potential of their invention and decided that their financial interests might suffer if they received publicity before their patents had been fully secured. So they decided to operate their aircraft well away from large crowds and, with the help of a friend named Torrence Huffman, created a base of operations at the Huffman Prairie, some 8 miles (13 km) from Dayton. Here, in the second half of 1904, the Flyer II took to the air about 75 times, the best flight covering just under 3 miles (4.8 km) in 5 minutes 4 seconds. Just as important, on September 20 Wilbur Wright succeeded in flying a circle, an achievement that had eluded the brothers up to that time because their aircraft had not climbed high enough to allow it to bank around turns.

In September 1904 the brothers had added a refinement to their takeoff system in the form of an accelerator device. This comprised a heavy weight winched to the top of a derrick and attached to the tail of a rope that was led via pulleys to the front of the launching rail and then back to the trolley. When the weight was released to drop to the ground the movement of the rope pulled the trolley swiftly forward along the rail. This device enabled the Wrights to fly on days when there was little wind, since the Flyer II was not capable of reaching flying speed relative to the wind along the rail without this aid.

In the 1904 flying season the brothers' flights were seen by hundreds of people, and on two occasions reporters came to the field to investigate. By a quirk of nature, the engine misperformed on both of these visits, and the pressmen went away skeptical.

FACING PAGE This classic photograph of a Wright Flyer A over the lawn in front of the White House reveals the asymmetric arrangement of the Flyer with the pilot to port and the engine to starboard.

The flying season of 1905 marked the appearance of the definitive, fully airworthy Wright airplane, the Flyer III. The same basic design was retained, this time with a span of 40 ft 6 in (12.34 m), but to improve their effectiveness the elevators and the rudders were moved farther from the wing cellule. The brothers completed some 40 flights between June and October, and in the process further enhanced their piloting skills. The one problem still plaguing them was the tendency of the airplane to stall in turns as the wing surfaces on the inside of the turn slowed and lost lift. The answer was to push the nose down slightly in turns and thus maintain speed. At the same time the permanent link between the warp cradle and the rudder controls was abandoned, enabling the pilot to use

With his brother Wilbur watching from a position off the starboard wingtip, Orville Wright makes the world's first successful powered and controlled heaver-than-air flight on December 17, 1903, at the brothers' test site in the Kill Devil Hills, near Kitty Hawk, North Carolina. The Flyer had just lifted off the takeoff rail with the biplane forward elevator in the raised position.

the two controls separately should he so desire, or to coordinate them in different ratios and thus produce a greater variety of banked turns. With the engine running reliably and powerfully, the Flyer III can certainly be called the first truly practical airplane in history.

The Flyer III was considerably better than the Flyer II, a fact readily proved by the large number of flights lasting more than 15 minutes that the brothers achieved during the summer: These six flights included two of more than 30 minutes. Coming on October 5, the brothers' best flight of the year lasted 38 minutes 3 seconds, in which time the Flyer III covered more than 24 miles (38.6 km). The increasing practicality of the Wrights' aircraft was also confirmed by the fact that the Flyer III suffered no significant damage in the course of 40 takeoffs and landings. Perhaps the most important factor, however, was that the two pilots were able to maneuver the airplane in a fully practical manner.

The Wright brothers were sure that they were on the edge of a commercial success to match what they knew they had already achieved at the technical level. The brothers therefore offered their Flyer to the U.S. and British governments.

Patents for the most important elements of the Flyer were pending, and the brothers now felt that they could begin to profit from their invention. In January 1905 the brothers had offered their machine to the U.S. Department of War, while they were still building the Flyer III: The department refused the offer without even considering it. The brothers then approached the War Office in the United Kingdom, but the administrative processes of that organization ground so slowly that in October, with the Flyer III now fully tested, the brothers abandoned their effort to interest the British and once more approached the U.S. Department of War. In their correspondence the brothers made it completely clear that they were offering a machine with guaranteed aerial capability and performance, but the Department of War insisted on treating the offer as a request for assistance, and again turned down the offer.

The first European airplane to fly, or rather to "hop" from the ground, did not take to the air for nearly another 12 months. Yet the Americans' lead was lost as a result of the shortsightedness of the government. The Wrights were discouraged, and also so concerned that their ideas might be stolen before their patents were approved in 1906 that they ceased flying and development work on their aircraft for the next 30 months. They locked away the Flyer III in a shed, and permitted no one to examine the airplane. The Wrights even refused to allow drawings of the Flyer III to be made, although a fairly accurate sketch appeared in the Parisian *L'Auto* on Christmas Eve 1905 after being stolen in Dayton. Even so, the Flyer III was still for sale: The brothers guaranteed the performance,

but would allow no one to see the machine or plans until they had bought them. Until 1908 the brothers made no more advances, except to build a few improved engines and a small number of Flyer III airframes, in the definitive form known as the Model A, pending the day that either the government or commercial interests decided to take seriously the concept of the airplane.

In just six years the American brothers had undertaken the research and designed and manufactured the airframes, engines, and propellers for an evolutionary series of gliders and powered aircraft culminating in the first practical airplane. They had also taught themselves to pilot their machines with great skill. But now they stopped.

FACING PAGE The factors that so impressed all who saw the flying of the Wright brothers in the period between 1904 and 1909 were, first, that the Flyer did rise into and then remain in the air, and second, the total assurance and ease with which the brothers controlled their machines in apparently effortless flight.

ABOVE The event that confirmed the fact that successful heavier-than-air flight had arrived was the great Reims aviation meeting of August 1909, sponsored by the champagne industry. The meeting was a technical success in that many aircraft were entered and a large number of these took to the air, but it was also a considerable social success that attracted large crowds who departed full of enthusiasm. The airplane that competed with the number 30 on its tail was the Farman III "box kite" flown by Henry Farman.

PRACTICAL AVIATION
TAKES OFF

The Curtiss F.5L was a Liberty-engined American development of a British flying boat, the Felixstowe F.3, and although designed for the maritime patrol task was also used in limited numbers for civilian transport during the 1920s. It also cropped up occasionally in publicity photographs, as nicely revealed here.

The birth of aviation was midwifed by a motley crew of dreamers, scientists, tinkerers, and governments. We remember the Wright brothers as isolated geniuses: In truth some of the world's leading minds were competing with them, along with some of history's most endearing frustrated visionaries.

The brothers' only rival in the United States was Samuel P. Langley, the eminent secretary of the Smithsonian Institution in Washington. Langley became interested in flight as early as 1886, and to test his theories used models that had inherent stability. Langley believed this to be a key to successful flight, and therefore neglected the problems of flight control. In 1894 Langley built his fifth and sixth models, both tandem-winged machines of considerable size. The two models made a large number of very successful flights, the best covering some 4,200 ft (1280 m). Langley's interest in flight was satisfied by his success with models, and he intended to hand over further development to a younger man. But in 1898 the U.S. government asked him to build a man-carrying "Aerodrome" (Langley's term). Langley built a quarter-sized model, powered by a small gasoline engine, in 1901. The success of the model paved the way for a full-sized airplane, completed by 1903. This was a large machine, with a span of 48 ft (14.63 m). It was powered by the first of the classic aero engines in the form of a remarkably light radial unit inspired, designed, and built by Langley's able assistant Charles M. Manly. The Aerodrome was structurally heavy but underpowered despite the good performance of the Balzer-Manly engine.

The Langley Aerodrome of 1903 was a tandem-wing machine with an elegant little engine. S. P. Langley hoped to provide his pilot, C. M. Manly, with a soft alighting by arranging for the Aerodrome to be launched over water by a catapult atop a houseboat on the Potomac River outside Washington, D.C. The Aerodrome is thought to have fouled the launching mechanism in its two attempted flights, but it is also possible that the structure failed for lack of strength to withstand the acceleration imparted by the catapult.

That there was some aerodynamic merit in Langley's thinking is revealed by the success of the powered models with which he proved his concept in 1901. This model was the first airplane to fly anywhere in the world with a gasoline engine.

Langley decided that flight trials by Manly should be carried out over water, and selected as the launching platform a houseboat on the Potomac River just outside Washington. Langley designed a catapult to accelerate the Aerodrome to flying speed, and had this installed on the short roof of the houseboat. On October 7 Manly attempted his first flight, but the Aerodrome fouled the launching device and crashed into the river. The same happened in the second trial, on December 8, and the Aerodrome was put into storage.

In Europe, only slow progress was made toward powered flight, in which the main protagonists between 1900 and 1905 were primarily Frenchmen: Ferdinand Ferber, Ernest Archdeacon, Gabriel Voisin, and Robert Esnault-Pelterie. None of these men achieved clear-cut success, but their efforts and others' did introduce four improvements: the aileron, better longer-term prospect for lateral control than wing warping; the box-kite layout developed in Australia by Lawrence Hargrave; the tractor biplane configuration; and the general relocation of the pitch control from the front to the rear of the airframe.

Another, and largely unsung, French hero of early aviation was Leon Levavasseur. Levavasseur originally created the Antoinette engine in 1903 for racing motorboats. He contributed more than anyone else to the final success of European avia-

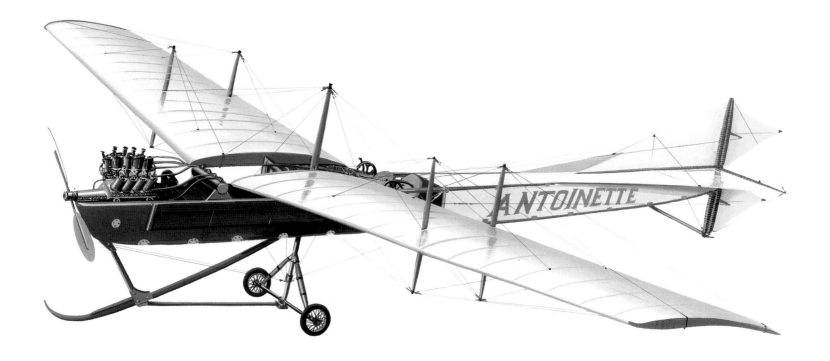

ABOVE Epitomized by the Antoinette VII of 1909, the Antoinette monoplanes designed by Leon Levavasseur, and powered by one of Levavasseur's V-8 engines, were among the most elegant of all early aircraft. Notable features were the long fuselage of inverted triangular section and the high-aspect-ratio dihedraled wing that was tapered on its leading and trailing edges. Wing warping was used for lateral control.

BELOW The Gnome rotary engine, seen here in the form of a seven-cylinder unit rated at 80 hp (59.6 kW), took the world of early aviation by storm when it appeared in the spring of 1909. The propeller was bolted to the crankcase/cylinder unit to create a mass that rotated in its entirety around the crankshaft, which was bolted to the airplane. The movement of the cylinders was good for air cooling, and the engine offered an excellent power/weight ratio by the standards of the day. Designed by the French brothers Louis and Laurent Seguin, the rotary engine transformed aviation in the period up to the later part of World War I.

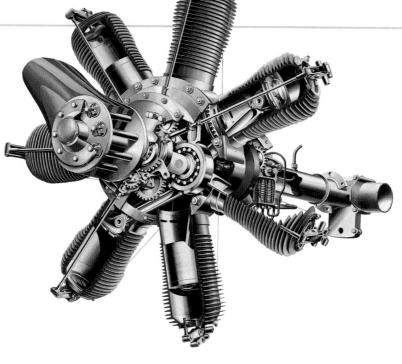

tion, and his two basic engines, of 25 and 50 hp (18.6 and 37.3 kW), powered most of the important European types up to 1909. By the standards of the day these engines were reliable, and their racing heritage gave them a good power/weight ratio. Only with the advent of the Gnome rotary engine, designed by Laurent and Louis Seguin in 1907 and introduced from late 1908 onward, would the Antoinette 50-hp (37.3-kW) engine be superseded as the prime mover of European aircraft.

The first man in Europe who can really be said to have flown was neither a European nor a pioneer previously interested in heavier-than-air flight. Alberto Santos-Dumont was a diminutive Brazilian who had settled in France and first worked on lighter-than-air craft. In 1905 Santos-Dumont became interested in heavier-than-air flying machines. His first effort, which was to be the first European airplane to fly, was a machine that was bizarre even by the standards of the times, and totally without further influence on the development of flight.

The Santos-Dumont 14-bis, tested under Santos-Dumont's No. 14 airship, was designed and built near Paris in 1906. It was what is known as "canard" style, with the normal positions of wings and tail assembly reversed. The control surfaces at the front of the fuselage took the form of a Hargrave, box-cell mounted on a universal joint to move up/down as an elevator and left/right as the rudder. The wings, spanning 36 ft 9 in (11.2 m), were attached to the rear fuselage at a considerable dihedral angle, and the pilot stood in a balloon basket just in front of the wings. The landing gear consisted of a pair of narrow-track wheels under the rear fuselage and a skid under the forward control surfaces. Power was provided by a 25-hp (18.6-kW) Antoinette engine mounted at the rear of the fuselage to turn a pusher propeller.

It was first tested in July 1906 and the initial attempt at free flight was made on September 13. After a hop of only 7 m (23 ft), the No. 14-bis came down heavily and suffered major damage. While the machine was being repaired, Santos-Dumont also changed the engine for a more powerful 50-hp (37.3-kW) Antoinette and then attempted his second flight on October 23. This time he managed to achieve a hop of 198 ft (60 m). Realizing that some form of lateral control was necessary, Santos-Dumont next modified the No. 14-bis with two large ailerons, operated by a harness worn around the pilot's body, mounted between the wings in the outermost bracing bay of each pair of wings. Santos-Dumont was ready for his greatest triumph. On November 12, 1906, after five short hops, the best of which covered 270 ft (82 m) in 7.2 seconds, Santos-Dumont finally achieved the first recognized flight in Europe by flying 722 ft (220 m) in 21.2 seconds. Although he achieved

ALBERTO SANTOS-DUMONT

ALBERTO SANTOS-DUMONT (1873–1932) Alberto Santos-Dumont was born at Cabangu near Palmyra (now Santos-Dumont), in the Brazilian state of Minas Gerais on July 20, 1873, to a family made wealthy by the coffee business. Throughout his youth he displayed a fascination with all things mechanical. Living in Paris from the age of 18, the diminutive and dapper Santos-Dumont soon became interested in aviation, and took his first flight in a balloon on May 23, 1898. He ordered a small 3,990-cu-ft (113-m³) balloon that he named *Brazil* and soon became one of the best aviators in Paris, although he was also involved in a number of accidents. A dedicated and comparatively wealthy young man, Santos-Dumont then moved to the dirigible airship as a more practical means of travel and developed his ideas through a series of little airships powered by small gasoline engines of the type that many had previously considered too dangerous for employment in hydrogen-filled vehicles.

Up to 1901 Santos-Dumont was little known outside Paris, but his fame began to spread after he had completed a flight around the Eiffel Tower, winning a 100,000-franc prize offered by the petroleum magnate Henri Deutsch de La Meurthe. At 2:42 in the afternoon of October 19, 1901, Santos-Dumont lifted off in his Airship No. 6, which was 108 ft 3 in (33.0 m) long and had a volume of 21,965 cu ft (622 m³). Just 29 seconds inside the maximum permitted time of 30 minutes, he returned to his starting point. Santos-Dumont donated 75,000 francs of his prize to the poor of Paris, and the other 25,000 francs to his team at Saint-Cloud.

In 1904 Santos-Dumont visited the St. Louis Exposition in the United States, where he met Octave Chanute and learned of the Wright brothers' success with heavier-than-air craft. Now drawn to this new means of aerial transport, Santos-Dumont in 1906 created his No. 14-bis machine (so named because it was first tested beneath his Airship No. 14). Powered by a 24-hp (17.9-kW) Antoinette engine, the No. 14-bis achieved a "hop flight" of just 23 ft (7 m) on September 13, 1906, but suffered damage in the "landing" that ended this effort. Repaired and powered by a 50-hp (37.3-kW) Antoinette engine, the airplane won the Archdeacon trophy for a "flight" of 82 ft (25 m) on October 23 with a "hop" of 198 ft (60 m) covered in 7 seconds. Then on November 12 of the same year, after the No. 14-bis had been fitted with primitive ailerons, Santos-Dumont achieved several flights, of which the best covered 722 ft (220 m) in a time of just over 21 seconds, reaching a maximum height of about 20 ft (6 m).

The Santos-Dumont Demoiselle was the world's first lightplane, an attractive but not very practical type in which the pilot sat below the wing just to the rear of the engine. This drove a two-blade wooden propeller turning ahead of the wing's leading edge and above the skids that prevented the machine from nosing over on landing. This Demoiselle is of the "rouleur" (roller) type with a truncated wing designed to prevent flight while allowing the tyro pilot to learn how to handle the machine on the ground.

The flight was credited in Europe as the world's first by a heavier-than-air craft, and was greeted with enormous enthusiasm. The basic impracticality of the No. 14-bis, however, is attested by the fact that Santos-Dumont attempted only one more flight in the machine.

Santos-Dumont continued with his experiments, building more little airships and also the No. 19, a precursor of the lightplane that weighed only 235 lb (107 kg). First named *Libellule* and then *Demoiselle* (both French words for "dragonfly"), the No. 19 was an elegant little machine of wire-braced high-wing layout with the pilot seated under the wing and power provided by a 20-hp (14.9-kW) Dutheil-Chalmers two-cylinder engine driving a tractor propeller. Santos-Dumont made only three flights in this 1907 machine, the best of them covering some 655 ft (200 m). This paved the way for the No. 20 of 1909 with a 35-hp (26.1-kW) Dutheil-Chalmers engine. In September this machine made a flight of 11 miles (18 km) in 16 minutes.

Santos-Dumont himself had retired from flying by the beginning of 1910 as he suffered from multiple sclerosis. Santos-Dumont never accepted that the airplane should or would be used for warlike purposes, and his faith was shattered by the events of World War I. He believed that the airplane should be used to foster social and economic development, for leisure, and as a means of transportation. Santos-Dumont returned to Brazil, and committed suicide on July 23, 1932, at Guarujà in the state of São Paulo.

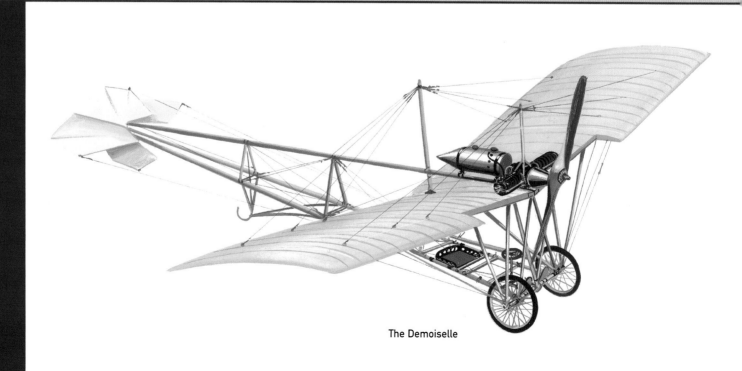

The Demoiselle

only a third of what the Wrights had managed on their first day's flying in December 1903, this flight was enough to win Santos-Dumont wild acclaim in Paris, and warm congratulations from all over the world.

Santos-Dumont's success inspired many flyers. And yet, in reality, only Henry (or alternatively Henri) Farman, a French resident of British parentage, managed to achieve anything significant. Farman bought a pusher biplane. Built by the Voisin brothers, the basic Voisin aircraft was essentially a Chanute type of biplane wing with a Wright forward elevator and a Hargrave box-kite tail.

The Voisin-Farman I was built by the Voisin brothers to the order of Henry Farman, who then introduced a sequence of improvements that turned this mediocre machine into one of the best flying machines of its time. The Voisin-Farman I first flew in September 1907, and is here seen after its revision as the No. 1-bis.

The Voisins' third powered airplane, built for Farman in mid-1907, was copied with increasing success by brothers Gabriel and Charles. It is now known as the Voisin-Farman I. Although generally happy with the first tests, Farman instructed the Voisins to rerig the airplane with dihedral and to replace the biplane elevators with a monoplane unit. With these alterations the Voisin-Farman I flew 2,540 ft (771 m) in 52.6 seconds on October 26. This was a European record, but it is worth noting that it took place just one month short of four years after the Wrights' first flights, and did not even equal the time of their fourth flight. Farman, not yet satisfied with his machine, ordered that the original large tailplane be replaced by a unit of reduced span.

After modifications, the Voisin-Farman I flew well. At last the Europeans could be said to have something approaching a practical airplane. The Voisins' combination of Wright, Chanute, and Hargrave elements and Farman's modifications proved to be a sound one, as evidenced by Farman's flight of 3,400 ft (1,030 m) in a circle, in a time of 1 minute 14 seconds.

During 1907, after several years of trials with aircraft of various types, Louis Blériot finally adopted the tractor monoplane, the type that he made famous. Blériot progressed cautiously and logically, and it was not until after he had discarded two designs that he arrived at the one now considered the definitive form. The aircraft had an enclosed fuselage, tractor engine, forward-mounted wing, and an empennage at the rear of the fuselage. Power was provided by a 50-hp (37.3-kW) Antoinette, which enabled the No. VII to take off several times, two of the flights covering more than 1,640 ft (500 m). The No. VII was not in itself a notably successful type, but with it Blériot had created the type of monoplane that his later success was to make famous all over the world.

THE AGE OF THE BIPLANE

With the de Pischoff I, built in 1907, the tractor biplane reached its definitive, if rudimentary, form. The airplane failed to fly, but was notable for two innovations. The more important of these was the propeller, designed and made by Lucien Chauvière. It was a built-up wooden structure of considerable efficiency and presaged the dominance of this propeller type for years to come. It was still not as advanced as the Wrights' propeller, but this deficiency would be rectified in the next two years. The de Pischoff I also introduced the 25-hp (18.6-kW) "arrowhead" three-cylinder Anzani engine. This efficient unit also revitalized Blériot's monoplanes.

It was 1908 when the world at large first saw that aviators could launch themselves into the air and stay there for considerable periods in full control of their aircraft. Among the devotees of the biplane, Léon Delagrange and Farman were best able to capitalize on their moderate previous successes. On January 13, 1908, Farman completed a round flight of more than 0.6 mile (1 km). Flying his Voisin-Farman I (Modified), he repeated the flight he had made at the end of 1907, witnessed this time by the requisite officials and won the Grand Prix d'Aviation Deutsch-Archdeacon of 50,000 francs. Actually, Farman's round trip of 1 km was in fact nearer 0.9 mile (1.5 km). Without lateral control he could not merely bank round the marker at the far end of his course, but rather had to skid around it in a wide curve.

Preparing for a flight in March, Farman took apart his Voisin-Farman I-bis for reconstruction and modification. Little had been done in the way of modifying the basic airframe, but a new engine, a 50-hp (37.3-kW) Renault unit, had been installed and the

Several types of control system were tried in the early days of flight. This Voisin biplane at the Farman flight school reveals the Voisin hands-only system: Back-and-forward movement of the control wheel moved the forward elevator by means of a push-rod, while rotation of the wheel operated the wires that moved the rear rudders. Voisin aircraft of the early period had inherent lateral stability, and therefore lacked any means of lateral control.

airplane was completely recovered with rubberized linen in place of the original silk. The Renault engine was used only once: Farman found it unsatisfactory and reverted to the original Antoinette. With the old engine once again installed, the Voisin-Farman I-bis showed its unspectacular paces compared to Wilbur Wright's machine.

Delagrange, meanwhile, was close on Farman's heels. With his Voisin-Delagrange I virtually written off in November 1907, Delagrange ordered another machine from the Voisins. Incorporating what could be salvaged from the Voisin-Delagrange I, this Voisin-Delagrange II differed little from the Voisin-Farman I (Modified). Later, as the Voisin-Delagrange III, it was modified with "curtains" on the two innermost sets of interplane struts. Delagrange then managed several useful flights in Italy. The best of these, on June 23, took Delagrange 8.87 miles (14.27 km) in 18 minutes 30 seconds.

The founding in the United States of the Aerial Experiment Association (AEA) during September 1907 by Dr. Alexander Graham Bell and Mrs. Bell, with the newcomer Glenn Curtiss as its prime mover, was of considerable importance. During 1908, the AEA built and tested three similar biplanes, the Red Wing, White Wing, and June Bug. The Red Wing, designed by Lieutenant T. E. Selfridge, was powered by an excellent Curtiss engine. The Red Wing had a span of 43 ft (13.11 m) and was fitted with skids instead of wheeled landing gear as it was tested from the frozen surface of Lake Keuka in upper New York State. With F. W. Baldwin as pilot, only two flights were made. The best was on March 12, and covered 319 ft (97 m). The second effort resulted in a crash and the Red Wing was abandoned in favor of the White Wing designed by Baldwin.

The White Wing was similar to its predecessor, but had conventional landing gear and ailerons. Five flights were made in May, the best covering 1,017 ft (310 m). But like the Red Wing before it, the White Wing was given up after a crash landing, to be replaced in turn at the center of the AEA's attention by the Curtiss-designed June Bug. Like the two previous aircraft, the June Bug was powered by the Curtiss engine, and retained the distinctive upward-curved lower wing and downward-curved upper wing. Four ailerons were fitted, and the tail surfaces were improved by being made into a biplane structure. Flown by Curtiss himself and by J. A. D. McCurdy, who, like Baldwin, was a Canadian, the June Bug proved itself far superior to the two earlier aircraft. Some 30 flights were made, the most notable being one of 2 miles (3.2 km) on August 29. With the June Bug, Curtiss won the prize offered by the *Scientific American* for the first flight of over 0.6 mile (1 km), with an effort of 5,360 ft (1,551 m) in 1 minute 42.5 seconds. Curtiss, who had recently fallen foul of the Wright brothers because of his infringement of their 1906 warping patent, was also soon able to bank the June Bug around in a circle.

After Blériot's introduction of the classic monoplane layout in 1907, further progress was made in 1908 toward turning this type into a viable flying machine. Blériot and Levavasseur separately made key innovations in the following two years. Blériot quickly moved toward the definitive form of monoplane with his No. VIII. In its first form of June 1908 the No. VIII spanned 36 ft 1 in (11.0 m); it was soon cut down to 27 ft 10 in (8.5 m). Power was provided by a 50-hp (37.3-kW) Antoinette. Although the fuselage was initially covered, the designer soon made an alteration, and the No. VIII took on the open-fuselage form so distinctive in Blériot monoplanes. The tail controls were conventional, except that it was the outer, rather than the rear portions of the tailplane that moved to give longitudinal control. Blériot turned in a flight of 2,997 ft (700 m) on June 29, the last day on which the No. VIII was flown in its original form before being taken in hand for modifications. Its original triangular ailerons were replaced by more effective rectangular units mounted as the trailing portion of each outer wing panel. On July 6 the No. VIII-bis stayed in the air for 8 minutes 24 seconds.

Still not satisfied, Blériot continued to experiment with the controls. In September he modified the No. VIII-bis into the No. VIII-ter by replacing the rectangular flap-type ailerons with differential elevons formed of the outer ends of the wings, and at

The airplane that in essence created the monoplane layout in its first definitive form was the Blériot No. XI, the airplane on which Louis Blériot made the first crossing of the English Channel in a heavier-than-air craft during July 1909.

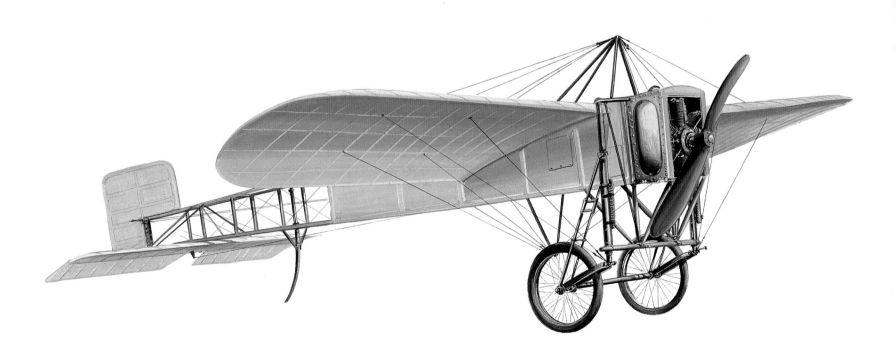

GLENN CURTISS

GLENN H. CURTISS (1878–1930) Glenn Hammond Curtiss was born on May 21, 1878, in Hammondsport, New York. His middle name was given in honor of the community's founding father. After the death of his father when he was only four years old, Curtiss was raised by his mother, and the family moved to Rochester during 1890. The interest and ability of the young Curtiss in mathematics and mechanics became clear at school, and after graduating Curtiss joined the Eastman Kodak company as a camera assembler. During 1906 his growing fascination with motorcycles and racing persuaded Curtiss to change careers with the acceptance of an opening at a local cycle shop, and

Glenn H. Curtiss is pictured in one of his so-called "wind wagons." These three-wheeled contraptions were initially developed for the evaluation of propellers for the airship ordered by "Captain" Thomas Scott Baldwin, but this example was based on the central structure of an airplane and was also used for the development of the forward elevator.

Wearing his habitual dour expression, Glenn Curtiss is pictured at the controls of one of his aircraft. Curtiss machines were well-engineered and nicely finished, and evident in this photograph are a Curtiss V-8 engine driving a pusher propeller and the overhanging aileron hinged to the midgap points on the outermost two pairs of interplane struts' rear units.

Curtiss later started his own business largely to provide the greater resources he needed to boost his chances as a racing driver. Curtiss expanded his interests into the design and manufacture of his own engines, and he was soon able to offer a range of one- and two-cylinder motorcycle engines. After attempting without success to gain the interest of the Wright brothers in his engines as powerplants for the Wrights' biplane aircraft, Curtiss secured an order from Thomas Scott Baldwin for use on the airship *California Arrow*.

On January 23, 1907, Curtiss established a world's motorcycle speed record of 136.3 mph (219.3 km/h) with the aid of a 40-hp (29.8-kW) V-8 engine. Later in 1907 the qualities of Curtiss's engineering so impressed Dr. Alexander Graham Bell that he asked Curtiss to become involved in the AEA (Aerial Experiment Association). Working with Frank W. Baldwin, Curtiss was responsible for the design of some of the world's first aircraft with lateral control by means of ailerons, but this led to a bitter wrangle with the Wright brothers over the infringement of the latter's patent: The legal case lasted for many years and ended only with the 1929 merger of Curtiss and Wright, forming the Wright-Curtiss Company.

During 1908 Curtiss learned to fly and became the AEA's director of experiments. In this capacity he designed aircraft including the June Bug, which used a Curtiss engine. On July 4 he secured the Scientific American Trophy for the first flight in the United States of 0.6 miles (1 km) or more. The Wright brothers, it should be noted, had made many superior flights, but not under the right type of scrutiny.

In March 1909 the AEA was dissolved and Curtiss began to manufacture aircraft for himself and others after bringing Augustus M. Herring into his company. In December 1910 he formed the Curtiss Airplane Company, and one year later the Curtiss Motor Company, which were combined into the Curtiss Airplane and Motor Company in January 1916. The classic Curtiss airplane of the early period was the Golden Flyer in which Curtiss won the speed event at the great aviation meeting at Reims, France, in August 1909, at a speed of 52.63 mph (84.71 km/h). He was also an organizational pioneer; the Curtiss company and flight school in Hammondsport were the first of their types in the United States. Meanwhile Curtiss invented the dual-control trainer and the "hydro-aeroplane" or flying boat in 1911.

At the 1910 Dominguez Hills Air Meet Curtiss won $6,500 in prizes in the speed, endurance, and quick starting categories. In the same year the U.S. Navy contracted with Curtiss for several flying boats as well as pilot training, which paved the way for experiments with ships at sea. In 1914 the Curtiss company manufactured a large multiengined flying boat for a planned flight across the Atlantic, which was canceled after the outbreak of World War I, but in World War I the company produced the classic JN "Jenny" trainer and immediately after the war the NC flying boat used in the first aerial crossing of the Atlantic in 1919. By 1918, however, Curtiss had retired from active participation in aviation to concentrate on real estate development in Florida. Curtiss died on July 23, 1930, at Buffalo, New York, as a result of complications following an operation to remove his appendix.

The Curtiss control system of 1909 combined elements of the Voisin and Wright systems: movement of the elevator and rudder was controlled respectively by fore-and-aft movement and rotation of the wheel, while the ailerons were activated by lateral swaying of the body in a shoulder fork.

the same time added a fixed horizontal tail surface. Yet again, Blériot's modifications proved efficient, the No. VIII-ter making a 2.78-mile (4.5-km) flight on October 2. On the last day of the same month Blériot made a round trip of about 17.4 miles (28 km), with two landings, in 22 minutes.

It was in 1908, too, that Levavasseur's monoplane first appeared. Although the first Antoinette aircraft were rather ungainly machines, Levavasseur developed his basic idea into a series of extremely elegant aircraft. The Gastambide-Mengin I, ordered by Levavasseur's employer and another member of the Antoinette firm in 1907, was delivered in February 1908. It was unsuccessful but nonetheless interesting in one very important respect: the airfoil section of the wings. Up to this date most early airfoils had consisted of parallel-sided cambered surfaces. Levavasseur, however, followed the example of Phillips and adopted a section with considerably less camber on the undersurface. This produced as much lift as the parallel-sided airfoils, but far less drag. Intended basically as a test vehicle, the airplane had no control surfaces. Only four tests were made, the best covering some 492 ft (150 m). After a crash landing, the airplane was rebuilt as the Gastambide-Mengin II, or more properly the Antoinette II, in July. Large triangular ailerons were added to the rear of the outer wing panels, and an elevator and twin rudders were installed. The Antoinette II proved moderately successful, its best flight lasting 1 minute 36 seconds.

Levavasseur's next airplane was the Antoinette IV, the world's first truly successful monoplane. This graceful machine was completed in October 1908, and in the course of a career that was lengthy by contemporary standards, it underwent a series of modifications, especially to the landing gear. Most attention at the time was concentrated on this machine's successor, the Antoinette V, but for lack of evidence, it is impossible to trace all the modifications. Nevertheless, the Antoinette IV ushered in the era of graceful Levavasseur monoplanes, the majority of them featuring a boat-shaped fuselage of triangular section, probably inspired by Levavasseur's earlier association with racing motorboats.

In 1908 Wilbur Wright arrived in France to reveal the extent to which the American brothers were still ahead of the Europeans. His visit altered the whole nature of European aviation. At the beginning of the year the Wrights' relationship improved with the aeronautical world when the brothers contracted to provide an airplane and pilot training for the U.S. Army's Signal Corps, and to have their aircraft built under license in France. Orville conducted the Signal Corps' evaluation and acceptance trials, and Wilbur

Sightseers wait at Sangatte near Calais on the French coast in anticipation of Hubert Latham's attempt to make the first crossing of the English Channel on July 19, 1909. The photograph shows the elegant Antoinette IV monoplane, complete with trapezoidal trailing-edge ailerons, to excellent advantage. Control of the airplane was exercised by means of the two hand wheels on the outer sides of the cockpit.

went to France to demonstrate the airplane already sent over in July 1907. Both the Signal Corps and French aircraft were of the modified Flyer III design called the Flyer Model A. Although the Wrights themselves did not use this appellation, they did call their next basic type the Flyer Model B.

Orville and Wilbur brushed up their flying techniques on the Flyer III, modified to Model A standard by the provision of two upright seats and other refinements, during May 1908. Immediately afterward, Wilbur left for France, where he erected the Model A at Le Mans. On August 8 the crowd at Hunaudières racecourse near Le Mans saw Wilbur supervise the take-off preparations and then give the launch signal to boost the Model A smoothly into the air. The pilot climbed and circled round twice, his superb banking showing off the degree of control possible with the use of warping and rudder control, and then landed after a flight of only 1 minute 45 seconds.

The crowd was astounded. Even those who had expressed a belief in the brothers' claims were overwhelmed by the magnitude of the event. The brothers were, in hard fact, on par with the Europeans, but it was the ease with which the first European flight had been accomplished that amazed the crowd. Delagrange summed up the event succinctly: *"Eh bien, nous sommes battus! Nous n'existons pas!"* ("Well, we are beaten! We do not even exist!")

Wilbur continued to astonish crowds for the next six days at Hunaudières, and then moved to the military training ground at the Camp d'Auvours, east of Le Mans. He flew from the Camp d'Auvours for the rest of the year, putting in some 26 hours in the air between August 8 and the end of 1908. On sixty of his flights Wilbur took up passengers. He made a few notable flights, six lasting between one and two hours, and on the last day of the year, he stayed aloft for a remarkable 2 hours 20 minutes 23 seconds. He also secured the world altitude record at 361 ft (110 m). By the end of the year, the Wrights' achievements in previous years had finally been recognized, and Wilbur Wright was a celebrity all over Europe. Indeed, other celebrities, not merely fellow aviation enthusiasts, flocked to the Camp d'Auvours to see the wonder of the year.

While Wilbur had his triumphs in Europe, Orville at first enjoyed similar acclaim in the United States. The Model A was assembled at Fort Myer outside Washington, D.C., and Orville began acceptance trials under Signal Corps supervision on September 3, immediately impressing all who saw him in the air with his complete mastery of flight. Progress was smooth and rapid: Orville made four flights of more than one hour, created two altitude records, and took up passengers on three occasions. But on September 17 all this came to an end. Late in the afternoon, Orville had taken Lieutenant T. E. Selfridge, one of the leading lights of the AEA, on an official flight. As they circled the field, one of the blades of the starboard propeller cracked along its length: The difference in thrust now produced by the two blades caused so much vibration that the bearings of the long propeller shaft loosened, allowing the propeller to waver back and forth. The propeller hit and cut one of the wires bracing the rudders, and as Orville throttled back and tried to land, the rudder structure collapsed, causing the airplane to dive into the ground. Selfridge was killed instantly, and Orville was grievously hurt. Selfridge was the first person to be killed in a powered airplane, and only the fourth aviator to be killed since serious work on heavier-than-air flight had begun during the last century. Orville, after recovering from the accident, went to France to join Wilbur.

Farman meanwhile set about modifying his Voisin-Farman I-bis into the Farman I-bis (Modified) by fitting four side curtains, and made some good flights, including three lasting over 30 minutes. Farman now realized that lateral control was the element missing from his Farman I-bis (Modified) and, early in October, installed four large ailerons, one inset into each of the outer wing panels. Although these could only move downward, Farman developed the first truly efficient ailerons ever fitted. Thus improved, the airplane performed creditably, and on October 30 Farman made the world's first true cross-country flight, of 16.8 miles (27 km) in 20 minutes.

The Wright brothers continued to play an important part in the realization of practical aviation over the next two years, but their basic Flyer design was fast approaching the end of its useful development life. They realized too late that they were falling from the van of aviation development, and by the end of 1909, Europe was firmly established as the center of the aeronautical world.

By now Farman had broken off all contact with the Voisin brothers, who had sold the Voisin-Farman II, for which Farman had already paid, to an English buyer. Farman established his own facility on the airfield at Camp de Châlons, south of Reims, where he had been flying since September 1908. Farman was now entirely free to pursue an aggressive and adventurous course in the development of aviation. The first result of this process was the Henry Farman III, destined to be one of the great aircraft of the period up to 1912. Three things made it stand out. First, Farman had moved away from the Voisins' concept of inherent lateral stability by means of dihedral and side curtains, and had adopted four large ailerons for lateral control. This was the first time such surfaces had been incorporated in a fully practical fashion, and was an advance of considerable magnitude. Second, he added a stabilizing tailplane to the trailing fin and rudder assembly, although he also retained the Wright type of forward elevator. Third, he replaced the bulky appearance of earlier machines with a sturdy yet practical look that presaged the pusher biplanes of the next few years.

Powered by a 50-hp (37.3-kW) Vivinus engine driving a primitive Voisin propeller, the airplane was ready in April 1909. Farman quickly set about intensive flight trials, which soon proved the new machine's practicality. He realized that the area of the ailerons was excessive, and disconnected the pair on the lower wings, locking them in place as extensions of the flying surfaces. Shortly thereafter, Farman incorporated four smaller ailerons, thus introducing the modern more balanced aileron/wing area ratio. By August Farman had modified the Farman III's large cellular biplane to an open configuration, and in this form the Farman III reached maturity as the progenitor of the classic European biplanes. Its best flight, on July 19, lasted 1 hour 23 minutes. The Farman III was so attractive two others were soon built for Roger Sommer and George Cockburn.

The Wrights continued to fly extensively in 1909, but with few modifications to their standard Model A machines, now obsolescent because of their forward elevators and lack of wheeled landing gear. Those in service were mostly Dayton-built, but late in the year French-built examples started to reach their buyers. As part of his French contract, Wilbur had taught three pupils to fly at his base at Pau in southern France, and meanwhile Orville, now fully recovered from the crash, restarted trials for the Signal Corps with a modified Model A featuring a smaller wing and taller landing gear skids. The tests had proved the satisfactory performance of the type by the end of July, and the American government bought the machine.

The practical possibilities of the monoplane had been clearly demonstrated in 1908 by the Antoinette and Blériot types, and in 1909 both lines came to maturity with a number of important designs and flights. Levavasseur continued the work he had started with the Antoinette IV and V the year before with further revisions to these two types. The exact details are not catalogued, but most important of all was the alteration of the aileron system. In their 1908 forms, the Antoinette IV and V had been restricted to downward-operating ailerons only, whereby the aileron on the downward-moving wing remained floating. Levavasseur now realized the inefficiency of this and provided differentially operating ailerons for 1909. On the following Antoinette VI, Levavasseur reverted to wing warping in place of the ailerons. The Antoinette VI was built for Capitache Binyeat, but its performance was no more than average in its 15 flights between April and July 1909. Its successor, the Antoinette VII, however, was the classic of the line and was excelled in performance only by the redoubtable Antoinette IV. Built for Hubert Latham, a Frenchman of British parentage destined to play a vital role in the popularization of flying, the machine first flew on July 27, 1909.

In the monoplane field, 1909 was to be Blériot's year, despite the courageous and ill-fated efforts of Latham. The Blériot No. XI was the foundation of Blériot's success as an aircraft constructor. In its original form, the No. XI looked very odd. This was a result of the stabilizing fin mounted on pylons above the pilot's head, near the front of the fuselage. Controls were the now-conventional warping, rear elevator, and rudder. The No. XI was ready toward the end of January 1909, but two months of effort yielded very little until Blériot transformed the No. XI into No. XI (Modified) with the central forward fin deleted, the rear rudder enlarged, and most important of all, an efficient Chauvière propeller fitted to the 25-hp (18.6-kW) Anzani engine that replaced the earlier 30-hp

LOUIS BLÉRIOT

LOUIS BLÉRIOT (1872–1936) Born at Cambrai in France on July 1, 1872, August Louis Blériot graduated from the École Centrale in Paris with a degree in Arts and Trades, and made his wealth in the manufacture of acetylene lamps for automobile use. He became an early devotee of powered flight at the age of 30 after visiting an exhibition and seeing one of Clément Ader's early, bat-wing aircraft. Blériot began to build, test, and crash numerous aircraft. Rather than follow one basic concept, Blériot worked by trial and error via gliders, box-kite biplanes, and, finally, monoplanes. By 1909 he had spent 780,000 francs on his passion for aircraft and was effectively bankrupt, but he also created an airplane that proved capable of remaining in the air for a useful time.

This was his No. XI machine, which made Blériot's fortune after he had achieved the world's first major over-water flight with a crossing of the English Channel on July 25, 1909. Only 24 days earlier, Blériot's plan had been saved from financial

Louis Blériot, conqueror of the English Channel, is pictured in the extremely rudimentary cockpit of his No. XI monoplane.

The competition number 22 on the long fin of this monoplane identifies this machine as the Blériot No. XII entered and flown by Blériot himself in the great Reims aviation meeting of August 1909. The machine was powered by a 50-hp (37.3-kW) ENV engine driving a four-blade Chauvière tractor propeller, and made nine flights during the meeting. The best of these covered 12.4 miles (20 km) in just under sixteen minutes, and the machine also took the "Prix de Tour de Piste" for speed over 6.2 miles (10 km) of 47.75 mph (76.95 km/h). The airplane was destroyed by fire on August 29 after a crash landing.

extinction. When the aviator's wife rescued the child of a rich planter from falling to his death, the boy's family lent Blériot 25,000 francs, which the pioneer used for the cross-Channel flight to win the prize of £1,000 offered by Lord Northcliffe's *Daily Mail* newspaper for the first person to complete a Channel crossing between sunrise and sunset in a heavier-than-air craft. Blériot was seriously injured at the time of his historic flight: As a result of a mechanical malfunction in a previous flight, his foot was badly burned, forcing him to use crutches and causing him severe pain when he operated the rudder bar. It was a dramatic story with a happy ending.

Blériot's competition in the race to cross the Channel consisted of the biplane of Charles de Lambert, a Russian aristocrat of French origins who pulled out of the race, and the Antoinette IV flown by Hubert Latham, an Englishman living in France. The No. XI had only about one-quarter of the Antoinette's wing area, and was powered by a 25-hp (18.6-kW) Anzani engine (the Antoinette IV used a 50-hp (37.3-kW) engine). Latham had attempted a Channel flight on July 19, coming down in the Channel only 7 or 8 miles (11 or 13 km) after takeoff from Sangatte and being rescued by a French tor-

The Blériot No. XI gained production orders after its creator's classic flight across the English Channel, and an airplane of this type is here captured by the camera during a flight near Brussels, the capital of Belgium.

pedo boat. At 3:00 on the morning of July 25, favorable weather conditions prompted Blériot to start the Anzani three-cylinder engine of his No. XI and await the arrival of dawn at Les Baraques near Calais. At 4:41 Blériot received the message that dawn had officially broken, and 36.5 minutes and some 23.5 miles (37.8 km) later he landed in the Northfall Meadow outside Dover Castle.

Without even a compass to guide him, Blériot had beaten the odds and gained worldwide fame. Latham made his second effort just four days later in the Antoinette VII powered by a 100-hp (74.6-kW) Antoinette engine, but was again forced down by engine failure, this time only 1 mile (1.6 km) from the English coast. Blériot's flight was not the longest of its time, but his achievement was huge, for its seized the attention of the world and further helped to boost the popularity of flight.

Blériot continued in aviation until his death in Paris on August 2, 1936.

(22.4-kW) REP unit. The result was an impressive airplane with capability much enhanced by the greater thrust of the Chauvière propeller. Blériot made some excellent duration and cross-country flights in this machine before turning his attention toward the English Channel.

Although basically unsuccessful, two other designs of 1909 were to have a profound influence on the future development of tractor biplanes. These were the Goupy II and Breguet I. Built by Blériot, the Goupy II was designed by Ambrose Goupy and Mario Calderera. It had staggered wings (the top wing being ahead of the lower wing) on a fuselage and empennage based on Blériot's designs. Designed and built by Louis Breguet, the Breguet I was not as advanced in appearance as the Goupy II, but it played a more prominent part in the development of tractor biplanes.

The United Kingdom was only now beginning to emerge from the aeronautical doldrums. American Samuel F. Cody and Englishman Alliott Verdon Roe were principally responsible for this. After the hesitant and minor successes of his first powered airplane, known as the British Army Aeroplane No. 1, Cody in the last quarter of 1908 rebuilt his machine into what may be termed the Cody 2, which made some 30 flights in the first half of 1909, the best of them covering 4 miles (6.4 km). Subsequent modification turned this machine into the Cody 3, on which its flamboyant creator made several successful flights, the best of them covering 40 miles (64 km) in just over 60 minutes on September 8, 1909. These Cody machines were large, sturdy, but clumsy machines, and exerted no real influence on the mainstream of aviation. They were, however, important in showing the British people that aircraft could fly, and that one designed in their own country, even if not by one of their own countrymen, could remain in the air for a considerable period. Cody's enthusiasm and determination were an encouragement to all would-be British pioneers and helped alleviate the unconscious British fears that the "Continentals" had stolen a march on them.

The only other British pioneer of the period to achieve anything like success was Roe, with a series of triplanes inspired by the unsuccessful Goupy I. Roe was desperately short of money and could at first only afford the 6- and 9-hp (4.5- and 6.7-kW) JAP engines. They limited him to powered hops in his otherwise promising machines.

In the United States the AEA continued its work with the Silver Wing, essentially a scaled-up version of the June Bug with a forward elevator, designed and flown by J. A. D. McCurdy. All these AEA aircraft, however, were built and tested in relative isolation near the American-Canadian border and had no direct influence on the course of aviation history apart from giving Glenn Curtiss his start in the field. Without his basic engineering and design skill, combined with his engines, it is questionable whether the AEA would have been as successful.

At the beginning of 1909 Curtiss started his own aircraft business in conjunction with Augustus Herring, Chanute's associate of 10 years earlier. The first machine, built for the Aeronautic Society of New York but soon lent to Curtiss, was the Gold Bug. Like the Silver Wing, this machine evolved from the June Bug and continued the basic design philosophy of the AEA, but it had parallel wings instead of the dihedral/anhedral curved wings of the AEA types. Powerful ailerons were installed at midgap, but otherwise the airplane was conventional by the standards of the day. The Gold Bug was flying successfully by the late spring of 1909, but by then Curtiss had decided to build a machine for himself, principally as a racing machine and record-breaker for himself. He had clearly foreseen that public enthusiasm for aviation would soon begin to pour hard cash into the sport, and that considerable sums could be secured by the first man to develop a specialized aircraft. The Golden Flyer, as Curtiss's machine was called, was similar in layout to the Gold Bug, but was powered by a new 50-hp (37.3-kW) Curtiss engine, although for tactical reasons Curtiss often stated that the engine could deliver only 30 hp (22.4 kW). The Golden Flyer was ready just in time for the Reims aviation meeting. Following its successes there, it greatly influenced other designers.

THE CROWDS GO WILD

Two 1909 events finally put aviation in the public spotlight. First, in July the first heavier-than-air flight was made across the English Channel, a primary symbol of British independence. The prospect of such a crossing had been in view for some time. The London newspaper, *The Daily Mail,* had offered a prize of £1,000 for the first man to do it. The two most likely contenders were Hubert Latham in an Antoinette and Louis Blériot in one of his own machines. It is noteworthy that both already were tractor monoplanes. Latham was the first to make an attempt, setting out from Sangatte near Calais early on the morning of July 19 in his Antoinette IV. Unluckily for him, however, the usually reliable 50-hp (37.3-kW) Antoinette engine cut out when he was about 8 miles (12 km) out to sea, and he had to ditch the airplane. Thanks to the generosity of the French government, however, the attempt had been escorted by the destroyer *Harpon,* which picked up both Latham and his machine.

Six days later, on July 25, Blériot was ready to make his effort. Although still suffering from the effects of burns on one of his legs from an earlier crash, Blériot set forth in his No. XI airplane and landed near Dover Castle after a flight of 23.5 miles (37.8 km) in 36 minutes 30 seconds. The airplane was by no means suitable for the attempt, but the success was Blériot's and he received a hero's welcome in London and on his return to France. The Channel flight ensured Blériot's financial success as an aircraft constructor, for within two days he had received orders for over 100 No. XI aircraft.

The other major event of 1909 was La Grande Semaine d'Aviation de la Champagne, the first great flying meeting. This grand affair attracted all the best pilots and machines in Europe and was held on the open spaces near Bétheny outside Reims between August 22 and 29. With many generous prizes offered by the champagne industry, the whole meeting was held under the auspices of the president of the French Republic and attended by many influential political and financial figures from all over Europe. There were 38 entries, of which only 23 succeeded in taking off. Of the 120 takeoffs achieved, 87 resulted in flights of over 3.1 miles (5 km) and 7 in flights of over 62 miles (100 km). The best flight recorded was by Henry Farman in his Farman III, now powered by the new 50-hp (37.3-kW) Gnome rotary engine, with a flight of 112 miles (180 km) in just over three hours. Curtiss took the speed prize at 52.63 mph with his Golden Flyer, and Latham took the altitude prize with a height of 508 ft (155 m) in the Antoinette VII. There were four other prizes for heavier-than-air craft, and two for lighter-than-air craft. The highest speed recorded at the event, though not during the competition for the speed prize, was in the special short sprint race, won by Blériot on his No. XII at a speed of 47.8 mph (76.95 km/h). This meeting, with its plethora of events, flights, and records, marked the beginning of Europe's acceptance of the airplane as more than just a toy.

On July 25, 1909, Louis Blériot sets off in his No. XI from Les Baraques near Calais for his successful attempt to make the first flight in a heavier-than-air plane over the narrowest point of the English Channel.

The meeting was a great success from every aspect, and set the style for similar events all over Europe in the next few years. It also spurred on men such as Roe who had not yet achieved true flight; by the end of the year he was able to coax his second triplane into the air for about 880 yards (805 m). Previously, European aviation had been principally a French story. Now other countries embraced it. In the United Kingdom only Roe, Cody, and J. W. Dunne had neared success with British machines. Most other aviators were content with French and American machines bought abroad or built under license in the United Kingdom. In 1909 Germany, Austria, Sweden, Rumania, Russia, Turkey, and Portugal all saw their first flights. Although these were mostly by touring French pilots, it would not be long before locals would join the fray.

In 1909 flights of considerable endurance had been made, and passengers had been carried. The next few years were to see an explosion in the development of the airplane's possibilities. The Wrights' basic layout would be eclipsed with the forward elevator beginning to lose its importance to a rear-mounted unit combined with the fin and rudder. The days of inherent instability were also waning. In the period between the Wrights' first flights and the great Reims aviation meeting, maximum speeds had risen slowly from some 25 to 31 mph (40 to 50 km/h) to 47.8 mph (76.95 km/h), and by the end of 1909 the world range and altitude records stood at 145.6 miles (235 km) by Farman and 1,486 ft (453 m) by Latham. In 1910 all the records were to be exceeded by handsome margins.

In 1910 flying became international in all its aspects, driven by races and competitions. This internationalism involved not only the number of places where the competitions took place, but also the nationalities of the competitors themselves. Although most of them flew French aircraft, an increasing number of British machines was evident. Despite the relatively small number of American pilots and designers, entrepreneurs in the United States were quick to realize the draw that flying had become, and in January 1910 the first international competition to take place in that country was held in Los Angeles. Honors were shared between France and the United States: Louis Paulhan in a Henry Farman set a world altitude record at 4,165 ft (1,269.5 m), and Curtiss established a world speed record at 55 mph (88.5 km/h) with a machine of his own design. Attendances were very large, and promoters in other cities were suddenly aware that aviation was a real money-spinner. In September there was a highly successful meeting in Boston, where most of the competitors were American and British. The United States was firmly in the grip of the flying "bug." Americans were soon also enthralled by daredevil flying, or "barnstorming."

In 1910 meetings were also held all over Europe: four in Italy, two in Germany, one each in Spain, Switzerland, Belgium, Denmark, Russia, and Hungary, and many in France and the United Kingdom. Crowds continued to flock to them. They were usually held close to large cities, sometimes on specially hired grounds and sometimes on airfields specially bought and built up by a few enterprising promoters. Claude Grahame-White established Hendon, one of the major flying areas for London. Flying displays became a regular feature of weekend life in the cities of Europe, attended by the aristocracy, the middle class, and the mass of working people who could get to the field alike. All were catered to in separate enclosures, and large fortunes were made by the entrepreneurs who were lucky enough to have their preparations and enterprise attended by good weather.

The flying displays so prominent in Europe and the United States before the start of World War I were particularly important for two reasons. First, they largely financed the growth and development of aviation: It was the public's money that put up the prizes and allowed manufacturers to expand their businesses, something that could not have been financed on sales of aircraft alone. Second, these displays and races provided the technical

The huge fillip given to powered flight by Blériot's flight over the English Channel in July 1909 and then the Reims aviation meeting in the following month led to a blossoming of interest in flight. This was strongest in Europe, but in 1910 there were three important air meetings in the United States. The first of these, in January of that year, took place at Los Angeles, California. The Los Angeles meeting included races, demonstration flights, and, as recorded here, joyrides for the more adventurous spirits among the large crowd.

BARNEY OLDFIELD   LINCOLN BEACHY
Col. O. 1914   1914

One of the greatest American "stunt" pilots of the period before World War I was Lincoln Beachey, who flew a special Curtiss pusher biplane. Before his death in a flying accident during 1915, Beachey made a huge name for himself with all manner of daredevil flying, including races against motorcars.

background and testing place for manufacturers; they were also a way to prove their abilities in public and sell aircraft to the growing number of pilots in the market. Prize money became increasingly important to the finances of most designers and constructors.

The number of constructors had grown considerably, and large companies with other basic interests were now taking an increasing share of the market. The best companies, however, were those that had gotten off to a sound start with aircraft in 1908 and 1909. When their own types were not selling very successfully, these companies could always undertake the building of a one-shot design, or the licensed production of aircraft whose output could not keep up with demand. By 1914, the building of aircraft was in the hands of a number of small builders, producing only a few aircraft a year, and a few larger companies, such as Bristol, Short Brothers, Blériot, Morane-Saulnier, Albatros, and Caproni, turning out a greater quantity of machines. These companies were to bear the brunt of the production race in the opening months of the war.

People who would never be able to afford aircraft of their own were now able to take part in the adventure of flight as passengers. The greatest passenger carriers of this time were the five German Zeppelin airships that, between 1910 and 1914, carried some 35,000 passengers over 170,000 miles (273,600 km). But aircraft also played their part. One or two passengers had already been carried on a variety of aircraft when Grahame-White, who always had a good sense of the future of aviation, decided that passenger flights should be added to the attractions of his displays and school at Hendon. The result was his extraordinary Charabanc, which flew for the first time late in the summer of 1913. On October 2 the type established a new world record by taking off with nine passengers and staying in the air for just under 20 minutes. On February 11, 1914 this record was bettered by the Sikorsky Bolshoi Bal'tiskii, which took up 16 people. This remarkable machine, which soon evolved into the world's first four-engined bomber, even had a promenade deck along the upper rear fuselage, with rails to prevent passengers from falling off as the huge machine lumbered along!

Uncertain as they were of the role aircraft could play in war, governments were at first hesitant to spend lavishly on air services. The British army had used balloons regularly since 1878. In 1907 the German army established its Zeppelin service. After the Reims meeting proved the practicality of aircraft in both a civilian and a military capacity, the United States paved the way with the purchase of a Wright biplane, *Miss Columbia,* for $30,000 on August 2, 1909. In 1910, France, Germany, and Russia each established an army air service, although the German service was not formally established until October 1912. The United Kingdom followed by forming the Royal Engineers' Air Battalion in 1911, transformed into the Royal Flying Corps with Military and Naval wings in May 1912. In July 1914 the Royal Navy established its own Royal Naval Air Service out of the RFC's Naval Wing.

The first use of aircraft in war, however, was by the Italians, who still lacked a proper air service. The Italian army fighting the Turks in Libya used a number of aircraft provided by the Royal Aero Club of Italy. On October 22, 1911, Capitano Carlo Piazza carried out the first air reconnaissance of Turkish positions near Aziziya in a Blériot; on November 1 history was made when Tenente Gavotti dropped four homemade bombs on a Turkish camp from his Etrich Taube; on November 24 Capitano Moizo carried out the first artillery spotting flight; and on February 23, 1913, Piazza flew the world's first photographic-reconnaissance mission. The four basic tasks to be fulfilled by aircraft in World

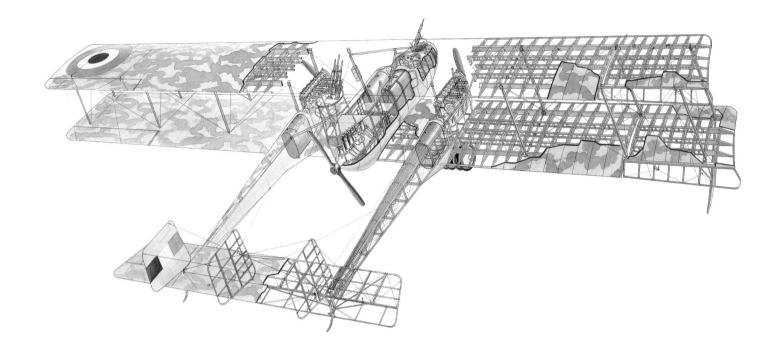

PLANES OF
GIORGIO CAPRONI

PLANES OF GIORGIO CAPRONI

The Caproni organization, established in 1908 by Count Gianni Caproni and destined to become a major force in the Italian economy of the first half of the twentieth century, became celebrated in World War I for its biplane and triplane bombers, which were notably large by the standards of the day. By the end of the war in 1918, Caproni was rivaled only by FIAT in the quantity and diversity of its types. The various subsidiaries of the Caproni organization, which grew rapidly in the period between the world wars, were responsible for more than one hundred different types of aircraft between 1919 and 1939 and in the process elevated Caproni to the forefront of Italian aviation. By the late 1930s, however, the designers of the Caproni empire had begun to fall behind the leading edge of aircraft design, and only a few modern designs of Caproni origin were in service with the Regia Aeronautica at the time of Italy's entry into World War II in 1940. These planes were not noted for their performance or general capability, moreover. Like another Italian company of the period, Breda,

FACING PAGE Italy was one of the pioneers of heaving bombing for strategic purposes, and for this task its air force relied heavily on the three-engined biplane bombers produced by Caproni. The most important of these were the Ca 3 and Ca 5 series, the former typified by the Ca 33 with 150-hp (112-kW) Isotta-Fraschini V.4B engines and the latter by the Ca 46 (sic) with 300-hp (224-kW) Fiat A.12-bis engines. The engines were arranged as two tractor units at the fronts of the booms that carried the tail unit, and one pusher unit at the rear of the central nacelle. The latter had a raised "pulpit" position for a defensive machine gunner just ahead of it, and there was another machine gunner in the nose of the central nacelle forward of the cockpit for the two pilots.

Caproni produced a large range of aircraft, equipment, components, and accessories, the most celebrated being probably the engines of the Isotta-Fraschini make. Caproni's primary airframe manufacturing facility, originally known as the Società per lo Sviluppo dell'Aviazione in Italia, was sited in Taliedo, Milan. The other elements of the Caproni organization were Cantieri Aeronautici Bergamaschi (later Caproni Aeronautica Bergamasca) at Ponte San Pietro, Bergamo; Caproni Vizzola S.A. at Vizzola Ticino, Varese; CNA (Compagnia Nazionale Aeronautica) at Littorio, Rome; Aeronautica Predappio S.A. at Predappio; Officine Meccaniche Reggiane S.A. at Reggio Emilia; and Società Anonima Industrie Meccaniche Aeronautiche Navali (SAIMAN) at Lido di Roma. Of these subsidiaries, only Bergamaschi and Reggiane produced modern aircraft in any significant numbers. After World War II the Caproni organization declined further, and Caproni himself died on October 27, 1957.

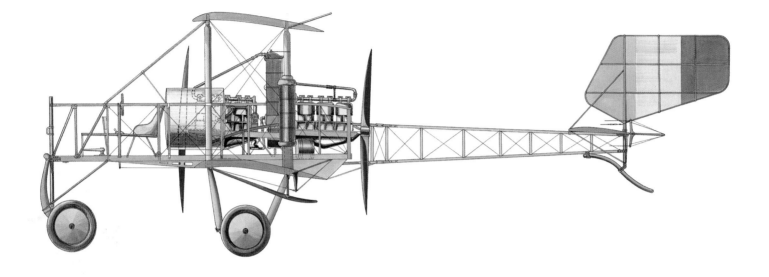

PLANES OF GIORGIO CAPRONI

ABOVE Ca 2 was the designation given by the Italian air service to the first production versions of the large three-engined Caproni bomber that entered service
in 1915. Italy was a pioneer of long-range bombing, initially by day and later by
night, and its first effective type was the Ca 2 variant known to its manufacturer
as the Ca 32 with the powerplant of three 100-hp (74.6-kW) Fiat A.10 engines
installed as one pusher and two tractor units.

FACING PAGE One of the most extraordinary and also ungainly aircraft ever developed, the "Capronissimo" was an attempt by the Italian Caproni company to create a flying boat airliner to carry one hundred passengers. The hull looked like a
houseboat, a tandem arrangement of three triplane wing cellules was designed
to provide adequate lift, and power was provided by four tractor and four pusher
Liberty 12 engines each rated at 400 hp (298 kW). Formally known as the Ca 60,
this monster was launched in January 1921, but crashed during its first flight in
March of the same year. The pilot escaped with his life, and while the wreckage
was salvaged for a proposed reconstruction, it was later destroyed by a providen-
tial fire.

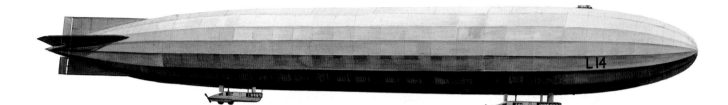

THE AGE OF THE ZEPPELINS

Ferdinand Adolf August Heinrich, Graf von Zeppelin, was born on July 8, 1838, at Konstanz in Bade, and died on March 8, 1917, at Charlottenburg near Berlin. Zeppelin was the world's first major constructor of rigid dirigible airships, and his name has since been popularly identified with this type of flying machine. Zeppelin was commissioned into the Prussian army in 1858 and made the first of several balloon flights at St. Paul, Minnesota, while attached to the Union army as a military observer during the American Civil War. He saw action in 1866 during the Seven Weeks' War and then in 1870–71 during the Franco-Prussian War, and served successively in the armies of Württemberg, Prussia, and the German empire. Retiring in 1890, he spent the rest of his life developing and promoting the lighter-than-air craft. The first flight of the LZ-1 on July 2, 1900, from a floating hangar on Lake Constance near Friedrichshafen in southern Germany was only partially successful, but caught the imagination of the public and paved the way for the subsequent funding of Zeppelin's work through public subscriptions and donations. The German authorities soon grasped the

FACING PAGE, TOP Operated by the imperial German navy as the L14, the LZ-46 was typical of the Zeppelin airships operated by the German forces in the middle part of World War I. The ship was one of the LZ-38 class of Type "p" airships, numbering 22 units delivered as 12 and 10 to the army and navy respectively. With a gas capacity of 1,126,530 cu ft (31,900 m³), the ship was 536 ft 5 in (163.5 m) long and was powered by four 210-hp (156.5-kW) Maybach C-X engines. First flown in September 1915, the ship had a crew of 18 and a range of 2,670 miles (4,300 km), and completed 526 flights including a last sortie on June 23, 1919, the day on which work on the ship's breaking up was started. The L14 was arguably the most successful airship ever built, and among her credits are scouting for the High Seas Fleet in the Battle of Jutland and 24 raids on targets in the U.K.

FACING PAGE, BOTTOM The need to keep the petroleum-fueled engines of airships well clear of the interior gas cells containing a Zeppelin airship's lifting agent of flammable hydrogen gas demanded the installation of the engines in exterior mountings. The engines were therefore installed in gondolas carried by struts outside the airship's envelope, and this arrangement also provided the room for the pusher propeller to turn. The engines were unsilenced and therefore very noisy, and provision was made for a mechanic to enter the gondola in flight to undertake any repairs or adjustments that might be needed.

ABOVE Early airships came in a wondrous assortment of sizes and shapes, practical and impractical. This cigar-shaped craft, apparently outpaced by people on the ground, has a nonrigid envelope stabilized by an underslung frame of triangular section with the small engine near the front, the vestigial control surfaces at the rear, and the pilot in the middle where he tried to maintain the airship's longitudinal balance by moving forward and rearward.

fact that lighter-than-air craft had greater potential, at least in the short term, than the still very primitive heavier-than-air craft of the period, and Zeppelin's achievement of a twenty-four-hour flight in 1906 sparked great interest. A passenger service was operated by Delag (Deutsche-Luftschiffahrts A.G.), established in 1910, before World War I, and during the fighting more than one hundred Zeppelin airships saw military service. The Zeppelin airships gained modest success in long-range bombing operations, which persuaded many thinkers that Zeppelin airships would become the major force in transport flight

after the war. Several Zeppelin airships were allocated to the victorious Allied nations as part of Germany's postwar reparations. The Zeppelin company managed to revive its transport operations in this financially difficult time, the organization's two most celebrated craft being the *Graf Zeppelin*, completed in September 1928, and the larger *Hindenburg*, completed in 1936. The *Graf Zeppelin* launched the world's first transoceanic services with flights across the North Atlantic; by the time it was taken out of service in 1937 it had completed 590 flights, including 144 ocean crossings, covering more than 1 million miles (1.61 million km) including, during 1929, 21,500 miles (34,600 km) in a round-the-world flight completed in a flying time of twenty-one days. In 1936 the *Hindenburg* carried a total of 1,002 passengers on ten scheduled round trips between Germany and the United States. Tragically, while trying to reach its mooring mast at Lakehurst, New Jersey, on May 6, 1937, the *Hindenburg* caught fire and was burned out with the loss of thirty-six lives. This ended the period of commercial airship operations, although attempts are being made in the first part of the twenty-first century to revive them, initially for freight operations.

Am Bodensee. Großflugzeug „Do X" und Luftschiff „Graf Zeppelin"

FACING PAGE Germany's hopes for European leadership in aerial passenger transport before World War I were centered on the use of airships rather than heavier-than-air craft. Here the Zeppelin airships were dominant, but other manufacturers were Parseval and Gross. This poster of the period before World War I reveals single examples of the largely unsuccessful airships of these two organizations over the German city of Cologne.

ABOVE The most famous of all commercial airships was the Zeppelin LZ-127, named *Graf Zeppelin*. This huge rigid airship was completed in September 1928 with hydrogen as its lifting agent, and carried up to twenty passengers as well as a crew of thirty-six. The ship offered exceptional levels of comfort, and logged 17,178 flying hours before being grounded in June 1937.

BELOW Even in its early days as a very underdeveloped type, the Zeppelin airship offered the promise of long-range air transport with levels of comfort that could not be matched by contemporary and later aircraft.

The Deperdussin Monocoque racing and record-breaking airplane was a clear portent of future design thinking in features such as its semi-monocoque fuselage and the aerodynamic "cleanliness" offered by its monoplane wing, low-drag fuselage, faired landing gear, and neatly cowled engine driving a propeller with a spinner.

War I were born. The Italians were impressed by the results, and they set up an army air service in June 1912. Further military uses for aircraft were discovered during the Balkan Wars of 1912–13.

Throughout 1910, 1911, and 1912 progress was continually made, especially in France and the United Kingdom, with the development of aircraft offering ever-improving levels of performance and reliability. Notable in 1913, though, was the appearance in France of the fastest airplane of the period before World War I. This was the Deperdussin Monocoque, a beautifully streamlined monoplane eventually capable of 126 mph (203 km/h). It looked forward to the racing aircraft of the 1920s with its monocoque (stressed "single-shell") fuselage, enclosed engine, and careful attention to the elimination of drag-producing factors. The advances made in the years before the world plunged into war in August 1914 are best made clear through a few statistics. Since 1909, the world speed record had improved from 47.8 to 126.7 mph (77 to 203.86 km/h), the range record had risen from 145.6 to 634.5 miles (234.3 to 1,021.2 km), and the altitude record had increased from 1,486 to 20,079 ft (453 to 6,120 m). But these advances were about to be utterly outstripped, for in the following four years aviation would receive its most profound, if perhaps regrettable, stimulus.

THE GREAT WAR IN THE AIR

The increase in the use of aircraft and their expanding roles in World War I inevitably altered both the nature of aviation and public opinion about flight and fliers. Although aircraft had seen limited use as military weapons in the last few years before World War I, in 1914 most Europeans still considered flight the province of adventurous spirits who flew for sport and for excitement. By the end of the conflict, on the other hand, aviation was very big business. Many thousands of aircraft and engines had been built in a multitude of factories, most of which had no connection with aviation before the start of hostilities in August 1914. The air forces of the combatant nations, too, had grown into potent weapons of war, revealing to the farsighted the era of total war in which every man, woman, and child, no matter how remote from the front, was at risk.

The various military aircraft competitions held in 1911 and 1912 had been intended to produce types that could be standardized for the squadrons, thus easing pro-

Even early pioneering flights revealed the potential of the airplane for the purposes of tactical reconnaissance.

The Avro Type 504 remains one of the classic aircraft of flight, for it was built in very large numbers and remained in service to 1933 even though it had first flown in July 1913. The Type 504 was first used as an operational airplane, but soon found its real niche as a very effective trainer. The example depicted is a Type 504K, which was introduced in 1918 as a variant able to use the Clerget, Gnome, or Le Rhône rotary engines in the power range between 100 and 130 hp (74.6 and 96.9 kW).

curement and maintenance problems. Yet it was one thing to select what was considered a type suitable for widespread use, and another to get it into mass production. The aviation industry of the period was just not geared to mass production: Most factories had experience only in the building of one-of-a-kind types for designers. The result, in military terms, was that chosen designs could not as yet be built in sufficient quantity and there could be little standardization of types within the squadrons. In this respect the Germans and French were better off than the British. The Germans fielded a large number of Taube (dove) types derived from the experiments of Igo Etrich and F. Wels, as well as units homogeneously equipped with tractor biplanes of Albatros and Aviatik design. The French had squadrons of Voisin biplane bombers, and Blériot and Morane-Saulnier monoplanes for reconnaissance work. The British, almost inevitably, went to war with several French aircraft plus a large miscellany of British types, the best of which were the Royal Aircraft Factory's B.E.2, Sopwith Tabloid, Bristol Scout D, and various marks of Avro Type 504.

At the outbreak of World War I, the Allied powers had some 233 aircraft (160 French and 73 British in France) against the Germans' total of 246. At first the weather was superb, but the aircraft had not been designed for intensive operations and their serviceability was low, a factor worsened by the number of different types and engines in service at a time when the Allies were in full retreat and all logistical backing was extemporized. Yet somehow or other losses were tolerable, and from August 19 the RFC began to turn in useful reconnaissance reports. At first, the high command distrusted the information received from this novel source, but when British reconnaissance aircraft brought in the first news of the Germans' great left-wheel sweep down past the east side of Paris, and this information was subsequently confirmed by orthodox methods, the generals at last began to realize that in aircraft they had an important new aid. The art of camouflage against air reconnaissance was as yet unknown, so the observers of the "recce-jobs" had an easy time and could turn in useful information.

J. BATCHELOR

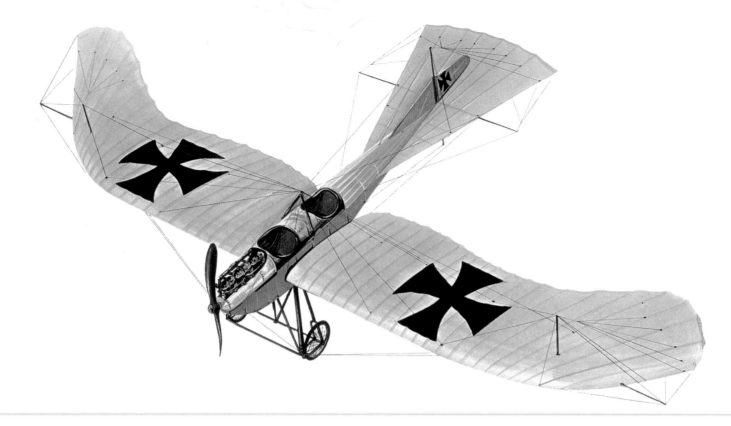

ABOVE Built by many companies to basically the same design, monoplanes of the Taube (dove) type were popular in Europe in the years before World War I, especially in Germany and Austria-Hungary. The large monoplane wings of such aircraft were certainly very appealing at the esthetic level, but required a mass of drag-producing wires to prevent their collapse under flying and landing loads.

BELOW The Morane-Saulnier Type L parasol-wing monoplane was a French airplane that entered service in 1914. The model is of great historical importance, for it was the type flown by Roland Garros when he became the world's first air "ace" in April 1915. The airplane depicted here in British markings was that flown by Flight Sub-Lieutenant R. A. J. Warneford on June 7, 1915, when he encountered the Zeppelin LZ-37 of the imperial German army air service as it was making for England on a bombing raid. Warneford managed to climb above the airship and drop six 20-lb (9.1-kg) bombs on it: The last bomb's detonation caused the LZ-37's hydrogen lifting gas to catch fire and explode, sending the airship to its destruction. The explosion also damaged Warneford's Type L, which came down behind the German lines: Warneford made a quick repair, took off, and returned safely, later receiving the Victoria Cross for his courageous effort.

It was not long before the first air weapons made their appearance. Initially these weapons consisted of personal equipment such as rifles and pistols. The resultant aerial duels of pilot against pilot stood little chance of inflicting mortal damage on either of the parties. But it was only a matter of time before effective aerial armament was introduced, and on October 5 a French gunner, Caporal Quénault, shot down an Aviatik two-seater with a Hotchkiss machine gun mounted in the front of the nacelle of a Voisin bomber. From this time onward the incidence of aerial combats, and also of aerial victories, began slowly to climb. But there remained one basic problem to be solved before air combat could reach a large scale: the interface between gun and propeller, not solved until 1915.

Biplane bombers of the pusher type from the Voisin stable were the mainstay of the French offensive air effort in the early part of World War I, but this example of the Voisin Type 3 (otherwise Type LA) was the machine on which the world's first air-to-air "kill" was scored on October 5, 1914, by the Hotchkiss machine gun manned by Caporal Quénault with Joseph Frantz as his pilot.

It had occurred to various pilots early in the history of aviation that if one could fly over a target, then one could also drop missiles on it, and early in the war practical work on the development of bombing got under way. As early as June 30, 1910, Glenn Curtiss had dropped dummy bombs on the outline of a battleship buoyed out on Lake Keuka. Bombing competitions, using bags of flour, had even become a popular feature of prewar flying meetings. The French and Germans, particularly the former, were concerned with bombing from the beginning of the war. On August 14, 1914, the French sent two Voisins to attack the Zeppelin sheds at Metz-Frascaty, and on August 30 a German Taube dropped five small bombs on Paris, killing one civilian and injuring another two. The RFC was not at first especially interested in bombing, but its naval sister service, the Royal Naval Air Service, showed more enterprise. It launched its first, ultimately abortive raid on the Zeppelin sheds at Düsseldorf with two aircraft from Antwerp on September 22. Another raid on the same target was launched on October 8, this time destroying the Zeppelin Z.IX.

Early bombs were extemporized affairs, usually based on an artillery shell with fins attached, and bombing sights were nonexistent. Nevertheless the will was there, and in the autumn of 1914 the French decided to build up a major bombing force of Voisins, which were too slow and ponderous for air combat, but which had reasonable range and load-carrying capacity.

Meanwhile, the location of the machine gun relative to the propeller hindered the development of true airfighting. The problem was easily solved on the pusher type of two-seaters. A light machine gun, usually on a simple pillar mounting, was placed at the front of the nacelle for the observer's use. Even on the newer tractor two-seaters, the observer could be provided with a light machine gun capable of upward, rearward, and lateral fire. The disadvantage of this was that the observer had to sit in the forward of the two seats so that the removal of his weight, on or near the airplane's center of gravity, would not affect the trim of the machine on solo flights. This meant that the observer was located between the wings, which seriously curtailed his fields of vision and of fire, surrounded as he was by a mass of rigging and bracing wires, many of which would be cut by bullets. The problem was later solved by reversing the positions of pilot and observer so that the observer had an improved field of fire over the airplane's rear.

Although armament was fitted to two-seaters from the earliest days of the war, two-seaters were not really suited to conversion into fighters, or scouts, as such aircraft

The majority of the aircraft used in the first part of World War I were unarmed two-seaters. These were generally flown in the short-range reconnaissance role with the pilot in the rear seat and the observer in the front seat. Typical of the breed was the Lohner B I, an Austro-Hungarian type with a swept-back wing cellule and a fully but somewhat clumsily cowled Austro-Daimler engine rated at either 100 or 120 hp (74.6 or 89.5 kW).

were then known. The two-seaters were too big, heavy, clumsy, and slow. What was needed was a single-seater fighter, but there remained the problem of the position of the gun relative to the propeller.

If the gun were fixed to fire forward along the airplane's longitudinal axis and pilot's line of sight, some of the bullets fired would almost inevitably hit one or more of the propeller blades. Various alternatives were tried, including the provision of guns angled out from the centerline of the aircraft by about 45°. Except for prodigiously capable men, however, these guns made accurate sighting so difficult it made the expedient next to useless. One rare success story was Captain Lanoe G. Hawker. In July 1915 Hawker took on three German aircraft in one flight, forcing one down, sending the second the same way with a knocked-out engine, and shooting the third down in flames, all in a Bristol Scout armed with an angled Lewis gun.

The only realistic option was to align the gun along the airplane's centerline so that all the pilot had to do was aim his whole machine at the target and press the trigger. But how to avoid the propeller? Experiments carried out before the war by Franz Schneider of the German LVG concern and Raymond Saulnier of the French Morane-Saulnier company helped develop primitive synchronizer gears, which linked the firing mechanism to the propeller's rotation. But both experiments had problems. Inconsistencies in the chemical compounds used as propellants meant that some bullets fired fractionally later than they should, undoing the work of the synchronizer and shattering a blade. To preserve these expensive items, Saulnier had fitted his experimental propellers with wedge-shaped steel deflectors bolted to the back of the blades to deflect any bullet.

Early in 1915 the idea was resurrected by Saulnier and the great prewar stunt pilot Roland Garros, who was serving in the French army air service. It was soon decided by the two men that the synchronizer gear should be omitted for the sake of lightness and simplicity, that the bullets that might hit a blade could be warded off by the deflectors. Preliminary tests proved successful, and in March 1915 Garros returned to his unit with his modified Morane-Saulnier Type L parasol-wing scout. All was ready on April 1, 1915, and Garros set off in search of prey. He soon ran into four German Albatros two-seaters,

A celebrated pioneer pilot in the period leading up to World War I, when he flew Morane-Saulnier aircraft, Roland Garros was the first true fighter ace in the history of air warfare. The kingpost ahead of the cockpit provided a centerline attachment for the wires that supported the outboard parts of the monoplane wing against landing loads and also carried the wires that controlled the warping of the wing for lateral control. The wires that helped brace the wing against flying loads mirrored the landing wires and extended from the main unit of the fixed landing gear.

EDDIE RICKENBACKER

EDWARD VERNON RICKENBACKER (1890–1973) Captain Edward "Eddie" V. Rickenbacker was the highest-scoring American air "ace" of World War I. He was born in Columbus, Ohio, on October 8, 1890, the son of William and Elizabeth Reichenbacher. His schooling ended when he left at the age of 12 following the death of his father, and his first paid employment, obtained after he had said he was 14, was with the Columbus Glass Company for the weekly pay of $3.50, which he handed to his mother. Later he worked in a foundry, a shoe factory, and the Frayer-Miller Air-Cooled Car Company and used his spare time for correspondence courses in mechanical engineering and draftsman-

"Eddie" Rickenbacker was the leading American fighter ace of World War I and a major figure in the development of American civil aviation in later years. He is here seen in nonchalant pose beside his French-built Nieuport Nie.28 fighter of the 94th "Hat in the Ring" Aero Squadron.

ship. He became fascinated with motor racing and from 1910 became a consistently successful racing driver. Early in 1914 he drove a specially built Blitzen-Benz racer to a new world's speed record of 134 mph (216 km/h). By 1917 he was bringing home some $40,000 per year as one of the United States' best racing drivers.

Early in 1917 Reichenbacher crossed the Atlantic to England to help build a racing team for the Sunbeam Motor Company, but the project was canceled after the United States entered World War I in April of the same year. In England Reichenbacher had developed a keen interest in aviation, and on his return to the United States proposed a flying unit manned by racing drivers, but could not win official support. In Washington, D.C., he met General John J. Pershing, who asked Reichenbacher to join the U.S. Army and come to France as his personal chauffeur. It was at this stage that Reichenbacher changed the spelling of his name to the less Teutonic Rickenbacker.

In August 1917, after several months as Pershing's chauffeur, Rickenbacker was able to transfer to Aviation Section, which taught him to fly at the 2nd Aviation Instruction Center at Tours. Seeing in Rickenbacker a very highly skilled engine specialist, the army posted him to the 3rd AIC at Issoudun as chief engineering officer: Rickenbacker apparently needed only to listen to an engine to tell what was wrong with it. On his own time, he managed to obtain advanced flying training and then persuade his commander to let him undertake an aerial gunnery course at Cazeau. Rickenbacker's many applications for combat service finally paid off, and on March 4, 1918, he joined the newly formed 94th Aero Squadron at Villeneuve-les-Vertus on the Marne sector of the front. Soon after this the 94th AS received its aircraft, and on March 19, Rickenbacker, in company with Major Raoul Lufbery and Lieutenant Douglas Campbell, made the first patrol over the enemy line by a U.S. air unit. Rickenbacker achieved his first aerial victory on April 29, and in little more than one month had become an "ace" by shooting down five aircraft. Rickenbacker was already displaying his tactical skill, for he always flew with a cool and logical attitude, never refusing to enter combat but always planning to use every advantage when he did so. In this he was aided by his earlier experience in the hazardous sport of motor racing, and also by his relative maturity.

During June Rickenbacker was afflicted with an ear infection, and during July and August recuperated in Paris from the resulting mastoid operation. Beforehand, Rickenbacker had become a flight commander, and on returning to service began to reveal his real skill. During the last two weeks of September he brought down six or more German aircraft, and during October added another 14 to his tally. On September 25 he became commander of the 94th AS, a command he held up to the Armistice of November 11, 1918, by which time he was credited with 26 victories and had received the Medal of Honor.

Upon his return to the United States, Rickenbacker was offered large salaries by companies wanting the services of this national hero for occupations as diverse as films and advertising. He refused all these offers and started an aerial survey operation with Major Reed Chambers, a seven-victory "ace." Rickenbacker later decided to sell his interest so that he could embark on a career in cars, and in 1921 he started the Rickenbacker Motor Company to sell the "Rickenbacker," which possessed several innovative features that later became standard. The company lacked adequate capital, however, and failed. During November 1927 Rickenbacker gained a controlling interest in the Indianapolis Motor Speedway Company, and was president of this company from 1927 until 1945. Early in 1928 he joined the Cadillac Motor Car Company as assistant sales manager of the La Salle Division, and a year later was transferred by General Motors from Cadillac to the General Aviation Manufacturing Corporation as vice president and sales director. In 1932 Rickenbacker became vice president of American Airways, and in the following year vice president of North American Aviation, Inc., successor to the GAMC. In 1935 he became general manager of Eastern Airlines, then controlled by North American. Rickenbacker was able to turn around Eastern Airlines' poor financial situation, and three years later arranged for the purchase of Eastern Airlines after NAA had decided to concentrate its effort on manufacture rather than operations. In 1953 Rickenbacker became chairman of the airline's board.

In World War II Rickenbacker visited combat groups of the U.S. Army Air Forces in the United States and also performed special missions for the secretary of war, traveling to China, Greenland, Iceland, Iran, India, the United Kingdom, and the U.S.S.R. as well as the Aleutian Islands, North Africa, and the South Pacific, receiving the Medal of Merit for his efforts. On one journey Rickenbacker's airplane crashed in the Pacific Ocean as a result of mechanical problems, and he and the crew survived 21 days in rafts before being rescued. Rickenbacker married Adelaide F. Durant in 1922 and the pair had two sons. Rickenbacker wrote *Fighting the Flying Circus* and *Seven Came Through,* a chronicle of his nearly disastrous World War II mission. He died in Zurich, Switzerland, on July 23, 1973.

which displayed no signs of fear or evasive action as the French scout closed in head-on. Suddenly a stream of bullets flew out from the nose of the Type L, and an Albatros plummeted down, its pilot dead at the controls. Before the astounded Germans could react, Garros had turned and fired at another Albatros, which immediately burst into flames and crashed. The remaining two Albatroses immediately fled, taking with them the first news of the arrival of the "era of the true fighter airplane."

German pilots, from the time of this success onward, gave a wide berth to any Type L plane, but in the next 17 days Garros managed to bag another three aircraft, thus becoming the world's first "ace" fighter pilot (defined by the achievement of downing five planes). The secret of the Frenchman's success soon fell into the Germans' hands. On April 19 Garros was forced down behind the German lines as the result of engine failure. In the course of almost three weeks of combat, the propeller blades of his airplane had been shaken many times as the deflectors forced away bullets. The consequent vibration was sent via the crankshaft to the already highly stressed rotary engine. Some form of engine failure had to happen, and Garros was unlucky that the prevailing westerly wind gave him no chance of gliding back over the lines. He was captured before he could set fire to his airplane and was bundled off to a prisoner of war camp.

The Germans immediately ordered Anthony Fokker, the enigmatic Dutch designer working for them, to copy the system on his recently introduced M.5 monoplane. Fokker was at best a mediocre designer, yet within 48 hours his able team had produced an efficient synchronizer gear for the 0.312-in (7.92-mm) Parabellum machine gun then in widespread use as the standard German aerial gun. The Fokker synchronizer system, which was tested on an M.5k monoplane, proved very effective, and the combination of the synchronizer gear and armed M.5k was ordered into service as the E I (Eindecker I, or monoplane type 1).

The new fighter entered service over the Western Front, and soon earned itself a fearsome reputation. Allied aircraft, which were mostly as agile and as fast as the German machine, could not cope with the technological advance of the synchronizer-controlled machine gun, and for the first time in aerial warfare, the Allies accrued severe casualties. The press was quick to name the problem the "Fokker Scourge."

Over the front, the Fokker Scourge was at first limited in its effect because the Germans had not evolved a tactical system to make full use of the new weapon. The E I, soon joined by the slightly larger and more powerful E II and E III, was issued at the rate

ANTHONY FOKKER

ANTHONY FOKKER (1890–1939) Anthony Herman Gerhard Fokker was born on April 6, 1890, at Blitar, Kediri, on the island of Java in the Dutch East Indies (now Indonesia), where his father was the owner and operator of a coffee plantation. In August 1894 the Fokker family came back to Haarlem in the Netherlands, and it was here that the young "Tonni" started to attend school. Fokker resented his formal schooling, for which he had little or no aptitude, and he exited the system before finishing high school. The young Fokker meanwhile invented a punctureless tire for car and motorcycle use, but unfortunately for the would-be entrepreneur there was already a French patent held on such an item.

The number and extent of the wires needed to brace Fokker's early aircraft made the name Spin (spider) most apposite. "Tonni" Fokker is here seen in the rear cockpit, which was the standard piloting position in the two-seat aircraft of the period before World War I so that the addition or subtraction of another person on the forward seat would not materially affect the airplane's center of gravity position. The piloting position looks, and indeed was, precarious in the extreme.

It was in 1908 that a fascination with flight was first instilled in Anthony Fokker by the visit of Wilbur Wright to France. Fokker had to wait for two years, until after he had completed his military service, before he could start to build his first aircraft. Fokker attended a school at Bingen in Germany to undertake a course in automobile engineering, but discovering that he was learning little from the course, he moved to the Automobil Fachschule at Zalbach, near Mainz in Germany, where a course in aircraft design, construction, and flying was offered. Here Fokker teamed with Franz von Daum, a former officer in the German army but now a fellow student despite being some 30 years older than Fokker, to design and finance his first machine. Von Daum supplied the 50-hp (37.3-kW) Argus engine for the Fokker-Daum Spin (spider), so named for the web of bracing wires used to ensure the structural integrity of this otherwise very frail low-wing monoplane. Construction started in the autumn of 1910 in the workshop of the school at Wiesbaden, possibly with assistance from the factory of Jacob Goedecker, a local manufacturer of Taube-type monoplanes. This primitive machine crashed during its first trial flight.

On June 7, 1911, Fokker was awarded his pilot's license. He started a factory and flying school at Johannisthal near Berlin, which he left in 1913 for Schwerin. There he stayed during World War I, building aircraft primarily for the imperial German army air service. Fokker was a superb, naturally gifted pilot who test flew all his company's designs. He also liked to claim that he had also designed both the aircraft and the classic gun-synchronization equipment that made the Fokker M.5k/mg the world's first true fighter. In fact the synchronizer was the work of several company engineers. Fokker's two most important designers, neither of whom ever received the accolade of chief designer, were Martin Kreutzer and Reinhold Platz. The latter was the more important of the pair, responsible for the great Fokker warplanes and civil aircraft from the middle of World War I to the time of his departure in 1931.

After World War I Fokker escaped to the Netherlands with his money and considerable quantities of equipment, materials, and even complete aircraft ferried over the border by train. This allowed him to establish the NV Nederlandsche Vliegtuigfabriek Fokker at Schiphol near Amsterdam. Here the new company designed, developed, and manufactured large quantities of aircraft for military and civil service, the former best exemplified by classics such as the C.V series of multirole biplanes, and the latter by high-wing passenger transports including the definitive F.VII. These and other Fokker aircraft gained sales and operating success in many parts of the world, and also secured a large number of world's records for range and endurance.

In October 1920 Fokker traveled to the United States, where he established the Netherlands Aircraft Manufacturing Company. The company was re-formed as the Atlantic Aircraft Corporation and Fokker Aircraft Corporation before becoming the General Aviation Corporation, the precursor of the North American Aviation Corporation. At the beginning of the 1930s Fokker was still an important name in world aviation, but Fokker aircraft were now beginning to fall behind the leading edge of modern technology: They were based on a fabric-covered welded steel tube fuselage with a plywood-covered wooden cantilever wing of thick section, which was the pattern established by Platz in World War I, but in the United States Douglas and Boeing had begun all-metal construction of the stressed-skin type, paving the way for a new generation of advanced aircraft.

Fokker was losing technical and commercial ground to his rivals, and it was only in the late 1930s, with the threat of war once again looming in Europe, that the Dutch armed forces and other European forces once more began to order more than penny-packet numbers of the latest Fokker warplanes. Fokker himself did not long outlive the start of World War II, for on December 23, 1939, the self-proclaimed "Flying Dutchman" died in New York from an infection after an operation on his nose.

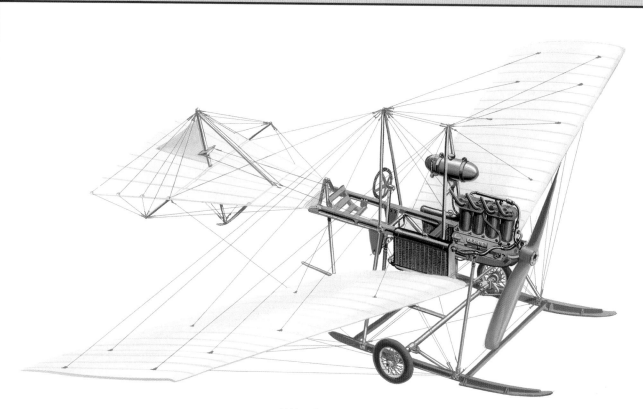

Fokker Spinner III

of about one or two to each flying unit. From the late summer of 1915 the Germans began to create dedicated fighter units. Backed by Max Immelmann, Oswald Boelcke, air warfare's first major tactician, created effective tactics.

The Fokker monoplanes dominated the air in the fall and winter of 1915, and it was only in the spring of 1916 the Allies were at last able to respond, albeit still without a synchronizer gear. The French produced the Nieuport Nie.11 Bébé (baby) sesquiplane, with a Lewis gun firing over the top wing to clear the upper arc of the disc swept by the propeller. The British introduced the Airco (de Havilland) D.H.2, a neat pusher biplane with a Lewis gun mounted at the front of the one-man nacelle. Side-by-side the Nie.11 and

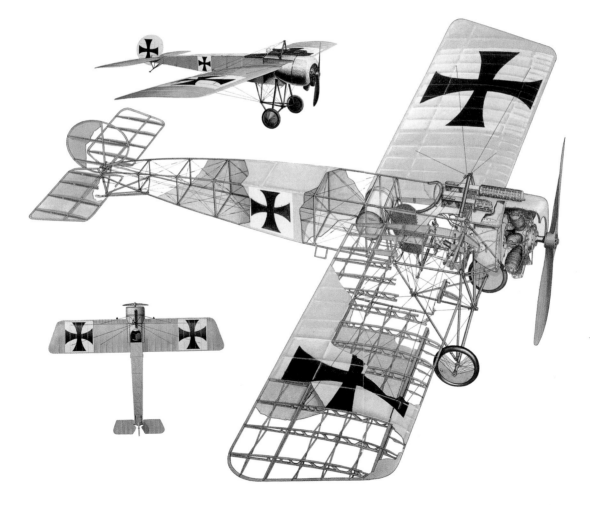

When introduced in 1915 the Fokker Eindecker (monoplane) series constituted the world's first true fighters as they included a fixed forward-firing armament of one or more rifle-caliber machine guns controlled via a synchronizer that allowed the guns to fire only when there was no propeller blade in the line of fire. Seen here is an E III, which was the definitive model of which up to 150 were produced with the 100-hp (74.6-kW) Oberursel U.I rotary engine.

D.H.2 fighters of the Aviation Militaire and RFC gradually seized command of the air from the Germans. Their own two-seaters worked more effectively against the German land forces, and their air warfare became more effective, driving the German observation machines virtually from the air. The Fokker Scourge was defeated by April, and the Allies quickly exploited their command of the air by pushing several new types into action in the second half of the year. At last synchronizer gears made a widespread appearance on the Allied side, on such excellent types as the Nieuport Nie.17 and SPAD S.7, both French, and the British Sopwith 1½-Strutter and Sopwith Pup. All four aircraft were fitted with one 0.303-in (7.7-mm) fixed forward-firing Vickers machine gun, and the 1½-Strutter also had a Lewis gun for the observer.

The Pup was the first adequate fighter. Its performance was excellent: It had a fixed machine gun with synchronizer gear, and its agility was phenomenal. Unlike many other aircraft, however, the Pup's maneuverability was not secured at the expense of other factors. Its control response was smooth, clean, and swift, allowing the pilot to place his machine exactly as he wished.

In the last part of 1916, Germany once again regained the lead in the inevitable technology race of war. Realizing that the Allies would produce a counter to the Eindecker by the middle of 1916, the Germans had set about developing a new generation of aircraft late in 1915. At the heart of the new German air superiority were the Albatros single-seat fighters, starting with the D I, D II and D III, the last of which entered service early in 1917. These sleek, sharklike biplanes with their wood-skinned, oval-section fuselages and well-cowled engines were capable of very good performance. Most important of all, however, they were armed with two machine guns, and in the spring of 1917 this gave them twice the firepower of Allied fighters.

The immediate consequence of the arrival of these new German fighters was what became known in the RFC as "Bloody April." The British suffered losses in aircrews and aircraft of some 30 percent, their highest losses of the entire war.

The only good news from the British point of view was the success of the handful of Sopwith Triplanes operated by the Royal Naval Air Service. Although armed with only one machine gun, these were clean aircraft that could combat the "Albatri" by means of their remarkable rate of climb and their general agility, both functions of the large wing area contained within the small overall dimensions of a triplane layout. The Germans immediately ordered triplane designs, resulting in the Fokker Dr I, but the era of the triplane was ending. The type ordered into production was the Fokker Dr I.

ABOVE LEFT In the absence of an effective synchronizer, the Allies had to respond to the Germans' E-series monoplanes with armament that avoided the propeller blades by other means. The primary French type was the Nieuport Nie.11, nick-named the Bébé (baby) for its small size. The Nie.11 was faster and considerably more agile than the E-series monoplanes, and carried its Lewis machine gun over the center section of the upper wing in a position above the disc swept by the propeller.

ABOVE RIGHT From March 1916 the Nie.11 was complemented and then replaced by the same company's Nie.17. This was slightly larger and more powerfully engined than the Nie.11, and possessed better performance, but was most notable for the introduction of a synchronized Vickers machine gun in the upper part of the forward fuselage, sometimes supplemented by a Lewis gun above the upper wing's center section.

BELOW The British response to the need to develop a fighter with fixed forward-firing armament was generally centered on the use of a pusher rather than tractor engine, leaving the front of the central nacelle free for armament. The best of these types was the Airco (de Havilland) D.H.2, but another type used in very small numbers was the Vickers F.B.12 seen here. This was powered by a number of rotary and radial engine types, and was armed with a Lewis machine gun.

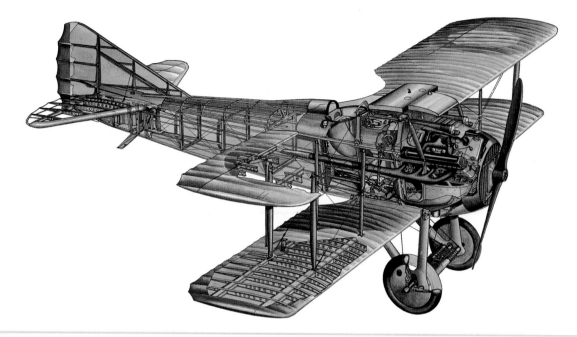

ABOVE From the summer of 1916 the water-cooled inline or V-type unit began to rival and then overtake the air-cooled rotary engine as the primary engine for fighter use. This allowed the creation of larger and stronger airframes, and brought to the fore the SPAD fighter with its two-bay wing cellule and high performance. The initial S.VII (or S.7) was powered by a 175-hp (130.5-kW) engine and was armed with a single Vickers gun, while the type illustrated here, the S.XIII (or S.13) that entered service in May 1917, had a 235-hp (175-kW) engine and was armed with two machine guns. The S.XIII served with eighty-one French, sixteen American, eleven Italian, and one Belgian squadrons.

BELOW The Sopwith 1½-Strutter was a remarkable British warplane that entered service early in 1916. The type was flown as a one- or two-seater, although the use of a Clerget rotary engine rated at only 110 hp (82 kW) meant that performance suffered when two men were embarked, and operated in the fighter, bomber, and reconnaissance roles. As an escort fighter, the 1½-Strutter was armed with one synchronized Vickers machine gun and one trainable Lewis machine gun. In the bomber role the 1½-Strutter could carry 130 lb (59 kg) of bombs, a figure that could be raised to 224 lb (102 kg) when the gunner and his Lewis gun were omitted.

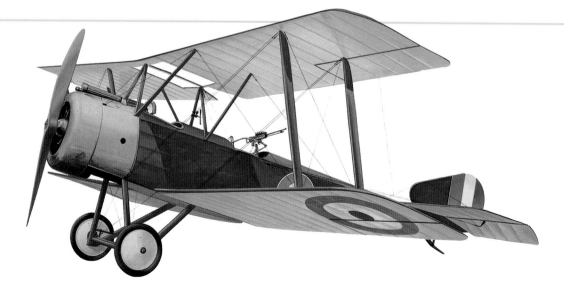

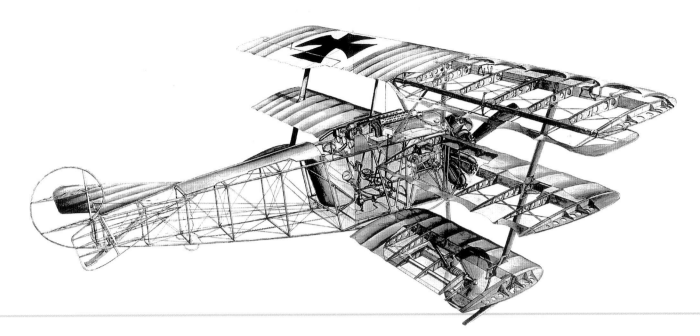

ABOVE The Fokker Dr I was manufactured only in small numbers and entered service in August 1917, when it was generally issued to elite units with pilots, such as Manfred von Richthofen and Werner Voss, who could gain maximum benefit from the fighter's good climb rate and superb agility. The armament was that which had become standard for German fighters since the closing stages of 1916, namely two LMG 08/15 rifle-caliber machine guns, but performance with the 110-hp (82-kW) Oberursel- or Thulin-built Le Rhône rotary engine was decidedly mediocre.

BELOW LEFT The Sopwith Camel was the most successful fighter of World War I and entered service in mid-1917 with the Royal Flying Corps and Royal Naval Air Service. The Camel was derived conceptually from the beautiful and agile single-gun Pup with twin guns and a considerably more powerful engine for greater firepower and performance. Like the Pup, the Camel was extremely agile, largely as a result of the grouping of the main masses in the forward fuselage, but lacked its predecessor's viceless handling characteristics.

BELOW RIGHT The Fokker Dr I triplane fighter was designed by Reinhold Platz and featured this great designer's standard combination of fuselage and tail unit of welded steel tube construction, thick-section cantilever wings of wooden construction with a single interplane strut on each side to prevent vibration, and a lifting surface on the axle of the main landing-gear unit.

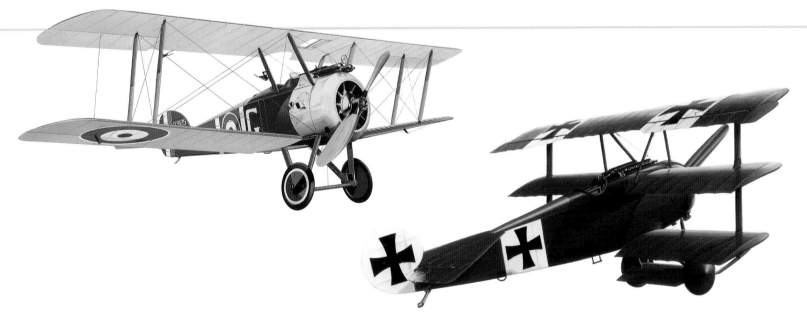

Back and forth went the airplane arms race, with new British, French, and German models introduced nearly every month. The Allies gradually exceeded their German competitors, however, with famous planes like the Sopwith Camel, which appeared in July 1917. This fighter combined great beauty—if beauty is defined as the marriage of form and function—with agility. Its appearance was slightly squat, pugnacious, belligerent. A "hump" over the breeches of the twin Vickers guns led to its nickname, which was later officially adopted. With the propeller, engine, fuel, oil, guns, ammunition, and pilot all squeezed into the front 7 ft (2.13 m) of the fuselage, where their inertia would least interfere with maneuverability, the Camel was supremely agile, especially in right-hand turns. The torque of the rotary complemented the turning moment of rudder and ailerons. The Camel's only fault was the result of this compactness and the torque of the rotary: Pilots unused to the new fighter were liable to allow the turn to become a spin, which at low altitudes was often a fatal mistake. In the hands of a skilled pilot, however, the Camel was a superlative fighter. Camels are officially credited with a staggering 1,294 kills of enemy aircraft before the end of the war, and the real total was considerably higher.

If the war had lasted much longer, the balance of air power might have swung back to Germany. Only in January 1918 did it order large-scale production of the Fokker D VII, possibly the war's best fighter, and the acme of the wartime designs of Reinhold Platz, Fokker's great designer. The hallmarks of Platz's designs were simplicity and sturdiness: welded steel tube fuselages allied to wings of wooden construction but great depth, allowing massive box structures to be used for strength, at a time when other designers preferred very thin sections that required masses of internal and external bracing by struts and wires. The D VII was feared by Allied pilots, and was the only airplane to be singled out by name to be surrendered in the armistice agreement of 1918. It had outstanding high-altitude qualities. Whereas Allied types would have stalled and spun, the D VII had the ability to hang on its propeller and fire upward. Yet the Germans were unable to rush this and other new types of fighters into service in sufficient numbers to prevent the British, French, American, and Belgian fighter forces from exercising almost total command of the air from spring 1918 on to the end of the war.

Unglamorous and unglamorized, it was in fact the work of machines rather than the fighters which was of primary importance in World War I. Artillery spotters and photo-reconnaissance aircraft, although in at least as much danger as the fighters, received little popular acclaim. The civilians at home preferred to read about dashing "scout" pilots. Yet the fighters were only there to protect their own two-seaters and bombers, and to prevent the enemy's machines from acting freely. Because they had to carry two men, armament, and their specialized equipment, artillery spotter and reconnaissance aircraft were usually heavy and fairly clumsy. And because they needed to be able to fly steadily for lengthy periods, a fair measure of inherent stability was called for. These machines had to operate in all weather, within reach of antiaircraft fire and enemy fighters, so anything that detracted from their maneuverability was a hindrance to survival. For all these reasons, the problems of designing a front-line two-seater were formidable, and it is remarkable how many good designs emerged in the second half of the war. The Germans produced the Albatros C X and C XII, DFW C IV and C V, the Halberstadt C V, the LVG (Roland) C V and C VI, and the Rumpler C IV and C VII. The French had the first-class Salmson 2 with an odd water- rather than air-cooled 260-hp (194-kW) radial

The Fokker D VII was the best German fighter to enter large-scale service in World War I. The type had a twin-gun armament and all the advantages of the Reinhold Platz design concept in its fully fledged form, and offered excellent performance and agility despite its use of a relatively low-powered engine.

Established just outside Berlin late in 1909, the Albatros Flugzeugwerke G.m.b.H. initially manufactured aircraft, most notably the Antoinette series from France, under license. Only after gaining this experience did the company begin to design its own aircraft. The early types were not distinguished, but after the appointment of Ernst Heinkel as chief designer in 1913 matters began to improve rapidly. The first notable airplane from the manufacturer was the L 1 that first flew in 1913 and entered production in 1914 for civil as well as military use, the latter with the designation B I. The B I was developed into the B II; later Albatros two-seat aircraft were C-class machines, with armament. The company's chief designer for most of World War I was Robert Thelen, a highly capable engineer who was responsible for the Albatros single-seat fighters that were numerically the most important aircraft of their type to serve with the German army air service in World War I. Albatros survived World War 1 to seek a reconstruction of its fortunes as the designer and manufacturer of sporting, touring, training, and transport aircraft, but was not notably successful and in 1931 lost its identity after merging with the Focke-Wulf company, then beginning to emerge as a force in the expanding German aircraft industry.

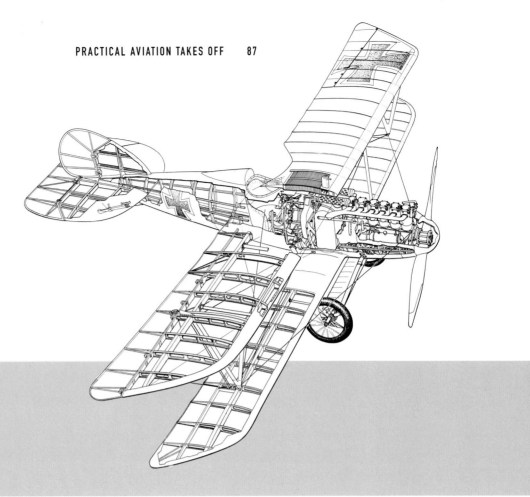

FACING PAGE, TOP Confident that its current fighters would be adequate to deal with Allied fighters into the second half of 1917, the imperial German army air service was shocked by the appearance of advanced types such as the Royal Aircraft Factory S.E.5, Sopwith Pup and Triplane, and SPAD S.VII and S.XIII. In an effort to regain air superiority over the Western Front, the imperial German army air service ordered Albatros to create an advanced version of the D III as the D V with a more powerful engine. The D V entered service in May 1917 and at first proved adequate for the task expected of it. For lack of an adequate purpose-designed replacement until well into 1918, however, the D V and closely related D Va had to soldier on into obsolescence and rapidly escalating losses.

FACING PAGE, BOTTOM The Mercedes engine, a product of the Daimler company, was one of the classics among early water-cooled inline engines and a mainstay of the German air arms in World War I. The six-cylinder type was produced in two series, the smaller 14.78-liter type evolving from the D.I of 100 hp (74.6 kW) to the D.IIIb of 185 hp (138 kW) for use mainly in fighters, and the larger 21.7-liter type as exemplified by the D.IVa rated at 260 hp (194 kW) and used mainly in larger warplanes. This engine is an example of the 160/180-hp (119/134-kW) D.III used in the Albatros D III and D V fighters as well as early examples of the Fokker D VII fighter.

ABOVE The D V, which appeared in 1917, marked the high point of the Albatros sesquiplane fighters so important to the German air war effort between 1916 and 1918. The oval-section laminated wood fuselage, large tail unit with curved leading edges, relatively powerful engine, and armament of two synchronized machine guns were all excellent, and the main limitation was the indifferent strength of the wing cellule, whose lower wing could twist and break away in the air.

engine. The Italians produced the sleek Ansaldo SVA 10, and the Austro-Hungarians the useful Ufag C I. These unsung aircraft worked because they were small and agile, and they gave the observer a good field of fire for his flexible machine gun.

The bomber and ground-attack aircraft, although at first less important than the spotter and reconnaissance machines, grew steadily in significance as the war progressed. For lack of any form of useful bomb sight and the very small weight of bombs that could be carried by early aircraft, the first attempt at bombing had only a token effect. But the Russians soon realized that large aircraft would be needed to carry a significant weight of bombs, and they already had such aircraft in the form of a four-engined machine, the Russkii Vitiaz, initially known as the Bolshoi Bal'tiskii. Designed by Igor Sikorsky, it was built in 1913 by the Russian Baltic Railway Car Factory in St. Petersburg. Early in 1914 the Russian technical bureau ordered 10 examples of an improved and enlarged version. This Ilya Muromets was used for the Russian army air service. Eventually some 80 of the type were built, but lack of suitable engines seriously hampered operational efforts. Nonetheless, over 400 sorties were flown with bomb loads of about 1,102 lb (500 kg).

Designed by Umberto Savoia and Rodolfo Verduzio for construction by the Ansaldo company (hence the designation) the SVA series of bomber, escort fighter, and reconnaissance aircraft were notable for their very high perform-ance, a fuselage that changed from a rectangular forward section to an inverted triangular rear section, and W-type interplane struts. The single-seat SVA 5 entered service in the fall of 1917 as a long-range reconnaissance airplane.

ABOVE Designed in Germany by Ernst Heinkel, who later established his own company to create aircraft that gained great fame in World War II, but built only in Austria-Hungary for the use of that nation's air services, the Hansa-Brandenburg D I single-seat fighter was generally known as the "Star-strutter" for its unique interplane strutting: On each side four short V-type struts were connected at their closed ends between the upper and lower wings in an arrangement that offered strength but also removed all need for rigging, flying, and landing wires. The D I was fast and climbed well but had handling problems and was poorly armed with a single unsynchronized Schwarzlose machine gun in a "baby coffin" fairing over the upper wing's centerline.

BELOW The imperial German army air service was an early exponent of bombing, and while it is the bombers from the Gotha company that have gained the greatest fame among German bombers of World War I, the Friedrichshafen G III was another type worthy of note. Operated by a three-man crew and powered by two 260-hp (194-kW) Mercedes D.IVa engines, the G III could carry 3,307 lb (1,500 kg) of bombs and was armed defensively with two or three LMG 14 Parabellum trainable machine guns. The type was used only over the Western Front.

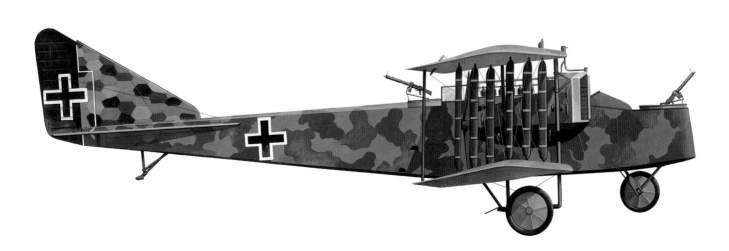

On Germany's behalf, World War I helped spur the development of the world's first serious bomber plane. Zeppelin airships had been launching sporadic attacks on targets in the southern half of the British Isles, principally London, since May 1915, but by 1917 the British defenses were so strong Zeppelin losses were no longer tolerable. The Germans therefore introduced the world's first long-range bombers, the Gotha G IV and G V. Raids were launched in June 1917, to the total consternation of the British public and government. Although the Zeppelin raids were the first "strategic bombing" ever attempted and had caused a great public shock, the aircraft raids proved a greater threat to life and property. The raids continued into 1918, causing a steady stream of casualties and damage. Only the deployment of aircraft such as the S.E.5a, which could climb fast enough to intercept the Gotha bombers before they flew out of range, curtailed the threat. The immediate result of these Germans raids was the total reorganization of the British air services. On April 1, 1918, the Royal Air Force was created from the RFC and RNAS. It was the world's first independent air force.

For the first time the British people, who had imagined themselves immune from war in the personal sense, found themselves embroiled in the "front line," an evil they had previously thought to be wholly the lot of those on the Continent. The realization that everyone, not just the fighting men or the unfortunate civilians living in the combat area, could be involved in the actual "fighting" ushered in the era of total war.

Although "heavy" bombers pointed the way to the future of bombing as a decisive strategic weapon, their military effect in World War I was very much less than that of the light bombers, which played an important part in land operations during the closing stages of the war. Considering their importance, it is surprising that the Allies used only two basic types: the Airco (de Havilland) 4 and its two derivatives, the D.H.9 and D.H.9a, and the French Breguet Bre.14.

The D.H.4 was in every respect one of the most remarkable aircraft of World War I. As well as being very agile and well-armed, it had a speed of 143 mph (230 km/h) at a time when most fighters were capable of speeds only in the region of 130 mph (209 km/h), and was able to carry a 460-lb (209-kg) bomb load. The D.H.4 entered service in 1917 and was joined in squadron use during 1918 by the supposedly improved D.H.9, which had the pilot's and observer's cockpits closer together. D.H.4's main tactical failing was the location of the fuel tank between the pilot's and gunner's cockpits in a location that effectively prevented communication. The D.H.4 was also fitted with an engine of notable unreliabil-

Fourth on the list of British aces in World War I, with a total of fifty-seven aerial victories, Major James McCudden was a great pilot and tactician who lost his life late in the war in a flying accident. McCudden's favorite mount was the Royal Aircraft Factory S.E.5a. Powered by a 200-hp (149-kW) Hispano-Suiza or Wolseley engine, the S.E.5a was notably strong and possessed good performance. The S.E.5a was not as nimble as the Camel but was a superior gun platform, and its armament combined a Vickers machine gun in the fuselage and a Lewis gun above the upper-wing center section.

ity, a factor only partially rectified by the development of the D.H.9a. The French equivalent of these de Havilland bombers was the Bre.14, which entered service in September 1917. Sturdy and fairly fast, this bomber played an important part in harrying the retreating Germans in the second half of 1918 and also proved a more than adequate reconnaissance aircraft.

The Germans placed more faith in ground-attack machines to support their land forces. These types were at first modified reconnaissance aircraft pending the arrival of more suitable types, with heavier armament and greater protection, such as the all-metal Junkers J I. The Junkers J I was designed under the supervision of Dr. Hugo Junkers, one of the pioneers of metal construction. In the fall of 1917, however, the need for a lighter type that could undertake both the ground attack and reconnaissance roles became evident. The first of the new models, the Halberstadt CL II and the Hannover CL II and CL III, were ready for service in the last-gasp German offensives in the spring and early sum-

After it had cut its bomber teeth with the pioneering Type O/100 and more fully developed Type O/400, Handley Page designed the altogether more capable Type V/1500. This was powered by four 375-hp (280-kW) Rolls-Royce Eagle VIII engines and offered the ability to carry a sizable bomb load on missions from England to targets in Germany, but only three had been delivered before the end of World War I.

ABOVE Entering service in August 1917, the Breguet Bre.14 was the best French two-seater of World War I. A sturdy two-bay biplane powered generally by a Renault engine rated at between 220 and 300 hp (164 and 224 kW), the Bre.14 was produced in two forms as a reconnaissance airplane and as a bomber: The former was armed with three machine guns (one Vickers fixed forward-firing and two Lewis trainable rearward-firing weapons), while the latter added 520 lb (236 kg) of bombs and, late in the conflict, a ventrally mounted Lewis gun.

BELOW The Airco (de Havilland) D.H.4 was a potentially first-class day bomber adversely affected by the location of the fuel tank between the two cockpits in an arrangement that hampered tactical communication and threatened dire conse-

quences for the pilot in any crash landing. This problem was removed in the D.H.9 by exchanging the positions of the pilot's cockpit and the fuel tank, but this type was hampered by its unreliable Siddeley Puma engine, replacing the D.H.4's excellent Rolls-Royce Eagle, of which there were inadequate supplies. The solution finally adopted was the combination of the D.H.9's airframe with the more powerful Eagle and later the American-produced Liberty 12 engine. The result was a restoration of performance and the ability to carry a bomb load increased in weight by almost 50 percent. This D.H.9A type (illustrated) saw only two months of full service over the Western Front in World War I, but was a mainstay of the Royal Air Force into the late 1920s.

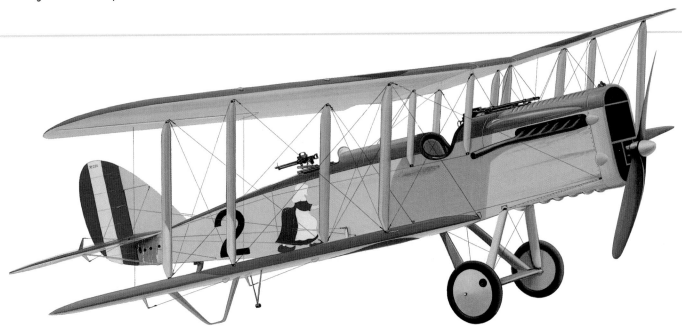

When it lifted off on its maiden flight on December 12, 1915, the Junkers J 1 cantilever monoplane was the first all-metal airplane to fly successfully anywhere in the world. Skepticism about the practical nature of the concept meant that Junkers could not obtain the aluminum alloy tube and sheet that he wanted for the airplane's construction, so instead he was forced to use steel tube and iron sheet. As a result the airplane was heavy, and therefore sluggish in the climb, but handled adequately and possessed a respectable turn of speed, reaching 106 mph (179 km/h) on the 120 hp (89.5 kW) generated by its Mercedes D.II inline engine.

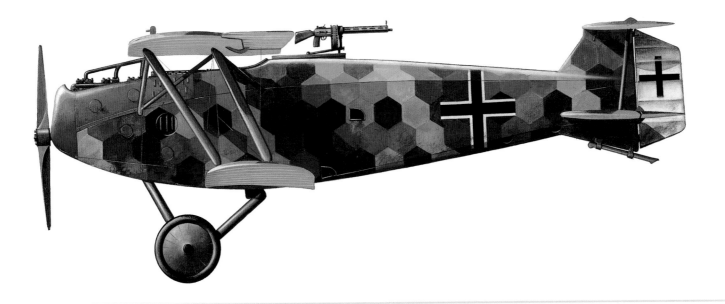

ABOVE Designed for the escort fighter and ground-attack roles, the Hannover CL II two-seater entered service in December 1917 with the standard German two-seater armament of one fixed forward-firing and one trainable rearward-firing machine gun. Notable features were the deep fuselage, powerful ailerons, and a compact tail unit with biplane horizontal surfaces to increase the gunner's fields of fire. The CL II was small enough to be taken for a single-seat fighter, an error that cost several incautious pilots their lives as they tried to make a stern attack.

BELOW The Halberstadt CL II was a contemporary of the Hannover CL II for the same basic roles, but was larger and lower-powered, had worse altitude performance, and possessed provision for a second fixed forward-firing machine gun.

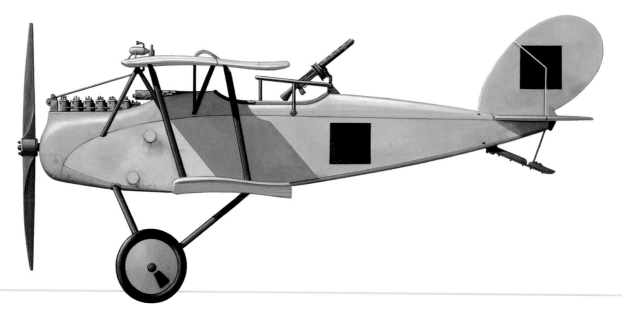

ABOVE Halberstadt's CL IV was a major reworking of the concept embodied in its CL II, with the same engine and similar performance, but the relocation of the wing cellule, the shortening of the fuselage, and the revision of the tail unit resulted in enhanced agility and crisper handling qualities.

BELOW The use of flying boats for maritime patrol and antisubmarine tasks grew steadily throughout World War I. One of the best types for this role was the Felixstowe F.2A, which was a British reworking of an American flying boat, the Curtiss H-12, with an excellent hull designed by Squadron Commander John C. Porte. The F.2A could lift 460 lb (209 kg) of bombs and carry between four and seven Lewis machine guns with which to defend itself and attack German coastal craft. On June 4, 1918, one of four F.2A machines was forced down onto the water by shortage of fuel, and the other three then fought off fourteen German aircraft, shooting down six of them without loss to themselves, as they protected their downed colleague.

mer of 1918. But useful as these new machines were in anticipating one of the major uses of armored aircraft in World War II, the novel tactics and aircraft deployed by the Germans in 1918 were unable to overcome the clear supremacy of the Allies.

Aircraft had entered World War I as unknown quantities: Their role was limited to reconnaissance and very light bombing. Yet by 1916 aircraft had altered out of all recognition and become durable, efficient fighting machines, capable of exerting some influence on the outcome of the decisive land operations. Two years later, toward the end of the war, aircraft had again advanced their overall performance, and were now the arbiters of the land battle.

When America entered into the war in April 1917, it had barely awoken militarily. The United States had had a useful navy but only a small army for years. It possessed enormous potential manpower strength as well an industrial base that needed only to be pointed in the right direction. Only in 1918, toward the end of the war, however, did American manpower finally begin to exert itself as a major force. The mobilization of U.S. industry also took longer than expected; American squadrons relied almost exclusively on British, French, and Italian aircraft types either procured directly in Europe or built under license in the United States. By the end of the war, though, the United States was geared up for technological advance and massive production. Soon the seat of aircraft history would return to the land of the Wright brothers.

THE RACE FOR SPEED
AND DISTANCE

World War I created aviation, but the peace that followed almost broke the new industry. The vast emotional, financial, and social cost of the war put aviation almost back to its 1914 state, at least from the point of view of manufacturers and pilots. In the last days before the war, the world had contained only a few hundred aircraft of perhaps 150 different types, and about three times that number of pilots. During World War I there was enormous growth: France had built 68,000 aircraft, the United Kingdom 55,000, Germany 47,600, Italy 20,000, the United States 15,000, and Austria-Hungary 5,400. Growth suddenly now slammed to a halt.

With the war ended, the European nations and the United States could start to take stock of the war and its cost. Stunned by the horrors of the war and the enormity of their losses, people wanted to believe that World War I had been the "war to end all wars." There was a natural revulsion for the majority of military machines, including aircraft, and the financial cost of the war had an enormous impact on aviation as an industry. Europe was almost bankrupt: France, Italy, and the United Kingdom had expended almost all of their resources on the war and were in debt to the United States. The countries of the former German, Austro-Hungarian, and Ottoman empires were also exhausted and broken financially and morally. There was no money in Europe for anything but essentials.

The drastic reduction in air strengths is best seen in the near elimination of the world's first independent air force, the Royal Air Force. In November 1918 the RAF totaled 188 operational squadrons, with 291,000 men and women to service them and keep them in the air; less than 14 months later, at the end of 1919, the RAF had been cut back to 12 operational squadrons, with manpower down to 31,500. Although the government soon realized that so small an air force was hardly worth having, only the most limited expansion was allowed, to a strength of 25 squadrons by March 1920 and 43 squadrons by October 1924.

A new generation of aircraft was just entering service at the time of the Armistice, and the machines of

Then as now, advertising material often claimed, or at worst insinuated, capabilities that the product did not in fact offer. This was sometimes the result of overenthusiasm rather than any attempt to deceive. The Christmas Bullet was the result of an attempt to create an advanced American fighter late in World War I, and was a cantilever sesquiplane. It was hoped that the lack of interplane struts and external wire bracing would reduce drag sufficiently to create high performance on only 185 hp (134 kW), but the hope was ill-founded.

CANTILEVER
AEROPLANES
MILITARY
NAVAL
COMMERCIAL
AERO CO.

ON DISPLAY AT THE

AERONAUTICAL EXPOSITION
MARCH 1st to 15th, 1919
MADISON SQUARE GARDEN

"Christmas Bullet"

The First Flexible Wing Aeroplane
SPEED OVER 180 MILES P. H.   MOTOR 185 H. P.   6 CYLINDERS

Maximum Speed, Maximum Lift, Minimum Horse Power

CANTILEVER AERO COMPANY
1269 Broadway   New York, U. S. A.

Here seen over the magnificent scenery of Yosemite National Park, the Curtiss B-2 Condor bomber was the mainstay of the U.S. Army Air Corps' heavy bomber capability in the late 1920s and early 1930s. The Condor represented one of the later iterations of the twin-engined biplane bombers in U.S. service and was notable for its ruggedness rather than its performance.

ABOVE Entering service in summer 1918, the Sopwith Snipe was clearly a descendant of the Camel with the earlier airplane's 150-hp (112-kW) Bentley BR.1 rotary engine replaced by a 230-hp (171.5-kW) BR.2 unit. Only some one hundred of the type entered service over the Western Front before the end of the war, but the Snipe was selected as a standard type for postwar service and remained in production up to 1919. The Snipe remained in first-line service up to 1926, and for a time after that as an advanced trainer.

BELOW LEFT Lack of military orders in the 1920s persuaded many manufacturers to try their hands at the creation of lightplanes for sale on the civil market. One of the most successful of these attempts was the de Havilland D.H.60 Moth two-seater. The airplane illustrated is *Jason*, the D.H.60G Gipsy Moth of the celebrated English flier Amy Johnson. With only one hundred flying hours in her log book, the twenty-seven-year-old Johnson took off from Croydon on May 5, 1930, and nineteen and one-half days later arrived at Darwin in Northern Australia as the first woman to fly from the United Kingdom to Australia.

BELOW RIGHT The culmination of de Havilland's series of Moth lightplanes was the elegant and wholly delightful D.H.82 Tiger Moth, here depicted in the type of flying trainer colors in which large numbers served the Royal Air Force during World War II.

this generation were thought to be sufficient for a lengthy time of peace. The RAF's equipment in the first years after the war consisted of the Bristol F.2B Fighter, the Sopwith Snipe, the de Havilland D.H.9a, and the Vickers Vimy. The first new bomber, the Fairey Fawn, did not enter service until 1923, and the first new fighters, the Gloster Grebe and Armstrong Whitworth Siskin, arrived one year later still.

Aircraft manufacturers thus found themselves in a tricky position. No new orders could be expected for some time, and production capacity was being gradually run down as the few orders that had survived the cutbacks were completed. Other work had to be found, but this was difficult while the market was glutted with ex-government machines being sold off at ludicrously low sums. Many companies could not cope and went out of business, and the survivors had to contract enormously.

Manufacturers had to decide what type of aircraft they should produce. With no military demand, the only possibility was civil aviation—but what sort of airplane would sell? The new aircraft would have to be cheap to buy and operate. None of the companies could afford much experimental and development work. Their only hope was the civilian lightplane.

A lightplane is an airplane intended purely for personal sporting use. Capable of lifting only one person, or later two people, and having no facility for a worthwhile payload, they were small and also cheap to build and run: Low performance levels would be acceptable, so a low-powered engine would be sufficient. The machine was for enjoyment rather than utilitarian purposes. Early contenders in the field were the Blackburn Sidecar and the Avro Baby, but with masses of wartime aircraft still on the market at very low prices their success was limited. Toward the mid-1920s, however, the British government decided to encourage these developments by sponsoring both lightplane competitions (and therefore designs) and flying clubs.

The first light airplane competition was organized by the Royal Aero Club, for which the Air Ministry provided some £3,000 in prizes. Among the entries were the Hawker Cygnet, the ANEC series, the English Electric Wren, and the de Havilland D.H.53. The competition was a technical success, but because the potential buyers wanted higher performance and greater aerial agility, the competition was not a commercial success.

One man who clearly understood the nature of the lightplane's initial failure was Geoffrey de Havilland. De Havilland, the designer of the D.H.60 Moth, was now heading his own company. The D.H.60 Moth combined reasonable performance and maneuverability with comparatively economical operation: It was powered by a 60-hp (44.7-kW) de Havilland Cirrus engine and carried two people in tandem. The Moth was an immediate success and became the standard airplane of flying clubs all over the United Kingdom. A

THE GREAT BARNSTORMERS

THE BARNSTORMERS Barnstorming is really a branch of stunt flying designed to entertain crowds on the ground with feats of a comic nature or of great skill and courage. It reached its zenith in the United States during the 1920s and early 1930s, as ex-military pilots sought to make a living for themselves in aircraft such as elderly Curtiss JN

"Wild Bill" Hopson epitomizes the character that barnstorming pilots generally possessed or, failing that, liked to suggest that they had. This photograph reveals William Hopson in the type of winter flying clothes used by him and other pilots while flying U.S. air mail services without the benefits of any cockpit enclosure or even cockpit heating.

PILOT Wm. C. HOPSON
U.S. MAIL SERVICE
WINTER FLYING CLOTHING

Jenny biplanes. The origins of stunt flying can be found in the daredevil stunts undertaken in early balloons, sometimes by such women as "Tiny" Broadwick (born Georgia
Ann Thompson), an early exponent of the parachute in the United States who jumped
many times between 1908 and 1914. The real training ground of the barnstormers, however, was World War I, when the dogfighting style of combat taught pilots to make tight
turns and daring maneuvers.

Perhaps the greatest of the early stunt flyers was Lincoln Beachey (1887–1915),
who learned to fly at the school run by Glenn Curtiss. Opinions about his flying differed
widely: Some said that he was mad to attempt the feats he did while others, including no
less an authority than Orville Wright, said that he was the greatest pilot of all time. What
is certain is that the crowds loved his stunts and flocked in great numbers to his appearances. Flying a Curtiss biplane, Beachey would perform such feats as vertical power dives
and the scooping up from the ground with one of his wingtips of a handkerchief or scarf.
He also performed the remarkable feat of flying low over the Niagara Falls and then under the suspension bridge just below them: He was watched by a crowd of 150,000.

Beachey was no headstrong youth. He was a man who had worked out the possibilities of his machine and his own skills with enormous detail. Increasingly worried
about the safety of the imitators of his work, Beachey retired in 1913, only to be persuaded to make further appearances when Alphonse Pégoud successfully flew a
loop-the-loop. In 1915, over Oakland Bay off San Francisco, the wings of his monoplane
folded at 2,000 ft (610 m), and a vast crowd watched in horror as Beachey and his
machine crashed to total destruction.

The other great person to catch the devoted attention of the American public at
this time was Calbraith Rodgers, already a celebrated racer of boats, cars, and horses. Late
in 1911 Rodgers decided to have a stab at the $50,000 prize offered by William Randolph
Hearst for the first coast-to-coast flight across the United States in 30 days. After two
months of practice on a Wright biplane, and accompanied by a chartered train carrying
spares and support personnel supplied by the Vin-Fiz soft-drink firm that was sponsoring
him, Rodgers set off from New York on September 11 with the intention of arriving in
Pasadena, California, by October 11. It soon became clear that the target date was impossible, but Rodgers decided that he would press on. The journey became an odyssey, and
Rodgers was beset by problems the whole way: He had many crashes, souvenir hunters
stole parts of his machine, he nearly collided in midair with an eagle, the weather was appalling in several regions, and his engine proved very temperamental, once blowing up in

the air. Yet Rodgers gamely pushed forward and finally arrived in Pasadena on November 5. The only parts of the machine he was flying that had been with him for the whole trip were the rudder and the engine drip tray, so many times had the machine been patched up and portions replaced. Like Beachey, Rodgers also met death in the air. While flying stunts in April 1912 he lost control of his machine and dived to the ground.

In the days of the barnstormers there was effectively no other commercial or private flying. Aerial circuses, flown both by men and women, played a key role in aviation history. World War I had shown the public what aircraft could do, but the barnstormers demonstrated the most hazardous of aerial exploits, including aerobatics, wing-walking, stepping from one airplane to another in flight, and parachuting. Needless to say, accidents were frequent and very often fatal, but public demand had to be met if these "flying circuses" were to stay in business. The barnstormers also took passengers aloft for short sightseeing flights. Charles Lindbergh was a barnstormer early in his flying career, undertaking wing-walking as well as flying. The men who operated and flew in the circuses were normally ex-service pilots who could not settle down to a humdrum existence after the war. The number of these pilots declined in the late 1920s and early 1930s, and the growth of civil aviation began to attract government supervision and regulation, so the flying circuses gradually died out.

FACING PAGE Roscoe Turner is rightly celebrated as one of the great figures in aviation history, as a brief biography confirms. Born in Corinth, Mississippi, in 1895, Turner moved to Memphis, Tennessee, in the first decade of the twentieth century and became an auto mechanic and truck driver, but in 1916 was rejected for lack of a college degree when he tried to enlist in the Aviation Section of the Signal Corps. He later joined the branch as a balloon observer before becoming a balloon pilot and then an airplane pilot. After World War I Turner went back to Corinth, bought a share in a Curtiss "Jenny" and established the "Roscoe Turner Flying Circus." In 1926 he bought a Sikorsky S-29 for use in publicity stunts and movies, and in 1928 started work for Howard Hughes on the movie *Hell's Angels*. In the following years Turner worked on many other movies, moving to Hollywood in 1929 and at about the same time starting to race aircraft. In 1929 Turner also organized, promoted, and flew for Nevada Airlines, mainly in a Lockheed Vega that he also raced, and established a transcontinental speed record between New York and Los Angeles in a time of eighteen hours thirty minutes. In the early 1930s Nevada Airlines entered bankruptcy, and Turner started work as a pilot for the Gilmore Oil Company. In 1930 Turner persuaded the company to buy a Lockheed Air Express, and in it gained third place in both the Bendix and Thompson trophy races under the Gilmore banner. In 1933 Turner had greater success, winning the Bendix trophy race in the Wedell-Williams Racer. During 1934 he won the Thompson trophy race in the Wedell-Williams Racer, and then placed second in the MacRobertson race from England to Australia in a Boeing Model 247D with Clyde Pangborn as his copilot. Turner entered and won many races during the 1930s, and took the Thompson trophy race in the Laird-Turner racer in both 1938 and 1939 before retiring from the racing arena and starting a flying school in Indianapolis, Indiana. In World War II this school trained more than thirty-three hundred pilots. After World War II Turner became president of the Roscoe Turner Aeronautical Corporation, which was a fixed base operator with a flying school in Indianapolis. During 1952 Turner was awarded the Distinguished Flying Cross for his contribution to flying. In June 1970 Turner died in Indianapolis.

The Supermarine Walrus amphibian flying boat first appeared in the 1930s but was the culmination of a design process that had begun in 1921 with the Seal Mk II. The type was initially operated by the Fleet Air Arm as a catapult-launched spotter, but found its real niche in World War II as an air/sea rescue type operating off the coast of virtually every theater involving British forces.

direct descendant of the Moth was the D.H.82 Tiger Moth, one of the most famous and best-loved machines ever built. The success of the first Moth, moreover, persuaded other aircraft designers that this was the type of machine wanted by most would-be buyers. Among several to follow in the Moth's footsteps were the Avro Avian, the Westland Widgeon, and the Avro Bluebird.

On the other side of the Atlantic, the United States initially displayed little or no attraction to private flying during the first half of the 1920s, and few light aircraft were produced. Commercial flying consisted mainly of aerial circuses, in which both men and women took part, largely in ex-military Curtiss Model JN Jenny aircraft. The war had shown the public what aircraft could do, and the latter-day "barnstormers" performed hazardous stunts, including aerobatics, wing-walking, stepping from one aircraft in flight to another, and parachuting. Accidents were frequent, but public demand had to be met if the circuses were to stay in business. The men who operated and flew in the circuses were normally ex-service pilots. As the number of these pilots declined in the late 1920s and early 1930s, and as the growth of civil aviation began to attract government supervision and regulation, the flying circuses gradually died out.

The first successful crossing of the Atlantic Ocean was not nonstop but was nonetheless a huge achievement. Three Curtiss Model NC flying boats of the U.S. Navy lifted off from Rockaway, New York, on May 1, 1919. Alighting several times before reaching Newfoundland, the three flying boats then set off for the Azores. Two came down on the water, one sinking after its crew had been rescued and the other taxiing the last 200 miles (320 km) across the water. The remaining flying boat flew to Lisbon and finally to Ferrol in Spain, where it arrived on May 31 after traveling almost 4,000 miles (6,440 km). This considerable achievement by the pilot, Commander A. C. Read, and his crew was proof that the Atlantic could be beaten.

Even more significant was the first nonstop crossing of the Atlantic. In a modified Vickers Vimy twin-engined bomber, Captain John Alcock and Lieutenant Arthur Whitten Brown set off from St. John's, Newfoundland, on June 14, 1919. Just under 16 hours later, on the fifteenth, the British officers crash landed in a bog near Clifden in County Galway, Ire-

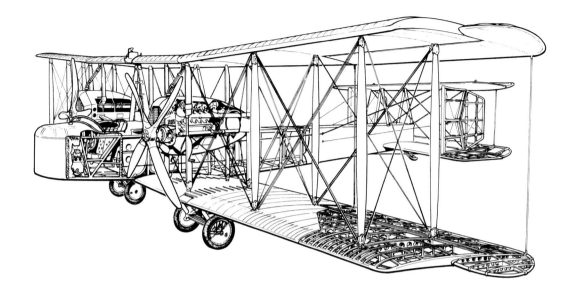

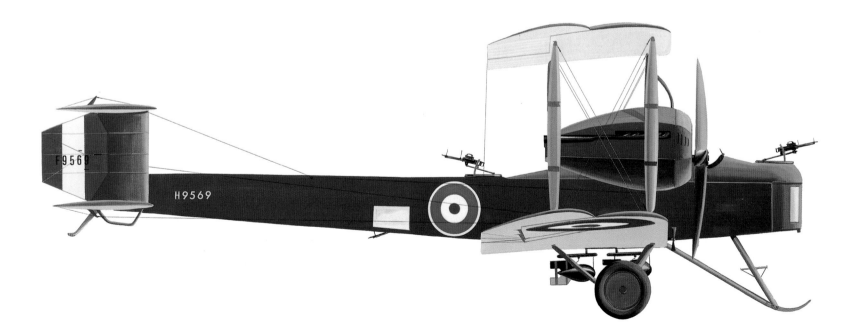

ABOVE AND BELOW Entering service just as the Armistice ended World War I, the Vickers Vimy was a three-seat bomber offering considerable capabilities. The type became a mainstay of the Royal Air Force in the years immediately follow- ing the end of the war, but is best remembered as the airplane in which John Alcock and Arthur Whitten Brown in June 1919 became the first men to achieve a nonstop aerial crossing of the North Atlantic.

land, after a flight of some 1,890 miles (3,050 km). The flight has become legendary, not only for the men's achievement, but also for their courage. The two men encountered appalling weather conditions, and Brown had to climb out six times onto the lower wing to attend to the engines. After receiving a welcome as heroes in London, the two men were knighted.

Even as individual airmen were attempting and achieving these heroic feats, commercial flight was still in its infancy. The first commercial flights in heavier-than-air craft took place before World War I. On July 4, 1911, Horatio Barber had flown a consignment of light bulbs across the county of Sussex in England, from Shoreham to Hove, for the considerable fee of £100. Air mail had been carried for the first time on February 18, 1911, when Henri Pequet delivered some 6,500 letters across the Jumna River from Allahabad to Naini Junction on behalf of the government of India. Just as important, although less well known, was the establishment by the Benoist company of the first regular schedule of passenger-carrying flights. Beginning in January 1914, the Benoist airline operated a flying boat designed by Benoist himself, on a service linking Tampa and St. Petersburg.

THE BIRTH OF CIVIL AVIATION

These early successes persuaded farsighted entrepreneurs that developments in the reliability and payload-carrying capability of aircraft would pave the way for the reemergence of commercial services after the war. George Holt Thomas registered the Aircraft Transport and Travel Ltd. in London in October 1916, one of the darkest periods of World War I. In 1919 AT&T began a mail service with D.H.9 aircraft between London and Paris, principally for those involved in the negotiations leading up to the Treaty of Versailles. Even before this, at least two regular mail services had been established. From March 1918 Hansa-Brandenburg C I biplanes had carried mail between Vienna and Kiev for the Austro-Hungarian armies in the region, and the U.S. Post Office Department had inaugurated a service between New York and Washington in August 1918.

The Deutsche Luft-Reederei company inaugurated the first postwar passenger service between Berlin and Weimar, homes of the old imperial and new republican governments, respectively, in February 1919. Other nations were quick to follow, with ex-service pilots flying hasty conversions of wartime bombers. There was virtually no regulation of the new industry, and the skies of northern Europe were soon buzzing with a growing number of bombers, such as the D.H.4, which was converted and could carry up

In numerical terms the Handley Page Type O/400 was the most important British heavy bomber of World War I, entering service early in 1918 and reaching a total of slightly more than four hundred by the war's end. The Type O/400 was retired from first-line service in 1919, seeing much of its postwar service in the transport role for which the civil Type O/10 and Type O/11 were also produced. The United States ordered fifteen hundred similar aircraft for manufacture in the U. S. A. by the Standard Aircraft Corporation with Liberty 12 engines, but only 107 had been completed before the program was canceled at the end of the war.

to four passengers. Larger machines such as the Vimy and two Handley Page types, the O/400 and V/1500, operated in the United Kingdom, while the Breguet Bre.14 and Farman F.60 Goliath operated in France.

The airline companies could initially carry any passenger who would take the risk, but during the 1920s regulations were introduced that increased safety requirements. Many of the little companies that had started up in the aftermath of the war closed down or were bought by larger concerns. Over a comparatively short period these little companies evolved into the national companies we know today. For example, Imperial Airways came into existence in 1924 as an amalgamation of Daimler Hire, Handley Page Air Transport, British Marine Air Navigation, and Instone Air Line, and eventually became the British Overseas Airways Corporation. Later it merged with British European Airways and became British Airways.

POSTAL PILOTS AND COMMERCIAL AVIATION

U.S. Air Mail One of the biggest boosts to early aviation—apart from World War I—came in the far-flung United States, where air mail turned part of the postal service into a band of brave airmen. By the middle of the 1930s regular commercial schedules would operate some 30,000 miles (48,280 km) of internal airways in the United States. These airways would be flown by 20 companies ranging in size from the great and steadily growing corporate operators flying coast-to-coast routes to the small companies flying short routes. Yet the commercial airlines did not spring into existence in a vacuum. The basis of their operations was air mail.

The first regular scheduled air mail service in the United States was launched on May 15, 1918, by aircraft of the U.S. Army, on the route linking New York City and Washington, D.C. Only three months later the Post Office Department perfected a civilian organization and assumed full charge of the air mail service. The initial sector of the transcontinental route was flown one year after the start of the first service, and on September 6, 1920, a scheduled coast-to-coast air mail service began between New York and

FACING PAGE The watchwords of military procurement in the period after World War I were low cost, in terms of procurement and operation, and small production batches. The U.S. Army, for instance, had procured only six examples of the Standard JR in World War I for use in the advanced trainer role, and after the war bought just another six aircraft to the revised JR-1B standard (illustrated) with a lower-powered engine and other changes for use in the service's fledgling air mail service.

ABOVE Night operations were still very much in their infancy, especially when a regular schedule in all weather conditions was attempted, but such was the general lot of the first American air mail pilots in aircraft such as this DH-4, which was essentially the Airco D.H.4, a British day bomber, built in the United States with a Liberty engine.

San Francisco. This was not a through service but rather the daylight relaying of mail that otherwise traveled by railroad. The standard practice was to fly the mail as far as possible during available daylight hours, and then load it onto railroad trains for continued movement through the night until another airplane could pick it up after dawn the next day.

The dangers of air mail flying are revealed by the 1921 statistics, when some 44.834 million letters were carried over 1.555 million miles (2.502 million km): In the course of this effort there were 56 crashes and 1,764 forced landings (810 as a result of mechanical problems and 954 due to the weather), leading to the deaths of 17 men and injuries to 36 more.

On July 1, 1924, the flying of mail by night began, ushering in the modern concept of air mail. In the spring of 1925 the postmaster general was authorized to contract for the operation of air mail routes by private companies, and during February 1926 the first contract air mail route was started. This first route linked Cleveland, Ohio, with Chicago, Illinois, via Detroit, Michigan, and by the end of August 1927 the Post Office Department had transferred to private companies the last of its routes.

POSTAL PILOTS AND COMMERCIAL AVIATION

Air mail was thus the basis of commercial flying in America. In 1934 all government air mail contracts were canceled. The government had tried to maintain an air mail service using U.S. Army aircraft and pilots, but the loss rate in aircraft and pilots was very high and the scheme was dropped. The Air Mail Act of 1934 established the pattern for American commercial aviation for years. Three bodies were responsible for civil air transport in overall terms: the Post Office, the Interstate Commerce Commission, and the Bureau of Air Commerce. The Post Office was responsible for awarding air mail contracts, fixing the routes to be flown by the various companies, and regulating schedules. The Interstate Commerce Commission was responsible for the establishment of fair rates. The Bureau of Air Commerce was entrusted with the task of licensing aircraft and the personnel to maintain and fly these aircraft, and as such was responsible for safety in the air.

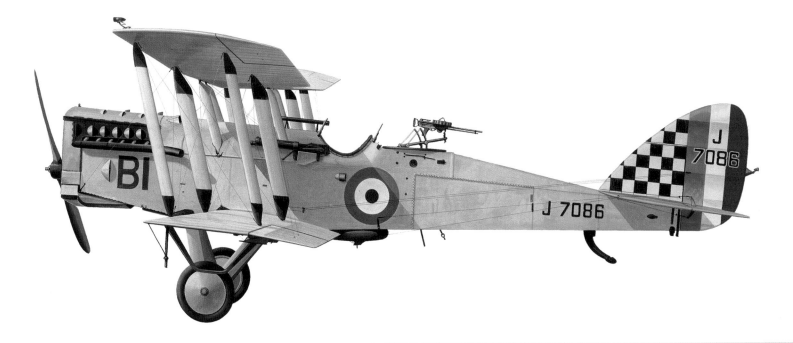

The Airco (de Havilland) D.H.4 two-seat day bomber was another British type ordered in World War I by the United States. No fewer than 12,248 "Liberty Planes" were ordered from a number of manufacturers with the 400-hp (298-kW) Liberty 12A engine, but 4,846 of these were completed by Dayton-Wright (3,106), Fisher Body (1,600) and Standard (140). The American-built model, known as the DH-4, remained in service up to the mid-1930s, many being upgraded to DH-4M standard with a welded-steel tube fuselage in place of the original plywood/fabric-covered wooden unit. The DH-4 was used for many tasks, including air mail flying.

The act also limited payment rates for the carriage of air mail. The result was that from 1934 the companies' income from the movement of air mail, at one time the lifeblood of civil aviation, fell steadily. Yet the air mail had served its purpose, for it had stimulated the creation of aircraft and routes to the point that the decline of air mail revenues was more than offset by the growth of revenues for the movement of steadily increasing numbers of passengers and freight. This growth permitted airline operators to reduce their charges to a point at which they became real competitors to railroads and roads for longer-distance transport.

The fifteen years following the end of World War I saw enormous advances in the theory and practice of flight. Speed, range, and altitude increased at an astonishing rate. Yet perhaps the most significant advances were made in the field of aerodynamics, where the Germans, British, and Americans led the field. Previously, designers' rudimentary appreciation of the effects of air pressure in flight had hampered the development of fast aircraft. Now considerable work was done both theoretically and in wind tunnels on the precise natures of lift and drag.

Reinhold Platz was a typical early designer. Platz's favorite airfoil was very thick, particularly at the leading edge. Such a section had obvious structural advantages and seemed an attractive aerodynamic feature. If lift is caused by the pressure differentials between air flowing over and under the wings, then an airfoil with a heavily cambered upper surface should give more lift by increasing those differentials. For Platz, such considerations outweighed the disadvantages of increased drag caused by the thick section. Later, engineers would understand far more precisely the trade-offs and optimal wing shapes involved.

Research was done on improving the ways in which airplanes could be flown safely, especially at low altitudes and low speed. The majority of fatal aircraft accidents, then and now, take place in the takeoff and landing phases of an airplane's flight. The most remarkable development for safety was the "slotted" wing, a solution to low-speed handling problems.

One of the major problems associated with aircraft of the time before and during World War I had been the stall, especially at low altitudes. When landing his airplane, the pilot would approach the airfield slowly with his engine throttled back and the nose of the airplane held high to retain as much lift as possible. This helped to maintain lift at slow speeds, but the extra area presented to the airflow had the effect of slowing the airplane. The pilot might then raise the nose still higher, and at an angle of attack of about 15° or slightly more, disaster often struck in the form of the stall. In aerodynamic terms the stall is easily explained. As the angle of attack gets higher, the pressure beneath it increases rapidly while that above it decreases. The result is greater lift. Eventually the airflow over the wing becomes increasingly turbulent, however, and develops less lift. At the critical angle, the airflow breaks away from the upper surface entirely and all lift is lost. The airplane then noses down and falls, yet while gathering speed, recovers lift. The pilot can usually resume his normal angle of flight. The stall is a major problem only at low altitudes: An airplane about to land will probably crash before it has regained flying speed.

Many methods of reducing the effect of the stall had been tried before World War I. Frederick Handley Page was one of the leading designers working on stall characteristics. His prewar aircraft were notable for a variety of antistall devices, but during the course of the war he came up with an enduring solution. The object had been to control the circulation of air around the wing. Handley Page reasoned that if air could be bled from the high-pressure area under the wing to the low-pressure area above the wing, the differential would be reduced and the stall would be delayed. The method he devised, the slotted wing, seems absurdly simple today. Yet it is still used and is one of the most important safety devices ever invented for aircraft.

The slot runs along the span of the wing just behind the leading edge, connecting the lower and upper surfaces of the wing; it is angled backward toward the trailing edge on the upper side. As the airplane approaches the situation in which its wing will stall, the pressure differential is kept down by high-pressure air forcing its way through the slot to the low-pressure area on the upper surface of the wing. Since the slot is angled backward, the air arriving on the upper surface streams backward and helps smooth the airflow, reducing turbulence.

Handley Page patented his idea in February 1918, but it did not see extensive use until Dr. Gustav Lachmann moved from the Göttingen laboratories and joined Handley Page in the late 1920s on the development of slotted wings.

Handley Page's simple type of slot then found favor almost immediately, and Hugo Junkers adopted it on many of his aircraft. The main disadvantage was that the slot was permanently open and produced drag. Handley Page and Lachmann therefore progressed one step further and developed the "automatic slot," which places no extra burden on the pilot but still reduces the drag. Using a floating slat just ahead of the wing's leading edge, Page and Lachmann's solution was a slot that opened only in response to high pressure differentials.

Similarly, the designers developed trailing-edge flaps for the rear edge of the wing. There are four basic types of trailing-edge flap, all of which made their appearance in the 1920s and were used universally in the 1930s. The plain flap consists of a long, relatively narrow portion of the rear of the wing. It is hinged so the pilot can lower it a few degrees and deflect the airflow downward. The plain flap dramatically affects the basic airflow over the upper surface of the wing. The split flap was designed to avoid this. Instead of the whole rear section of the wing hinging down, in the split flap only a portion of the wing's lower surface does so, deflecting the airflow under the wing but leaving the airflow over the upper surface intact.

The Fowler flap is far superior to the plain or split flaps, both of which increase lift solely by deflecting the airflow downward. The Fowler flap consists of one or more high aspect ratio "winglets," which drop down and back from the wing when operated, thus increasing both its area and its lift. Fowler flaps can double the lift of a wing, with great advantages at the lower end of the airplane's speed range.

The slotted flap works on the same principle as the Handley Page leading-edge slot. At the trailing edge, slots are combined with the Fowler type of area-extending flaps to provide a smooth airflow over these high-lift devices. Flaps served two purposes: At takeoff they were depressed only slightly (about 12°) and served as high-lift devices only, but for landing they were depressed through a greater arc (about 20°) in the final-approach stage and served both as high-lift devices and airbrakes.

All these developments took place within a few years of one another, but it was some time before designers took full advantage of slots and flaps. After a resurgence of aviation in the 1920s, Americans were soon making extensive use of both devices, particularly for their airliners. Because the public was increasingly sensitive to questions of safety, flaps and slots found favor quickly. Flaps and slots also improved the efficiency of the new aircraft.

REVOLUTION IN THE COCKPIT

World War I planes had been remarkably free of navigational instruments. Everyone was flying blind, forced to avoid cloudy days and moonless nights. Then Elmer Sperry, an American, exploited the particular characteristics of the gyroscope to solve the problem. Sperry, beginning work in 1912 on an automatic pilot, devoted much of his life to the perfection of the gyroscope and other instruments. Sperry was funded by the Guggenheim Fund for the Promotion of Aeronautics and received help from James Doolittle, and excellent analytical pilot, and Paul Kollsman, a brilliant instrument maker.

In 1928 Sperry finally perfected his artificial horizon. A pilot could fly in a cloud using a gyrocompass and a gyroscopically stabilized artificial horizon as his primary external reference. A year later, on September 24, 1929, Doolittle took off in thick fog in a modified Consolidated NY-2 trainer with a hood over its cockpit and landed safely 15 minutes later. He used his Sperry instruments along with specially arranged radio beams for direction. Swift progress was made in the early 1930s. The rapid development of rate

The Bristol Racer was a generally unsuccessful British attempt of 1922 to create a high-speed racing airplane with a midset monoplane wing and a fuselage faired to the shape of the powerful radial engine. The type has a place in aviation history as one of the world's first aircraft with retractable main landing-gear units of the type first developed in practical form for an American airplane, the Wright RB racer of 1920.

of climb and descent indicators, fast-reacting aneroid altimeters, good turn-and-bank indicators, and efficient radios made it safe to fly even in the very worst of weather.

Significant improvements were also made in controlling aircraft in the air. By the middle of World War I controls were standardized as a fin-mounted rear rudder for control in yaw, tailplane-mounted rear elevators for control in pitch, and wing-mounted ailerons for control in roll. The control surfaces themselves had also been improved.

Except for aircraft designed by Junkers and Dornier, aircraft structures up to the end of World War I were wire-braced and wooden, and covered with fabric. Wood possessed great advantages as the primary structural material: It is light, cheap, and easily worked, and also has a good strength/weight ratio. Large quantities of well-seasoned wood were available. Typical materials were light but strong spruce for fuselage longerons and spars; plywood for fuselage formers and wing ribs; and ash or hickory for the landing gear, where great strength was needed regardless of weight. The use of metal in the airframe was largely restricted to fittings and bracing wires.

Yet from the earliest days of heavier-than-air flight designers and engineers knew that wood had its drawbacks, especially for larger aircraft. Large machines could be built of wood, but in structural terms they were too heavy and complex. Metal offered distinct advantages, particularly when light alloys started to become readily available during World War I. A switch from wooden to metallic structures therefore seemed inevitable at some stage, not only because of the weight and complexity of large wooden structures but also because they permitted only modest aerodynamic refinement.

There were three basic components to the structure of early aircraft: a basic frame (fuselage, monoplane or biplane wings, and tail unit), layout-controlling (struts for the wings, tail unit, and landing gear), and a fabric covering. The problem was that wood made it difficult to design aircraft in which the three basic elements could be combined into one, or at most two. Progress had been made just before the war by Louis Béchereau, Deperdussin's chief designer and the man responsible for the Deperdussin Monocoque racer. Monocoque, an improvised word that means "single shell," is a term that combines the three components of earlier structures. In these prewar types, the fuselage was a hollow shell of plywood, sometimes stiffened with internal formers and stringers, which supported the structural load and also provided a nicely streamlined shape. The advantages were obvious: good shape, rigid structure, and relative simplicity. Béchereau had set aircraft construction on the road toward the modern fuselage.

Unfortunately, the same sort of construction could not be used for the wing. Before Dr. Adolph Rohrbach devised his concept of wings with "stressed skins," Junkers half-solved the problem during World War I, with his cantilevered monoplane wings of metal construction. In Rohrbach's stressed-skin structure, the wings were covered in metal, which bore a considerable part of the load. Inside the stressed skin were spars bearing the main part of the loads, and ribs to give the skin its shape. The concept differed radically from that of Junkers, whose corrugated skinning bore little of the load, but depended on a wing structure of conventional design. Rohrbach's structure featured a smooth covering that could support a considerable load, allowing the inside structure to be lightened, while at the same time producing a reduced amount of drag because of improved streamlining.

Rohrbach's ideas had been paralleled in Germany during World War I by Claude Dornier, one of the Zeppelin company's chief designers. In 1917 he designed the CL I experimental fighter, which had conventional wings but a metal monocoque fuselage.

The Short Silver Streak (first called the Swallow), built in 1920 and exhibited at the Olympia Aero Show, was the first airplane to combine stressed-skin flying surfaces and a metal monocoque fuselage. Although the principle of stressed-skin and monocoque construction received positive feedback, it remained no more than an oddity.

In the United Kingdom the concept fell almost immediately into a temporary limbo. Traditional structures still seemed to offer sufficient scope to the designer, although metal came to be used increasingly in place of wood for the main structural components for two reasons. First, the increased availability of light alloys offered the designer and engineer the chance to build conventional aircraft out of modern materials that would last and were easy to make. Second, the British Air Ministry was disturbed at the scarcity of high-quality seasoned timber after World War I. In 1927, the Air Ministry decided that the main structure of all British military aircraft would be metal.

Another aspect of aircraft design that received considerable attention from the early 1920s was the landing gear, which conventionally comprised two wheels at the ends of an axle attached to the closed ends of two wire-braced V-struts under the fuselage. The growing size and weight of aircraft soon forced a major reassessment of this increasingly weighty and drag-producing part of the airframe. Two solutions were either "cleaning up" the fixed landing gear for reduced drag, or introducing a mechanism that retracted the landing gear into the fuselage or under the surface of the wing, thus removing the drag entirely.

The first retractable landing gear had been developed as early as 1908 by an American, M. B. Sellers, but he had worked in almost total isolation and had no effect on subsequent developments. Experiments with semi- and fully retractable landing gear continued intermittently up to the end of World War I, and later began to appear on a number of racing aircraft. The weight of such units was too great for conventional aircraft, however, until the new breed of American transport aircraft appeared in the late 1920s and early 1930s.

In the 1920s more powerful engines appeared. They made the weight penalty of such landing gears steadily more acceptable and made high-speed flight a possibility. The two most important types of engine used in World War I had been the water- and air-cooled inline (and related V units) and the air-cooled rotary unit. The latter slowly declined in importance as it approached its theoretical limits. There were problems with the torque of the rotating assembly that included the crankcase, cylinders, and propeller. The inline and V engines were steadily developed for more power, but were cooled by water. The weight of the water together with that of the radiators, pumps, and all the associated "plumbing" became almost too much to bear.

The closing stages of World War I heralded a number of high-powered engines based on the radial layout, in which the cylinders are arranged radially around the crankshaft. Its devotees claimed the engine's cylinders could easily be exposed to the slipstream and cooled as the airplane passed through the air. This offered the possibility of a much improved power/weight ratio; it also removed the weight, drag, and cost of the water-cooling system.

Work to develop these engines was done during the 1920s, particularly by Bristol and Armstrong Siddeley in the United Kingdom, Wright and Pratt & Whitney in the

The de Havilland D.H.80A Puss Moth was typical of the European concept of the late 1920s for a monoplane touring airplane with three-seat accommodation. The type was used for a number of classic flights by pilots such as J. A. "Jim" Mollison, whose machine *The Heart's Content* is illustrated here. At one time married to Amy Johnson, Mollison used this airplane, with single-seat accommodation and much-enlarged fuel tankage, for the first solo east/west crossing of the Atlantic on August 18/19, 1932, between Portmarnock Strand outside Dublin in Ireland and Pennfield Ridge in New Brunswick, Canada.

The mid-1920s saw the launching of the U.S. Navy's first two true aircraft carriers, the USS *Saratoga* and *Lexington*, completed from incomplete battle-cruiser hulls. This photograph reveals the large flight deck of the *Saratoga* covered with Vought O2U Corsair observation aircraft. Introduced to U.S. Navy service in 1927, the O2U could be operated with wheeled landing gear from shore bases and aircraft carriers, or with float alighting gear from battleships and cruisers. The versatility of the floatplane version was later enhanced by the introduction of retractable wheels to provide an amphibian capability.

United States, Siemens and BMW in Germany, Gnome-Rhône in France, and Alfa-Romeo in Italy. The only major disadvantage of the radial engine compared to its inline and V counterparts was its greater frontal area, which made for greater drag, especially when the upper part of each cylinder extended beyond the lines of the forward fuselage. The consequences were minor for commercial aircraft, where power, reliability, and fuel economy were more important than performance, but it was a serious disadvantage for military aircraft.

The Americans had the fuel and metallurgy skills to exploit the advantages offered by the radial engine and soon became dominant in the field to the extent that most American civil and military aircraft from 1925 to 1945 were radial-engined. With the exception of the Italians, the Europeans generally stuck with inline and V engines for military aircraft, to their disadvantage.

As a group, pilots of the period before World War I had been seen as adventurous and fascinating eccentrics. In World War I many airmen had become "personalities" through the accomplishment of singular acts of bravery or attainment of ace status in air combat. In the period after World War I, daring pilots pushed themselves and their aircraft to the limit. Public interest centered on endurance pioneering flights over great distances, such as that of Alcock and Brown over the North Atlantic, and also around short-duration speed contests. Most countries with any significant interest in aviation held their own races, but the United States held the most.

THE GREAT RACES

The Pulitzer Trophy race was first held in 1920 and produced a rivalry between pilots of the U.S. Army and U.S. Navy. Although the series lasted only until 1925, it saw such legendary machines as the Verville-Sperry racer and a series of great Curtiss racers. The other major competitions were the National Air Races, the two most important being the Thompson Trophy for speed around a closed-circuit course and the Bendix Trophy for speed in a transcontinental race. U.S. Army and U.S. Navy aircraft entered these and other races, but they are remembered mostly for odd machines like the Gee Bee sportsters built by the Granville brothers, the Travel Air "Mystery Ship," and other out-and-out racers. All of these possessed very high speeds by the standards of the day, largely as a result

Great things were expected for the world of aviation after the end of the "Great War" in November 1918, and exhibitions such as the Paris air show of 1919 featured large numbers of advanced aircraft. Experience then revealed that the victorious Allied powers had no political or popular stomach for new military aircraft, and no financial resources for the development of commercial aviation.

Through the 1920s and 1930s there was great enthusiasm for racing aircraft, especially among the European and American public as well as designers and small-scale manufacturers who saw success in this exotic field as a means of publicizing their capabilities. Air racing therefore witnessed the creation of a number of radical aircraft optimized exclusively for high-speed flight, and one marque that really captured the public imagination was the "Gee Bee" series created by the Granville Brothers. The most extreme of these was the Super Sportster of the early 1930s, built in Model R-1 and Model R-2 forms, of which the latter is illustrated. The key to the Super Sportster was the use of the most powerful engine possible in the smallest airframe that could be packaged around it.

of the shoehorning of the most powerful possible engine into the smallest possible airframe. Although popular at the races, these fascinating aircraft were of distinctly dubious airworthiness.

The "blue ribbon" of all international competitive racing, however, was the Schneider Trophy. Now possessed by the Royal Aero Club in London, the Schneider Trophy was a magnificent prize for seaplanes. The series was instituted in December 1912 by Jacques Schneider, the son of a leading French armaments manufacturer. Schneider had a vision of the world united by great flying boats. He confidently expected that competition for his trophy would spur the development of seaplanes.

To be held annually over a course of not less than 150 nautical miles (172.75 miles, 278 km), the contest was to be organized by the winner of the previous race. There were to be flotation and water navigation tests, and the series was to end when one team had won the contest three times in five years. As the series proceeded, the structures of flying boats and later floatplanes were driven past their natural limits. New aerodynamic thinking was incorporated, and larger and considerably more powerful engines ran on new fuels and were cooled by novel radiators. During the interim period between the two wars, the Schneider races (see summary table on page 130) single-handedly motivated a steady stream of technical improvements in aircraft.

The Schneider races also fostered the split between American and European aviation. The competition spurred innovation on both continents, but set the Americans and Europeans on different paths. The Americans' 1923 victory, for example, completely changed the character of the race. Realizing that valuable information about the technical

In one of the classic photographs of the golden age of American air racing, a Gee Bee (Granville Brothers) Model R-1 Super Sportster passes a pylon. The only event that the Model R-1 won was the 1932 Thomson Trophy race. This airplane represented one of the extremes of trying to pack maximum engine into minimum airframe.

and physiological problems of high-speed flight could be gained from racing, as well as great prestige, the U.S. Army and U.S. Navy both decided to invest in entrants. The Curtiss firm produced a series of excellent racers, conventional in layout but compact in size and superbly streamlined. The designers' efforts in streamlining were aided in the choice of engine. This was the Curtiss D-12, one of the classic engines of aviation history. The D-12 featured a remarkably low frontal area for its power, enabling the airframe designers to build a racer with low profile drag. This, combined with good detail design, was primarily responsible for the CR-3's high speed.

In 1926, confident they would outright win the Schneider Trophy, the Americans wanted to end their involvement with international racing and focus on commercial aviation. They had already established the Aircraft Board in 1925. The board's sole purpose was to supervise trends in American aviation. After they were upset in the 1926 race by the Italians, the Americans split off and pursued aircraft optimized for high-performance commercial and medium-performance military purposes, using new aerodynamics and structures and air-cooled radial engines, while the Europeans pursued aircraft offering high performance using aerodynamic refinement and liquid-cooled engines.

The Schneider Trophy races continued into the 1930s and spurred the development of aviation, most notably in the development of high-powered engines and to a lesser extent aerodynamics, fuels, and propellers. The races motivated the great British and Italian designers to develop their thinking about high-speed aerodynamics. Particularly brilliant were Reginald Mitchell and Mario Castoldi, two of the most significant designers of the middle and late 1930s. Apart from the technical benefits, the Schneider Trophy races helped to keep aviation in the public eye at a time when there was little money for aviation and passenger flying was only for the few.

Racing series such as the Schneider Trophy competitions were largely responsible for the construction of the "ultimate aircraft" of the period in terms of speed. Yet the same period, from the mid-1920s to the mid-1930s, also witnessed another type of flying that was competitive without the presence of one-on-one competition. This involved record-breaking flights over increasingly long distances. While the speed contests required advanced technology and received government sponsorship, long-distance flying was generally the province of manufacturers and private pilots. Despite the fact that they did not receive the same level of public attention as the speed races, long-distance flights were just as important to the development of flight. They promoted the development of low-drag airframes and reliable and fuel-efficient aircraft.

The U.S. Army and U.S. Navy were keen rivals during the 1920s for the landplane races that dominated the American air-racing scene, but collaborated in the premier international seaplane racing series for the Schneider Trophy. In this series it was the floatplane racers from the Curtiss stable that almost enabled the United States to take the trophy outright for three successive wins. The last of the Curtiss racers was the Model 42 that was known to the services as the R3C. Two were built for the U.S. Navy and one for the U.S. Army.

THE SCHNEIDER TROPHY RACES

DATE	LOCATION	WINNER
4/16/1913	Monaco	Maurice Prévost, France, in a Deperdussin
4/20/1914	Monaco	Howard Pixton, U.K., in a Sopwith Tabloid
9/10/1919	Bournemouth	No winner
9/20/1920	Venice	Luigi Bologna, Italy, in a Savoia S.12
8/11/1921	Venice	Giovanni de Briganti, Italy, in a Macchi M.7
8/12/1922	Bay of Naples	Henri Biard, U.K., in a Supermarine Sea Lion II
9/28/1923	Cowes	Lt. David Rittenhouse, U.S. Navy, in a Curtiss CR-3
10/26/1925	Baltimore	Lt. James Doolittle, U.S. Army, in a Curtiss R3C-2
11/13/1926	Hampton Roads	Maggiore Mario de Bernardi, Italy, in a Macchi M.39
9/26/1927	Venice	Flt. Lt. S. N. Webster, U.K., in a Supermarine S.5
9/7/1929	Southampton Water	Flg. Off. H. R. D. Waghorn, U.K., in a Supermarine S.6
9/13/1931	Calshot	Flt. Lt. John N. Boothman, U.K., in a Supermarine S.6B

The primary beneficiaries of speed racing were the military, and in particular their fighter arms, while the swelling numbers of civil airlines benefited from the distance record-breakers. Air forces with a major interest in transport and heavier bombing also gained benefit from the experience of long-distance flying and aircraft. As a direct result, navigational skills increased and machines capable of carrying a significant payload began to appear on the designers' drawing boards.

There had been several notable long-distance flights immediately after World War I, the two most celebrated being the first crossing of the Atlantic by Curtiss seaplanes and the first nonstop crossing of the Atlantic by a Vickers Vimy, both in 1919. The aircraft used in these flights were World War I designs modified for the specific demands of these epoch-making flights. From the early 1920s onward long-distance flights were made by newer aircraft.

In 1924, four Douglas "World Cruisers" belonging to the U.S. Army departed on the first flight around the world. Departing from Seattle, Washington, on April 6, the aircraft flew via the Aleutian Islands, Japan, and India, through Europe to Scotland, Iceland, and Greenland, and then back to Seattle. Two of the aircraft arrived in Seattle on September 28 after a remarkable 175-day journey. The flight's average speed was slow, but in every other respect the achievement was extraordinary. The mere fact that two of the four aircraft, operating from wheeled landing gear or float alighting gear, had even managed to fly around the world was amazing.

The Atlantic remained the chief lure for long-distance fliers. Even as the "World Cruisers" were still on their great flight, the Italian pioneer Locatelli attempted a transatlantic flight in a Dornier Wal flying boat. Forced down into the sea, the flying boat stayed afloat, and three days later Locatelli and his crew were rescued by a passing ship. Two years later, Major Franco and a crew of three used the same type of flying boat in the first successful crossing of the South Atlantic from Spain to Rio de Janeiro in Brazil via the Canary Islands, the Cape Verde Islands, and Pernambuco. The Wal was an ungainly machine, but proved a popular model for long-distance flights because it had good range and well-proved survivability qualities on the water.

The greatest of all early long-distance flights, of course, took place on May 20 and 21, 1927, when Captain Charles A. Lindbergh flew across the North Atlantic from Long Island, New York, to Paris. The world was astounded by the achievement and heroism of this unknown American pilot. The flight was a landmark in every respect. It was the first solo nonstop transatlantic flight, and unlike earlier pioneers, Lindbergh had effectively flown from

ABOVE The Loening Aeronautical Engineering Company of New York, later taken over by the Keystone Aircraft Corporation that then became a component of the Curtiss-Wright Corporation, specialized in the design and manufacture of amphibian floatplanes that were used by the U.S. Army and U.S. Navy. Illustrated here is an example of the OA-1A in U.S. Army service as an observation type but often flown for utility and rescue purposes. This was one of six such aircraft flown on a goodwill trip to the southern tip of South America in 1926.

BELOW Sherman Fairchild was a specialist in aerial photography for the survey role, and failing to find an airplane suitable for the carriage of his camera, decided to produce his own, with a capacious fuselage under a high-set braced monoplane wing. The result was the FC that later became known as the Model 51, as it was Fairchild's first five-seat airplane. This 1925 type also secured success as a rugged light transport for "bushplane" services, and development of the concept led to the Model 71 (first seven-seat airplane) that appeared in 1928 and could be operated on wheels, skis, or floats. This particular example was operated by Reeve Aleutian Airways, an Alaskan bushplane operator that started services in April 1946.

one major city to another. He secured the Raymond Orteig $25,000 prize for the first flight in either direction between New York and Paris. Desperately short of money to commission and buy an airplane for the attempt, Lindbergh had received great assistance from a group of businessmen in St. Louis, Missouri. Designed to his own specifications by the Ryan company of San Diego, California, the NYP *Spirit of St. Louis* was an advanced and attractive design powered by a Wright air-cooled radial, which was a type of engine currently gaining great favor in the United States for its light weight and mechanical reliability.

Lindbergh's success spurred on other aviators who wanted to secure a place in history. Shortly after Lindbergh's flight, Clarence Chamberlin, with C. A. Levine as his passenger, attempted a nonstop flight from just outside New York to Berlin. Taking off in their Wright-Bellanca W.B.2 *Columbia* monoplane on June 4, 1927, the two men came down in Eisleben, somewhat short of Berlin, after a two-day flight that covered 3,911 miles (6,394 km).

The flights of Lindbergh and Chamberlin had been made from west to east, thereby securing the advantages of the prevailing winds. The first successful east-to-west flight over the North Atlantic came only in 1931, when Captain Hermann Kohl, Colonel James Fitzmaurice and Günther Graf von Hünefeld left Baldonnel, Ireland, in the Junkers F 13 *Bremen,* a pioneering low-wing cantilever monoplane transport of all-metal construction, and touched land again on Greenly Island off the coast of Labrador one day later on April 13, 1928.

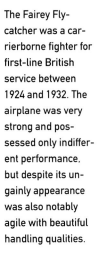

The Fairey Flycatcher was a carrierborne fighter for first-line British service between 1924 and 1932. The airplane was very strong and possessed only indifferent performance, but despite its ungainly appearance was also notably agile with beautiful handling qualities.

CHARLES LINDBERGH

CHARLES A. LINDBERGH (1902–1974) Charles Augustus Lindbergh was born in Detroit on February 4, 1902, and spent most of his early life in Little Falls, Minnesota, and in Washington, D.C., while his father served as a congressman. The formal part of Lindbergh's education ended with his second year at the University of Wisconsin, when his increasing fascination with flight led him to switch his allegiance to a flying school in Lincoln, Nebraska, and also to buy a war-surplus Curtiss Jenny with which he barnstormed in the South and the Midwest. In 1924–25 Lindbergh attended army flying schools in Texas, and then in the following year became an air mail pilot. Lindbergh flew the route linking St. Louis, Missouri, and Chicago, Illinois.

Charles Lindbergh was certainly no "one-success wonder," for he followed the great 1927 nonstop flight over the North Atlantic with the exploration and proving of possible airline routes. This made full use of Lindbergh's qualities as a pilot and mechanic, emphasized his capabilities as a planner, and in the process opened the way for the enlargement of the route network flown by American airlines.

During his time as an air mail pilot, Lindbergh decided to try to win the $25,000 prize offered by the hotelier Raymond Orteig in 1919 for a nonstop flight between New York and Paris, and gained the financial support of a group of St. Louis businessmen. With this backing Lindbergh sent a telegram to T. Claude Ryan in San Diego, California, on February 3, 1927, asking if his company could design and build the required airplane in just two months. Ryan responded in the affirmative, asking for $6,000 excluding the engine and instruments. The capabilities of the *Spirit of St. Louis,* as the plane was named, were revealed when Lindbergh arrived outside New York on May 12, 1927, after a nonstop transcontinental flight even though he himself had never previously flown more than 500 miles (800 km) nonstop.

On May 20 and 21, in a time of 33 hours 39 minutes, Lindbergh flew from New York to Paris, covering 3,610 miles (5,809 km) at an average speed of 107.5 mph (173 km/h). He immediately received a hero's accolades on both sides of the Atlantic Ocean, which led to a series of goodwill flights in Europe and America. In May 1929 Lindbergh married Anne Morrow, daughter of the U.S. ambassador in Mexico, and Mrs. Lindbergh then flew as her husband's copilot and navigator on flights to many parts of the world.

Lindbergh soon became the technical adviser to two airlines, Transcontinental Air Transport and Pan American Airways, and in this capacity proved many of the routes that the two operators wished to undertake. His fame took a tragic leap, however, in March 1932, when the Lindberghs' son, then aged only two, was kidnapped and killed in what was for many years the world's most notorious crime. In April 1936, Bruno Richard Hauptmann was executed for it. The distressed Lindberghs tried to escape from the blaze of publicity by taking shelter in Europe.

Here Lindbergh came into contact with the reviving military strength of Germany, and in 1936 he started to issue reports about the power of the Luftwaffe. In 1938 he was decorated by the German government, which drew great criticism. This sit-

Named *Spirit of St. Louis,* the Ryan NYP (New York– Paris) flown by Charles Lindbergh in his epic solo flight between New York and Paris was a braced high-wing monoplane with fixed tailskid landing gear. One of the keys to Lindbergh's success was the reliability of the engine, a 237-hp (177-kW) Wright Whirlwind J-5C radial unit supplied with 450 U.S. gal (1.703 liters) of fuel mainly from a large tank immediately ahead of the cockpit. This meant that Lindbergh had to resort to a periscope for forward vision.

The Ryan NYP *Spirit of St. Louis* flown by Charles Lindbergh was typical of aircraft design "best practices" in 1927, and was a braced high-wing monoplane with fixed tailskid landing gear. A key feature of the design and the airplane's eventual success was the Wright Whirlwind J-5C air-cooled radial engine, which was supplied with 450 U.S. gallons (1,703 liters) of fuel carried one-third in two wing tanks and two-thirds in one fuselage tank immediately ahead of the cockpit.

uation became worse in 1940–41 when, after his return to his native country, Lindbergh urged the United States to remain neutral in World War II. President Franklin D. Roosevelt publicly condemned the opinions of Lindbergh, who resigned his Air Corps Reserve commission in April 1941. Lindbergh nonetheless devoted all his energies to the American war effort after the United States joined the battle in December 1941, working as a consultant to the Ford Motor Company and the United Aircraft Corporation. He flew 50 unofficial combat missions in a tour of duty in the Pacific and, after Germany's surrender in May 1945, was part of a U.S. Navy technical mission to assess German aviation developments.

After the war the Lindbergh family lived in Connecticut, and later in Hawaii. Lindbergh still worked as a consultant to Pan American World Airways and the Department of Defense, was a member of the NACA (National Advisory Committee for Aeronautics), and also served on several other aeronautical bodies. Lindbergh died on Maui in the Hawaiian Islands on August 26, 1974.

The Universal was the first airplane from the Fokker stable to be designed, built, and certificated in the United States. This braced high-wing monoplane was intended for the utility transport role and based on the standard Fokker combination of a welded-steel tube fuselage and a plywood-covered wooden wing. The Universal was certificated in June 1927 with the Wright Whirlwind J-4 radial engine, and this example was operated in Canada with the Whirlwind J-5 engine and float/ski alighting gear after modification by Western Canada Airways. The pilot was located in an open cockpit ahead of the wing's leading edge, while freight or six passengers were carried in the enclosed cabin.

Though other long-distance fliers now shifted their attention to other unconquered distance, the Atlantic still exerted a strong pull on the adventurous, including many pilots who won their aviation "spurs" over the Atlantic before moving to still more demanding efforts. Fokker high-wing cantilever monoplane transports were now at their peak. In 1928, for example, the American Amelia Earhart crossed from west to east as passenger in a Fokker, while the Australian Charles Kingsford-Smith made an east-to-west crossing, also in a Fokker. Pilots were now attempting increasingly lengthy routes. On July 15/16, 1931, for example, the Hungarians Gyorgy Endres and Alexander Magyar flew from Newfoundland to Budapest in their Lockheed Model 8 Sirius, and on July 28/30, 1931, Russell Boardman and John Polando flew a Bellanca from New York to Istanbul. By August 10, 1934, the North Atlantic had been flown 41 times by heavier-than-

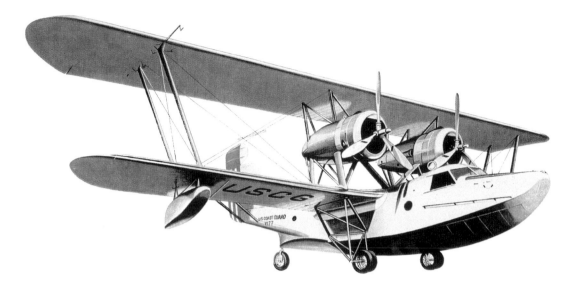

ABOVE One of the features of military aircraft procurement in the 1920s and early 1930s was the revision of existing designs into more capable forms. Thus the Hall PH-3 patrol and air/sea rescue flying boat, ordered by the U.S. Coast Guard in 1939 and here seen on its beaching gear so that it could be moved into and out of the sea, stemmed ultimately from a design of 1914. This was a large flying boat ordered from Curtiss by Rodman Wanamaker for a planned transatlantic flight but never completed. In 1916 the U.S. Navy ordered an improved version as the H-12 and then, with more powerful engines, as the H-16. The Royal Naval Air Service also procured the type, which was then developed in the United Kingdom as the Felixstowe F.2, F.3, and F.5. The U.S. Navy saw the advantages of the F.5 over the H-16 and ordered this British model from Curtiss as the F-5L with Liberty 12A engines, and the F-5L was later improved to a marked degree by the Naval Aircraft Factory for production as the PN-7, which was then upgraded in a

number of forms up to the PN-11. The Hall Aluminum Aircraft Corporation was then entrusted with further development, resulting in the PH-1 of 1931, the PH-2 of 1936 and finally the PH-3 that served in World War II.

BELOW Production of the Latécoère 28 began in 1929 to meet the requirement of Aéropostale, the French national air mail operator, for a transport to carry mail and passengers. The airplane was typical of European design and manufacturing concepts at this time, and was thus a strut-braced high-wing monoplane with fixed landing gear and fully enclosed accommodation. The airplane illustrated was a Laté 28-1, which carried eight passengers and was powered by the 500-hp (373-kW) Hispano-Suiza 12Hbr engine. The Laté 28 also appeared in seaplane form with twin-float alighting gear.

The pioneering work of Lindbergh and other route-proving pilots led to the establishment of the first overseas services by American airlines. These first extended south into the Caribbean and then Central and South America, and then west into and finally across the Pacific Ocean. The key to long oceanic flights was the use of large flying boats, mainly of Boeing, Martin, and Sikorsky design. Flying boats were, of course, independent of paved runways, and could therefore alight at islands where support facilities were built for limited repairs, refueling, and overnight accommodation of the passengers. Reliability on long over-water flights virtually dictated the use of a four-engined powerplant, and the need to carry a substantial fuel load made it feasible to create luxurious accommodation and facilities for limited numbers of passengers.

air craft and four times by lighter-than-air craft. By the end of September 1934 the South Atlantic had also been flown 31 times, all of them by heavier-than-air craft.

There were, of course, many other long-distance flights that were just as challenging as the Atlantic, if not more so. As early as 1920 a group of Italian aircraft (four Caproni multiengined and seven SVA single-engined machines) attempted to fly from Rome across much of Europe and Asia to Tokyo, in the process passing over some of the most inhospitable parts of the world. After almost three months, only two of the SVA machines finally reached Tokyo. One of the aircraft was flown by Masiero and the other by Ferrarin, who later made a great name for himself in the Schneider Trophy races and in several record-breaking flights over long distances.

Other great flights to the Far East were those of Pelletier d'Oisy and Bésin, who took a little less than seven weeks to fly a Breguet Bre.19GR from Paris to Tokyo in 1924, and de Pinedo and Campanelli, who in 1925 flew from Lake Maggiore to Tokyo and back in a Savoia-Marchetti flying boat. The outward leg of this 34,000-mile (54,720-km) journey included a flight around Australia. In the same year, Pelletier d'Oisy flew from Paris

ABOVE A British experimental development to investigate a means of maximizing the range of floatplanes for tasks such as the high-speed delivery of air mail, the Short Mayo composite of 1936 produced excellent if not altogether practical results. Developed by Robert Mayo, the concept was based on the use of the large S.20 *Maia*, basically a scaled-up S.23 "Empire" class flying boat, to lift a heavily laden floatplane, the four-engined S.21 *Mercury*, which could then depart on its journey with a full fuel load. Once the composite had reached cruising altitude and speed, the S.21 lifted off its motherplane, which then returned to base, and cruised out to its maximum range. On October 6, 1938, the S.31 was launched to establish a record as yet unbroken, namely a seaplane distance figure of 5,997.5 miles (9,652 km) from a point in the air near Dundee in Scotland to the Orange River in South Africa.

to Peking in the remarkably short time of one week. The Bre.19 was the most celebrated French long-distance airplane of the time and made many great flights, including two crossings of the Atlantic. The most famous single airplane was the *Point d'Interrogation* (question mark), a Bre.19 in which Costes and Bellonte flew from Paris to New York September 1/2, 1930.

The great challenge of long-distance flight after the North and south Atlantic was the Pacific Ocean. The first crossing had been made during the U.S. Army's round-the-world flight in 1924, when the four Douglas "World Cruisers" had flown from the Aleutian Islands to Japan. A gap of almost three years followed before the next attempt. On June 1, 1927, Lieutenants Lester Maitland and Albert Hegenberger of the U.S. Army Air Corps flew a Fokker C-2 "Bird of Paradise" transport 2,400 miles (3,850 km) from Oakland, California, to Honolulu in the Hawaiian Islands in a fraction under 26 hours.

The distances were so great that few dared to fly nonstop across the full breadth of the Pacific Ocean. The main routes between land masses therefore became important factors. The first man to cross from the United States to Australia was Squadron Leader Charles Kingsford-Smith. He flew with another Australian, Flight Lieutenant Charles Ulm, and two Americans, Harry Lyons and J. W. Warner, as his crew. In the Fokker *Southern Cross,* Kingsford-Smith and his crew lifted off from Oakland, California, on May 31, 1928, and in a remarkable feat of navigation involving intermediate refueling points in Hawaii and Fiji, reached Brisbane, Queensland, nine days later on June 10.

On June 28/29, 1931, Harold Gatty and Wiley Post flew over the North Pacific from Solomon Beach, Alaska, to Khabarovsk in Siberia in their Lockheed Model 5 Vega. The trip was only one stage in their epic flight around the world. An even greater land-mark was the first nonstop flight across the North Pacific on October 4/5, 1931, by Hugh Herndon and Clyde Pangborn in a Bellanca called *Miss Veedol.* This flight reached Tokyo from Wenatchee, Washington, part of the two men's round-the-world flight. In a Lockheed Model 8 Altair, Kingsford-Smith, now knighted and with Captain Taylor as his crew, made the first crossing of the Pacific (in fact the reverse of his Fokker flight) in a single-engined airplane between October 22 and November 4, 1934.

Women played their own part in the conquest of the Pacific when, on January 11/12, 1935, Amelia Earhart became the first woman to fly across the ocean when she took a Lockheed Model 5 Vega from Oakland to Honolulu. On May 21/22, 1932, as Mrs. Putnam, she had also made the first solo west-to-east crossing of the North Atlantic by a woman, flying from Harbour Grace, Newfoundland, to Londonderry in Northern Ireland.

AMELIA EARHART

AMELIA EARHART (1897–1937) Amelia Mary Earhart was born on July 24, 1897, in Atchison, Kansas. At the age of 10 she caught her first glimpse of an airplane at the Iowa State Fair. A popular misconception is that this sparked a lifelong devotion to flight, but in fact it was a further 10 years or more before Earhart began to develop a fascination with aviation. After visiting her sister, who was studying at a Canadian college, she remained in Toronto and trained as a nurse before serving as a Voluntary Aid Detachment nurse in a military hospital until the end of World War I in November 1918. Earhart next enrolled

Amelia Earhart worked as a nurse in a Canadian military hospital during World War I and then as a social worker in Denison House, Boston, after the war. She then won the first part of her enduring fame on June 17/18, 1928, when she became the first woman to cross the Atlantic by air, albeit only as a passenger. Determined to gain a personal justification for her fame, Earhart achieved a solo flight over the Atlantic on May 20/21, 1932. This led to a series of flights across the United States, and in January 1935 she recorded the first solo flight from Hawaii to California, a distance greater than that between North America and Europe.

as a premed student at Columbia University in the fall of 1919. Yet some months later, at an air meeting in California, she took a 10-minute joyriding flight. "As soon as we left the ground I knew I myself had to fly!" she later reported. Soon after this she started to take flying lessons with one of the United States' pioneer women pilots, Anita Snook.

By October 1922, after gaining her "wings," Earhart started to become involved in attempts to break flying records, her first success being a women's altitude record of 14,000 ft (4,267 m). She was also involved in the organization of the first Women's Air Derby race. During this race, Earhart was tied for first place with the great woman pilot Ruth Nichols at Columbus, Ohio, the event's penultimate intermediate landing point. Nichols crashed while trying to take off and Earhart, awaiting her turn to take off, jumped out of her machine and dragged Nichols, badly shaken but without any injury, from the cockpit of her wrecked airplane. Only then returning to her own airplane and lifting off, Earhart finished the race at Cleveland, Ohio, in third place. Earhart continued her racing and record-breaking career, securing personal satisfaction but also making a major contribution to the further popularization of flying and the role of women in the field.

In 1928 her life was permanently changed by Captain H. H. Railey, who had been asked by George Palmer Putnam, a New York publisher, to find the person to become the first woman to complete a transatlantic flight. Caught by Earhart's resemblance to Charles Lindbergh, Railey coined the nickname "Lady Lindy" for Earhart. Just one week later Earhart and Putnam met in New York, and Putnam quickly decided that Earhart was the woman for the flight, on which she would be a passenger, with the formal designation commander, rather than a real member of the crew as she lacked multiengined and instrument flying experience. The task of flying the three-engined Fokker F.VII, named *Friendship,* was entrusted to Wilmer Stultz and Louis Gordon. On June 3, 1928, following a delay of several days as the weather improved, the *Friendship* left for Halifax, Nova Scotia, where adverse weather again imposed a delay to June 18. Flying through dense fog for most of the trip, the *Friendship* landed at Burry Port in South Wales and not in Ireland, as had been planned. Earhart entered the aviation history books.

Earhart entered three Bendix transcontinental air races, and during 1933 took a special prize for the first woman to complete the course. In the early 1930s Earhart also set women's speed and distance records with 181 mph (291 km/h) and 2,026.5 miles (3,261.25 km) respectively, and also secured an Autogiro altitude record of 18,415 ft (5,613 m). Then on May 21, 1932, Earhart entered the "big time" of flying when she completed the first solo flight over the Atlantic by a woman, in the process becoming the first person to have crossed this ocean by air on two occasions. This flight also qualified

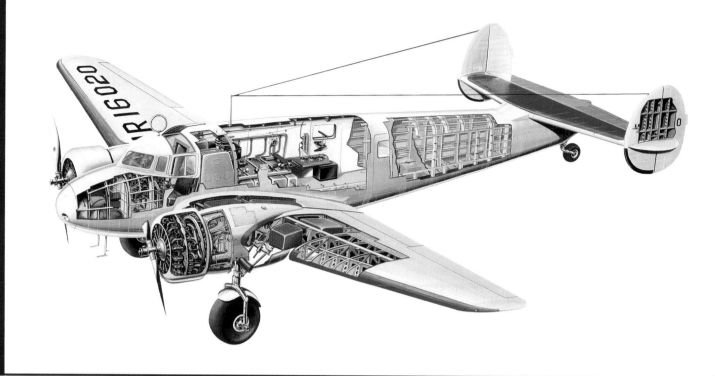

While Boeing and Douglas fought it out for the upper end of the airline market with their pioneering Model 247 and DC-3. Lockheed was carving out a niche for itself in the lower-capacity end of the market with the high-performance Electra and its successors. This particular airplane was the machine flown by Amelia Earhart.

for two records, for the longest nonstop distance by a woman and for the most rapid crossing. Earhart additionally set and then improved some women's transcontinental speed records, and achieved many point-to-point records.

In 1931 Earhart married Putnam, and after this became a part-time counselor to women students at Purdue University. On June 1, 1937, Earhart and her navigator, Fred Noonan, lifted off from Miami, Florida, in their Lockheed Electra twin-engined monoplane on a flight round the world. The flight progressed via San Juan in Puerto Rico, the northeast coast of South America, across the Atlantic to Africa and then the Red Sea before progressing to Karachi, Calcutta, Rangoon, Bangkok, Singapore, Bandoeng, Port Darwin, and Lae in New Guinea. This was the last point at which anyone saw Earhart and Noonan, who failed to arrive at their next staging point, Howland Island in the Pacific. On July 2, President Franklin D. Roosevelt authorized a $4-million search by nine ships and 66 aircraft, but this failed to find the Electra or its crew.

Many theories about her fate have been advanced over the years, including the suggestion that she was involved in a reconnaissance authorized by Roosevelt to determine Japanese military developments in the Pacific. It has also been claimed that she deliberately crashed her Electra into the ocean; that she was captured by the Japanese and forced to broadcast to American GIs as "Tokyo Rose" in World War II; and that she lived for years on an island in the South Pacific with a native fisherman. More recently, the results of a series of four archaeological expeditions to uninhabited Nikumaroro atoll suggest that Earhart's and Noonan's Electra may have landed there, out of fuel, and that the two perished for lack of water.

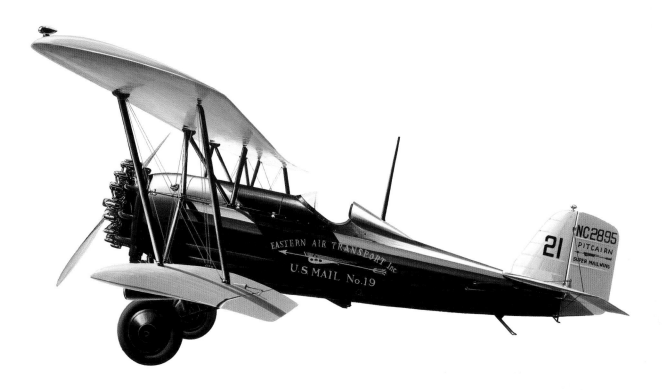

The Pitcairn Super Mailwing was created specifically for the carriage of air mail on the growing network of routes throughout the United States, and was flown from 1928 by a number of operators such as Eastern Air Transport, precursor of Eastern Air Lines, in this striking black and chrome yellow color scheme.

A significant advance in long-endurance rather than long-distance flight was achieved in January 1929, when a Fokker C-2A of the USAAC remained airborne for 150 hours with the aid of air-to-air refueling. The *Question Mark* was crewed by Major Carl Spaatz, Captain Ira Eaker, Lieutenants Harry Halverson and Elwood Quesada, and Sergeant Roy Hoe: All four commissioned officers later rose to high command in World War II. In the course of the flight, the C-2A was refueled no fewer than 37 times from a Douglas O-2C, which also supplied oil and other necessary items. The technique was rudimentary, to say the least, requiring someone in the C-2A to seize the hose as it was lowered from the O-2C and then place the nozzle into the opened filler of the fuel tank before reversing the process at the end of the refueling.

Other air forces began to acquire a real interest in long-distance flight during the 1920s. As Mussolini's air minister, General Italo Balbo thought flights by massed aircraft over record-breaking distances would bolster the reputation of the world's first Fascist state. The first such flight, with Balbo in personal command, was composed of 10 Savoia S.55 flying boats that flew from Portuguese Guinea in West Africa to Natal in Brazil on January 6, 1931. Balbo then planned a formation flight of no fewer than 24 S.55X twin-hulled flying boats from Italy to the World's Fair in Chicago in July 1933.

Several private individuals were setting their sights on greater objectives during this period. Perhaps the most adventurous of these men were Wiley Post and Harold Gatty. Post was blind in one eye, and habitually wore a black patch. Flying possibly the best long-range type of the period, a Lockheed Model 5 Vega named *Winnie Mae of Oklahoma,* Post and Gatty set off from New York early on June 23, 1931. Stopping to refuel at Harbour Grace in Newfoundland, Chester in England, Berlin, Moscow, Novosibirsk, Blagoveshchensk, Khabarovsk, Fairbanks in Alaska, and Edmonton in Canada, Post and Gatty returned to New York on July 1 after a heroic flight of eight days.

Without a doubt, however, the greatest long-distance flight of the period was Wiley Post's solo round-the-world flight in 7 days, 18 hours, and 49 minutes on July 15/22, 1933. Flying at optimum speed and optimum altitude and staying on the right course was an extraordinary flying accomplishment, especially considering the physical demands of solo flight. The achievements of men such as Post and Gatty showed the public how small the world was, when even single-engined aircraft could circle it in just over seven days.

Most of the famous long-distance flights were achieved in monoplanes. By the mid-1920s the United States and Italy had taken a distinct lead over the rest of the world in the development of long-range monoplanes. The British, on the other hand, were concentrating on developing the tried and tested biplane formula that had proved so successful during World War I. Some interesting monoplane designs had reached prototype form, but these had been either very large machines such as the Beardmore (Rohrbach) Inflexible technology demonstrator and Fairey Long-Range Monoplane, or very small lightplanes such as the Blackburn Sidecar (dating from 1918), the Short-Gnosspelius Gull, and a variety of other Short machines. In both these categories, monoplane design was the only practical possibility, for biplane construction was too heavy and clumsy for large aircraft, and produced too much drag for very small aircraft.

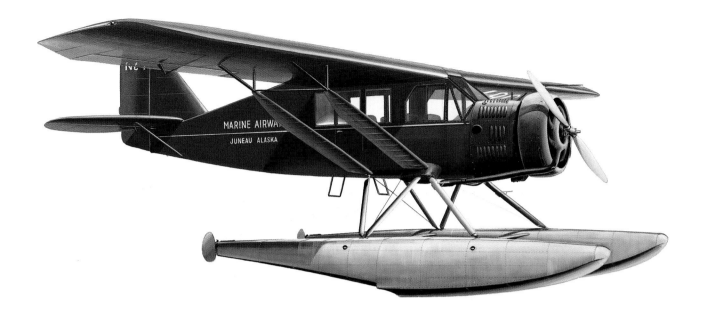

ABOVE One of the most distinctive features of Bellanca aircraft in the 1920s and 1930s was the use of a high-set wing braced on each side by struts faired to an airfoil section for the provision of additional lift. The CH-300 Pacemaker was powered by a 220-hp (164-kW) Wright Whirlwind radial engine and provided six-seat accommodation, and entered service in August 1929. The airplane was rugged and could be operated on twin-float alighting gear as an alternative to its standard fixed tailskid landing gear, and this fact commended the type to "bushplane" operators such as Marine Airways, based at Juneau in Alaska, from the launch of its services in 1936 and its 1940 link with Alaska Air Transport to create Alaska Coastal Airlines, now part of Alaska Airlines.

BELOW The basic design thinking that was to reach a massive maturity in the class Republic P-47 Thunderbolt fighter of World War II was evident in the first design from the Seversky Company, Republic's precursor. This was the SEV-3 amphibian, a three-seat floatplane with a very substantial fuselage and modern features such as all-metal construction, cantilever flying surfaces, and fully enclosed accommodation. The SEV-3 first flew in June 1933, and only small numbers were produced.

There is little that needs to be said about the celebrated Douglas DC-3, the transport that can rightly be claimed to have kick-started the "modern" airline industry. There was nothing radical about this magnificent transport, which was based on the blending of all the best in current thinking in just the right proportions. NC16013 was the fourth example of the DST-114 to be built for American Airlines, the launch customer for this truly classic airplane with a July 1935 order for an initial ten examples of this Douglas Sleeper Transport at a unit price of $79,500.

The DST was based on a cabin laid out for fourteen double seats each 36 in (0.91 m) wide and possessing the facility to be made up into seven lower berths, and seven upper berths each 30 in (0.76 m) wide with the facility to be folded into the ceiling when not needed. The DST therefore had provision for twenty-eight day passengers or fourteen night passengers, but the sleeper provision was little used as the DST quickly became the DC-3 with facilities for up to twenty-eight passengers.

The growing emancipation of women after World War I was strikingly apparent from the relatively large number of women taking part in these pioneer long-distance flights. Amelia Earhart and Jacqueline Cochran were two of the American heroines, while Amy Johnson was perhaps the most remarkable of all the many British women pilots. While working as a shorthand typist, Miss Johnson got the flying "bug" after seeing the 1928 film production *Wings*. She took out all her savings, and learned to fly. Although she showed no more than an average ability at first, Johnson gradually became a good, if cautious, pilot. Determined that nothing should stand in her way, she made a number of excellent long-distance flights, the first of which was to Australia, winning the hearts of a nation. Johnson's popularity grew after she met and married another extraordinary pilot, James Mollison. Together the two made a number of great flights across the Atlantic as well as on the empire routes. Ironically, Mollison was the very opposite of Johnson as a pilot, being noted for extremely risky enterprises. While they were married, the couple did a great deal to popularize flying.

The 1920s and 1930s will be forever remembered as a romantic age for aviation, with international celebrities, record-breaking feats, and popular competitions. Along the way, the aircraft industry switched from its World War I military focus to a civil and commercial enterprise capable of world-circling distances. Modern aviation had arrived.

FROM BIPLANE
TO MONOPLANE

FACING PAGE The nature of the U.S. Army Air Forces' daylight bombing effort over Europe in World War II is more than evident in this photograph of a Consolidated B-24 Liberator heavy bomber against a backdrop of bursting German "flak" shells. Despite the fact that it was a four-engined machine, the Liberator was built in larger numbers than any other American airplane of the period, and its versatility meant that it was also used for transport and for maritime patrol and antisubmarine roles, among others.

Warfare has been one of the great drivers of historical change, for better and for worse, for centuries. The bigger the war, the greater the transformations wrought in technology, politics, economics, and culture. Many of mankind's greatest achievements in the past sixty years (antibiotics, computers) and many things that define daily life (national highway systems) owe their origins to the great conflagration of World War II. The story of aviation in the 1920s, 1930s, and during the war is a story of steady improvement at first, only to be interrupted in 1939 by massive, unprecedented change.

Commercial transport in heavier-than-air craft began right after World War I's end, but neither the machines nor the routes were satisfactory. The aircraft were modified World War I bombers, which meant that the interior of the wooden-framed and fabric-covered fuselage was converted to accommodate a limited number of passengers, while the rest of the airframe was left unaltered. Passenger conditions were spartan, for the cabin was both cold and drafty. The routes served short-term political rather than long-term economic interests. Connecting mainly the capitals of the victorious Allied nations, starting with Paris and London, they at first shuttled the peacemakers, but were soon opened to the general public. But private passengers needed to be wealthy and interested as much in the novelty of air transport as in getting to their destinations quickly.

GERMANY REBUILDS

As the airlines that survived the first months of operation started to rationalize their routes in the early 1920s, converted wartime machines were being retired in favor of newer types designed for the air transport role. Germany made the fastest progress. By the terms of the Treaty of Versailles in 1919, Germany was not allowed to design, build, or possess any military aircraft, so German designers were limited to lighter civil types. This led to the world's first true airliner, the Junkers J 13, later redesignated F 13, that appeared in 1919 and entered service with Deutsche Luft-Hansa (shortened to Deutsche Lufthansa in 1934) soon after this.

The F 13 bore a clear family relationship to the low-wing cantilever metal fighters and ground-attack aircraft that Junkers had produced toward the end of the war, and was so different in overall concept that it met with considerable resistance at first. But the F 13 was years ahead of its time: Apart from its clumsy engine installation and the

ABOVE Even before the end of World War II, aircraft manufacturers began once more to prepare for production of revived and new models to meet what was expected to be a booming market for lightplanes. Aeronca's response was Model 7 Champion, which was the first U.S. lightplane to receive civil certification after World War II. The type shared the same general high-wing configuration and structural ideas as most other lightplanes of the period. The Champion first flew in mid-1944 but was not officially revealed until November 1945. Immediately after World War II, the U.S. lightplane market experienced a boom and the Champion proved very successful: Demand was so high, indeed, that Aeronca manufactured no fewer than seventy-two hundred examples of the Champion, generally known as the "Champ" and the "Airknocker," between 1946 and 1948. The lightplane boom started to collapse in 1948, and in 1950 the Champion series went out of production after Aeronca had produced some ten thousand examples. Production of the Model 7 Champion resumed in June 1954 when the Champion Aircraft Corporation acquired the manufacturing rights to the type. Remarkably, production of the Champion was again reinstated in 1977 after Champion had merged with Bellanca.

BELOW Appearing in 1919 as a radically modern low-wing cantilever monoplane of all-metal construction, the Junkers F 13 was an extraordinarily far-sighted transport design. The type gained considerable commercial success in terms of sales to the airlines of many countries or, as illustrated here, as executive transports for large companies.

standard fixed landing gear, the F 13 had lines that were sleek by the standards of the day, and it carried four passengers, and later the pilot, in the relative comfort of enclosed accommodation.

Hugo Junkers went on to produce other very successful airliners, most of them covered (or "skinned") with corrugated Dural metal. By comparison, British and French transports of the period were clumsy and old-fashioned in appearance, their biplane layouts requiring a mass of rigging and bracing wires. The only other manufacturer to match the conceptual advances of the Junkers airliners was Anthony Fokker. Fokker had realized in 1918 that Germany was about to lose the war and prepared for flight to his native Netherlands. He managed to cross over into the neutral Netherlands at the end of the war with a train carrying large numbers of dismantled aircraft, engines, tools, machines, and plans. Here Fokker was able to set up in business again, finding a ready market for his World War I designs in the Netherlands and Sweden, and setting about the development of new military and civil aircraft.

Fokker still had as his chief designer Reinhold Platz, one of the ablest designers to emerge from World War I. Platz saw no reason to abandon the constructional features that had contributed so much to the success of his three great fighters of World War I and set about producing civil airliners with the same clean lines, simplicity, and strength. The first such airliner to enter service was the F.II, which appeared in 1920. This was a typical Platz design: a welded steel-tube fuselage of rectangular section skinned with fabric except on the engine cowling, which was covered with metal sheeting; sturdy but simple landing gear; and a massive cantilever wing covered with plywood.

Like the F 13, the F.II carried a crew of one and up to four passengers, but was considerably slower than the Junkers machine despite being powered by the same type of 185-hp (134-kW) BMW engine. Yet the F.II proved the forerunner of a great line of Fokker airliners that would dominate European and American airline operations until the early 1930s. Next came the F.III, capable of carrying five passengers; the F.IV 10-passenger transport that failed to attract airline orders; the F.V that was built only in prototype form as an eight-seat airliner; and then the great F.VII, first of the most famous Fokker series of the period. The F.VII family (comprising the original single-engined F.VII, aerodynamically improved F.VIIa, three-engined F.VIIa-3m, and long-range F.VIIb-3m) represented possibly the most successful airliner and long-distance record breaker of its day, and contributed beyond measure to the acceptance of long-distance flying as a normal part of airline operations. The F.VII's basic concept was maintained without significant alteration

up to the F.XIX project, and of the later Fokker airliners built before the start of World War II, the F.XX had a retractable landing gear and the F.XXII was a clean four-engined airliner with, oddly enough, fixed landing gear.

Platz left the company in March 1931. Nonetheless, in the 1920s and 1930s there were very few European airlines that did not use some Fokker aircraft at some time. Because of its connection with the Germans in World War I, though, the American authorities felt that the name of Fokker would not be popular with the American people. When Fokker started to build aircraft for the U.S. Army and U.S. Navy, and to supply these services with technical assistance in the manufacture and maintenance of steel-tube airframes, it was decided to call the new company the Netherlands Aircraft Manufacturing Company, later changed to the Atlantic Aircraft Corporation. Between 1925 and 1929 it was briefly called the Fokker Aircraft Corporation; finally, however, the name was settled as the General Aviation Manufacturing Corporation.

The influence of Fokker airliners on other designers was nowhere more apparent than in the best American airliner of the 1920s, the Ford Tri-Motor. This appeared in June 1926 and combined what the designer, William Stout, thought to be the best features of both the Fokker and Junkers type of aircraft: The Tri-Motor resembled the F.VIIa-3m in appearance, but was built with the Junkers type of corrugated skinning.

The Ford Tri-Motor was in essence an all-metal American development of the concept embodied in the mixed metal and wood Fokker F.VII-3m transport created in the Netherlands. The type proved very successful in a number of forms, and that seen here is the Model 4-AT-15 *Floyd Bennett*, which took part in Admiral Byrd's expedition to the Antarctic and on November 28/29, 1929, became the first airplane to fly over the South Pole.

Junkers had not been standing idle all this time: The company had produced a series of typical aircraft, culminating in the G 31 of 1926. This transport was powered by three 450-hp (335.5-kW) radial engines, and could carry 16 passengers at 100 mph (160 km/h). Like the F.VII, it had a wide-track split landing gear, and in turn was the starting point for further Junkers aircraft, which culminated in the single-engined Ju 52 of 1930 and its three-engined derivative, the Ju 52/3m, which became the most famous and numerous German transport of the 1930s and World War II. Like the Tri-Motor, the Ju 52/3m remained in service for many years, and its ruggedness and wide-track landing gear proved invaluable for operations to and from indifferent airfields.

By the middle of the 1920s, most European nations had established their own national airlines. Companies such as Fokker sold transports to the airlines of most technically advanced nations, but the general tendency was for the national flag-carrying airline to operate machines built in the same country. Britain had Imperial Airways; Germany started Lufthansa in 1926; France acquired Air France in 1933. The United States was the only major ally who did not create a government-run airline, and its commercial aviation at first lagged behind the others.

The aircraft used by these companies in the twenties and early thirties were lumbering machines capable of carrying only 10 to 20 passengers. Imperial Airways operated a variety of types, the most important early machine being the de Havilland D.H. 66 Hercules. This was typical of the design practices used in British transport aircraft in the mid-1920s: It was a large machine with wide-track landing gear, a slab-sided fuselage mounted over the lower unit of the biplane wing cellule, and a tail unit carrying triple fin-and-rudder units mounted above the monoplane tailplane and elevator. The spacious 14-passenger cabin was located over the lower wing, and the three engines were mounted in the nose of the fuselage and above the main landing-gear wheels, one in each lower wing. With a cruising speed just under 100 mph (160 km/h), the Hercules was employed mainly on "intercontinental" flights, first to Egypt, then in 1927 to Basra in southern Iraq, and finally to Karachi in northwestern India during 1929.

So poor was the payload/range performance of these and comparable airliners into the early 1930s that passengers undertaking longer journeys were faced with the need to change aircraft several times, and on some routes to complete part of their travel by railway in sectors where airfields had yet to be completed. Imperial Airways saw its primary role as the flying of services on colonial routes, to the outlying parts of the empire, and the demands of European travel were virtually ignored. As the only airline flying passengers and mail over long-haul routes, Imperial Airways could afford to concern itself not with speed but with the delivery of a relatively small number of passengers steadily and in comfort. In many respects Imperial Airways was operating in splendid isolation at a time when virtually every other airline in the world was beginning to consider a switch to monoplane transports with their considerably higher performance.

Imperial Airways ordered two versions of one basic biplane type for its European and intercontinental routes: These four-engined Handley Page aircraft were the H.P.45 carrying 38 passengers on European routes and the H.P.42 carrying 24 passengers over long distances. In their way these were great aircraft, for in their years of service not one passenger suffered an injury. Both variants had the triple fins and rudders that were almost the trademark of British airliners in this period.

Air France, in the 1930s, similarly focused on services to the farther-flung parts of the French empire and was thus politically as much as commercially motivated. Unlike the British, however, the French had relatively few stepping stones to the Far East, and so placed great reliance on a series of old-fashioned Lioré-et-Olivier (LeO) and Breguet flying boats, the best means of air travel to the remoter parts of the world, as they required no airfields of the type that were and still are the single most expensive item in the infrastructure required to support airline operations. Italy used the excellent tri-motor monoplanes (most of them produced by Caproni and Savoia) as well as a miscellany of smaller types for its airlines' routes within Europe and across the Mediterranean to Libya and thence to Italian Somaliland.

In common with countries such as Germany, Italy made great efforts to produce transport aircraft that were highly cost-effective, as they could be used as airliners in times of peace and as troop transports or even primitive bombers in times of war. Another attraction of this operational philosophy for the Germans and Italians, moreover, was the fact that the relevant production lines could quickly be adapted to produce a dedicated warplane modeled on the basic transport. This had obvious advantages in the rapid production of military aircraft, not to mention reduced development and production costs. For Germany, prohibited by the Treaty of Versailles from developing or producing any military aircraft, these dual-role aircraft could be passed off as civil transports rather than bombers. Germany was the first European state to realize the economic advantages of an air route network that was both extensive and well-organized. By the early 1930s Lufthansa had the most comprehensive network in Europe, linking Germany's centers of industrial production with the most important financial and trading hubs on the rest of the continent. Lufthansa also employed more personnel per plane than did its counterparts, which would prove useful in the next world war.

AMERICA'S DECENTRALIZED INDUSTRY

On the other side of the Atlantic, the American airline industry was almost nonexistent during the 1920s. The main regions of population were linked by an extremely efficient network of roads and railways, and mass production was already making the car an everyday item. With the exception of those to Canada, Mexico, and the closer islands in the Caribbean, there were no external air routes for the Americans to launch, for the distances involved in intercontinental routes were far beyond the technology of the time.

Even so, there were several small private operators, and these operated limited services in heavily populated areas and places where transport by road and rail proved difficult, as well as services to the holiday centers of the Caribbean. Moreover, the Americans did develop a remarkable and forward-looking route network for the carriage of mail. Organized by the U.S. Post Office, the air mail service soon expanded beyond its 1918 New York–Washington, D.C., origins, right across the continent to San Francisco. The inauguration and subsequent development of the network was beset by a number of technical and operational problems, but by 1925 a serviceable navigation system was available across the center of the continent, dotted with searchlight-lit private airfields every 25 miles.

In that year, in one of the extraordinary reversals that characterize the early years of flight, the government took over all these private-enterprise airfields, while at the same time offering the mail flights themselves out to commercial tender. The change was ultimately to the benefit of U.S. commercial aviation since the government was in a position to improve airfields and navigational aids such as radio; it also ensured adequate maintenance for all the mailplanes. The mail had to be delivered in all weather to meet the terms of the contract, which paid by the ton of mail collected and delivered, and this had a great effect in spurring the development of fast all-weather aircraft capable of carrying a reasonable payload.

The production of such aircraft, even in the limited numbers required, was the foundation on which American civil aviation began to grow: Manufacturers produced the technical developments needed; the routes created the best courses between the main cities; nocturnal and all-weather flying improved piloting and navigational skills and also showed the need for blind-flying instruments; and the whole operation provided the American people with proof of the benefits of fast and reliable air services.

The Travel Air Manufacturing Company came into existence late in 1924 at Wichita, Kansas, with Walter Beech, Clyde Cessna, and Lloyd Stearman among its creators. The company concentrated the bulk of its efforts on the design and manufacture of light transport aircraft, but under the impetus of Beech created the Model R Mystery Ship as a dedicated racer for participation in the Open Class race of the National Air Races at Cleveland, Ohio. A wire-braced monoplane with fixed landing gear and an enclosed cockpit, the Mystery Ship was faster and generally more agile than the U.S. Army's biplane fighters of the period. The Mystery Ship was powered by a 425-hp (317-kW) Wright Whirlwind J-6 radial engine offering somewhat less power than the V-12 engines used in the U.S. Army aircraft. The race was flown over ten laps of a 5-mile (8-km) triangular course, and in the hands of Doug Davis, the Mystery Ship won at the average speed of 194.9 mph (313.6 km/h), thereby ending the racing domination of military biplanes. Five examples of the Mystery Ship were built, this illustration detailing the fourth machine, which was built for Captain Frank Monroe Hawks with sponsorship from the Texaco Oil Company. This airplane set more than two hundred city-to-city records, but was written off after a bad landing in September 1932 near Worcester, Massachusetts.

ABOVE The aerodynamic "cleanliness" of the Boeing Model 200 Monomail, with its all-metal construction, neatly cowled radial engine, low-set cantilever wing, and retractable main landing gear units, heralded a new era for American civil aviation, as the airplane could operate profitably without the subsidies paid by the federal government for air mail services.

BELOW Seen here in its definitive Model 247D form with a windshield sloped rearward rather than forward, Boeing's Model 247 was the world's first "modern" airliner of low-wing cantilever construction in light alloy with features such as retractable main landing gear units. The Model 247 was successful in performance terms, but was too small to satisfy the market that it helped to create and was therefore overshadowed by the later, larger, and generally more capable Douglas DC-2 and DC-3.

In 1927 Boeing, soon to emerge as a giant of the aeronautical world, made an extremely low tender for the Chicago to San Francisco route and managed to make a profit on the contract using aircraft of its own design. The type was the Model 40A, for its time a remarkably efficient and economical airplane, designed as a very clean machine whose low drag was enhanced by subtle design details and the reduction of structural weight. The age of World War I aircraft and their derivatives was finally ending.

In 1930 Boeing produced the Model 200 Monomail, the most advanced mailplane yet built. It was the first American plane to use a circular-section fuselage of metal monocoque construction, a neatly cowled radial engine offering good power and reliability with low fuel consumption, a cantilever low-set wing of metal stressed-skin construction, and retractable landing gear. The Monomail was a revelation, for its full use of stressed-skin metal was both practical and beautiful.

A year later Boeing used the same design formula at a larger, twin-engined size, to produce a bomber. This was the B-9, the immediate predecessor of the first truly modern airliner, the Model 247, in 1932. The Model 247 was a remarkable airplane, and perhaps deserved to enjoy greater commercial success than it did. Powered by a pair of 550-hp (410-kW) Pratt & Whitney Wasp radial engines inside clean wing-mounted nacelles, the all-metal Model 247 was based on stressed-skin and semi-monocoque construction with an oval fuselage, enclosed cockpit as well as accommodation, and main landing-gear units that retracted into the engine nacelles. To improve the safety factor at high altitude, rubber deicing "boots" were fitted to the wings and tail surfaces. The airplane's one limiting factor was that it was just slightly too small, with capacity for only 10 passengers at a time when the airlines were just beginning to look for something larger.

The Model 247 entered service with United Air Lines, formed in 1934 from Boeing Air Transport and two other companies, and did much to make this new giant airline a major force in American air transport. Other major American airlines already in existence were Pan-American Airlines, founded in 1927, and Transcontinental and Western Air, otherwise known as TWA (today the letters stand for Trans World Airlines), founded in 1930 through an amalgamation of four smaller airlines. Not to be outdone by United Air Lines' Model 247 fleet, TWA asked Douglas to produce a similar but superior machine.

The result was the Douglas DC-1 (Douglas Commercial 1), of which only one was built for a first flight in July 1933. The performance of this 12-passenger machine was so encouraging that Douglas immediately decided that the basic design could be easily "stretched" for 14-seat accommodation. This DC-2 went straight into production for a first

flight in May 1934. The DC-2 could carry 14 passengers at almost 170 mph (274 km/h) by comparison with the Model 247's 10 passengers at 155 mph (250 km/h), and also had greater range. The success of the DC-2 was immediate. By the middle of 1934 Douglas had orders for 75 of his new transport, including orders from KLM, previously a staunch purchaser of Fokker aircraft. It was one of these DC-2 machines that KLM entered in the great MacRobertson race from England to Australia in 1934, winning handily.

From the DC-1 in 1933 to today's DC-10 and beyond, Douglas (later McDonnell Douglas) has been a mainstay of the industry. If the monocoque, metal-skinned, monoplane DC-1 was revolutionary, however, everything after has been evolutionary. More powerful engines, longer cabins, fancier navigational equipment, and other features have increased speeds, altitudes, and distances dramatically. But the major design questions were solved by 1933. The commercial smash hit DC-3 made its maiden flight in December 1935 and won immediate approval from the airlines. Essentially a scaled-up DC-2, the DC-3 was offered in its production form with two 1,000-hp (746-kW) Wright Cyclone or 1,200-hp (895-kW) Pratt & Whitney Twin Wasp radial engines in place of the DC-2's 710-hp (529.5-kW) Wright Cyclone units. The DC-3 carried 21 passengers at about the same speed as the DC-2 but over the longer stage length of 500 miles (805 km).

The DC-3 rapidly met airlines' increasing number of orders, and by 1938 it dominated American airline operations. By the time production ceased in 1946, about 13,000 DC-3 civil airliners and military C-47 Skytrain/R4D military transports had been built, making this the most prolific transport plane ever put into production.

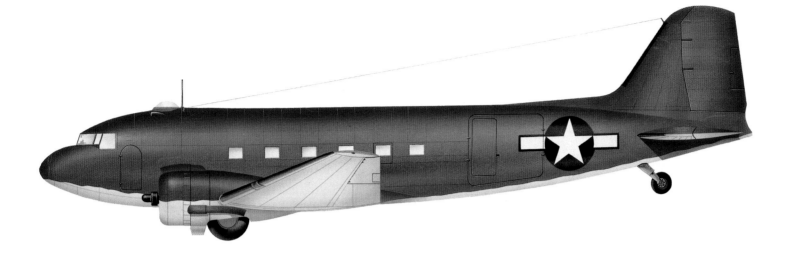

ABOVE AND BELOW The DC-3 came into its own in World War II as the Allied powers' most important transport airplane, with great prominence as the C-47 Skytrain series that was known to the British as the Dakota. There were a host of other designations for the series, the best known being the R4D bought for the U.S. Navy and the Lisunov Li-2, which was the version made under license in the U.S.S.R.

ABOVE The growth of the aircraft manufacturing industry, especially in World War II, paved the way for large numbers of women to break into what had previously been a male-dominated field. Seen at a Lockheed plant, these women are working on the riveted light alloy skinning of an airplane approaching completion.

The DC-3 did much to popularize air travel in the United States as part of everyday life, with comfort not much less than that of the train but speed very considerably higher.

While Douglas was securing the upper end of the market, however, Lockheed was concentrating on the middle level with transports offering lower capacity but higher performance. From the mid-1920s onward, Lockheed had concentrated its efforts on small, very fast aircraft of considerable range for mailplane and other long-distance operations: The classic example was the cantilever high-wing Vega with its all-wood construction, monocoque fuselage, and radial engine, produced in four-passenger Model 1, 2, and 5 variants. With the growth of civil air transport in the late 1920s, Lockheed produced another fascinating design, the Model 9 Orion. This was a very advanced machine with sleek lines, mixed metal and wood construction, a low-set cantilever monoplane wing, a nicely cowled radial piston engine, and retractable landing gear.

Lockheed then decided to risk all on an advanced but small twin-engined airliner. The new machine emerged in February 1934 as the Model 10 Electra, a trim low-wing monoplane of all-metal construction that carried eight passengers at high speed thanks to two 450-hp (335.5-kW) Pratt & Whitney Wasp Junior radial engines. Lockheed pressed on, with a slightly smaller and faster Model 12 Electra Junior, and then the definitive light transport of the period, the Model 14 Super Electra. Appearing in 1937, the Super Electra was aerodynamically the most advanced civil airplane to appear before World War II. It was also the first airliner to use two-speed superchargers for its engines, and the first civil airplane with constant-speed propellers, which helped save fuel by constantly adjusting the pitch of the propeller blades to the air speed and power output of the engine: This feature was later to become standard on all but the smallest and lightest piston-engined aircraft.

With the Douglas and Lockheed airliners, the United States took a commanding lead in the field of civil aviation. A healthy rivalry in engine manufacture matched the rivalry in aircraft design. Some of the Wright company's ablest engine designers resigned in 1925 and secured financial backing to create the rival company of Pratt & Whitney. The days of daredevil pilots were over; the engineers and businessmen had taken over.

American advances were so comprehensive in concept and scale that U.S. transports had virtually cornered the market for civil transports in the mid- and late 1930s. This is not to deny, however, that the Europeans could and did indeed develop and produce some good aircraft. Junkers, for example, realized that with the Ju 52/3m the day of corrugated metal skinning and fixed landing gear was over, and therefore switched to smooth skinning and retractable main landing-gear units. The Ju 60, of 1933, designed to compete with the Model 9 Orion, and the Ju 86, a larger transport designed to compete with the DC-2, enjoyed mixed fortunes. The Junkers design was used fairly extensively by Lufthansa, but the Heinkel He 111 was apparently more suitable for carrying bombs than passengers, and so became one of the Luftwaffe's principal medium bombers throughout World War II. The Ju 86 was also used as a bomber, and with wingtip extensions as a high-altitude reconnaissance airplane.

In the United Kingdom designers also tried to match the Americans, and in the mid-1930s developed some interesting transport aircraft. In the same class as the Lockheed light airliners was the Bristol Type 142, designed in 1933 and rolled out in 1935. With a top speed above 300 mph (483 km/h), the Type 142 was faster than any fighter in current first-line service with the Royal Air Force, which eventually led to Bristol's Type 143 Blenheim light bomber.

Part of the British problem lay in Imperial Airways, the largest customer for British transport aircraft. Supported by the government and lacking any real competition, Imperial Airways demanded and received small numbers of several types of airliners sufficient for the tasks required of them but expensive to build. So their transport aircraft were conservative in design and possessed only marginal export potential. There were a few successful British airliners in this period, but these resulted wholly from private enterprise. The three most important of these successful transports were the Airspeed AS.6 Envoy, a pretty little twin-engined monoplane with retractable main landing gear and accommodation for six or eight passengers, and two de Havilland twin-engined biplanes, the D.H.84 Dragon and D.H.89 Dragon Rapide with fixed landing gear and accommodation for six and eight passengers respectively. All three of these transports were built in quite large numbers for British and foreign operators.

French aviation had started to decline in the 1920s. There were too many small companies, few of them with adequate capital to finance major new projects and set up the necessary production tooling and jigs. A succession of short-lived French governments had seen the problem but lacked the time in office to devise and effect any solution, so by 1936 France, the world leader in 1918, was in the humiliating position of trailing behind the United States, United Kingdom, Germany, and even Italy. In 1936, partly out of fear of German rearmament and territorial ambition, the French government nationalized the country's aviation industry and launched a major reorganization into large regional

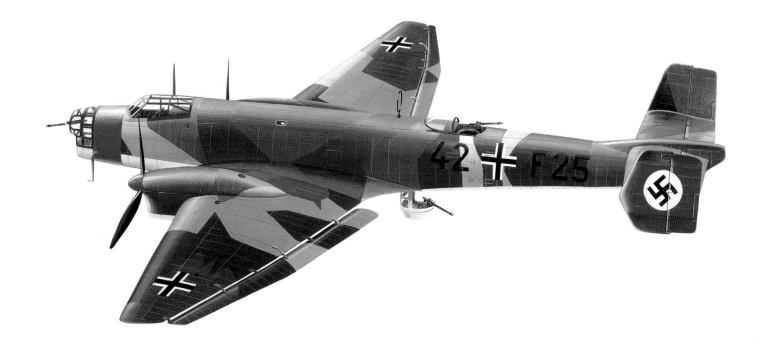

ABOVE One of the new generation of Junkers aircraft of the 1930s with smooth rather than corrugated skinning, the Ju 86 was planned as a bomber but then additionally developed as an airliner. The type could be powered by air-cooled radial engines or liquid-cooled Diesel engines, and was later developed with long-span wings for the very high-altitude reconnaissance role. A notable feature of the wing was the Junkers type of "double-wing" aileron and flap below and behind the wing's trailing edge.

BELOW Seen here in the form of an Mk I airplane of the initial production type, the Bristol Blenheim light bomber was some 40 mph (65 km/h) faster than the current lineup of British fighters, but was more useful for proving the concept of the high-speed monoplane bomber than for combat operations, in which it was soon found to be too lightly built and lacking in adequate defensive as well as offensive capability.

ABOVE In its civil transport aircraft of much of the 1930s de Havilland plowed a singular course, offering supremely elegant biplane light airliners with fixed landing gear and the company's own air-cooled engines. This is a Rapide, undoubtedly one of the most beautiful aircraft ever to have flown.

FACING PAGE The much-increased production of aircraft in World War II opened the way for more extensive use of definitive mass-production techniques, including the extensive use of components and assemblies built by subcontractors and delivered to primary production centers only when needed. Looking like surreal items of sculpture, these are dorsal fins awaiting the moment for addition to Boeing B-29 Superfortress heavy bombers.

groupings. The effect was immediate. An increasing number of excellent military and civilian aircraft started to flow off the drawing boards and then out of the experimental shops. By the late 1930s Air France was extending its routes all over the world with a number of first-class aircraft, mostly of Dewoitine, Farman, and Potez design. It is worth noting, however, that the very excellence of these new designs and prototypes was something of a problem, for the French authorities could not decide which types to produce and which to cancel, leading to the production of several types in small numbers rather than wholehearted concentration on a single type in each class with all the advantages that would have accrued from larger production runs.

Meanwhile, in the United States manufacturers were forging ahead to extend their world lead. With a new generation of very high-powered engines not yet available, designers saw that the next step in performance would require four-engined powerplants. These, it was hoped, would allow aircraft to carry more passengers at higher speeds over longer stages. Boeing had a head start in this process as by 1935 it had already designed two four-engined bombers, the Model 294 and the Model 299, later built in large numbers as the B-17 Flying Fortress.

ABOVE THE CLOUDS

Up to the mid-1930s, civil aircraft had operated at relatively low altitudes, in the region of 10,000 ft (3,050 m) or lower. The advantages of high-altitude operation, however, were tempting: Supercharged engines could allow higher cruising speed with greater fuel efficiency. The problem, of course, was passenger comfort: At the required altitude of 20,000 ft (6,095 m) or more, the air is thin and cold. The new generation of civil transports would therefore have to be pressurized with warm air. Provision of air at the right temperature and at the correct pressure was relatively straightforward, for the air could be tapped from the supercharger and warmed by the heat emitted from the engines. The main problem lay with the construction of the fuselage itself, which would have to be made airtight in order to maintain a positive pressure differential between the cabin and the outside air.

In theory it is comparatively straightforward to make a monocoque fuselage airtight. In theory this is easy. In practice, it was impossible until the Lockheed XC-35 (a much-modified Model 10 Electra) flew in 1937.

Boeing had success with its Model 307, which used the same wing and tail unit as the Model 209 bomber but with a new circular-section fuselage. Entering service in a developed form as the Model 307B Stratoliner in 1940, this transport could carry 33 passengers over long distances in the comfort of a fully pressurized cabin. Five such machines were delivered to TWA before the United States entered World War II, and these were subsequently used by the U.S. Army Air Force as VIP transports.

On the other side of the Atlantic, Germany produced two interesting unpressurized aircraft designed to cruise at about 8,200 ft (2,500 m). These were the Focke-Wulf Fw 200 Condor and Junkers Ju 90. The Ju 90 saw little commercial use before World War II but the Condor, which first flew in 1937, made an excellent flight from Berlin to New York in 1938 and paved the way for nonstop flights between major cities on opposite sides of the Atlantic. The war intervened before the Condor had been able to make its mark as a civil transport, and it soon evolved into a maritime patrol plane and reconnaissance bomber.

Two British four-engined airliners were the de Havilland D.H.91 Albatross of 1937 and the Armstrong Whitworth A.W.27 Ensign of 1938. The Albatross was a very beautiful airplane with excellent performance and was built using the type of wooden construction pioneered by the D.H.88 Comet and eventually brought to fruition by the superb Mosquito multirole aircraft of World War II. The Albatross could carry some 35 passengers over moderately long routes, but airlines were deterred from large-scale orders by the type's wooden construction. The Ensign was a high-wing type of more workaday conception and could carry 40 passengers, but the outbreak of war ended any civilian chances it may have had.

The mystery aeronautical powers of the period were Japan and the U.S.S.R. Japan's aviation industry and airlines grew steadily during the late 1920s and 1930s as the country extended its empire on the Asian mainland. Starting virtually from scratch after World War I, Japan was at first happy to purchase the latest Western types for examination and licensed production. Impressed by some of these aircraft, the Japanese also built extensively developed versions. The Japanese concentrated on military aircraft but their civil aircraft were very well made and in general somewhat lighter than the Western types from which they derived. By the start of World War II, their bombers and fighters would be far superior to America's, which nearly proved disastrous at Midway.

Soviet aviation remained essentially unknown. Comparatively few Soviet aircraft were seen in the West before the Spanish Civil War, which broke out in 1936, but these appeared to be poorly made. The Western authorities failed to notice that many of these aircraft, even if poorly made and finished, were of advanced design and incorporated several novel ideas. With little need for international air transport and only marginally more for internal air services, Soviet civil aviation had not flourished. There had been a considerable expansion in the numbers and activities of flying clubs, so a number of sporting types and trainers had been produced, but for the moment the Soviet authorities were content to let air transport develop slowly. Meanwhile, a major part of the country's aeronautical resources were concentrated on record-breaking and experimental aircraft, both of which would help keep aeronautical science up to date.

Though built largely of wood, the de Havilland D.H.88 Comet was of advanced low-wing cantilever concept with retractable main landing gear units, but other features, such as the two-position propellers actuated by air pressure, represented interim technology. The type was created in great haste as a dedicated long-distance racing airplane, and in this capacity edged out an airline standard Douglas DC-2 in the 1934 MacRobertson air race from England to Australia.

In the 1920s and 1930s many people expected that long-distance airliners of the future would be water- rather than land-based types to avoid the need for expensive air-fields, to eliminate landing gear in favor of a sturdy pair of floats or a boat-shaped hull, to boost load-carrying capacity for the payload or fuel within the large hull/fuselage, and to offer floatability in the event of the machine being forced down by engine failure over water. These mistaken assumptions led to a flurry of great seaplanes.

The first of the classic airliner flying boats was the Short Calcutta, built in 1928 to the specifications of Imperial Airways for its routes to Africa and India, on which the three-engined Calcutta carried 15 passengers at a cruising speed of 90 mph (145 km/h). In 1931 there appeared the Short Kent, powered by four radials, which could carry 16 passengers. The prewar British flying boats reached their peak with the Short "Empire" class of four-engined monoplane flying boats. So impressive did the design look that Imperial Airways ordered no fewer than 28 such flying boats "off the drawing board" for use on all the routes of the imperial air mail scheme. From 1937 onward, the "Empire" class flying boats were a regular and well-loved sight on all of Imperial Airways' more important routes.

Germany also developed an early interest in flying boats, and the great successes of a number of Dornier Wal boats did much to impress on the world that the German aviation industry had not faded away in the 1920s. But Dornier had greater things in mind, and in 1929 unveiled the monstrous Dornier Do X, a huge flying boat spanning 157 ft 6 in (48.0 m) and powered by no less than 12 engines. Driving six tractor and six pusher propellers, these engines were mounted in pairs in nacelles above the wing. The Do X was too big and heavy for its engines, and was not a success.

Like the British, the Germans were interested in swift mail delivery, and they hit on an ingenious scheme: Fast liners would cross the ocean toward the mail's destination, and when within range would catapult off a floatplane loaded with the mail. The primary type selected for this exercise was the Blohm und Voss Ha 139, an attractive four-engined twin-float machine. The Ha 139 went into operation during 1938, but was abandoned a year later when the Dornier Do 26 entered service. The Do 26 was one of the most beautiful flying boats ever built. The hull was wonderfully streamlined and the four engines (two tractor and two pusher units) were installed in the angle of the gulled wings. To reduce airborne drag and thereby improve speed and range, the stabilizing floats were designed to retract into the undersurfaces of the wings once the Do 26 had taken to the air.

Prevented by the United Kingdom from operating a transatlantic flying boat service, American interests concentrated on routes in the Caribbean, South America, and the Far East, where American flying boats had been operating with increasing success since the middle 1920s. Three classic American flying boats appeared in the 1930s and operated services that were to become legends in their own time: the Sikorsky S-42 and Martin Model 130 of 1934, and the Boeing Model 314 of 1938. These three established a reputation for luxury travel, especially across the Pacific, rivaled only by the British "Empire" class flying boats. Various routes crossed the Pacific to Australia, New Zealand, the Philippines, and China, via the islands of the Pacific.

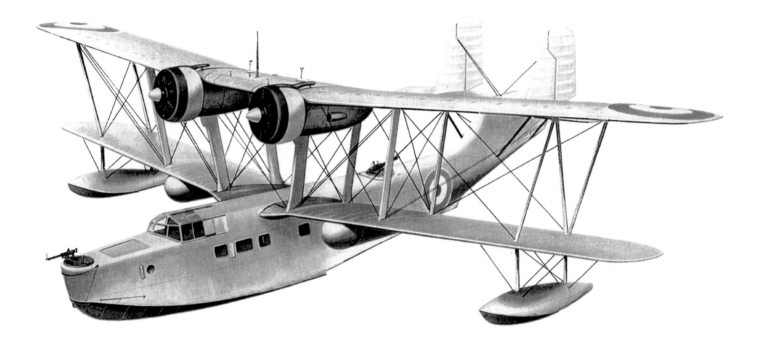

The Supermarine Stranraer was the last biplane flying boat to serve with the forces of the United Kingdom and its empire, equipping two British and a few Canadian squadrons until the middle of World War II. The type was flown in the medium-range maritime patrol task and marked the culmination of a series of civil and military flying boats that Supermarine developed right through the 1920s and 1930s.

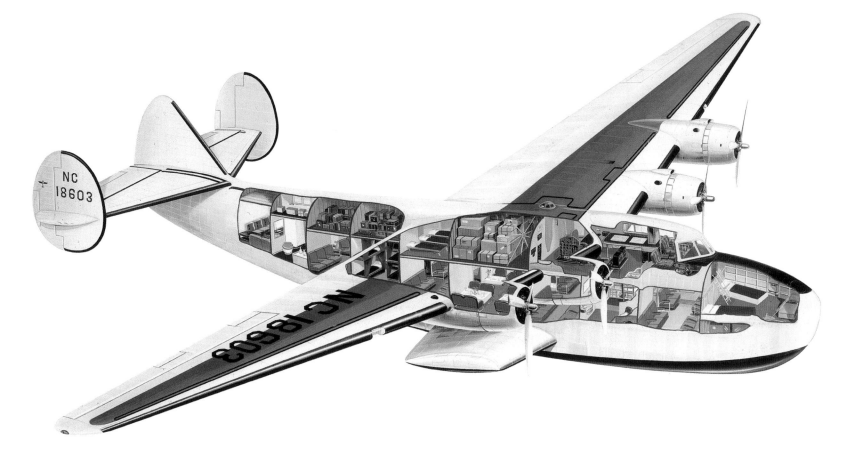

The Boeing Model 314 was perhaps the finest civil flying boat ever placed in production. Only small numbers of the type were produced as the days of the civil flying boat were already numbered, but in its time the Model 314 offered excellent performance and very high levels of comfort for small numbers of passengers.

The outbreak of World War II halted European expansion just at the time that American airlines were accelerating their aircraft development. The 1930s had seen a rapid expansion of commercial flying. In 1929, for example, the world's airlines flew 96.3 million passenger miles, of which European and North American airlines contributed 48.9 million and 44.2 million respectively. By 1934 the figures had grown to a grand total of 421.9 million passenger miles, represented by 151.7 million in Europe and 231.6 million in North America. By 1939 the figures had again increased enormously: Total passenger miles flown were 1,395.5 million, with the Europeans responsible for 434.5 million and the North Americans for 771.3 million. Within five years, therefore, the North Americans had boosted their passenger flying by a factor of 3.33 and the Europeans by 2.8. Yet by 1941 European passenger miles had fallen to 292,600, while the North Americans had again increased their total, to 1,602.7 million.

Nevertheless long-distance travel was arduous. The first scheduled crossing of the Pacific was an air mail flight by a Model 130 of Pan American Airways on November 22, 1935. The flying boat departed from San Francisco and arrived at Manila in the Philippines by way of staging points in the Hawaiian Islands, Midway Island, Wake Island, and Guam. The first commercial survey flight across the North Atlantic was not made until July 1937, when both Pan American and Imperial Airways launched flights, one from west to east and the other from east to west. Scheduled passenger operations did not begin until 1939, when Pan American started a service from New York to Southampton via Bermuda and Lisbon with Model 314 flying boats. Within the United States the first passenger transcontinental flight, using a number of staging points, had taken place on June 15, 1929. This Universal Air Lines System crossing had taken some 60 hours from New York to Los Angeles and had involved several stages by rail. Even by the end of the 1930s airline flights across America were little faster than train trips.

FACING PAGE Now known universally as the "Kaydet" from its nickname in World War II, the X70 design by the Stearman Aircraft Division of the Boeing Aircraft Company was a truly classic primary trainer. Viceless in its handling and rugged in construction, the type was produced in a multitude of variants, of which the PT-13 and PT-17 were numerically the most important. Many thousands of these aircraft survived World War II to enter civil life as sporting and agricultural aircraft.

THE GREAT CATACLYSM

Aviation's technical progress had been led by racing aircraft (in speed) and by civil aircraft (in payload/range and reliability). Air forces had suffered through lean times in the late 1920s and early 1930s. The Royal Air Force received small numbers of specialized fighters and bombers, but the majority of service aircraft were general-purpose machines. While the RAF's success in imperial policing operations did secure the service's continued existence as an independent arm of the British military forces, it also had unfortunate consequences. The type of aircraft needed for such work required great reliability, good range, and the ability to carry a modest but varied bomb load and other armament: In other words, the aircraft were general-purpose types. The result was a number of good general-purpose aircraft, from the F.2B and D.H.9 machines left over from World War I to the Westland Wapiti and Hawker Audax machines of the early 1930s.

These aircraft were ideally suited to policing the British empire, where there was little or no serious opposition, but were wholly inadequate for the type of aerial combat that would be encountered over a European battlefield, where even good general-purpose machines could not compare with machines optimized for a single role.

A similar policy held sway in France and Italy, which respectively had large and small parts of the world to police, and in combination with the consequences of the "10-year rule" this meant that European military aircraft gradually began to lag behind civilian machines. It has often been noted that the air forces of the United Kingdom, France, Italy, and also the United States in the early 1930s were well-prepared to fight the air battles of World War I again. Fighters and bombers had limited offensive and defensive armament, and in layout they were still biplanes with fixed landing gear.

Oddly enough, the gradually increasing technical inferiority of military aircraft relative to their civilian counterparts was balanced by major advances in the theory of air warfare. Three officers—the British Hugh Trenchard and the Americans "Billy" Mitchell and William Moffett—advocated the development of the bomber as the decisive factor in any future war. They believed that bombers, flying in mass formation, would fight their way to targets deep in enemy territory. Strategic bomber theory held that such forces would destroy both the ability and the will of the enemy to wage war: smashing war industries, transportation systems, and power production and demoralizing civilians with devastating raids on residential areas.

Marking one of the high points of biplane fighter development in Europe at the time of its entry into service during May 1931, the Hawker Fury Mk I interceptor was of all-metal construction but still covered largely with fabric and armed with the standard pair of rifle-caliber machine guns. The Fury Mk I was powered by a liquid-cooled V-type engine, the Rolls-Royce Kestrel IIS, cooled by a radiator in a neat installation between the legs of the main landing-gear unit.

Billy Mitchell was forceful and persistent, and was finally court-martialed and driven to resign his commission in the U.S. Army for his constant attacks on established Army and Navy dogma. He is best remembered today as the first man to demonstrate the obsolescence of the battleship as the arbiter of sea power. In 1921, to the amazement of most of the U.S. Navy, aircraft under his command succeeded in sinking the surrendered German battleship *Ostfriesland,* widely believed to be unsinkable. While Mitchell was in disgrace, Admiral Moffett worked with greater discretion to encourage the gradual emergence of the U.S. Navy as a major offensive air arm. By the late 1920s the American military establishment was well on the way to accepting the concept of strategic air power and had subscribed fully to it by the mid-1930s. The first real American heavy bombers, the Boeing B-9 and Martin B-10, were advanced monoplanes of metal construction with performance equal or superior to that of contemporary biplane fighters.

"HAP" ARNOLD

H. H. "HAP" ARNOLD (1886–1950) Henry Harley "Hap" Arnold was born on June 25, 1886, in Gladwyne, Pennsylvania. He graduated from the U.S. Military Academy at West Point in 1907 and was commissioned into the infantry. Arnold served for two years in the Philippines and two more at Governors Island, New York, before transferring in April 1911 to the aeronautical division of the Signal Corps. In June 1911 Arnold received his pilot's certificate after taking instruction from Orville Wright in Dayton, Ohio, for a period of almost one year. He served as an instructor at the U.S. Army's first aviation school at College Park, Maryland. In September 1911 Arnold flew the first U.S. air mail. In 1912 he was posted onto the staff of the aviation school at San Diego, California, and during February 1917 he was dispatched to establish and lead an air service detachment in the Panama Canal Zone.

In May 1917, the month after the United States' entry into World War I, Arnold was recalled to Washington, D.C. where as a staff officer he was charged with supervising the U.S. Army's aviation training schools throughout the war. After the Armistice, Arnold saw service at a number of posts in the states of the United States' western seaboard, and in 1934 he led a flight of 10 Martin B-10 bombers from Bolling Field, D.C., to Fairbanks, Alaska, and back. In December 1935 Arnold became the assistant com-

"Hap" Arnold, seen here at the controls of a Burgess biplane, was one of the pioneers of American aviation, gaining the twenty-ninth pilot's license issued in the United States.

mander of the U.S. Army Air Corps, and in September 1938 he became the USAAC's commanding officer. As evident by his championing of Colonel "Billy" Mitchell, Arnold had long been an advocate of air power as a decisive factor in modern war and was now in the right position to push forward the task of making the USAAC as capable a force as possible in terms of equipment and combat readiness. Money was still in relatively short supply, but Arnold was extremely adroit at the task of wringing every last vestige of "give" out of his resources. An early feature of Arnold's leadership of the USAAC was the creation of an ever-larger pilot pool by sending future pilots to civil flying schools. Arnold also used every means at his disposal to push aircraft manufacturers to prepare for production of their latest aircraft types on a much larger scale.

When the United States entered World War II in December 1941, thanks to Arnold, the American aircraft-manufacturing industry was capable of producing six times as many aircraft as it had been able to manage in 1939, and there were pilots ready for these new aircraft. In March 1942 the Department of War underwent a major reorganization, and Arnold was designated as the commanding general of the Army Air Forces, now given the same status within the War Department's structure as the other two major commands (Army Ground Forces and the Army Services Forces).

In World War II Arnold served on the U.S. Joint Chiefs of Staff and also on the Combined Chiefs of Staff within the equivalent Allied structure. In these parallel tasks Arnold helped to create and conduct the overall strategy for the prosecution of the war and was also a key player in the establishment of the strategies and organization that opened the way for the Allied powers to gain and keep overall superiority in all the theaters in which they were engaged. Arnold insisted that there should emerge a U.S. air force wholly independent of the U.S. Army. A first step in this direction was his establishment in April 1944 of the 20th Army Air Force as a strategic bombing force with a limited global capability through its equipment of Boeing B-29 Superfortress long-range heavy bombers. Arnold was directly responsible for control of the 20th AAF as the agent of the Joint Chiefs of Staff, with General Curtis E. LeMay as the force's field commander during most of its existence in World War II.

During December 1944 Arnold was one of four senior army officers promoted to the five-star rank of general of the army. Arnold turned over command of the USAAF to General Carl Spaatz in March 1946 and, though he retired in June 1946 to a farm near Sonoma, California, during May 1949 he was named General of the Air Force, the first such commission ever made. Arnold died in 1950, rightly remembered as a founding father of the American concept of independent air power.

In the 1920s a comparatively high level of public and political antipathy to things military combined with low levels of public finance and a measure of military conservatism to check the development of military aviation. One result was that the fighters that remained in service into the mid-1930s were little changed at the conceptual level from those at the end of World War I. The armament was still two machine guns, the accommodation an open cockpit, and the layout that of the biplane with fixed landing gear, with improvements limited to a metal rather than wooden structure and a higher-powered engine for modestly improved performance. Typical of this breed was the type seen here, the Bristol Bulldog Mk IIA as flown by the Royal Air Force.

France also adopted the concept of heavy bombing and produced a number of such aircraft in the late 1920s. Almost all were notable for a singular lack of streamlining and a slab-sided appearance of great ungainliness. The twin-engined Amiot 143 and Bloch MB.200 bombers, together with the four-engined Farman F.221 bomber, were the most notable examples. Yet even these French machines seem modern by comparison with a British contemporary, the Handley Page Heyford, a large biplane with the fuselage attached to the underside of the upper wing.

Fighters, on the other hand, remained little better than their World War I predecessors. The first such machines to enter service with the RAF after World War I were the Armstrong Whitworth Siskin and the Gloster Grebe, both of which made their service debuts during 1924. Several companies produced experimental monoplane fighters during the decade, but the RAF adhered rigidly to biplanes, usually with a radial engine, for a period of some 15 years after World War I. Later types such as the Bristol Bulldog, Gloster Gauntlet, and Gloster Gladiator continued this tradition, and the only notable exception was the Hawker Fury. Powered by a Rolls-Royce Kestrel V-12 engine, this was the first British fighter to exceed 200 mph (320 km/h) in level flight.

In America, competition between the Navy and Air Force proved a useful spur to the development of superior combat aircraft. By 1927, the U.S. Navy had received its first two large aircraft carriers, the USS *Saratoga* and USS *Lexington,* sister ships that could each accommodate and operate a large number of high-performance aircraft. Moffett's steady pressure for a naval air arm capable of confronting land-based air power had produced dramatic results.

The most important carrier-borne fighters of the U.S. Navy were the Boeing F2B and Curtiss F6C, each possessing a maximum speed of 155 mph (250 km/h), later supplanted by the Boeing F4B, which was capable of 190 mph (305 km/h). The U.S. Army Air Corps' fighters of the period were the Boeing PW-9 and Curtiss P-6, capable of 155 and 108 mph (250 and 318 km/h) respectively, later joined by the Boeing P-12 (the landplane counterpart of the F4B) and in 1933 by the Boeing P-26 "Peashooter," the first American monoplane fighter, which was capable of 235 mph (380 km/h). Of these only the P-26 represented a major advance on its predecessors, but they were all good aircraft notable for their sturdy construction and high agility.

The development of aircraft had not yet become prohibitively expensive, so it was normal for all but the very poorest countries to try their hand at the design and production of fighters and other small aircraft. In 1932 Poland produced the PZL P.7 fighter using an inverted gull-wing monoplane layout. Later Polish planes would perform well in the hands of Polish and Greek pilots against the Luftwaffe in 1939 and 1941.

Czechoslovakia and Yugoslavia also produced indigenous fighters in this period, and Italy, despite an aviation decline in the late 1920s, built world-class aircraft starting with the Fiat CR.32 in 1933. The CR.32 was very strong and maneuverable, and for its time was fast, with a top speed of 230 mph (370 km/h).

By 1933 the design philosophies of World War I had been completely revised. There were still believers in the biplane formula, including the Italians, but this design concept's practical limits had been reached by fighters such as the Gloster Gauntlet and Gladiator in the United Kingdom, Fiat CR.42 in Italy, and Polikarpov I-15 and I-153 in the U.S.S.R. Even before this, however, the nature and shape of the biplane's inevitable successor had been proven effective, and monoplanes with retractable landing gear were the norm.

ABOVE One of the classic fighters operated by the U.S. Navy for the carrierborne role in the first part of the 1930s was the Boeing F4B, which was the naval version of the P-12 landplane fighter. The first production version was the F4B-2, seen here in the form of an airplane operated by the VF-5B squadron that flew from the aircraft carrier USS *Lexington*.

BELOW The F4B-4 was the naval counterpart of the P-12E landplane fighter, which introduced a new tail unit and a fuselage of semi-monocoque aluminum alloy construction. This airplane was flown by the U.S. Navy's VF-2 squadron, one of the units embarked on the aircraft carrier USS *Lexington*. The blue band around the fuselage indicated that this was the airplane of the leader of the squadron's third three-plane element.

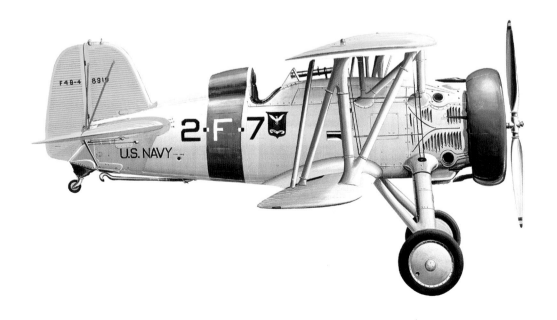

ABOVE The PW-9 was the first fighter designed by Boeing for the U.S. Army, the company's previous fighter experience having been limited to manufacture of the MB-3A designed by the Thomas-Morse company. First appearing in September 1924, the PW-9 was of mixed construction, with a steel-tube fuselage and wooden wings all under a covering of fabric, and was powered by one of aviation history's classic engines, the Curtiss D-12, known to the military as the V-1150. The airplane illustrated is a PW-9D of the last production variant with a horn-balanced rudder of the type later retrofitted to surviving examples of earlier variants.

BELOW The first monoplane fighter to enter service with the U.S. Army, late in 1933, was the Boeing P-26, generally known as the "Peashooter." This fascinating type must be seen as only an interim step in the U.S. Army's progress toward true monoplane fighters, for its thin wing required the use of flying and landing wires to brace it, and other obsolescent features were the fixed main landing-gear units and the pilot's open cockpit. The P-26A illustrated here bears the celebrated black/white-trimmed olive drab colors of the 34th Attack Squadron of the 17th Attack Group.

When Adolf Hitler came to power in Germany in January 1933, he was able to order an immediate expansion and acceleration of German rearmament, and in 1935 he renounced the military terms of the Treaty of Versailles and revealed a full-sized Luftwaffe. At first the German air force was not equipped with particularly advanced aircraft, the standard fighter and bomber being the Heinkel He 51 biplane and Junkers Ju 52/3m monoplane, respectively. But great leaps forward were soon in coming.

After lengthy evaluation, the Germans selected the Messerschmitt Bf 109 as the Luftwaffe's primary fighter, the Dornier Do 17 and Heinkel He 111 as its standard medium bombers, and the Junkers Ju 87 Stuka (abbreviated from *Sturzkampfflugzeug,* or dive bomber) as its basic tactical support airplane. The last of the Luftwaffe's mainstay aircraft to appear before World War II was the Junkers Ju 88 medium bomber of 1939. A classic airplane of great if not unrivaled operational versatility, the Ju 88 was originally intended as a fast medium bomber with limited dive-bombing capability, but served with great distinction in a variety of roles throughout World War II.

The Germans tested their concept of tactical air power in the Spanish Civil War, which started in 1936. German aircraft were involved from the beginning, when Ju 52/3m transports were used to ferry General Francisco Franco's Nationalist troops from Spanish Morocco into southern Spain. As a bomber, however, the Ju 52/3m proved a failure, as did the He 51 as a fighter when opposed by the formidable Soviet I-15 and I-16 fighters.

German engineers responded quickly, however, and as a result the Luftwaffe was a confident and experienced air force by the start of World War II in 1939. With the 1936 death of Generalleutnant Walther Wever, the Luftwaffe's first chief of staff and Germany's primary advocate of strategic bombing, Germany devoted virtually its full attention to the development of tactical air power to be used as "flying artillery" in support of the German army's new fast-moving, hard-hitting armored divisions.

The cockpit of the Junkers Ju 87B-2. "Stuka" reveals the state of the art so far as instrumentation and controls were concerned in the mid-1930s.

ABOVE The advent of the "modern" airplane, of all-metal construction with a cantilever wing, retractable main landing-gear units, and enclosed accommodation, as well as other advanced features, sparked a phenomenal spurt of design and production that created new civil and military aircraft. One of the latter, and a type that was of huge importance to the German air effort in World War II, was the Junkers Ju 88 high-speed bomber. This was an extraordinarily "developable" airplane that rivaled the de Havilland Mosquito in overall versatility.

BELOW The Junkers Ju 87 "Stuka" was created to provide the German army's mobile divisions with "flying artillery" support. By 1942 the dive-bomber concept was obsolete, especially in the face of advanced fighter opposition, but Germany had nothing with which to replace the Stuka in the ground-attack role, and the type therefore had to soldier on. The variant seen here is a Ju 87G-6, which was optimized for the antitank role with a pair of 37-mm cannon in large underwing fairings.

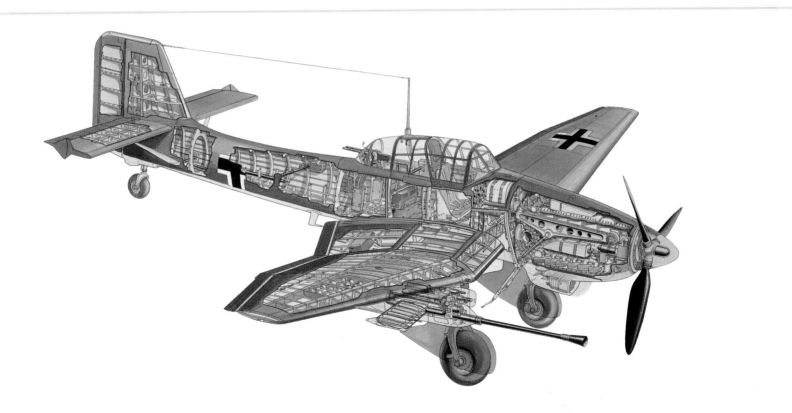

The initial success enjoyed by the Axis powers (Germany, Italy, and Japan) was due in part to the fact that all three nations had gained genuine operational experience before the outbreak of World War II. Italy had supported the Nationalists in Spain and had also been able to test its forces in the conquest of Abyssinia, which began in 1935. The Italian bombers, principally the Savoia-Marchetti SM.79 tri-motor monoplane, distinguished themselves in Spain, but the CR.32 and CR.42 fighters seemed better than they were because their phenomenal agility enabled them to keep out of trouble. The Regia Aeronautica emerged from these two campaigns with a misplaced belief in the continued operational viability of its first-line biplane fighters. Three very promising monoplane fighters, the Fiat G.50 Freccia, Macchi C.200 Saetta, and Reggiane Re.2000, were nonetheless developed just before World War II, but all three were fitted with low-powered radial engines. Speed and rate of climb were also sacrificed to the pilots' preference for maneuverability, and their armament was poor, especially in comparison with the standards set in German fighters, in which a battery of machine guns was complemented by one or two 20-mm cannons firing explosive shells.

Although the army and navy had each possessed their own air arms since 1911, Japan began to develop modern aircraft industries and air forces in the 1930s. Western observers mistakenly believed that the Japanese were relying solely or heavily on Western designs; in fact, by the mid-1930s, Japanese engineers produced their own designs. These planes were skillfully designed to take advantage of Japan's capacity for producing light-weight structures with heavy armament, superior agility, and good performance especially in speed, climb rate, and range.

Some inkling of Japan's success could have been gained from reports coming from China, where the Japanese had started a full-scale war in 1937, but Western intelligence staffs were amused rather than impressed by high assessments of Japanese aircraft. The Mitsubishi A5M and Nakajima Ki-27 low-wing cantilever monoplane fighters had very good performance despite their fixed landing gear arrangements, and the next generation of fighters was even better. The Mitsubishi A6M Reisen (zero fighter), later known as the "Zeke," received a glowing assessment from Americans flying against them in China, as did the Mitsubishi G3M "Nell" and G4M "Betty" bombers. All such warnings were disregarded, as were first intimations of the capabilities offered by the Nakajima Ki-43 Hayabusa landplane fighter.

By 1936 the United Kingdom and France had become highly alarmed by the pace of German rearmament and decided to launch major rearmament efforts in which aircraft

ABOVE Lacking liquid-cooled V-type engines of adequate power to make possible single-engined fighters and twin-engined bombers of high performance, Italy opted for the continued use of medium-power radial engines in single-engined fighters notable for their agility, and in three-engined bombers. Typical of these latter was the Savoia-Marchetti SM.81, a dual-role bomber and transport intended for the colonial role against negligible air opposition. This airplane of the 11a Squadriglia operated over Abyssinia from 1936, and the upper-surface markings indicate the desire for high visibility as a primary aid to discovery in the event of any forced landing. The dual-role concept and the retention of fixed landing gear were attractive in the hard times of the 1930s, but made the aircraft incapable of making an effective offensive contribution to Italy's air effort in World War II.

BELOW Mitsubishi created its G3M bomber, which later received the Allied reporting name "Nell", to provide the imperial Japanese navy air force with a land-based bomber able to operate over long range to seek out and destroy enemy ships using bombs or torpedoes carried under the fuselage. This G3M3 was operated by the 2d Hikotai (squadron) of the Genzan Kokutai (Genzan naval air corps) from a base in Thailand in December 1941, when aircraft of this type sank the British capital ships HMS *Prince of Wales* and HMS *Repulse* off the coast of Malaya.

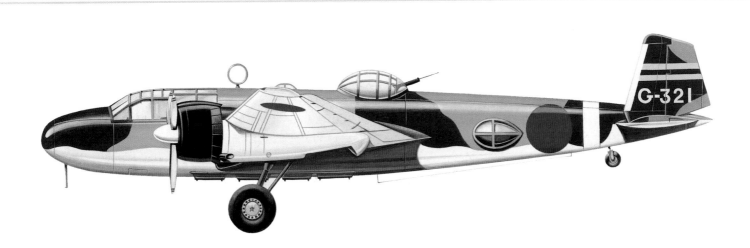

PLANES OF
THE LUFTWAFFE

The Luftwaffe, or German air force, was geared primarily for tactical air operations in World War II, and the German high command only belatedly came to appreciate that its lack of long-range heavy bombing capability was a strategic error. German fighter capability was instead based on the protection of home airspace for use over the battlefield and the enemy's lines of communications. This offensive air superiority, won by the Messerschmitt Bf 109 single-engined short-range and Bf 110 twin-engined long-range fighters, opened the way for the Luftwaffe's tactical attack and bomber aircraft to destroy the enemy's military cohesion and will to resist. This offensive capability was vested in aircraft such as the Henschel Hs 123 close-support warplane, the Junkers Ju 87 dive bomber, and the Dornier Do 17, Heinkel He 111, and Junkers Ju 88 medium bombers. The support of these tactical warplanes was seen as essential to the success of the German army's Blitzkrieg (lightning war) operations, in which a gap was torn through the enemy's front line by fast-moving armored forces that then plunged into the enemy's rear areas to shatter his artillery concentrations, supply dumps, reinforcements, and lines of communication. The concept also involved the use of paradropped or glider-landed airborne forces to take and hold key points pending the arrival of the surfaces forces.

Germany was the first great exponent of airborne warfare, making extensive use of such forces in the initial years of World War II. The glider that was used primarily in the assault transport role was the DFS 230 (facing page), which carried an infantry squad. In an effort to provide its airborne forces with support weapons and equipment larger and heavier than anything that could be carried in direct assault gliders and aircraft such as the Junkers Ju 52/3m transport (right, center), the Germans ordered the design of huge logistic support gliders. The only type to enter production was the Messerschmitt Me 321 Gigant (giant) (above), capable of carrying large numbers of men as an alternative to equipment (including vehicles and artillery).

PLANES OF
THE LUFTWAFFE

FACING PAGE, TOP LEFT Early use of the Me 321 Gigant heavy transport glider revealed problems with the provision of a tug sufficiently powerful to get this monster into the air when fully loaded. Messerschmitt therefore developed the glider into the Me 323 powered transport with six radial engines (using captured stocks of French engines), and this also had the advantage of being able to fly itself back to base.

FACING PAGE, TOP RIGHT The Junkers Ju 52/3m was a real workhorse of the German air effort in World War II. Technically obsolescent by the outbreak of the war, this three-engined transport was built in large numbers for all the transport roles including the support of the German air force's airborne arm. In this latter capacity the Ju 52/3m was used for paratrooping and for glider towing.

FACING PAGE, BOTTOM Like other countries, Germany in the 1930s saw a role for the twin-engined heavy fighter. This emerged as the Messerschmitt Bf 110, which was an adequate but in no way exceptional type with a two-man crew. Too large to tangle with more agile single-seat day fighters on a basis of equality, the Zerstörer (destroyer), as the type was known to the Germans, was then successfully developed into a night fighter. The model illustrated here is a Bf 110G-4 night fighter with flame-damped exhausts and radar with a cumbersome antenna.

ABOVE Germany's most important medium bomber of World War II was the Heinkel He 111. This had been designed ostensibly as a civil transport, but then emerged in its true colors as a dedicated bomber with limited transport capability. For lack of any adequate replacement, the He 111 was maintained in production right into 1944, and the type remained in service to the time of Germany's surrender in May 1945.

had a high priority. France had at last divorced the air force from the army by creating an independent Armée de l'Air in 1933, but the new air force was still tragically short of modern aircraft and was not ready for the German invasion of 1940. The main burden of aerial defense fell on aircraft designed by the few successful private firms: Dewoitine's beautiful little D.520 fighter, Morane-Saulnier's angular M.S.406 fighter, Bloch's stubby but powerful MB.151 fighter, Breguet's promising Br.690 twin-engined fighter, and Potez's useful Type 63 twin-engined fighter-bomber.

The British were almost equally unprepared and barely survived initial German attacks in 1940. But their engineers responded quickly, with low-wing monoplanes. The two that became best known were the Hawker Hurricane and the Supermarine Spitfire, each powered by the magnificent Rolls-Royce Merlin, a descendant of the "R" racing engine, and armed with eight rifle-caliber machine guns. Both these interceptors had top speeds in the order of 350 mph (565 km/h), about 100 mph (160 km/h) faster than the Gladiator, and their features included retractable landing gear, trailing-edge flaps, and enclosed cockpits.

The British bomber force was also given completely new equipment in the shape of the Armstrong Whitworth Whitley, Handley Page Hampden, and Vickers Wellington, each a low-wing cantilever monoplane with two engines and retractable landing gear. There was also the Fairey Battle single-engined light bomber, which was to prove almost worthless in combat, and the twin-engined Bristol Blenheim light bomber, an advanced and speedy airplane for its time though somewhat flimsy and underarmed.

Before the war the Americans were producing some very advanced aircraft, including the first B-17 Flying Fortress four-engined heavy bomber in 1935. But American fighters were inferior to the Japanese. Even so, American production capability was considerable, and the European powers were happy to order large quantities of such aircraft as the Curtiss P-36 and P-40 fighters, and the Douglas DB-7 and Martin Maryland twin-engined bombers. Meanwhile American engineers were hard at work on a new generation of aircraft that would make great and enduring reputations for themselves in World War II.

FACING PAGE The most famous British fighter of World War II is without doubt the Supermarine Spitfire, which was conceptually more advanced than the Hawker Hurricane and therefore remained in development and production right through the conflict. The type is here exemplified by a Spitfire Mk XII, which was the first mark in which the original Rolls-Royce Merlin engine was replaced by the same company's more potent Griffon engine.

BELOW One of the two great British fighters in the first years of World War II was the Hawker Hurricane, seen here in the form of the airplane of No. 257 Squadron flown by the celebrated ace R. S. Stanford Tuck, who eventually amassed twenty-nine aerial victories. The Hurricane bore the brunt of the fighting in the Battle of Britain, concentrating its efforts on the German bombers that were causing so much damage to London and other English cities, and was ultimately responsible for the destruction of more German aircraft than all the other British aircraft involved in the battle.

ABOVE Created by Mitsubishi as successor to its pioneering A5M carrierborne monoplane fighter with an open cockpit and fixed landing gear, the A6M was the first carrierborne fighter anywhere in the world to offer parity with its land-based counterparts, and became celebrated in World War II as the Reisen (zero fighter) or, to the Allies, as the "Zeke." The A6M was introduced in the Japanese year 2600 (hence the Japanese name), and by the standards of 1940 offered an excellent blend of performance (especially in speed and range) with firepower and agility.

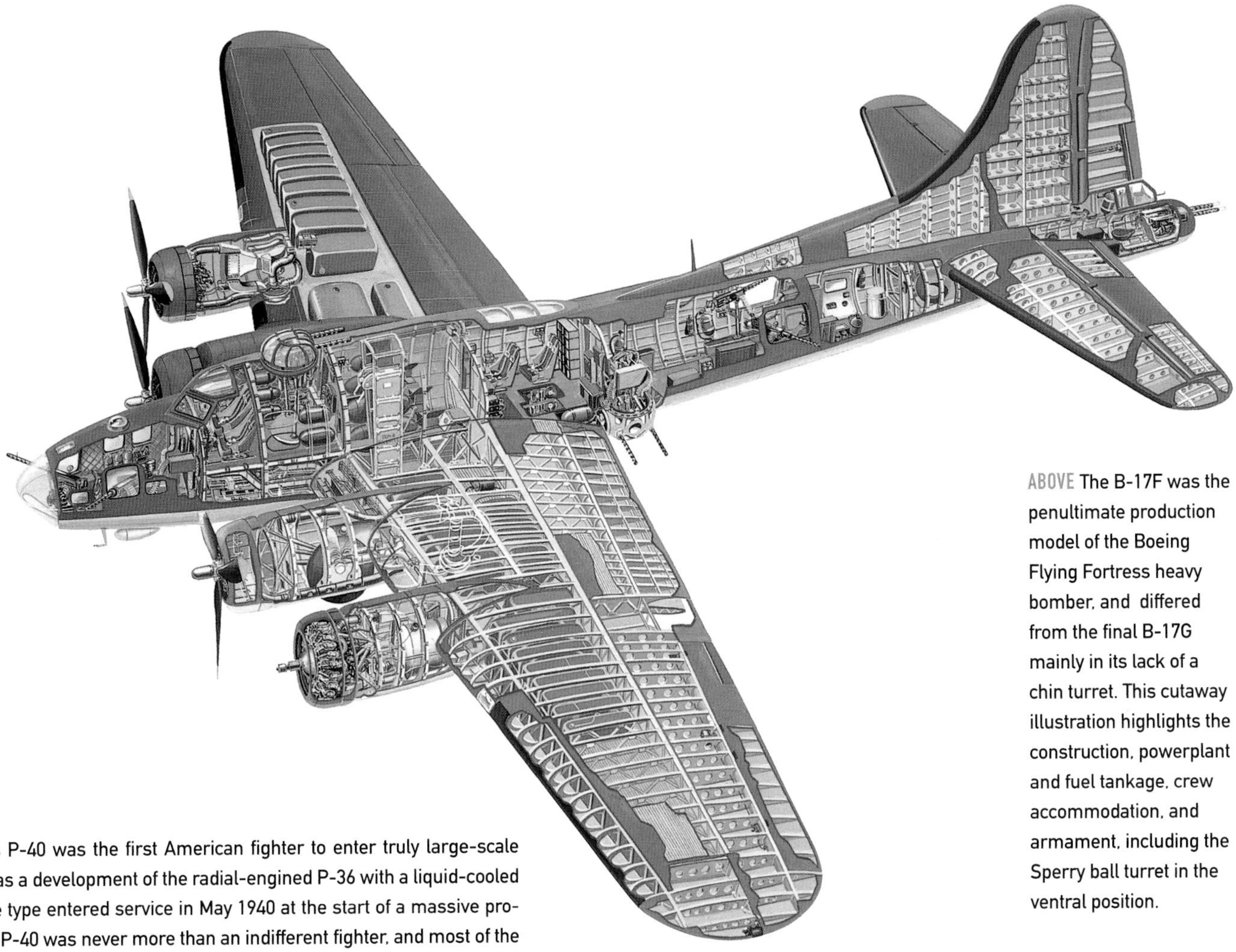

ABOVE The B-17F was the penultimate production model of the Boeing Flying Fortress heavy bomber, and differed from the final B-17G mainly in its lack of a chin turret. This cutaway illustration highlights the construction, powerplant and fuel tankage, crew accommodation, and armament, including the Sperry ball turret in the ventral position.

BELOW The Curtiss P-40 was the first American fighter to enter truly large-scale production, and was a development of the radial-engined P-36 with a liquid-cooled V-type engine. The type entered service in May 1940 at the start of a massive production effort. The P-40 was never more than an indifferent fighter, and most of the aircraft were therefore used with considerable success in the fighter-bomber role with Allison V-1710 and Rolls-Royce V-1650 engines. The final major production model, illustrated here, was the P-40N development of the lightweight P-40L, and production amounted to more than fifty-two hundred such aircraft.

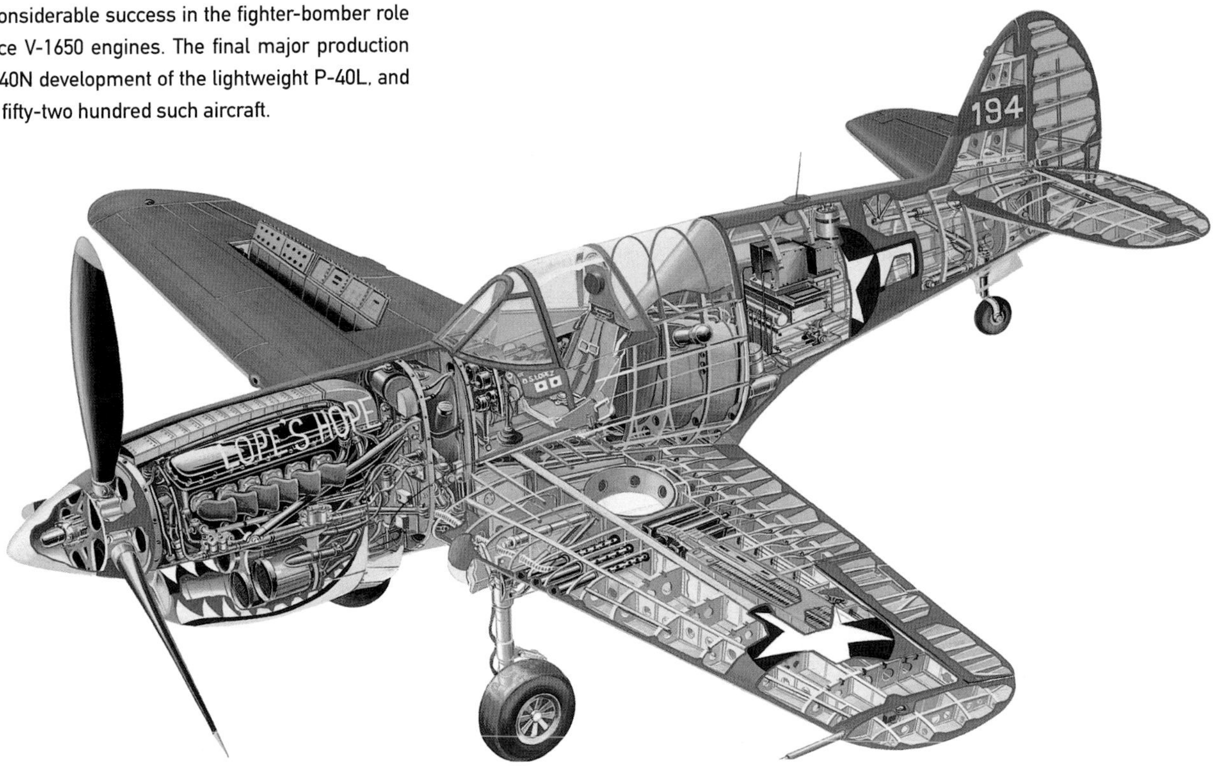

ABOVE The importance of Frank Whittle in the transformation of the airplane from the piston engine to turbine propulsion cannot be overstated. Whittle applied for his first turbojet patent in 1930 and overcame enormous technical problems and official indifference to design the WU as his first turbojet, which made its initial run on April 12, 1937. The WU paved the way for the much improved W.1X experimental turbojet of 1940 and then the W.1 flight-capable unit that first ran on April 12, 1941, and was used in the United Kingdom's first jet-powered airplane, the Gloster E.28/29. The Whittle engines were of the centrifugal-flow type.

BELOW LEFT The first airplane to fly anywhere in the world solely with turbojet power was the Heinkel He 178, a purely experimental type that made its first true flight on August 27, 1939.

BELOW RIGHT Work on the turbojet in the United Kingdom was paralleled in Germany by the efforts of a Heinkel team under the leadership of Hans-Joachim Pabst von Ohain. Von Ohain's first concrete success was the hydrogen-burning HeS test rig that first ran in March 1937 and paved the way for the supposedly flight-capable HeS 2 of 1938 with an axial/centrifugal-flow compressor and then the HeS 3A that was first tested in the air, under an He 118 airplane, in the early summer of 1939. Finally there came the HeS 3B intended for the He 178 jet-powered airplane.

One of the fascinating—if often overlooked—arms races of the war pitted British scientists against German scientists in search of a new type of engine that would revolutionize aircraft design and operation. This was the turbojet, which exhausts a stream of fast-moving gases to thrust the airplane forward. Frank Whittle's early prototype for Britain ran for the first time in April 1937; Hans von Ohain's model a month later for Germany. These two pioneers were working independently of each other and they evolved radically different types of engines. In August 1939, less than one week before the outbreak of World War II, the Heinkel He 178 became the world's first jet-powered airplane to fly. If Germany had exploited its new achievement immediately, the war might have turned out differently. But the authorities in both Germany and the United Kingdom were slow to see the possibilities of the new type of engine, and operational jet aircraft did not appear until late in the conflict.

Both Allied and Axis strategists employed tactical air support extensively for the first time in history. Today, Western ground troops can easily "call in strikes" and even reverse the flow of support, with ground troops providing tactical support for precision bombers. In the 1940s, however, bombing was far more haphazard. Germany, led by World War I ace Hermann Göring, held the advantage in this theater. The dread of Allied infantry was the Ju 87 Stuka dive bomber, which was used to provide the Panzer units with extremely accurate support at close ranges, thus replacing conventional horse- and tractor-drawn artillery. The Stuka dive bombers were armed with bombs up to 500 kg (1,102 lb) in weight and were capable of dealing with most of the enemy's defensive positions and tanks.

Nonetheless the key roles for aircraft remained as fighters or long-range bombers. The Polish campaign that opened the war on September 1, 1939, involved heavy air battles. Using combat aircraft such as the single-engined P.11 gull-winged fighter, single-engined P.23 Karás light bomber, and twin-engined P.37 Lós medium bomber, the Polish air force fought gallantly and in the initial stages of the fighting inflicted some severe losses on the Luftwaffe. But the weight and experience of the Luftwaffe was far greater. After a few days the Poles could offer no large-scale aerial resistance, and the main weight of the Luftwaffe was switched to tactical support of the Panzer divisions, whose pincer movements were biting deep into Poland. German aircraft losses to ground fire were moderately heavy, but not prohibitive. The fate of Poland was hastened, perhaps, by the devastation of Warsaw on September 25, when high explosive and incendiary bombs rained down on the city.

Any possible doubts about the efficiency of the German armed forces were soon dispelled by the capture of Denmark and the most important strategic points in Norway by airborne and seaborne landings on April 9, 1940. The subsequent Luftwaffe operations

JAMES DOOLITTLE

JAMES DOOLITTLE (1896–1993) James "Jimmy" Harold Doolittle was born in Alameda, California, on December 14, 1896, was educated in Nome, Alaska, and also at Los Angeles Junior College, and spent a year at the University of California School of Mines. In October 1917 Doolittle enlisted as a flying cadet in the Signal Corps Reserve and received his training at the School of Military Aeronautics, University of California, and Rockwell Field California. He was commissioned as a second lieutenant in the Signal Corps' Aviation Section on March 11, 1918, and then served at Camp Dick, Texas, Wright Field, Ohio, and Gerstner Field, Louisiana, before returning to Rockwell Field as a flight leader and gunnery instructor. He then went to Kelly Field, Texas, for duty first

Photographed here in 1922, "Jimmy" Doolittle was one of the small group of men responsible for the development of American aviation during the lean years of the 1920s and 1930s, and also for the increase in the American public's "air mindedness" during the same period. Doolittle was a superb flier, but more than that he was an excellent analyst of the way that aircraft and their systems perform in the air, and also a highly capable commander with a flair for bringing out the best in his men.

with the 104th Aero Squadron, and next with the 90th Aero Squadron undertaking the border patrol duty at Eagle Pass, Texas.

Doolittle remained in the U.S. Army after World War I, and on July 1, 1920, received a regular commission and promotion to first lieutenant. He then took the Air Service Mechanical School and Aeronautical Engineering courses at Kelly Field and McCook Field, Ohio, respectively. On September 4, 1922, Doolittle became the first pilot to fly across the United States in a single day, taking off from Pablo Beach, Florida, in a modified DH-4B and arriving at San Diego, California, in a flying time of 21 hours 19 minutes, excluding a refueling stop of 1 hour 16 minutes at Kelly Field, Texas.

In 1922 Doolittle gained his bachelor of arts degree from the University of California, and in July of the following year he entered Massachusetts Institute of Technology for special engineering courses, graduating the following year with a master of science degree and getting his doctor of science degree in aeronautics one year later, one of the first men in the country to earn this degree.

In March 1924 he served at McCook Field, where he flew aircraft acceleration tests. In June 1925 Doolittle was posted to the Naval Air Station in Washington, D.C., for special training in flying high-speed seaplanes, serving for a time with the Naval Test Board at Mitchel, New York. In the same year Doolittle won the eighth Schneider Trophy seaplane race in a Curtiss R3C-2 floatplane at 232.56 mph (374.27 km/h). During April 1926 Doolittle received a period of furlough to demonstrate aircraft in South America, and, after breaking his ankles, nonetheless managed to display the Curtiss P-1 fighter with both ankles in casts. On return to the United States Doolittle was kept at the Walter Reed Hospital until April 1927, when he was posted to McCook Field for experimental work and additional duty as an instructor with the Organized Reserves of V Corps Area's 385th Bomb Squadron. Returning to Mitchel Field in September 1928, Doolittle was involved in the development of blind-flying equipment, such as the artificial horizontal and directional gyroscope, at the Guggenheim Flight Laboratory: On September 24, 1929, this process reached an early peak when, in a Consolidated NY-2 trainer adapted with Sperry instruments in a completely blacked-out cockpit, Doolittle was able "to take off, fly a specific course, and land without reference to the earth."

In January 1930 Doolittle became the U.S. Army's adviser on the building of Floyd Bennett Airport in New York City, but on February 15 of the same year he resigned his regular commission, being commissioned instead as a major in the Specialist Reserve Corps. Doolittle became the manager of the Shell Oil Company's aviation department, and in this capacity was instrumental in the development of high-octane fuel for aviation purposes. With Shell as a sponsor, Doolittle became probably the most important single figure in American air racing, and in 1931 he won the Bendix Trophy race at a speed that also constituted a new transcontinental record: Flying the Laird Super Solution, Doolittle lifted off from the Union Air Terminal in Burbank, California, landed for fuel at Albuquerque, New Mexico, and Kansas City, Missouri, before completing the course at Newark, New Jersey, in an elapsed time of 11 hours 16 minutes 10 seconds for an average speed of 217 mph (349 km/h), knocking no less than 1 hour 18 minutes off the time set earlier in the same year by Frank Hawks in the Texaco 13 Mystery Ship. On September 3, 1932, Major Doolittle flew the extraordinary Granville Brothers (Gee Bee) Super Sportster R-1 to a new world's landplane speed record of 294.42 mph (473.82 km/h), and just two days later won the Thomson Trophy race in the same machine, thus becoming the first man to win all three of aviation's "big-name" events, the Schneider, Bendix, and Thomson trophy races.

Doolittle went back to active service on July 1, 1940, with the rank of major and worked on plans to adapt car plants for the manufacture of aircraft. After Pearl Harbor, on January 2, 1942, Doolittle was promoted to lieutenant colonel in the HQ, Army Air Forces, and ordered to start planning the United States' first attack on the Japanese home islands. Taking off from the aircraft carrier USS *Hornet* on April 18, 16 North American B-25 Mitchell twin-engined medium bombers attacked targets in Tokyo, Kobe, Osaka, and Nagoya in a one-way raid that greatly boosted American morale. Like others who failed to find a landing spot, Doolittle bailed out of his machine and landed in a Chinese rice paddy. He received the Medal of Honor and was promoted to brigadier general.

Doolittle was assigned to the 8th Army Air Force in July 1942, but in September of the same year moved from England to North Africa as commander of the 12th Army Air Force, only to be given command of the North African Strategic Air Forces in March 1943. Doolittle assumed command of the 15th Army Air Force in the Mediterranean theater in November 1943, and between January 1944 and September 1945 led the 8th AAF in Europe and then the Pacific. He was promoted to lieutenant general on March 13, 1944, but on May 10, 1946, he left regular service and rejoined Shell as a vice president and later as a director.

Doolittle retired from Air Force duty on February 28, 1959, but continued to serve as consultant to the U.S. Air Force as well as on the boards of several U.S. corporations. Doolittle died on September 27, 1993.

in Norway followed the pattern set for them in Poland. The Norwegian air force was negligible, and the only major air support sent by the Allies was a number of British aircraft, most of them obsolete compared with the German opposition.

While the Germans were tackling the last Allied pockets in central and northern Norway, momentous events were taking place in western Europe. On May 10, 1940, Hitler unleashed a huge offensive against the Netherlands, Belgium, and France. Germany again relied on breakthrough and deep exploitation by the Panzer formations. These struck through the "impassable" Ardennes to reach the Channel coast, splitting the Allied armies in two. The Germans then concentrated on eliminating the two halves in detail. With the Dutch, Belgians, and French defeated to the north of the "Panzer corridor," and the British and a number of their allies escaping from Dunkirk, the Germans turned their full weight on the remnants of the French army holding that portion of France south of the corridor, and the last elements of the French army surrendered toward the end of June.

Again it had been the Blitzkrieg combination of Panzer formations and aircraft that had proved decisive. But losses in this campaign had been proportionally even heavier than in the Polish campaign. In the north, against the Netherlands and Belgium, Germany had used its airborne forces on a major scale for the first time, and losses had been severe.

The northern sector of the Allied defeat also suffered the kind of raid that had destroyed Warsaw. This time the victim was Rotterdam, whose old quarter was razed in the attack of May 14. The Germans had threatened this raid as a means of forcing a capitulation in the area, and the Dutch had in fact surrendered. But a communications failure prevented the local German commander from calling off the attack, and Kampfgeschwader 54 burned out the mainly wooden quarter of the historic city for no military purpose whatsoever.

The few Hurricane and Fokker D.XXI fighters of the Belgian and Dutch air forces fought valiantly, but courage and determination were not enough to halt the larger and better-equipped Luftwaffe, which enjoyed considerable numerical as well as qualitative superiority. The air war over France was similar but larger. Here the Germans were faced by the Armée de l'Air and elements of the Royal Air Force as well as a few units manned by Czech and Polish personnel. Despite the mixed assortment of good and mediocre aircraft they were flying, the French fought the Germans with determination at least for the first few days.

Below the air arena, the Panzer divisions were forcing the French into ever-deeper withdrawals. As the French fell back, their airfields, depots, and factories fell into German hands, further weakening the Armée de l'Air. When France signed an armistice on June 25, most of the French pilots flew their aircraft to the unoccupied zone in the south of France or even to the French territories in North Africa.

War-time urgency has often opened the way for aircraft designers with unorthodox ideas. The other side of this particular coin is the belief that something that has served well can, despite its basic obsolescence, be transformed by the addition of limited improvements and a more powerful engine. This was certainly the case with one British type, the Fairey Albacore, which was seen as a way of improving on the well-established Swordfish carrierborne torpedo bomber. Yet the Albacore was not a success, and was accordingly outlived by the type its was supposed to succeed. A concept that had received lukewarm British approval in the 1930s was represented by the Pterodactyl series of tailless aircraft designed by Geoffrey T. R. Hill and built by the Westland company. The Okha was a Japanese attempt to create a cost-effective kamikaze airplane made out of non-strategic materials and made as small as could carry a large warhead, the pilot and the powerplant of three rocket motors.

Another aspect of wartime experiment was the use of scaled-down or lightweight aircraft for the evaluation of advanced aerodynamic and structural concepts. This breed of airplane is represented by the fabric-covered wooden Vought V-173 and the F5U carrierborne fighter offering an exceptional speed range and great agility. The XF5U-1 prototype was built of Metalite, a material in which a balsa core was sandwiched between two layers of aluminum alloy, and the prototype was so strong that it proved difficult to destroy after the program had been canceled.

FACING PAGE Having adopted the kamikaze concept of diving manned aircraft loaded with explosives onto American warships, the imperial Japanese navy decided in 1944 that the concept of using obsolete warplanes was tactically inefficient and also a waste of resources. The service therefore ordered the creation of a low-cost expendable airplane that took form as the basically wooden Yokosuka MXY7 that the Japanese named Okha (cherry blossom) but the Americans nicknamed Baka (fool). The MXY7 was powered by three solid-propellant rockets and carried a 2,646-lb (1,200-kg) explosive warhead, and first flew in the fall of 1944.

BELOW First flown in November 1942, the V-173 was a test platform for the aerodynamic validation of the planned Vought F5U carrierborne fighter, of which a single example was completed for the U.S. Navy but never flown. Trials of the V-173, which had a truly remarkable geometry, suggested that the F5U would have possessed excellent performance, including the ability to fly at extremely low speed while still under full control, as well as a very high level of agility with a twin-engined powerplant of only modest power.

BELOW One of the oddest aircraft to fly in World War II was the Blohm und Voss Bv 141 asymmetric airplane. This was schemed for the reconnaissance role, and the desire to provide the crew with the best possible fields of vision led to the incorporation of the accommodation in a very extensively glazed nacelle offset to starboard of the centerline and balanced by a long boom-type fuselage, carrying the tail unit and single radial engine, offset to port. Only small numbers were built, and while these saw limited service for evaluation purposes, the Bv 141 did not enter full-scale production.

STRANGE PLANES BEFORE AND DURING WORLD WAR II

BELOW The Westland Pterodactyl Mk V, which first flew in May 1934, was a bold but not altogether successful British attempt to create a tailless fighter, in this instance of sesquiplane layout, offering good performance and agility but pro- viding the gunner behind the pilot with superb fields of fire for his two machine guns, which were to have been installed in an electrically powered turret for high rates of traverse.

The British part in the French air campaign was relatively small. Serving with the British Expeditionary Force were a number of fighter and light bomber squadrons of the Advanced Air Striking Force, supported from England by the main part of Fighter Command and the medium and heavy bomber squadrons of Bomber Command. Uncertain about the probable course of events in France, the Air Ministry had given the AASF only "semi-expendable" types such as the Hurricane fighter, considered slightly inferior to the Spitfire, and the Fairey Battle light bomber. The AASF played a forlorn part in the defense of France and suffered very heavily in the process. The Hurricane performed well but the Battle proved a disastrous failure. The British bomber force in France was virtually wiped out in the first few days of the campaign, and the few British fighters could only harry the German bombers ineffectively.

The biggest surprise of the early months of the war came in the East, where Finland resisted the Soviet Union far more effectively than anyone could have hoped. Finland's fight was nowhere more successful than in the air. Despite using the Polikarpov I-16 monoplane fighter, Tupolev SB-2, and Ilyushin DB-3 twin-engined monoplane bombers, and other fairly modern aircraft, Soviet pilots were very severely handled by the excellently trained and highly dedicated pilots of the small Finnish air force, which had at its disposal only a limited and motley collection of obsolescent fighters. The D.XXI and Gladiator were notably successful. Soviet air operations were undertaken in clumsy formations, and the Finnish pilots exacted an enormously heavy price from the Soviet bombers. Only in February 1940, the last month of this "Winter War," did the Soviets win the skies.

ALL-AIR WARFARE: TERROR FROM THE SKIES

World War II's most famous air campaign, of course, was the Battle of Britain, the world's first strategic all-air campaign. It comprised three phases: attacks on convoys and coastal installations; an assault on Fighter Command's bases and fighter production centers; and finally a campaign against urban areas. The coastal shipping phase began as France fell and was typified by raids, usually by a few bombers and a heavy fighter escort, against British coastal convoys and the ports and naval installations on the English south and east coasts. The Germans were trying to avoid civilian casualties while engaging the RAF's fighters on favorable tactical terms. Yet with the aid of radar—one of the war's crucial technological achievements—the RAF was able to meet the Germans on equal terms.

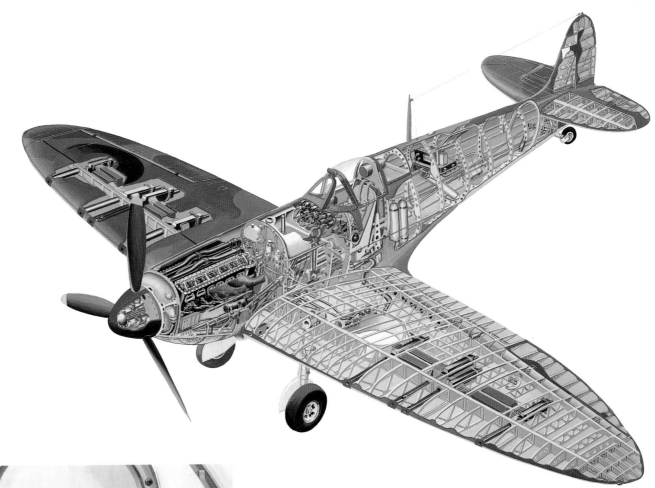

ABOVE One of the most beautiful and justly celebrated aircraft of all time, the Supermarine Spitfire was the United Kingdom's most important fighter of World War II. The type remained in development and production right through this conflict, and is here exemplified by a cutaway example of the Spitfire Mk IA, as the original Mk I with the armament of eight fixed forward-firing machine guns was redesignated after the 1940 appearance of the Mk IB with two 20-mm cannons and four machine guns. The Spitfire Mk I entered service in August 1938.

BELOW The Supermarine Spitfire was the most advanced fighter in British service at the start of World War II. Its cockpit reflected the current state of the art, and included a comparatively large number of analog dial instruments as well as a bulletproof panel on the windshield and a reflector gun sight just behind this.

The Luftwaffe high command decided at the start of August 1940 to concentrate on British fighter bases and radar stations. Bombers would be used to lure the British fighters into the air, and could also cause considerable damage to industrial areas and air bases, but the Germans believed that it would be their fighters that would inflict the main damage as the British fighters clawed for altitude. This second phase of the battle revealed major flaws in the German air machine, however, as the vaunted Bf 110 was easy prey for the faster and nimbler British fighters. Losses were severe on both sides, but with the slower Hurricane fighters taking on the bombers and Bf 110 heavy fighters, and the Spitfires holding off the Bf 109 single-seat fighters, the RAF slowly but inexorably gained the ascendancy over the Luftwaffe.

By the start of August's last week, Luftwaffe attacks were extended to inland fighter bases and centers of fighter production. Fighter Command's most serious problem was now pilot fatigue rather than shortage of fighters, but Air Vice Marshal Keith Park, commanding No. 11 Group in southeast England, showed tactical genius in handling his front-line squadrons, and Air Chief Marshal Sir Hugh Dowding, leading Fighter Command, constantly replaced exhausted squadrons with units that had been rotated to less threatened areas for rest as they undertook the defense of these secondary areas. Even so, losses continued to rise, and on September 15, now remembered as Battle of Britain Day, Fighter Command had no reserves left.

Already, a week earlier, the Germans had switched their focus to London and the other great British industrial cities. This would prove a strategic error, as British air defenses were strong, and the Germans made things worse with a very ill-considered tactical alteration that replaced the fighters' free-roving loose escort with a tight escort of bombers. This stripped the fighters of their freedom to exploit speed and agility, and also forced them into a flight regime that was less fuel-efficient and therefore reduced their endurance over England.

By the end of September daylight raids on London had proved to be prohibitively expensive and were replaced by a fighter-bomber campaign of low-level sneak raids. By November, the night-bombing Blitz was on. But the British had already won the Battle of Britain. Hitler turned against his ally the Soviet Union rather than invading the United Kingdom.

Both the British and the Germans learned valuable tactical and technical lessons from the Battle of Britain, and in the spring of 1941 both sides made strenuous efforts to update existing designs and rush forward new combat aircraft. Cannon appeared in

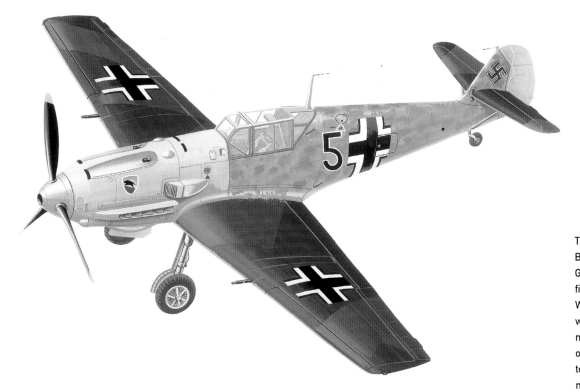

The Messerschmitt Bf 109 was Germany's standard fighter throughout World War II, and was built in larger numbers than any other fighter in history. One of its primary advantages, especially in the early part of the war, was its Daimler-Benz DB 601 engine, which was a fuel-injected unit that allowed the pilot of a Bf 109 to initiate a negative-g maneuver such as a bunt by pushing the stick forward, whereas the pilot of a fighter such as the Spitfire with the Merlin engine fitted with a standard carburetor had first to half-roll and then pull back on the stick as a means of maintaining positive g.

British fighters, and new models of both the Bf 109 and the Spitfire were fitted with more powerful engines and better superchargers, raising maximum speeds by some 50 mph (80 km/h) to about 400 mph (645 km/h). The Luftwaffe kept up its night attacks on British cities until the end of spring 1941, and RAF Bomber Command also began a campaign of nocturnal raids on German cities. While the German bombers found it relatively easy to find London and other major British cities from their bases in northern France and the Low Countries, British bombers found it far more difficult to find German cities. An operational research report at the end of 1940 showed that only a very small percentage of British bombs was falling anywhere near their intended targets. This night-bombing campaign was the only means available to the British for direct attack, so the effort was continued with a gradual increase in strength if not initially in accuracy.

The Blitz ended in May 1941 for two reasons. First, the twin-engined Bristol Beaufighter night fighter, fitted with the new AI (airborne interception) radar, was taking an increasingly heavy toll of the raiders, and second, German air formations were being transferred east for the invasion of the U.S.S.R. By June 1941 the United Kingdom was faced by only two fighter wings, but these managed to check British offensive operations over

Large, heavy, and well-armed, the Bristol Beaufighter was based on the same configuration as the Blenheim light bomber and Beaufort torpedo bomber. This British twin-engined heavy fighter was first used as a radar-equipped night fighter, but then matured as a superb maritime attack warplane with an armament of cannon, rockets, torpedoes, and bombs.

northwest Europe with the aid of the latest German fighter, the Focke-Wulf Fw 190. Powered by a closely cowled radial piston engine, this structurally sturdy fighter was highly maneuverable, carried very heavy armament, and was generally superior to any British fighter.

Hitler's invasion of the U.S.S.R. was helped by the self-inflicted weakness of his new opponent. Standards had declined radically during Stalin's purges of the Soviet armed forces during 1937 and 1938, and the Red air force was only just emerging from the shock of its mauling by the tiny Finnish air force in the Winter War. Worse still, at the time of the start of hostilities with Germany the Red air force was saddled with vast numbers of obsolete aircraft that the government was unwilling to scrap. The Luftwaffe did the job for the Soviets, and in the process forced the communist leadership to accelerate the design, development, and production of new aircraft.

The Soviets were already producing one of the war's finest ground-attack types, the single-engined Ilyushin Il-2 Shturmovik, and this was soon joined by the excellent twin-engined Petlyakov Pe-2 tactical medium bomber and the improving series of single-engined fighters designed by Semyon Lavochkin and Alexander Yakovlev. With just these four series as the core of their operational inventory, the Soviets were able to produce vast numbers of aircraft that were, by Western standards, austerely equipped but that were nonetheless ideally suited to the U.S.S.R.'s climatic extremes and simple military tactics.

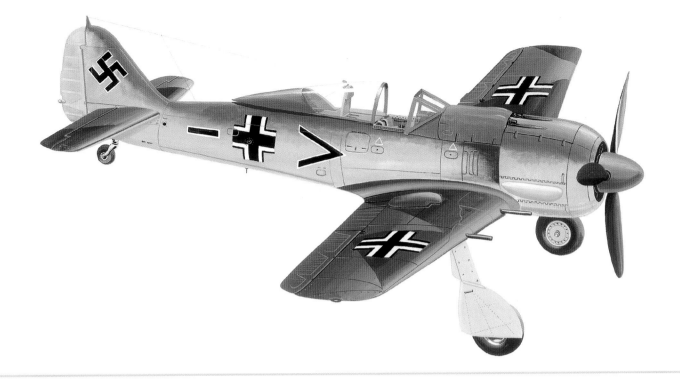

ABOVE The Focke-Wulf Fw 190 entered service in the spring of 1941 and completely outclassed the British fighters opposing it. The type was then further developed with more powerful radial engines before switching in the Fw 190D model to a V-type engine cooled by an annular radiator that left the radial-engined appearance basically unaltered.

BELOW The Yakovlev Yak-3 was developed in parallel with the Yak-9, which was slightly larger and heavier, and entered service in 1944. The Yak-3 was one of the best low- and medium-altitude fighters of World War II, offering phenomenal agility.

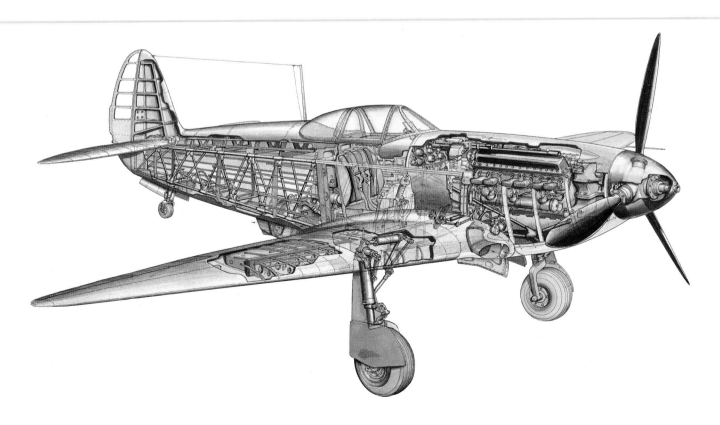

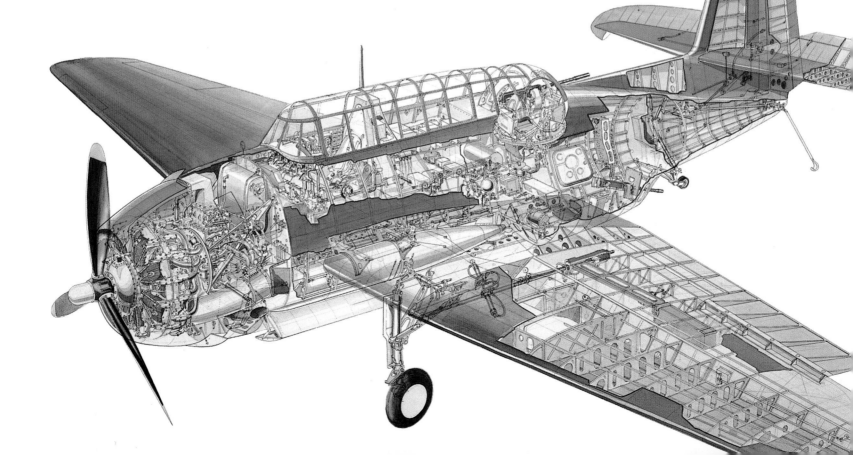

ABOVE Operated by the U.S. Navy with the designation SBD, the Douglas Dauntless partnered the Grumman Avenger in the role of carrierborne dive-bombing up to 1945, although it was supplanted in first-line service from 1943 by the Curtiss SB2C Helldiver.

BELOW The Grumman Avenger was the U.S. Navy's standard torpedo and attack bomber from the middle of 1942 onward, and proved itself a very capable warplane after a disastrous start in which virtually a whole squadron was lost in the Battle of Midway. The type was built by the parent company as the TBF, and also manufactured in large numbers by the Eastern Aircraft Division of General Motors as the TBM.

The Germans enjoyed general air superiority over the Eastern Front from June 1941 to the Battle of Kursk in July 1943. But from that time on, the Red air force gradually won superiority at the low and medium altitudes that mattered most. Right to the end of the war the Luftwaffe could generally regain temporary command of the air in a particular area, but the huge size of the Soviet general offensives between July 1943 and May 1945 meant that such limited setbacks were no more than pinpricks. The Soviet planes won with quantity not quality.

Realizing the importance of tactical aircraft in the Soviet campaign, the Germans deployed two special types in this theater, the Henschel Hs 129 tank-buster and the Focke-Wulf Fw 189 tactical reconnaissance airplane. Suffering from lack of power and poor flying qualities, but well protected and carrying heavy armament, the Hs 129 was a potent antitank weapon that performed very creditably in the Battle of Kursk. So too did late-model Ju 87G attack aircraft fitted with a pair of underwing 37-mm antitank cannon, but as soon as the Soviets discovered the poor performance of the Stuka, their fighters kept a constant watch for them.

Although the Germans tried a number of weapons in their efforts to find the ideal antitank type, they found in the end that heavy cannons provided the best solution. The Soviets, on the other hand, found high-velocity cannons in 20- and 23-mm calibers were usually effective, and that rockets, although unguided, were also very useful. The Soviets had undertaken much experimental work with rockets in the years before the war, and most of their fighters could carry a number of 82- or 132-mm (3.2- or 5.2-in) rockets.

THE TRIUMPH OF THE BOMBERS

During the war with the U.S.S.R., the Germans came to appreciate their error in abandoning the development of a heavy bomber capability. Without this they now found themselves in the position of being unable to attack the main centers of Soviet armament production, relocated from the western regions of the U.S.S.R. to locations east of the Ural Mountains. German designers responded with the four-engined Heinkel He 177 Greif (griffon). It had two engines buried in each wing and geared together to drive a single propeller. The idea offered interesting possibilities, but development of the coupled engines and their associated gearbox proved intractable. The He 177 was plagued with engine fires, making it very unpopular with aircrews

ABOVE The Hawker Typhoon was schemed as successor to the same company's Hurricane for British service, but lacked the climb and high-altitude speed performance for the pure fighter role. The type suffered structural problems and was nearly canceled before emerging as one of the definitive ground-attack fighters of World War II with bombs or rocket projectiles under its wing. The scene shows Flying Officer James Kyle and his No. 197 Squadron flying low into the coast of Europe at 6:15 a.m. on D-Day.

BELOW The Douglas DB-7 secured its initial success in the export market, where France and the United Kingdom were the two main customers, and was only later ordered for American service as the A-20 in the attack bomber rather than medium bomber role.

The de Havilland Mosquito remains one of the classic and most beautiful warplanes of all time. Schemed as a private venture and employing in its structure the plywood/balsa/plywood "sandwich" material that the company had developed before World War II, the Mosquito was planned as a light bomber that would be too fast for any opposing fighter to catch and would therefore require no defensive armament. The result was an immensely capable warplane that was very cost-effective for production and service. The Mosquito proved very versatile and was therefore developed for a host of roles, and is here seen in its initial unarmed bomber variant, the Mosquito B.Mk IV that entered service in 1941.

The Allies, though at first behind both Germany and Japan in aircraft quality, managed to overtake them even while British backs were against the wall. The most fascinating aircraft to enter widespread service in the RAF during 1940, for example, was the de Havilland Mosquito, which, with the possible exception of the Ju 88, may have been the war's most versatile airplane. Conceived as a private venture, the Mosquito was planned as a high-speed bomber based on a plywood/balsa/plywood sandwich structure. Among its features was a maximum speed so high that the Mosquito would need no defensive armament. At first the Air Ministry was dubious, but after the November 1940 appearance of the prototype, the Mosquito's beautiful lines, very high speed, and superb handling ratified its vision. The Mosquito's performance was phenomenal on two Rolls-Royce Merlin engines, its handling was delightful, and the type could outpace any German fighter in service. By the end of the war it had appeared in a virtually nonstop stream of variants optimized for tasks as diverse and important as bombing, fighter-bombing, night-fighting, photo-reconnaissance, maritime attack, meteorology, high-speed transport, training, and target-towing.

By the autumn of 1941 Britain produced crucial new bombers as well. Three four-engined heavy bombers entered service with Bomber Command: First was the Short Stirling, able to carry 14,000 lb (6,350 kg) of bombs for 590 miles (949 km); second was the Handley Page Halifax, carrying 5,800 lb (2,631 kg) for 1,860 miles (2,993 km); and finest of the trio, the Avro Lancaster, with 14,000 lb (6,350 kg) for 1,660 miles (2,671 km) and incorporating a weapons bay large enough to carry considerably heavier special weapons over shorter ranges for specific missions such as dam-busting, bridge destruction, and the penetration of reinforced concrete U-boat pens. With the Halifax and Lancaster as its primary weapons, Bomber Command could finally begin to take the air war to Germany successfully.

In 1941 Bomber Command was learning the lessons of area bombing by night and building up its strength and skills for the heavy bombing campaign. Unlike the Americans, who were confident that their heavily armed bombers could fight their way through the German defenses and use their advanced Norden bomb sights to succeed in pinpoint attacks on small targets of strategic importance by day, the British believed that night bombing was the only solution to operations with acceptable losses to antiaircraft guns and fighters. The targets would have to be large industrial areas, in which bombing would damage industry and demoralize the civilian population, while keeping to a minimum the number of bombers lost to the German night fighters. Led by Air Chief Marshal Sir Arthur Harris, Bomber Command attacked Köln on the night of May 30, 1942, in the world's first 1,000-bomber raid. The city was not devastated, for as usual the bombers crossed the target in a long straggling stream, dropping their loads haphazardly in the target area. Yet the raid was a considerable boost for British morale at a time when little other success had been achieved.

Accurate navigation and bombing were thorny problems. Two clear advances came with the introduction of radar aids and "pathfinder" forces. The first truly successful radar aid was H2S, a special downward-looking radar: This provided a moving map of the land or water directly below the airplane, allowing a navigator to check his position with some accuracy. A valuable navigation as well as bombing aid, H2S was used throughout the war. In combination with the earlier "Gee" and "Oboe" radio navigation aids, H2S allowed Bomber Command to attack German cities accurately, especially after the crews of the Pathfinder Force had been trained in their operation. The concept was for Pathfinder Force crews to use Oboe and mark the target accurately with special pyrotechnic bombs, and for the rest of the bomber force to then bomb these flares. There were problems with development and implementation, but the system proved its worth with the destruction of a large part of Essen on March 5, 1943, by 400 Bomber Command aircraft.

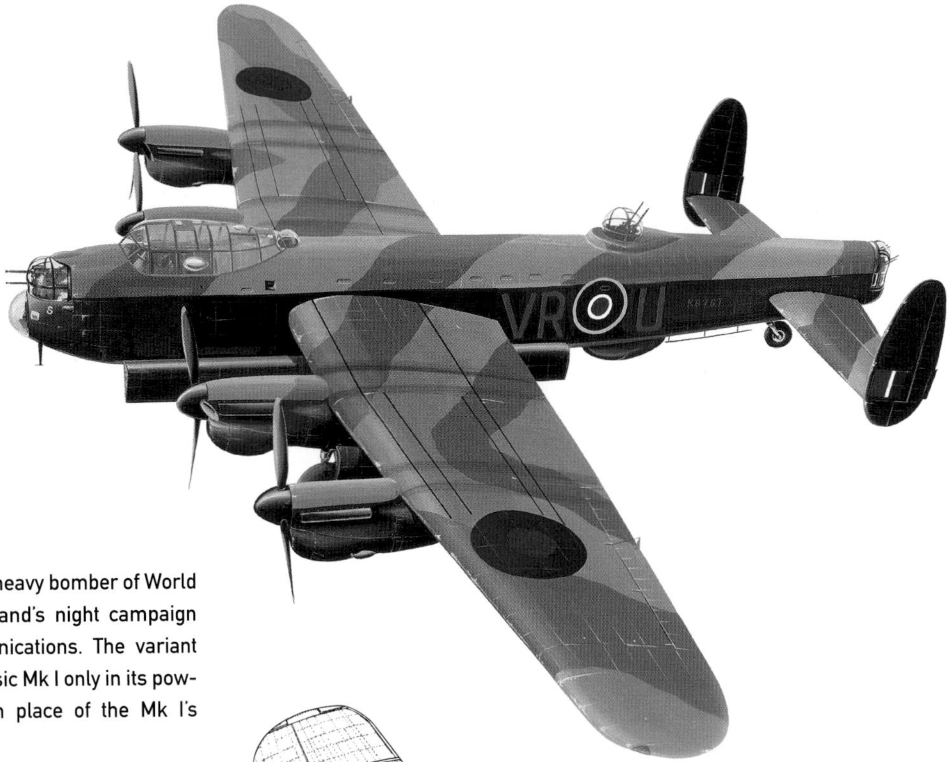

ABOVE The Avro Lancaster was the most important British heavy bomber of World War II, and carried the main weight of Bomber Command's night campaign against Germany's industrial areas, cities, and communications. The variant seen here is a Lancaster Mk III, which differed from the basic Mk I only in its powerplant of four license-built Packard Merlin engines in place of the Mk I's Rolls-Royce Merlin units.

BELOW The Lancaster heavy night bomber was little different from its American counterpart, the Boeing B-17, in terms of available power, but carried a heavier bomb load over a slightly longer range at only marginally lower speed but considerably lower altitude.

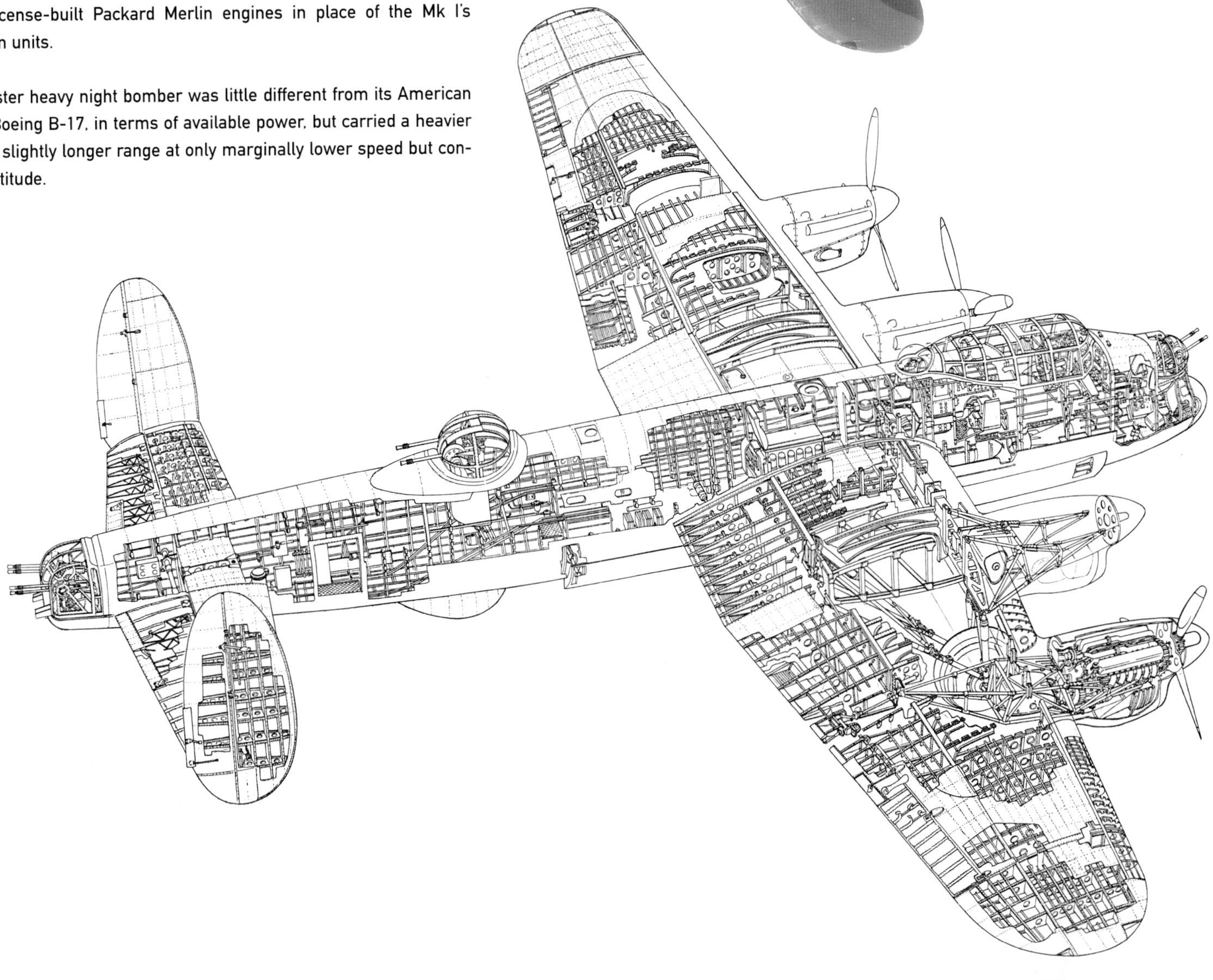

ABOVE With the Martin B-26 Marauder, the North American B-25 Mitchell was the United States' standard medium bomber of World War II. The example seen here is that flown by "Jimmy" Doolittle when he led the "Tokyo raid" from the U.S. Navy carrier USS *Hornet*, and included features such as extra fuel (including fuselage tanks topped up by hand from cans carried in the fuselage) and lightening measures including the removal of much armor and armament, with a pair of broomsticks poking out from the tail position to simulate machine guns.

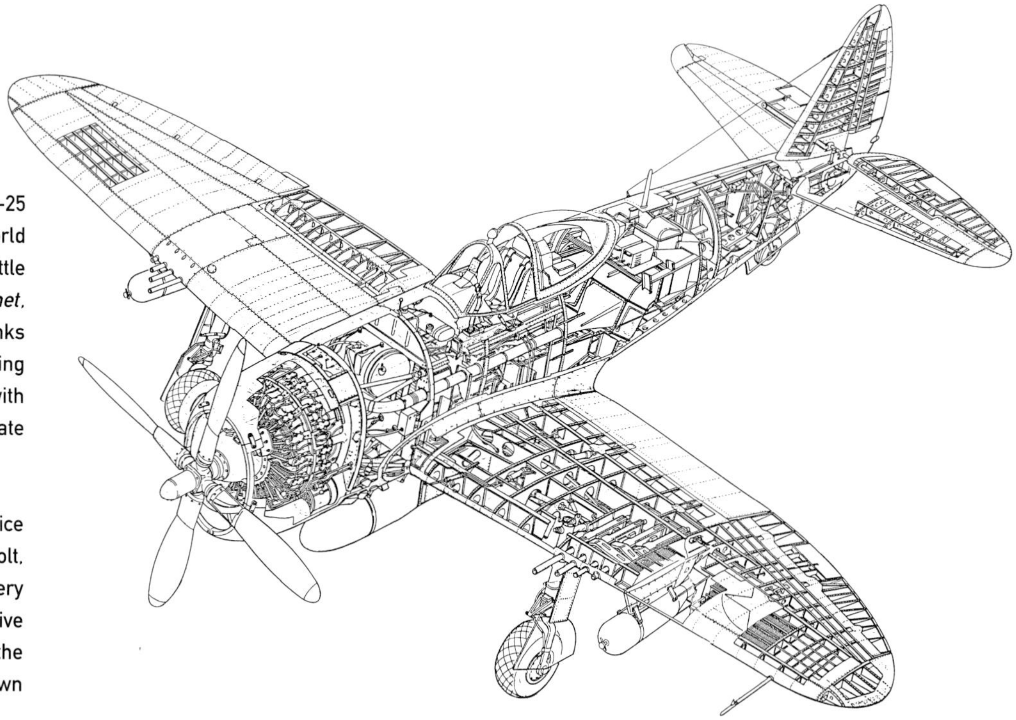

BELOW The heaviest single-engined American fighter to see service in World War II was the magnificent Republic P-47 Thunderbolt, which secured excellent performance through the use of a very potent turbocharged engine. The variant seen here is the definitive P-47D, in which the framed canopy and "razorback" turtledeck of the earlier variants was replaced by a "bubble" canopy and cut-down rear fuselage to provide the pilot with superior fields of vision.

When German planes began employing a similar system, the Allies responded with chaff—specially sized strips of metal foil, which were dropped in the millions to reflect the German radar beams and so cause a totally confused picture. By 1943 British bombers could destroy Hamburg and turn their attention to the Battle of Berlin in a series of 16 great raids launched against the German capital in the winter of 1943 and spring of 1944.

America also had some catching up to do, once it entered the war in December 1941. Most of 1942 was spent building up the U.S. air forces in England, but from the summer B-17 Flying Fortress and Consolidated B-24 Liberator heavy bombers started daylight probes into northern Europe. Convinced that the quickest and surest way to defeat Germany was to destroy its factories and other point targets in its war-making capabilities, the Americans flew in great three-dimensional "box" formations. Their bombers could thus cover each other with their many trainable heavy machine guns, and thus ensure that enough bombers got through to destroy small but vital targets with accurate bombing using optical bomb sights. The U.S. forces initially enjoyed some successes. Then, in August 1943, the 8th AAF launched its first raid deep into Germany. Warned by radar of the American build-up over the English Channel, the Germans scrambled large numbers of fighters to attack the bomber formations, which were cruising at high altitude and leaving highly visible vapor trails. The fighters found the bombers en route to Schweinfurt, the target, and there followed a running battle. American bombers suffered crippling losses. A second attempt in October proved even more disastrous and deep penetration raids were temporarily halted.

The problem was that the bombers lacked the weight and concentration of defensive fire to beat cannon-armed fighters. They needed long-range escort fighters to protect them, and these were not available until the end of the year. At the time, the 8th AAF's fighter squadrons were equipped with the single-engined Republic P-47 Thunderbolt, which was later to gain an enviable reputation as a heavy attack fighter, and the twin-engined Lockheed P-38 Lightning, which was too large and heavy to dogfight with single-engined fighters. There was also an increasing number of North American P-51 Mustang fighters, but these were of the early American-engined variants that offered their best performance only at low altitude. Moreover, none of the American fighters had sufficient range to escort the heavy bombers deep into Europe.

The first key new American plane to emerge in response was the Mustang. Designed to a British specification and produced in prototype form over a period of just 117 days, the Mustang was a departure from standard radial-engine design in being pow-

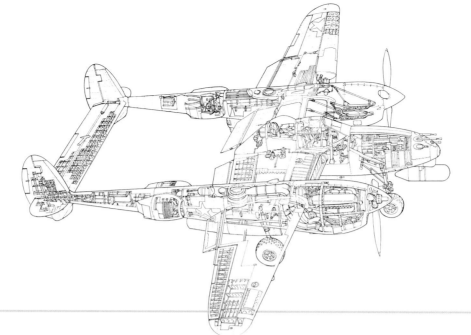

ABOVE The design of the P-38 single-seat fighter, whose success transformed Lockheed from the small-scale manufacturer of advanced twin-engined transports into a major defense contractor, was intended to provide very high performance through the use of a twin-engined turbocharged powerplant as well as concentrated firepower by the grouping of the fixed forward-firing armament in the nose of the central nacelle that otherwise carried only the pilot.

BELOW Designed by North American Aviation to meet a British requirement, the P-51 Mustang was almost certainly the finest all-round fighter of World War II. This magnificent cutaway illustration reveals the major structural and armament features of the definitive P-51D with a clear-view canopy and the Packard V-1650 American-made version of the Rolls-Royce Merlin, the most important British-designed engine of World War II.

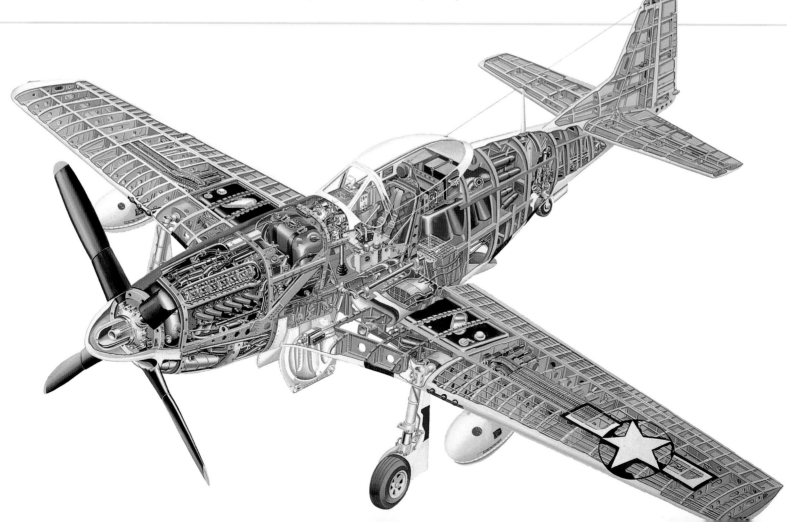

ered by a V-12 engine. With the British Merlin engine, the Mustang became perhaps the best fighter of the war. Armed with six 0.5-in (12.7-mm) machine guns and able to use drop tanks to supplement its considerable internal fuel, the Mustang had excellent range and, once the drop tanks had been released, a combination of superb performance and agility that allowed it to dogfight on equal terms with the best of the opposing German fighters. The Americans now had a fighter that could escort bombers as far as Berlin and back, and from December 1943 the 8th AAF ranged deep into Europe with ever-increasing success.

The booms that supported the tail unit of the Lockheed P-38 Lightning each carried, from front to rear, one of the two Allison V-1710 engines, one of the two rearward-retracting single-wheel main landing gear units under an upper-surface turbocharger, and an engine coolant radiator based on two lateral units.

This success could be measured not only in the number of targets attacked and destroyed by the bombers, but also in the swelling total of German fighters dispatched to oblivion by the escort fighters.

Only in the closing stages of World War II did the radical new advance to jet power see the light of day. By 1943 both the British and Germans had experimental combat jets in the air. Not only were they fast, but they allowed the designer to do away with the large, vibrating piston engine in the nose of fighters, giving the pilot a much better field of vision and simplifying the task of installing a heavy battery of forward-firing cannon. By 1944 Germany had the Messerschmitt Me 262 twin-jet fighter and Arado Ar 234 twin-jet bomber in service.

These were both greatly superior to Allied aircraft, but tactical misuse, shortages of fuel and of top-class pilots, and a variety of teething problems meant that the few German jets produced could do little more than startle the Allies. The only Allied jet fighter to see service was the Gloster Meteor, which was rushed into service in time to help defeat the V-1 flying bomb menace and enter the fray over northwest Europe.

Before the jet engine reached a fully practical stage, however, several superb piston-engined fighters were developed as the last generation of such aircraft. They all possessed a maximum speed in the order of 475 mph (765 km/h). British versions included the Supermarine Spiteful, Hawker Fury, and de Havilland Hornet; the

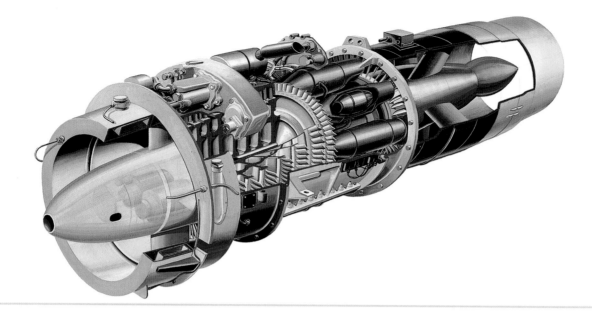

ABOVE Junkers began work on the development of gas turbine engines in 1936, but the finalization of its first design, the Jumo 109-006 axial-flow engine that first ran in the fall of 1938, was then transferred to Heinkel. Thus the first Junkers turbojet to make it into the air purely as a Junkers effort was another but more conservative axial-flow unit, the 109-004A turbojet that first ran in November 1940 and was developed into the production-standard Jumo 004B for the Messerschmitt Me 262 twin-engined fighter and Arado Ar 234 twin-engined bomber.

BELOW Much delayed by engine development problems and political difficulties, the Messerschmitt Me 262 single-seat fighter entered service with the German air force in June 1944 as the world's first turbojet-powered operational warplane. The Me 262's British counterpart was the Gloster Meteor that entered service less than one month later, but the German machine was in every respect a superior type.

Americans had the Republic XP-47J Thunderbolt and North American P-82 Twin Mustang; the most highly developed German contender was the Focke-Wulf Ta 152. None of these aircraft saw full-scale service.

The Pacific war witnessed a similar turnaround, with Axis air superiority giving way to new Allied planes. At first, on a one-for-one basis, Japanese aircraft were more agile than their Allied counterparts, especially in the first year of the war. Although a number of Japanese fighters had only machine guns for armament, the redoubtable Mitsubishi A6M Reisen also had cannon, and this enabled it to decimate more limited Allied fighters such as the U.S. Navy's Brewster F2A Buffalo and Grumman F4F Wildcat as well as the U.S. Army's Bell P-39 Airacobra and P-40. New planes, along with a swelling number of aircraft carriers that created mobile "airfields" all over the Pacific, gave the Americans air superiority from mid-1942 onward.

Another twin-turbojet warplane that entered German service in the middle of 1944, in this instance during the month of July, was the Arado Ar 234 Blitz (lightning). The first two series were the Ar 234B-1 and -2, dedicated to the reconnaissance and bomber roles respectively, and these would have been followed in 1945 by the much-enhanced Ar 234C with the powerplant upgraded to four BMW 003 turbojet units.

ABOVE Though designed for carrierborne service with the U.S. Navy, the Vought F4U Corsair was initially deemed to possess unsuitable flight deck characteristics and was used as a land-based type by the U.S. Marine Corps until the British proved its feasibility for flight deck use. The Corsair was the most powerful naval fighter at the time of its introduction in 1943, and was also destined to become the last piston-engined fighter to remain in American production. The example illustrated here is an F4U-1D fighter-bomber with attachments under the fuselage for two 1,000-lb (454-kg) bombs or two drop tanks, and under the outer wing panels for eight 5-in (127-mm) rockets.

BELOW The Mitsubishi Ki-21 was part of the imperial Japanese army air force's first-line strength throughout World War II after entering service in 1941. The Japanese classified the type as a medium bomber, whereas the Allies would have regarded it as little more than a light bomber. Thus a seven-man crew was required for the delivery of only a modest bomb load, although the crew complement did allow the incorporation of a defensive armament that was adequate by the standards of 1942 but soon fell well below the requirement for effective defense against ever more capable American fighters. The Allies knew the Ki-21 as the "Sally."

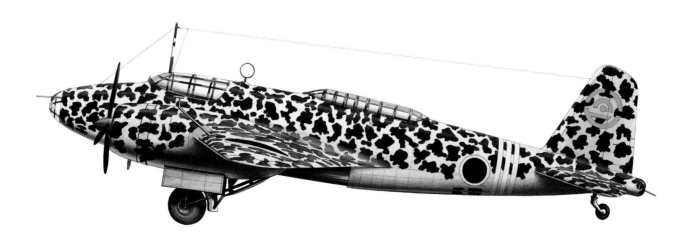

ABOVE The first airplane with retractable main landing-gear units to enter car- rierborne service with the imperial Japanese navy, the Nakajima B5N was known to the Allies as the "Kate." The B5N and the Aichi D3A "Val" dive bomber were the two types of Japanese attack warplanes involved during December 1941 in the attack on Pearl Harbor, where the "Kate" operated as a torpedo bomber and level bomber.

BELOW The "Emily," as the Allies knew the Kawanishi H8K, was perhaps the finest long-range patrol bomber flying boat to see service with any of the combatants in World War II. The H8K possessed very good performance, adequate offensive armament, very potent defensive armament, and, somewhat unusually in Japanese aircraft of the period, good passive defensive features such as armor and protection for the fuel tanks.

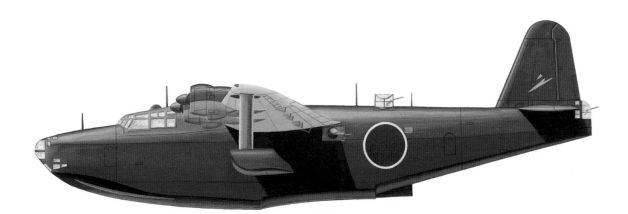

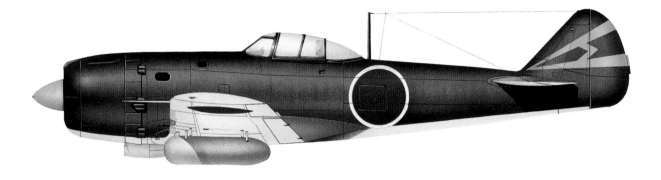

ABOVE Based conceptually on the Ki-43 Hayabusa (peregrine falcon) known to the Allies as the "Oscar," the Nakajima Ki-84 Hayate (gale) was known to the Allies as the "Frank." Entering service in 1944 as a land-based warplane, the Ki-84 was one of the best fighters and fighter-bombers fielded by the imperial Japanese army in the later stages of World War II, for it was fast, agile, and, by Japanese standards, sturdily built and well-protected.

BELOW The *Enola Gay* was the Boeing B-29 Superfortress heavy bomber that dropped the first A-bomb on the Japanese city of Hiroshima on August 6, 1945. The bomber's flight deck reveals the state of the aeronautical art in the latter stages of World War II. The accommodation was pressurized for comfort in high-altitude, long-range flight, and this very extensively glazed forward compartment carried the bombardier in the extreme nose, the pilot and copilot side by side behind and slightly above the bombardier, and then the flight engineer, radio operator, and navigator in its rear portion. A tunnel over the weapons bays linked this forward compartment with the midships compartment for the gunners who remotely controlled the power-operated machine-gun barbettes (two above and two below the fuselage). The tail gunner occupied a separate pressurized tail position.

The Japanese wanted agility and range above outright performance in their warplanes, but in general these possessed adequate performance and became increasingly well-armed. By comparison with those of the Allied nations, however, Japanese aircraft lacked sufficient structural strength, self-sealing fuel tanks, and pilot protection. At first the A6M fighter, twin-engined Mitsubishi G4M "Betty" bomber, single-engined Aichi D3A "Val" dive bomber, and single-engined Nakajima B5N "Kate" torpedo bomber dominated the Pacific and eastern Asia, supported over land by the single-engined Nakajima Ki-43 "Oscar" fighter, twin-engined Kawasaki Ki-48 "Lily" bomber, and twin-engined Mitsubishi Ki-21 "Sally" bomber. By 1942 the Spitfire and American F4F had begun to shift the balance. The 1943 Grumman F6F Hellcat fighter marked a new American dominance. The Japanese never produced a suitably powerful radial engine. Moreover, American heavy bombing had begun to cripple Japanese industry, and once the submarine fleet had destroyed most of Japan's tankers, there were no ships left to bring crude oil from the East Indies in large enough quantities.

It was the Pacific war that finally proved that strategic bombing had arrived. On August 6 and 9, 1945, B-29 bombers dropped single atomic bombs on the Japanese cities of Hiroshima and Nagasaki, where the truly terrible devastation finally persuaded Japan that the war had to be ended without further delay. Just a few bombers with this devastating weapon could destroy a nation. Air power was now supreme.

THE JET AGE

An airplane that still excites controversy for its initial development with a downward-firing ejection seat and the commercial skullduggery that helped to secure the commitment of a group of four European nations to large-scale procurement, of the F-104G multirole development, the Lockheed F-104 Starfighter was often called the "manned missile" for its long, cylindrical fuselage and tiny, essentially straight and very thin flying surfaces. The two machines nearest the camera are the pair of XF-104A prototypes pictured against a Lockheed T-33 two-seat trainer being used as a chase plane.

4

The jet engines produced at the tail end of World War II would quickly come to dominate all forms of flight, both civil and military. The postwar era also saw a jet-powered revival of the swaggering heroism of World War I aces. Fighter pilots were back at the center of military aviation, and "the right stuff" was required for any of them to outduel his enemies. Famous flyers from Chuck Yeager to Robin Olds would be celebrated in books and movies.

INITIAL HURDLES

It took several years, however, before the engineering challenges of turbojets were fully ironed out. One key limitation was fuel consumption. One of the turbojet's great advantages is that it will run on a fuel as simple and inexpensive as kerosene, but the early turbojet's consumption was enormous. Air arms wanting to introduce turbojet-powered aircraft faced a considerable dilemma. The U.S. Navy, for example, had long worked on the principle that its aircraft carriers should operate warplanes qualitatively equal to land-based aircraft they might fight, and decided in the middle of World War II to start funding the development of turbojet-powered aircraft for carrierborne employment. Aircraft carriers frequently operate at long distance from their targets. This requires their aircraft to have long ranges. The U.S. Navy thus resorted to the odd combination of a hybrid power-plant. This was first used in the Ryan FR Fireball, a carrierborne fighter that allowed the U.S. Navy's carrier air groups to gain experience with turbojet-powered flight. The hybrid powerplant comprised an economical radial engine in the nose for long-range cruising and a turbojet in the tail for the power boost needed for high performance in combat and enhanced takeoff capability.

Similar ideas were tried over the next few years. In the 1950s the British Saunders-Roe SR.53 combined a turbojet and a liquid-propellant rocket. The turbojet's specific fuel consumption had been improved, and a rocket motor was added to provide a major boost in climb rate, ceiling, and maximum combat speed. The fighter could now cruise on its turbojet but use the extra power of the rocket engine for high performance in combat and at high altitudes. These ideas were tested extensively in the 1950s and 1960s, but few hybrid powerplant designs ever went into production. One notable exception was the French Dassault Mirage III, whose early models had a rocket booster pack under the rear fuselage.

Increased power was causing difficulties for designers even before the turbojet had been widely accepted. The last generation of piston engines, which included the Rolls-Royce Griffin V-12, Pratt & Whitney R-4360 Wasp Major 28-cylinder radial, and Wright R-3350 Duplex Cyclone 18-cylinder radial units, each produced more than 2,500 hp (1,864 kW). To absorb this tremendous power, designers had to fit propellers with four or five blades, or even a pair of three- or four-blade coaxial propellers turning in opposite directions so that the torque reaction of each unit counteracted that of the other.

Aerodynamicists were also discovering that at high speeds the air approaching and hitting the airplane's wings and fuselage was being compressed around the leading edges of the wing and other airflow entry areas. Compression resulted in shock waves causing considerable turbulence and drag, leading in turn to extreme buffeting that could cause structural failure. The Germans solved the problem. They swept the wings back out of the line of the shock wave. The Messerschmitt Me 262 twin-turbojet fighter that entered service in 1944 had a top speed of 540 mph (870 km/h) and a slightly swept wing.

The Germans also had made great strides researching high-speed flight for both manned aircraft and missiles. After the war the Soviets and Americans made every effort to apply German research and recruit German engineers and theoreticians. Yet even with the German research, there was still much to be discovered before aircraft would be capable of approaching and then breaking the so-called "sound barrier." The United States and U.S.S.R. took a quick lead in devoting a large proportion of their research effort to high-speed flight and soon emerged with some formidable combat aircraft and impressive research types. Yet while they were absorbing German engine technology, most of the world's military powers used British turbojet engines, either imported or built under license.

The first American swept-wing fighter to enter service, in the course of 1949, was the North American F-86 Sabre. This possessed very good performance and generally viceless handling characteristics, and was the instrument with which the U.S. Air Force gained long-lasting and almost total air superiority over the communist fighters in the Korean War of the early 1950s.

EARLY JET PLANES

The world's first turbojet-powered aircraft marked the emergence of a technology that was to transform military and then civil aviation. Yet the transition period was inevitably marked by a measure of hesitation, for aircraft designers and the authorities funding their designs were skeptical of combining something as novel as the turbojet engine with a new type of airframe that might present aerodynamic or structural difficulties. The designers were also concerned about the limited capabilities of the first generation of turbojet engines, for these were of limited power, had suspect reliability, and possessed a prodigious thirst for fuel. The first jet fighters developed by the Allies were the Gloster Meteor in the United Kingdom and the Bell P-59 Airacomet in the United States, based on "piston-engine thinking" with a single piston engine replaced by two turbojet units to provide adequate power and reliability. The Ryan FR Fireball was even more of a hybrid, for it combined both a turbojet and a piston engine in an effort to secure power, reliability, and range. The twin-boom de Havilland Vampire and flying wing D.H.108 were attempts to reduce friction-generated power loss and aerodynamic drag respectively, and as such were notably successful in performance terms.

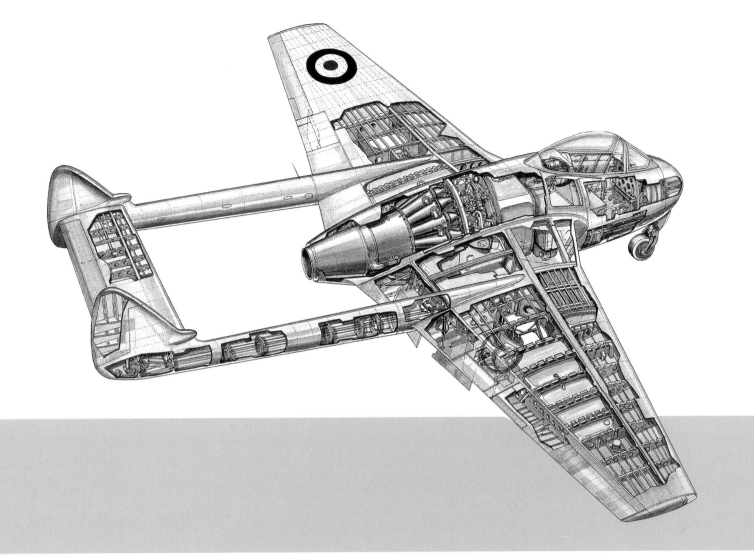

FACING PAGE Although Bell, under contract to by U.S. Army, led the American way to the "sound barrier" with its air-launched and rocket-powered X-1, this company was soon rivaled by Douglas, under U.S. Navy contract, with the more practical D-558 Skystreak. The D-558-1 first flew in May 1947 with straight flying surfaces, retractable tricycle landing gear, and the powerplant of one Allison J35 turbojet drawing its air through a circular nose inlet, and as such was more typical of the high subsonic warplanes that the United States was trying to develop. On August 20, 1947, the D-558-1 raised the world air speed record to 640.74 mph (1,031.18 km/h), and only five days later boosted this to 650.91 mph (1,047.54 km/h). The other D-558 design was the rocket-powered D-558-2 with swept flying surfaces and altogether more advanced capability.

ABOVE In the United Kingdom de Havilland was dedicated to the idea of extracting as much performance as possible from its aircraft by reducing weight and drag, and this was evident in the design of the Vampire turbojet-powered fighter with a mixed structure of metal and plywood/balsa/plywood sandwich material. Initially known as the Spider Crab and first flown in September 1943, the Vampire was based on a central nacelle carrying the armament, pilot's cockpit, and centrifugal-flow engine. The D.H. 100 design was specially chosen to remove the need for a long and weighty jetpipe, with all its attendant friction losses to the thrust, and meant that the tail unit had to be carried by slender booms.

EARLY JET PLANES

FACING PAGE TOP LEFT The United States' first jet-powered fighter was the Bell P-59 Airacomet, seen here in the form of one of three XP-59A prototypes. The Airacomet was little more than the standard type of straight-winged fighter, typical of the period late in World War II, with power provided by two General Electric I-A turbojet engines in the angle between the wing roots and the lower fuselage. The Airacomet possessed only indifferent performance, and was used only for development work and the familiarization of pilots with jet-powered handling.

FACING PAGE TOP RIGHT The turbojet offered fighters a virtually quantum leap in speed capability from the time of this engine's introduction, but this was only at the expense of very high fuel consumption and slow response to the throttle. This was unacceptable for a carrierborne fighter, and the U.S. Navy therefore entered the jet-powered age with a hybrid type built only in small numbers. This was the Ryan FR-1 Fireball, which had a standard radial engine in the nose for reliability at takeoff and landing as well as fuel efficiency in the cruise, and also a turbojet in the tail for boosted power under adverse conditions and in combat.

FACING PAGE BOTTOM The Gloster Meteor entered service in July 1944 as the second turbojet-engined fighter to enter service anywhere in the world, and was powered by a pair of Rolls-Royce engines in nacelles on its large and essentially straight wing. The aerodynamic concept embodied in the Meteor was not as advanced as that in the Messerschmitt Me 262, but the type served the British well over a long period of development, production, and service as a fighter, night fighter, trainer, and reconnaissance airplane.

ABOVE De Havilland went two steps further than the Vampire it its D.H.108, often known as the Swallow: This did away with the booms and tail unit and introduced modest sweep in the wing and centerline fin-and-rudder unit. The D.H.108 was created for investigation of the handling characteristics of the swept wing for the planned D.H.106 Comet turbojet-powered airliner, and one of the three aircraft may have been the first in the world to exceed Mach 1 in June 1946, but the airplane broke up in the air during this flight and therefore no confirmation was possible.

SWEPT-WING WARRIORS

In 1947 North America produced one of aviation history's classic fighters, and this succeeded largely because it incorporated the results of German research. The F-86 Sabre was the West's first swept-wing fighter. The Sabre's lines looked just right and, despite its lack of a suitably powerful engine, it was transonic (on or about the speed of sound) in level flight and marginally subsonic in a shallow dive. A year later it was in service with the newly independent branch of the U.S. armed forces, the U.S. Air Force. Far more advanced than other Western planes, 10,000 Sabres would eventually see the light of day. Yet the Sabre had been preceded by what would become its greatest foe, the Soviet Mikoyan-Gurevich MiG-15 "Fagot." Although not as neat as the Sabre, the MiG-15 fully incorporated German as well as Soviet research and featured swept flying surfaces. Like most Soviet aircraft of the 1930s and 1940s, the MiG-15 was crude in finish and equipment, but was rugged and an excellent performer in the air.

Although the MiG-15 had entered widespread production and service use as early as 1948, the Soviets had been more than normally secretive about their new fighter's performance. American pilots were completely startled when they first encountered the MiG-15 after the outbreak of the Korean War in 1950. The success of the MiG-15 persuaded the U.S. Air Force to deploy the Sabre, yet pilots soon discovered that the Sabre was marginally inferior in overall combat terms to the MiG-15. One lesson of the jet age soon emerged: Good pilots are worth more than good technology. The American pilots' superior training enabled them to turn the tables entirely on their Soviet opponents. They learned, however, that the standard battery of 0.5-in (12.7-mm) machine guns was inadequate for high-speed fighter combat. While pitted against the MiG-15, for example, many of the better American pilots discarded their radar gun sights, thereby removing a frequent cause of technical failure and saving weight.

By the early 1950s, the development cost of new aircraft had risen so sharply that governments and manufacturers alike were determined to exploit existing designs for all they were worth. In the West the basic airframe and engine were rarely altered; avionics (aviation electronics), on the other hand, was constantly improving. The F-86D Sabre featured an advanced avionics package that provided an all-weather capability and also enabled the fighter to engage targets automatically after the pilot had selected his objective. Once locked on to the target, the F-86D's radar and computer instructed the pilot

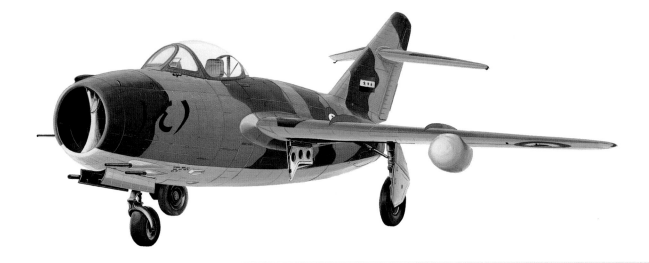

ABOVE The Mikoyan-Gurevich MiG-15 was the U.S.S.R.'s counterpart to the F-86 Sabre, and in some respects was the better fighter. In air combat over Korea, however, the much superior flying skills of the Sabre pilots predominated and allowed the USAF to attain an eleven-to-one kill/loss rate.

BELOW With the Convair FY "Pogostick," the Lockheed FV "Salmon" of 1954 was an ambitious effort to provide the U.S. Navy with a fighter able to operate from small ships as a result of its vertical takeoff and landing capability. The XFV-1 prototype was based on a cruciform arrangement of tail surfaces with small castoring wheels at their tips, was controlled by a pilot in a gimbaled seat, and was powered by a turboprop engine driving a large contra-rotating propeller unit that provided vertical thrust for takeoff and landing. The engine was very troublesome and the practicality of the configuration was very suspect, so development of the FV and FY was cancelled.

In the period following the end of World War II, Bell and Douglas were the companies that took the lead in developing research aircraft to approach and then break the "sound barrier." But it was North American and Republic that played the key roles in providing the U.S. Army Air Forces, and then from 1947 the U.S. Air Force, with transonic and finally supersonic warplanes. The service's initial fighter with genuinely supersonic performance was North American's F-100 Super Sabre, which was also the first of a series of impressive "century series" of supersonic fighters.

about course and speed until the target was in range; the computer/radar complex then extended the retractable rocket pack under the nose, fired the requisite weapons at the target, and retracted the pack.

From the Korean War until the late 1960s, the U.S. Air Force preferred a primary armament of missiles. At first these were unguided rockets rather than true guided missiles and were fired at the target in salvoes in the case of the 2.75-in (70-mm) caliber FFAR (Folding-Fin Air Rocket) series, or individually in the case of the MB-1 Genie with its command-detonated nuclear warhead. Developed in the early 1950s, guided missiles with heat-seeking IR (Infra-Red) or radar guidance were in common service by the late 1950s.

Another improvement introduced on the F-86D was the use of afterburning. Afterburning produces more thrust for little extra weight and complexity, but considerably higher fuel consumption. Even with afterburning and a fully developed engine, however, the Sabre was limited by its aerodynamic layout to transonic speeds. The first American fully supersonic flight plane came next. With wings of increased sweep and reduced thickness/chord ratio and a beautifully streamlined fuselage, the F-100 Super Sabre was the first of the U.S. Air Force's "century" series of supersonic fighters. It entered service in 1954.

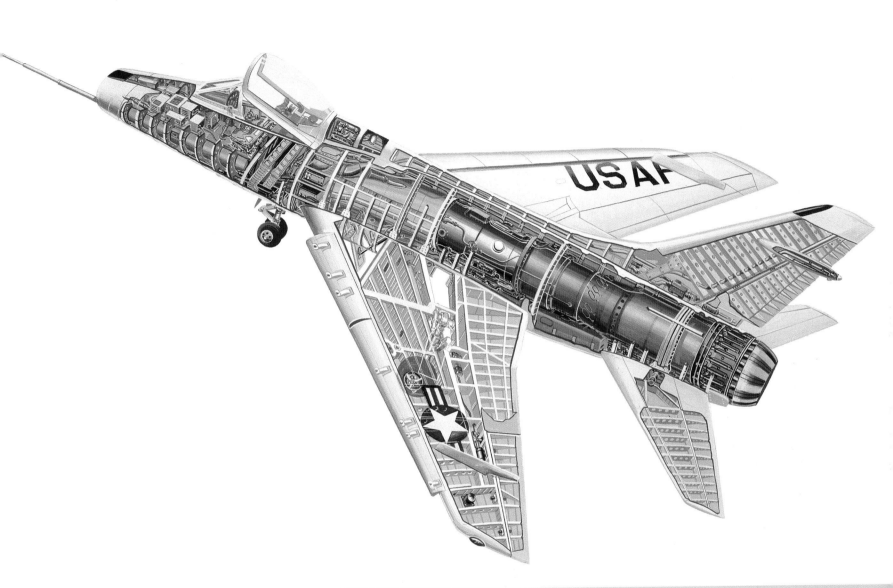

North American followed its F-86 Sabre with the F-100 Super Sabre, characterized by more sharply swept flying surfaces and a more powerful afterburning
turbojet. The F-100 entered service late in 1953 as the world's first warplane with
genuinely supersonic performance.

CHUCK YEAGER

CHARLES E. "CHUCK" YEAGER (1923–) Born on February 13, 1923, Charles Elwood "Chuck" Yeager grew up in Myra, West Virginia, and enlisted in the U.S. Army Air Corps after graduating from Hamlin High School in 1941. He was initially a mechanic who disliked flying after being sick during his first flight. Facing the prospect of better pay and conditions as a pilot, however, Yeager applied for flight training. He was accepted, and his excellent coordination, mechanical skills, and memory all proved useful. After qualifying as a pilot, Yeager was assigned to the 363rd Fighter Squadron (357th Fighter Group),

Two of the "exhibits" in any aviation hall of fame have to be Charles "Chuck" Yeager and the Bell X-1 *Glamorous Glennis*. This was the combination that on October 14, 1947, achieved the world's first officially recognized supersonic flight when they reached Mach 1.015 at an altitude of 42,000 ft (12,800 m).

flying the Bell P-39 Airacobra fighter. Yeager remained with the squadron as it moved from Tonopah, Nevada, to Casper, Wyoming. On October 23, 1943, after the engine of his Airacobra had blown up, Yeager took to his parachute but suffered a fractured spine. He recovered and was with the 357th FG when it left the United States for Europe in the winter of 1943–44, equipped with the new North American P-51 Mustang. Yeager shot down his first Messerschmitt Bf 109 on only his seventh mission, flown on March 4, 1944, but on the following day he was caught by three Focke-Wulf Fw 190 fighters and, in turn, shot down. Yeager managed to avoid capture, and French resistance forces helped him to escape into Spain and eventual repatriation.

Although the operational procedures of the time ordained that escaped pilots should not return to combat duty, in case they were shot down again, captured, and somehow induced to talk about the resistance, Yeager appealed the matter all the way up to General Dwight D. Eisenhower, who said that he would try to have the rule overturned. Meanwhile his group commander allowed Yeager to fly training missions, and during one of these he caught and shot down a Junkers Ju 88, giving the credit to another pilot. In the summer of 1944 it was decided that Yeager could return to combat. Flying a P-51D and promoted from sergeant to lieutenant, Yeager at first found little "trade." He became an "ace" on October 12: Leading an escort for bombers attacking Bremen, Yeager closed in on a Bf 109 whose pilot broke sharply and collided with his wingman, both the Bf 109s crashing, while Yeager went on to shoot down another three German fighters.

In the later part of 1944 Yeager caught a Messerschmitt Me 262 jet fighter as it was coming in to land, and he shot it down. Yeager flew his last mission on January 14, 1945, ending with 11.5 victories. In February he got married, and in July Yeager was posted to the test establishment at Muroc Field (later Edwards AFB), California, the location of the testing of the Bell XS-1 (soon X-1) rocket-powered research airplane designed to reach and then break the "sound barrier." The pilot chosen for the attempt on October 14, 1947, was Yeager. Dropped from a Boeing B-29 Superfortress motherplane at 25,000 ft (7,620 m), the X-1 *Glamorous Glennis* (named for Yeager's wife) dropped clear, and Yeager ignited the rocket motor. The X-1 soared to a height of 42,000 ft (12,800 m) and a speed of 670 mph (1,078 km/h) or Mach 1.015. Yeager had become the first man to be credited with exceeding the speed of sound.

Because of his superb skill as a pilot, his cool performance under dangerous conditions, and his technical ability to see, analyze, and solve problems, Yeager was selected to fly later experimental aircraft, including the Bell X-1A and Douglas X-3. Yeager was also involved in the testing and evaluation of aircraft being considered for service with the U.S. Air Force and, when possible, examples of aircraft against which these new machines might have to fight. In 1953, for example, Yeager flew a Mikoyan-Gurevich MiG-15 jet fighter in which a North Korean pilot had defected. In the period between 1947 and 1954 he regularly logged more than 100 hours per month in the air, and in one month alone flew 27 different types of aircraft.

During October 1954 Yeager became commander of the 417th Fighter Squadron in Germany and then in France. On his return to the United States in September 1957, he commanded the 1st Fighter Squadron at George AFB, California, and later became director of the Aerospace Research Pilot School at Edwards AFB. He suffered bad burns when forced to bail out of a Lockheed NF-104 Starfighter that got out of control and doused him with burning rocket fuel as he ejected. In 1966 Yeager went to South Vietnam as commander of the 405th Fighter Wing, flying 127 combat missions. In February 1968 Yeager became commander of the 4th Tactical Fighter Wing at Seymour Johnson AFB, North Carolina, and during February 1968 led the move of this wing to South Korea after North Korean forces had seized the intelligence-gathering vessel USS *Pueblo*. During July 1969 Yeager was appointed vice commander of the 17th Air Force with its HQ at Ramstein AB, Germany. After 34 years with the USAAF and USAF, Yeager retired in March 1975 in the rank of brigadier general after accumulating more than 10,000 hours in the air and flying more than 330 types of aircraft.

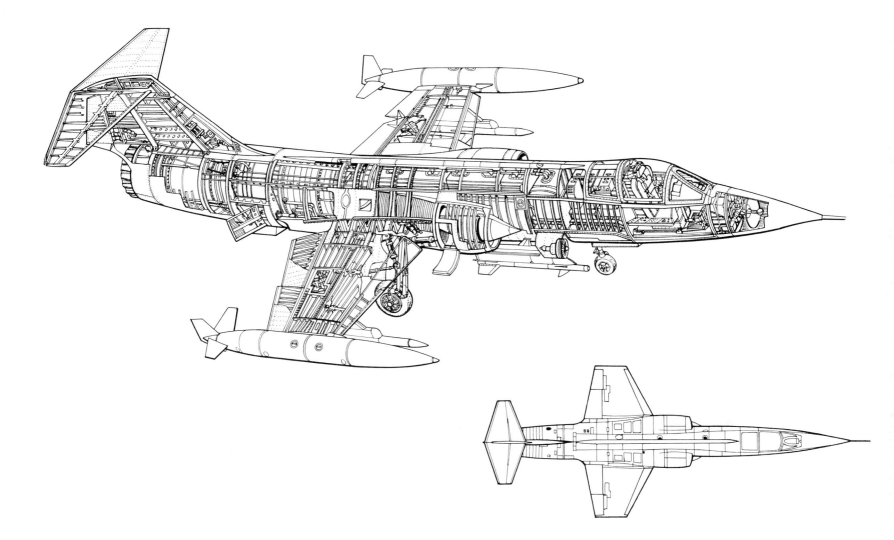

Entering service in January 1958, the Lockheed F-104 Starfighter was sometimes called the "missile with a man in it" as its large cylindrical fuselage and small but basically straight flying surfaces bore more than a passing resemblance to those of a missile. The Starfighter was designed for the interception role and for its time possessed excellent climb performance as well as a maximum speed, for the first time in an operational type, of more than Mach 2. The type was also the first airplane ever to hold the world speed and altitude records simultaneously.

Lockheed was also well aware of the limitations suffered by the current straight-winged F-80 and improved F-94 Starfire fighters. The company now also produced a thoroughly supersonic fighter. The design concept was radically different from the Super Sabre. Rather than use a high sweep angle, the Lockheed design team opted for an extraordinary layout that made its fighter, the F-104 Starfighter, resemble a missile.

Soviet avionics were markedly inferior to those of the United States or even the European nations during the 1950s. Like their counterparts, they also did little to change the basic designs of their planes. There was a marked similarity between the MiG-15 and the MiG-17 "Fresco." A much-improved powerplant was installed, producing major improvements in handling and performance. Roughly contemporary with later models of the F-86, the MiG-17 performed better than its rivals, but was not met in combat by its Western contemporaries. The MiG-17 was later passed to a number of Soviet allies and clients, including North Vietnam and many Arab states. The North Vietnamese used the type with some success against the American "century" series fighters in the early part of the Vietnam War; the fighter's agility and heavy firepower were effective in turning fights.

Just one year after the appearance of the MiG-17, the Mikoyan-Gurevich design bureau produced its MiG-19 "Farmer." This was the first Soviet fighter capable of super-sonic performance in level flight, and in most respects it was equal if not superior to the F-100. The MiG-19 featured a more refined design than the MiG-17, with improved aero-dynamics and a much-improved powerplant. The U.S.S.R. had also begun to catch up with advanced avionics, and the MiG-19 appeared in a number of models with different avion-ics packages for a variety of roles including limited all-weather interception with radar and up to four primitive air-to-air missiles. Like the F-100, the MiG-19 enjoyed a long operational career. While the F-100 was soon switched from the pure fighter to a tactical fighter role, the MiG-19 generally retained its pure fighter role. Even after it had been superseded in the U.S.S.R. by more advanced fighters, the MiG-19 was still a mainstay of most Soviet allies, clients, and satellites.

By the mid-1960s Western analysts thought the MiG-19 obsolescent. Events in the Vietnam War and the Arab-Israeli Wars of 1967 and 1973 showed otherwise. The heavy cannon armament and light wing loading made the MiG-19 an excellent air-combat fighter at high subsonic speeds, a factor important up until the mid-1990s.

In the early 1950s an American company, Republic, responded to the MiG-19 with the F-84F Thunderstreak. Its swept surfaces improved performance at minimal cost, but the Thunderstreak was at best only an interim type, despite a long and distinguished career as a fighter-bomber and reconnaissance airplane with the U.S. Air Force and several allied nations.

BEYOND THE SPEED OF SOUND

To create a truly supersonic type, Republic adopted highly swept flying surfaces, a sleek fuselage, and a powerful turbojet with full afterburning. First flown in 1955, the F-105 Thunderchief became one of the classic USAF aircraft of the period after World War II. Although categorized as a fighter, the Thunderchief was really a strike/attack warplane with high supersonic performance and an internal weapons bay to supplement the so-called hardpoints under the wing.

By the late 1950s, their powerful engines and advanced aerodynamic features made it possible for multirole fighters to carry on offensive load far greater than could be stowed inside the airframe, even if it had been possible to locate a weapons bay among the masses of avionics equipment scattered through the fuselage. Pioneered during World War II, streamlined pylons under the wings and fuselage could accept an ever-widening assortment of stores (equipment as well as weapons).

During this period the Europeans had been advancing more slowly than the Americans and Soviets. World War II had devastated Europe, and of the major aeronautical powers before World War II only the United Kingdom and France were in any position to create advanced combat aircraft. Yet the British government had ceded Cold War leadership to the United States, and with finance in short supply, accorded a low priority to the development of new warplanes. In France the work of reconstruction after World War II took top priority. Despite a number of interesting experiments, the French focused primarily on combat aircraft selected for basic serviceability rather than high-performance or advanced designs.

The limitations of the Meteor and Vampire as front-line fighters became obvious to the British in the Korean War, but they were ill-prepared to do anything about them. In 1954, even as several supersonic types were being introduced in the United States and U.S.S.R., two swept-wing but only transonic British fighters entered service after prolonged development. The first of these was the Supermarine Swift, whose production program was curtailed as a result of the type's severe aerodynamic problems, and the second was the Hawker Hunter, perhaps the best transonic fighter and ground-support aircraft of its kind. With clean lines, excellent handling characteristics, and a good load-carrying capacity, the Hunter was built in greater numbers than any other postwar British airplane and remained in first-line service with several smaller air forces into the early twenty-first century.

In the period after World War II, French fighters were produced almost exclusively by the firm set up in 1945 by Marcel Bloch. Returning from Germany, where he had been incarcerated during the war, he changed his surname to Dassault and created the company bearing his new name. It became the biggest military aircraft manufacturer in France. The first Dassault turbojet-powered fighter was the Ouragan (Hurricane), which was built in moderate numbers for the French and Indian air forces before being replaced by the more advanced swept-wing Mystère. The Mystère was built both for the home market and for export and was the first French aircraft to exceed the speed of sound in a shallow dive. With its more streamlined fuselage, a Rolls-Royce Avon axial-flow afterburning turbojet, and a thin wing, it proved a first-class fighter.

In the mid-1950s several NATO forces became interested in the idea of a lightweight fighter that would be cheaper than the current generation of aircraft, offer high performance with smaller engines than those used in the heavyweight U.S. fighters, and provide the tactical advantage of being able to use grass or semiprepared airstrips, rather than NATO's vulnerable concrete runways. Several very interesting designs appeared, including the minuscule Gnat built by the Folland company in the United Kingdom, the Taon (Horsefly) from Breguet in France, and, winning the design competition for a modest production run, the G91 from Fiat (later Aeritalia, later Alenia) in Italy.

Dassault produced two designs, the conventional-looking Etendard (Battle Standard) and the delta-winged Mirage. Both of these had started life as small, lightweight fighters with a pair of low-powered turbojet engines. Initial trials revealed that the designs would realize their full potential only if they were scaled up and powered by a single large turbojet. The results were the Etendard IV transonic carrierborne attack fighter and the Mirage III, Europe's second Mach 2 fighter to enter service.

The first Mach 2 European fighter was the English Electric (later British Aircraft Corporation, then British Aerospace) Lightning. It reached service in 1960 after a 13-year development period in which a supersonic research airplane had been turned into a phenomenally fast-climbing but short-ranged interceptor. Adopted in 1961, the Mirage III came six years after the first flight of the Mirage I lightweight prototype. The Mirage III has been the most successful European combat airplane since World War II and has formed the basis of a large number of advanced and high-performance combat aircraft. Essentially a scaled-up Mirage III, the Mirage IV was a Mach 2 bomber for the delivery of France's atomic bomb; the Mirage 5 was designed to an Israeli requirement as a simplified clear-weather version of the Mirage III for use as a ground-attack fighter but later upgraded in most cases to Mirage III standards or higher as miniaturized avionics became available; and the Mirage F1 was designed as a multimission fighter and attack airplane based on the Mirage III's fuselage but with new swept wing and tailplane.

Israel was concerned that delivery of its Mirage 5 force might be delayed by Arab political and economic pressure on France, and set in hand a program of indigenous but wholly unlicensed production and further development of the Mirage III. This foresight paid handsome dividends when delivery of the Mirage 5 was embargoed rather than just delayed, and Israel Aircraft Industries was able to respond with its Nesher (Eagle) version of the Mirage III as work continued on the much-upgraded Kfir (Lion Cub) derivative with an American turbojet and an advanced suite of Israeli avionics. Israel used its Mirage III warplanes to stunning effect in the 1967 Six-Day War, and introduced the Nesher in time for the Yom Kippur War of 1973. Surplus Nesher aircraft were later exported to Argentina with the name Dagger, and were used against the British during the latter's successful 1982 campaign to retake the Falkland Islands.

In Israel, further development of the Kfir produced the Kfir-C2 with canard horizontal foreplanes to supplement the surfaces on the trailing edge of the rear-mounted wing as a means of improving field performance and enhancing maneuverability in air combat. Israel has continued to develop this useful type in variants with more refined aerodynamics, greater power from a "tweaked" engine, and most important of all, much more sophisticated electronics in single- and two-seat variants. Many exported Mirage III and Mirage 5 warplanes have been upgraded to a comparable standard. South Africa, similarly, produced the Atlas Cheetah by rebuilding French aircraft delivered before the imposition of a United Nations embargo of arms supplies to that apartheid regime.

Fearing that France might be unwilling to make further deliveries of the Dassault Mirage III and 5 aircraft it had ordered in the 1960s, Israel decided to manufacture the type indigenously without a license. Further development of this Nesher saw the introduction of more advanced Israeli electronics and the American J79 turbojet engine to create the much improved Kfir, and then the addition of canard foreplanes to enhance agility in what thus became the Kfir-C2 (illustrated) and then the upgraded Kfir-C7 and Kfir-C10. Aircraft surplus to Israeli requirements have been exported to Colombia, Ecuador, and Sri Lanka.

JACKS OF ALL TRADES

Smaller combat aircraft have had to accomplish a wide range of tasks in modern warfare. Up to about the middle of World War II, it was possible to build a combat airplane for one specific role, but development costs soon became prohibitively high for any nation other than the two superpowers. The result: multirole aircraft.

Each role demands its own electronics package and specialized weapons, but this has actually eased the designers' task. As long as the electronics packages for the all-weather interception, reconnaissance, and ground-attack roles can all fit into the same fuselage, the basic airplane can be used in a number of roles. Reduced to its simplest terms, the designer's task from the mid-1950s onward has generally been the creation of a warplane capable of high performance at all altitudes and in all conditions, but with the ability to carry a heavy offensive load on its exterior combined with sufficient internal volume for accommodation of the relevant avionics. Although simple in concept, such design is vastly complex in practice, and has been made still more complicated by the realization that missiles have some disadvantages in combat. Internally mounted guns, with all their bulky ammunition and fire-control radars, quickly returned to fighter design.

Advanced combat aircraft are so expensive that the economies of the United Kingdom and France were severely strained by the development and production of machines such as the Lightning and Mirage. Other European countries, apart from Sweden, could not match this expenditure, and bought aircraft from one of the main producers or concentrated on less-advanced types with limited

Although designed for operation by just one man, the pilot who occupied a cockpit above the forward fuselage with excellent fields of vision, the Douglas AD Skyraider carrier-borne attack warplane was a formidable machine with a very powerful engine. In 1962 the type was redesignated as the A-1, and could carry a massive and very diverse load of drop stores under its fuselage and wing, and the fuselage was large enough to allow development of the type in multicrew electronic warfare and airborne early warning variants, and also as a carrier onboard delivery airplane with seating for up to twelve passengers.

Two of the piston-engined warplanes that were still of vital importance to the carrierborne efforts of the U.S. Navy and U.S. Marine Corps in the Korean War during the early 1950s were the Vought F4U Corsair fighter-bomber (foreground) and Douglas AD Skyraider (middle distance), with a Sikorsky planeguard helicopter in the background.

Grumman developed the F-14 Tomcat for service from 1972 as a carrierborne long-range fleet defense fighter using much of the technology that had been developed for the unsuccessful F-111B naval version of the General Dynamics F-111 tactical fighter. These inherited features included the wing's variable-sweep system, the powerplant, and the weapons system (radar fire-control system and Hughes AIM-54 long-range air-to-air missile). The result, seen here in its F-14A initial production version, offers unrivaled capabilities, including the ability to destroy aerial targets at ranges of more than 115 miles (185 km).

capabilities. Italy transformed its two most important turbojet-powered trainers into useful but limited light attack types: the single-seat attack version of the Aeromacchi MB-326, and the two-seat MB-339. Such machines have been and still are sold to Third World nations as primary combat aircraft, while providing only a secondary attack capability for the home air forces.

The USAF's modern combat aircraft designed between the late 1940s and late 1950s, ranging from the F-86 Sabre to the Convair F-102 Delta Dagger and F-106 Delta Dart interceptors, were impressive. The Navy, meanwhile, produced one truly superlative type, the McDonnell (later McDonnell Douglas) F-4 Phantom II multirole fighter (later adopted by the USAF). By 1960 the Phantom II was clearly the best all-round American warplane since World War II. Conceived initially as a carrierborne attack type, the Phantom II was then recast as a two-seat carrierborne fleet defense fighter, the first machine of its type able to complete an entire interception mission without support from surface ships. It eventually matured into strike, attack, close support, electronic pathfinder, defense suppression, and reconnaissance variants. The Phantom II is still in limited service.

The main strength of the U.S. Navy's air arm immediately after World War II rested with piston-engined warplanes such as the Grumman F8F Bearcat fighter, the Vought F4U Corsair fighter and fighter-bomber, and the Douglas AD Skyraider attack bomber, the last of which was operational in Vietnam into the early 1970s. Interim turbojet-powered types were under development, however, and by the early 1950s the U.S. Navy and U.S. Marine Corps had accepted a number of new aircraft such as the Grumman F9F fighter (in its straight-winged Panther and swept-wing Cougar forms), the McDonnell F2H Banshee and F3H Demon fighters, and the Douglas F3D Skyknight all-weather fighter. Later in the decade two other Douglas aircraft, the A3D Skywarrior attack bomber and A4D Skyhawk light attack airplane, appeared, and then the U.S. Navy moved into the supersonic age with the Vought F8U Crusader fighter, whose configuration was later scaled down to create the LTV A-7 Corsair II strike and attack warplane.

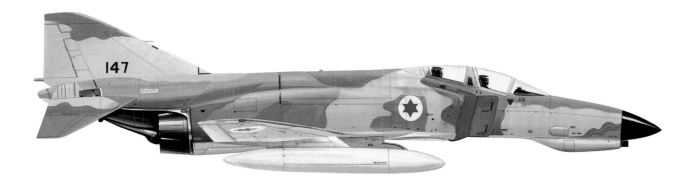

The fighter whose role the F-14 assumed was the McDonnell Douglas (originally McDonnell) F-4 Phantom II, the first carrierborne fighter able to undertake the whole air-defense mission, from target detection to destruction, without support from the electronics of its parent carrier. Entering service in 1961 and eventually built in larger numbers than any other Western warplane since World War II, the Phantom II was one of the most important warplanes of the Vietnam War, and was so capable that the U.S. Air Force took large numbers of aircraft optimized for the land-based role.

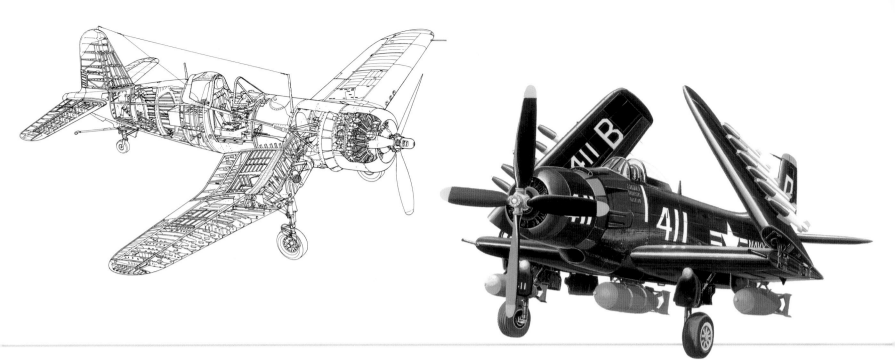

ABOVE LEFT The Vought F4U Corsair fighter-bomber and the AU, its dedicated attack derivative, may be regarded as definitive exemplars of the piston-engined fighter of World War II. The basic configuration and structural medium were cantilever monoplane and aluminum alloy respectively, and the incorporation of an inverted-gull wing layout allowed the optimum 90° junction of the wing root and fuselage and the use of shorter and therefore lighter main landing gear legs without sacrifice of the adequate propeller clearance required for safe takeoff and landing.

ABOVE RIGHT The Douglas Skyraider piston-engined attack warplane was developed in the last stages of World War II and entered service in December 1946 as the AD. The Skyraider proved itself immensely capable and versatile, saw land-based as well as carrierborne service, and enjoyed a career so long that its later variants were redesignated in the A-1 series after the 1962 rationalization of the U.S. services' separate designation systems into a single system. The machine illustrated here in the markings of the U.S. Navy's VA-194 squadron is an AD-4.

BELOW Created by the team that had been responsible for the Skyraider, the Skyhawk was an extraordinary achievement in packing huge capability into a very small airplane. A light attack warplane intended for carrierborne operation, the Skyhawk entered service in October 1956 with the designation A4D and in 1962 became the A-4. As with the Skyraider, the Skyhawk has enjoyed a long and very successful career as a carrierborne and later as a land-based type, and not inconsiderable numbers remain in service into the first part of the twenty-first century.

U.S. JETS OF THE 1960S

Designers in the 1960s combined fixed thinking with radical reevaluation. The fighters of the period had reached a plateau, inasmuch as they were large and heavy aircraft generally powered by two afterburning turbojet engines and possessing a maximum speed of about Mach 2.25. This upper limit was fixed not by any shortage of power but rather by the capabilities of the period's aluminum alloys, which began to lose strength as friction at higher speeds heated the skin. These magnificent aircraft, typified by the McDonnell Douglas F-4 Phantom II multirole fighter and Republic F-105 Thunderchief strike/attack warplane, were extremely expensive to buy and to operate, and were also costly to maintain in terms of money and man hours, largely as a result of their complex electronic and other systems. The OV-10 Bronco was designed by North American (soon to become part of Rockwell) as a light and reliable warplane powered by two small turboprop engines but still offering an effective tactical reconnaissance and attack capability. Altogether more advanced were two Mach 3-plus types, the North American (Rockwell) B-70 Valkyrie strategic bomber and the Lockheed SR-71 "Blackbird" strategic reconnaissance platform. Both were based on advanced aerodynamic and structural thinking, and each was powered by advanced engines to provide massive thrust in combination with a measure of fuel economy so that considerable range could be achieved on internal fuel capacity.

FACING PAGE The idea behind the OV-10 Bronco was to create a light, cheap, yet effective STOL warplane for battlefield roles such as reconnaissance and attack in the hands of the U.S. Marine Corps and U.S. Air Force. Convair and North American (soon to be Rockwell) each developed a contender for the anticipated production order, which went to the North American type as the OV-10A.

TOP North American's program for the B-70 Valkyrie bomber, capable of Mach 3 at high altitude, was extraordinarily ambitious in nearly all of its aspects and looked as though it would result in the warplane the U.S. Air Force had specified. The service then revised its thinking and decided that the high-altitude supersonic bomber would be vulnerable to Soviet defenses. The program was

canceled, and of the two XB-70A prototypes, the first was lost after a midair collision and the second was used for test purposes.

BOTTOM Still the holder of the world's absolute records for aircraft in the sustained-altitude, closed-circuit speed and straight-line speed categories, the last at a figure of 2,193.17 mph (3,529.56 km/h) set in July 1976, the Lockheed SR-71A was a phenomenal strategic reconnaissance airplane until its final retirement in 1998. The type was based on the airframe of the A-12, operated in very limited numbers by the CIA but then developed into both the M-12 for the carriage of a ramjet-powered reconnaissance drone and also the F-12 Mach 3 interceptor with advanced radar and missiles. The F-12 paved the way for the magnificent SR-71.

All these aircraft operated in Vietnam, and constant updating kept them in the forefront of military technology into the later 1970s. More than those of the USAF, perhaps, these U.S. Navy types were resilient and versatile machines, disproving the theory that turbojet-powered aircraft and their avionics would be susceptible to battle damage.

Meanwhile, for Great Britain's Fleet Air Arm (FAA), three swept-wing aircraft were under development by the late 1950s, entering service as the Supermarine Scimitar interceptor and strike fighter, the de Havilland (later Hawker Siddeley) Sea Vixen interceptor, and the Blackburn (later Hawker Siddeley) Buccaneer strike airplane. The Buccaneer was a particularly good machine, yet the Royal Air Force long resisted its blandishments. It was only in the mid-1960s, after the cancellation of a competing program, that the RAF belatedly accepted it; much to its surprise, the RAF found the Buccaneer to be a truly great airplane that was then ordered in larger numbers whose last examples were retired only in 1994.

The U.S.S.R.'s air force moved into the Mach 2 era with the Mikoyan-Gurevich MiG-21 "Fishbed," the successor to the MiG-19. Small and compact for a Mach 2 aircraft, the MiG-21 has a delta wing but conventional, highly swept tail surfaces, and it proved both popular and successful. Lacking the size, weight, and versatility of the Phantom II, the MiG-21 was designed for short-range interception in clear weather conditions. Total production in the U.S.S.R., several Warsaw Pact countries, and India reached more than 6,500 aircraft, and large but unspecified numbers were also produced in China as the J-7 series.

Planned for a clear-weather interception role and first flown in 1955 with comparatively light armament, the MiG-21 evolved into a limited all-weather plane capable of ground attack as well as interception. The MiG-21 family also included several reconnaissance models and three tandem-seat operational conversion trainers, and such was its versatility that during its long production career it was built in many variants.

The nearest Soviet equivalent to the F-105 Thunderchief in the strike and attack role was the family of immensely strong swept-wing aircraft from the Sukhoi design bureau. The first of these was the Su-7 "Fitter" that served with the air arms of many nations in the Soviet sphere of influence. Offering speed comparable to the F-105, the Su-7 was limited by its inability to carry a comparable offensive load and by its shorter range. The Su-7 was in effect a short-range tactical strike and close-support fighter whereas the F-105 was a long-range strike and attack fighter with strategic capabilities.

ABOVE In the United Kingdom de Havilland developed its concept of the twin-boom fighter, first expressed in the Vampire late in World War II, first into the straight-winged Venom fighter-bomber with a single engine, and finally into the swept-wing Sea Vixen carrierborne all-weather fighter warplane with twin engines. The Venom entered service in September 1952 and the Sea Vixen, illustrated here, in July 1959.

BELOW Whereas the MiG-15 (and derived MiG-17) and MiG-19 had been created as the Soviet counterparts to the North American F-86 Sabre and F-100 Super Sabre respectively, the following design from the Mikoyan-Gurevich design bureau had no exact American equivalent at the time. This was the MiG-21, which was planned as a light air-combat fighter with Mach 2 performance and considerable agility, but only short range and limited "developability" into other roles, although modest reconnaissance and ground-attack facilities did appear in later variants. Even so, the MiG-21 was admirably suited to the production capabilities and tactical requirements of the U.S.S.R., and was accordingly built in very large numbers for its parent nation as well as the U.S.S.R.'s satellites and clients.

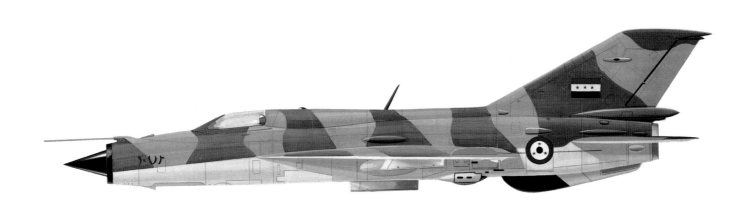

BELOW The 1950s saw a host of very varied attempts to create high-performance warplanes by combining ever more powerful turbojet engines with advanced airframes exploiting any and all aerodynamic as well as structural advances. One result was the Douglas F4D (later F-6) Skyray carrierborne fighter with a modified delta wing. Armed with four 20-mm cannon and able to carry 4,000 lb (1,814 kg) of stores on six hardpoints, the Skyray was just capable of exceeding Mach 1, and is here seen in the form of one of its two XF4D-1 prototypes.

In the 1960s the Soviets worked to improve jet ranges and payloads, succeeding with the 1971 Su-17 "Fitter-C" and revised Su-20 and Su-22 planes. With the outer wing panels in the minimum-sweep position, the Su-17 had much-improved field performance and greater tactical radius, while the sweeping of these panels into the maximum-sweep position yielded speed comparable to that of the Su-7.

It was not only fighters that exercised the capabilities of the world's design teams in this period. With the destruction of Hiroshima and Nagasaki, the strategic bomber had made a lasting impression on the world. The invention of an enormously destructive device such as the "Fat Boy" nuclear bomb dropped on Hiroshima opened the possibility of true strategic air power in the form of just a few aircraft each crewed by fewer than a dozen men. Strategic bombing as the arbiter of war was then made still more terrible by the development of the enormously more powerful fusion or thermonuclear bomb shortly after the end of World War II.

THE RISE AND FALL OF STRATEGIC BOMBERS

It was inevitable that these weapons would dominate military thinking in the late 1940s. Strategists assumed that long-range guided missiles, based on the German V-2 of World War II, would eventually serve as a delivery system for them, but in the short term the only practical solution was the long-range manned bomber and the long-range unmanned bomber, which was really a surface-to-surface missile of the type now called a cruise missile, though then of much larger size than anything in service today. The manned bomber quickly became the single most important type of weapon in the arsenals of the United States, U.S.S.R., and United Kingdom, the only three countries with nuclear weapons in the 1950s.

The only turbojet-powered bomber in service when World War II ended was the Arado Ar 234. The Germans had been experimenting with several other types, most notably the Junkers Ju 287. This extraordinary airplane had a forward-swept wing, with a power-plant comprising four turbojets: two under the wing and two on the sides of the forward fuselage. Fascinating experimental data on the use of forward-swept wings as a means of combating the worst effects of high-speed compression were obtained by the Americans and Soviets, but as yet no warplane with a forward-swept wing has entered production.

By 1946 both superpowers had instituted top-priority programs to develop a strategic bomber capable of carrying nuclear bombs over very long ranges, the Soviet effort signaling that the U.S.S.R. was abandoning its virtually exclusive concentration on tactical air power for a more mixed tactical and strategic approach. The Soviets were starting almost from scratch, since the Petlyakov Pe-8 long-range bomber used in the war years had been only a limited design. Nonetheless, they were hardly ignorant of the problems involved. In the 1930s they had led the world in the production of very large aircraft, and the forced landings of three Boeing B-29 Superfortress bombers in Siberia had given them good examples of the latest Western technology. They started by building the Tupolev Tu-4 "Bull," a reverse-engineered derivative of the Superfortress, and then proceeded apace.

The United Kingdom's main heavy bombers at this time were the well-proved but obsolete Avro Lancaster and the new Avro Lincoln, which was a more heavily armed derivative of the Lancaster with considerably more powerful engines. Worthy as the Lincoln was by the standards of World War II, it was obsolete by the time it entered production. By the end of the 1940s, therefore, the British heavy bomber force was completely obsolete and the United States had to lend the RAF's Bomber Command a number of B-29 bombers.

The United States had become convinced during World War II that it needed a completely new generation of bombers and had already started a large-scale research and development program. At first it relied on the Boeing B-50 under the direction of the newly formed Strategic Air Command. Soon that plane was superseded by one of the oddest and most controversial aircraft of all time, the Convair B-36. The pace of technical development in these years was so fast that the new bomber was almost instantly obsolete in everything but its ability to deliver a very heavy bomb load over intercontinental ranges. Development and procurement of the B-36 nonetheless continued, and the type entered service in the late 1940s. With a wing spanning no less than 230 ft (70.1 m), the huge B-36 was powered by six 3,500-hp (2,610-kW) radial engines buried in the wings, driving pusher propellers located behind the wing's trailing edges. In the B-36D model the six piston engines were supplemented by four turbojets in a pair of two-engine pods under the outer wing panels. This boosted the maximum speed to 435 mph (700 km/h), which was considerably below the figure attainable by current fighters, but was thought to provide adequate survivability as the B-36D also carried the potent defensive armament of six pairs of 20-mm cannon in remotely controlled barbettes.

Among the notable experiments carried out to improve the B-36's combat survivability was the installation of a McDonnell F-85 Goblin fighter, which could be launched from the bomber in flight in order to deal with opposing fighters, before being picked back

ABOVE The B-36 remains the largest bomber that has entered service with the U.S. Air Force, and was designed and developed by Consolidated-Vultee (later Convair) from 1941 to provide the United States with a strategic weapon able to deliver a bomb load of 10,000 lb (4,535 kg) over a radius of 5,000 miles (8,050 km). The type entered service in August 1947 and remained operational to February 1959, and could carry a maximum bomb load of 86,000 lb (39,010 kg). Power was provided in early models by six radial engines driving pusher propellers, but speed and altitude performance was so poor that later models added four turbo-jet engines in two podded pairs under the under wing panels.

BELOW The B-36's defense rested in six barbettes each carrying two 20-mm cannon, but this was considered too little for a bomber of this size and weight, so consideration was given to an extraordinary development. This was the carriage of a small fighter on a trapeze that could be extended below the fuselage to launch the fighter over enemy airspace and then recover it at the end of its defensive sortie. The fighter planned for this role was the McDonnell F-85 Goblin, a true oddity of the air that was so demanding in its handling characteristics that only test pilots could fly this minuscule machine. No production followed trials of the two XF-85 prototypes.

up by the parent bomber. The F-85, of which only two were built, was an extraordinarily compact and ugly little airplane that proved only marginally controllable in the air. Yet its development shows the extremes to which the Americans went in their efforts to capitalize on their possession of the Bomb.

The Americans reasoned that the B-36's successor should be a smaller bomber that would be faster and less detectable by radar. But a smaller airframe meant reduced fuel capacity and therefore less range. New measures were needed to provide the range required for SAC's worldwide strategic mission.

The answer lay in inflight refueling, which had been attempted as early as the 1920s. The British had undertaken a fair amount of experimental work with air-to-air refueling before World War II and had reached a similar conclusion about the need for this procedure for their new generation of bombers. The two nations arrived at different solutions. In the American system, an operator in the tanker airplane "flies" a rigid but telescopic boom, with its own control surfaces, into a receptacle located on the upper surface of the receiving airplane. He (for pilots were all men in those days, something that has fortunately changed of late) then opens the valve that releases fuel down the boom. The British system, on the other hand, is based on a long, flexible hose, with a drogue at its end, trailed from the tanker airplane: Once this has been extended to its full length, the receiving airplane noses its refueling probe into the drogue, completing a fuel-tight lock and initiating the flow of fuel, which is halted when the receiver airplane drops back and breaks the connection. The British system is much simpler than the type adopted by the U.S. Air Force and is better suited to the demands of smaller combat aircraft. It was also adopted by the U.S. Navy and other nations with their own tanker aircraft, notably the U.S.S.R. As inflight refueling became more important for tactical as well as strategic aircraft, the USAF began to see the advantages of the hose-and-drogue system, and the majority of its tankers now operate a dual system with a single flying boom under the rear fuselage and two hose-and-drogue units under the wings.

Tanker aircraft must have a large internal volume in which to carry fuel, and civil transport aircraft have proved ideal for conversion to this exacting role. In the United States the pioneering Boeing KC-97 tanker was derived from the C-97 transport (itself derived from the B-29 bomber). The KC-97 proved air-to-air refueling could be done, but the system really came into its own with the adoption of a turbojet-powered tanker possessing much the same speed capability as the aircraft it was intended to support. The classic machine of this type has been the Boeing KC-135 Stratotanker.

With its sleek lines and powerplant of six turbojet engines, the B-47 Stratojet medium bomber from Boeing offered performance unprecedented in strategic bombers up to the time of its introduction in 1950. Seen here at takeoff with the aid of RATO (Rocket-Assisted Take Off) units in the sides of its fuselage between the wing and the tail unit, the B-47 had wings too thin to carry the main landing gear units, which therefore comprised a pair of twin-wheel trucks that retracted into the lower fuselage in front of and behind the weapons bay.

CURTIS LEMAY

CURTIS E. LEMAY (1906–90) Curtis Emerson LeMay was born in Columbus, Ohio, on November 15, 1906, and was educated in Columbus public schools and Ohio State University. In 1928 LeMay joined the armed forces as a flying cadet. After completing his training as a pilot at Kelly Field, Texas, he received his commission as a second lieutenant in the U.S. Army Air Corps Reserve during October 1929. LeMay received a regular commission in January 1930.

LeMay's first posting as an operational pilot was to the 27th Pursuit Squadron at Selfridge Field, Michigan. He remained a "fighter officer" until transferring to the bomber arm in 1937. Before the United States' entry into World War II, LeMay helped

The man most responsible for the development of the U.S. Air Force's Strategic Air Command was General Curtis E. LeMay. Under LeMay's driving leadership, SAC became a mainstay of the United States' strategic deterrent force, operating both manned bombers and land-based long-range missiles.

to establish air routes over the South Atlantic to Africa and over the North Atlantic to the United Kingdom. In 1942 he organized and trained the 305th Bombardment Group, which he then led to operational service with the 8th Army Air Force in the European theater. LeMay was also responsible for the creation, proving, and dissemination of the procedures for "combat box" formation flying and pattern bombing that became standard for Boeing B-17 Flying Fortress units in the European theater. LeMay then developed the same basic concepts for use by the Boeing B-29 Superfortress units that flew in the Pacific theater.

As commander of the 8th AAF's 3rd Bombardment Division, LeMay led the celebrated but costly raid on Regensberg, a shuttle mission that lifted off from bases in England, attacked a target deep in Germany, and landed in North Africa. In July 1944 LeMay was moved to the Far Eastern theater to command the operations of the 20th Bomber Command's growing B-29 force in the China-Burma-India theater. From January 1944 he led the 21st Bomber Command from his HQ on Guam in the Mariana Islands, until he finally became chief of staff of the Strategic Air Forces in the Pacific. As leader of the 21st Bomber Command, LeMay planned and introduced the low-altitude raids with incendiary bombs that burned out parts of Tokyo and a number of other Japanese cities in an effort to force a surrender before the Allied invasion of Japan planned for the end of that year.

LeMay's first posting after World War II was to the HQ Air Materiel Command, but he then moved to the Pentagon in Washington, D.C., as first deputy chief of air staff for research and development. During October 1947 LeMay was appointed commander of the U.S. Air Forces in Europe, and from his HQ at Wiesbaden, Germany, was instrumental in the successful organization and operation of the Berlin Airlift that kept the city in food and fuel in the face of the 1948 Soviet land blockade. One year later LeMay took command of the new Strategic Air Command with his HQ at Offutt Air Force Base, Nebraska, which rapidly became the hub of control of a worldwide bomber and missile force. LeMay concentrated on the development of SAC as a force based on the latest jet-powered aircraft crewed and maintained by highly professional personnel. LeMay led SAC for almost 10 years.

During July 1957 LeMay became vice chief of staff of the U.S. Air Force. He was named the fifth chief of staff in July 1961. LeMay retired in February 1965, and in 1968 was the vice presidential candidate on the unsuccessful third-party (American Independent) ticket headed by George C. Wallace. He died on October 3, 1990.

As the value of inflight refueling tankers became increasingly clear, other nations started to buy them, generally in the form of surplus Model 707 transports converted to any of several tanker configurations. The United Kingdom and somewhat later the U.S.S.R. (now C.I.S.) had used converted transports and bombers. It is hard to exaggerate the importance of these tankers. Without them most of today's fighting aircraft would be incapable either of flying long missions into enemy territory or of covering the considerable distances between theaters required by modern combat.

The B-36 was replaced from the early 1950s onward by the remarkable Boeing B-47 Stratojet and Boeing B-52 Stratofortress turbojet-powered bombers. The B-47 was a

Entering service with the U.S. Air Force in December 1950, and offering fighter-type performance as well as considerable aerial agility, Boeing's B-47 Stratojet was the first genuinely effective turbojet-powered American strategic bomber, albeit of the medium type with a bomb load of 20,000 lb (9,070 kg).

superbly clean airplane whose swept-wing design was given its final form only after the Americans had digested the implications of German research data captured at the end of World War II. The Stratojet revealed how aerodynamics hitherto applied only to small fighters could be successfully used on a large airplane with its wing swept at 35°. Although it was classified as a medium bomber, its range of 4,000 miles (6,435 km) and maximum speed of 600 mph (965 km/h) made the B-47 far more formidable than the larger and theoretically more devastating B-36. The wings were very thin, but able to support six turbojet engines installed in four pylon-mounted pods under the wings: The two inner pods each carried a side-by-side pair of engines, while the two outer pods each carried a single engine. The wings were so thin that they could not accommodate the main landing-gear units, however, which came in the form of two pairs of wheels in tandem under the fuselage. The weapons bay allowed for a maximum 22,000-lb (9,979-kg) load of nuclear or conventional bombs. The airplane's stability on the ground was provided by small outrigger units that retracted into the inner engine pods. The Stratojet's normal crew comprised only three men arranged in tandem on ejection seats under a fighter-type canopy, although three more were carried in the fuselage of the electronic reconnaissance version.

The Americans followed the Stratojet with the famous and long-lasting B-52 Stratofortress, which entered service with SAC in 1955. The B-52 was based on the B-47 in aerodynamic and structural terms, but it was much more powerful. Its maximum speed was 660 mph (1,060 km/h), its range was 10,000 miles (16,095 km), and its normal bomb load of up to 27,000 lb (12,247 kg) of nuclear weapons could be increased in some models to a maximum of 75,000 lb (34,020 kg) of conventional weapons. Powered by eight engines and fitted with the same sort of landing-gear arrangement as the B-47, the B-52 has proved an enormously versatile strategic bomber. Curtis LeMay ran a fleet of nuclear-bomb-equipped B-52s of which a certain number was always in the air, thanks to constant refueling. It was thought to be the ultimate deterrent. The B-52 was used to devastating effect for conventional tactical bombing in the Vietnam War, the 1991 Gulf War against Iraq, and the 2001–02 campaign against terrorist forces and their local supporters in Afghanistan. Although the B-52 was supplanted in 1986 as SAC's most important strategic bomber by the Rockwell B-1 Lancer, it is still in major service as a conventional bomber and sea-control airplane.

By 1964 the United Kingdom had two primary V-shaped bombers in service. These were the Avro Vulcan, the first large so-called delta-wing airplane to enter service

The B-47 paved the way for the B-52 heavy strategic bomber, which was essentially a much-enlarged airplane with eight more powerful engines to provide greater range as well as a much-increased bomb load of conventional and nuclear bombs, supplemented in later models with two large or smaller numbers of smaller cruise missiles. The B-52 entered service in June 1955 and the final B-52H with turbofan rather than turbojet propulsion is still in very effective service in the first years of the twenty-first century.

anywhere in the world, and the more conventional Handley Page Victor, whose "crescent" flying surfaces featured a sweep angle that gradually reduced from root to tip. The last few Vulcan bombers were rescued from retirement in 1982 to participate in the Falklands campaign, when very long multiple inflight-refueled missions were flown against the runway at Argentine-held Stanley Airport from a forward base on Ascension Island in the South Atlantic. The last Victor tankers were retired only in the mid-1990s when their airframe hours were exhausted by intensive operations in the 1991 UN-led campaign to expel the Iraqi occupiers from Kuwait.

Apart from refueling, the next most urgent challenge to keeping strategic bombers in the air was to avoid interception by missiles or other planes. Initially American planners focused on very high-speed and high-altitude planes as the solution. They also offered the greater range capability that was a key element in the USAF's ability to strike at targets deep in the U.S.S.R. from bases in the continental United States. The Convair B-58 Hustler supersonic bomber, which entered service in 1960, was powered by four podded turbojet engines and capable of 1,385 mph (2,230 km/h) with a service ceiling of 60,000 ft (18,290 m). To keep the Hustler's fuselage as small and as clean as possible in order to minimize drag and maximize speed, the designers opted to locate the fuel for the outward leg of the mission and the weapon load in a streamlined pod. Carried under the fuselage, the pod was to be released over the target, leaving the unencumbered bomber to fly home on its internal fuel.

The Hustler was a fascinating undertaking but was beset by a host of technical problems, and it was superseded in the late 1960s by the General Dynamics F-111, the first major warplane to enter service with a variable-geometry wing. Powered by a pair of advanced turbofan engines, the F-111 had a maximum speed well in excess of Mach 2 and proved itself capable of undertaking the strike, attack, and reconnaissance roles previously performed by a number of different planes. In many respects the F-111 lived up to expectations from the beginning of the program, but rising costs, engine limitations, and airframe weight all caused problems. Nonetheless the F-111, first flown in 1964, proved itself a flexible and hard-hitting warplane.

The variable-geometry concept is basically simple. At low speeds, such as those needed for takeoff and landing, the wings are shifted into their minimum-sweep position to present as much area to the airflow as possible and so bring down the stalling speed; at medium speeds, when the airplane is cruising, the wings are moved to their intermediate-sweep position to secure the optimum combination of low drag with maximum wing area to ensure fuel economy; and for combat or high-speed dashes, the wings are moved to their fully swept position to minimize drag and reduce buffet. The concept offers great advantages in fuel economy and aircraft performance, and became completely accepted in the 1970s.

Similar progress in the design of strategic bombers was achieved in the U.S.S.R. With its most likely opponent clearly the other great superpower, the U.S.S.R. was faced with the problem of how to deliver a greater weight of conventional bombs, or a smaller weight of powerful nuclear weapons, over the long distance separating the U.S.S.R. and United States. The Tu-4 copy of the American B-29 was in service in 1947, less than two years after work on the project began and eloquent testimony to reverse engineering, as Soviet designers had dismantled the American aircraft, produced working drawings of every component, and supervised all the modifications that had to be effected for Soviet production techniques and methods. Metallurgists had to discover what alloys the Americans had used. Soviet manufacturers had to imitate them. And the engineers and planners had to produce entirely new factories and techniques to build a plane markedly different from any of their own. Yet the advantages were colossal: In the B-29 the Soviets found good examples of all the latest American systems, which they could copy and modify quickly.

This treasure trove was quickly exploited in the Tu-16 "Badger," the first Soviet turbojet-powered strategic bomber, which appeared in 1954 and inherited much from Tupolev's continued effort to evolve bombers, transports, and even airliners from the basic Tu-4. The wing of the Tu-16 was well swept, and the two Soviet-designed engines were buried in the wing roots. The Tu-16 was a match for its Western contemporaries in every respect, and more than a match in defensive armament. The Soviet designers had eagerly accepted both the German research into swept wings and the British experience with turbojet engines.

The Tupolev bureau sprang a further surprise in 1955 with the magnificent Tu-95 "Bear" bomber. Powered by four 14,795-hp (11,031-kW) Kuznetsov turboprop engines driving very large contra-rotating propeller units, the Tu-95 was very sleek and had moderately swept flying surfaces. The type had an excellent range of 7,455 miles (12,000 km) and a maximum speed in the order of 560 mph (900 km/h). The Tu-114 civil transport version of the Tu-95 appeared slightly later, and set a number of world range-with-payload records. The Tu-16 remained in service with the Russian air force into the mid-1990s, and the Tu-95 is still in service and has been modernized and upgraded into the Tu-142 for long-range maritime patrol and antisubmarine roles.

ABOVE The General Dynamics F-111 was born of a politically and economically ambitious scheme of the late 1950s to create a multirole tactical fighter with a variable-geometry wing platform for service with the U.S. Air Force and U.S. Navy. Trials revealed that the proposed naval version was too heavy for carrierborne service, and work on the F-111 program was then concentrated on the land-based variant that was produced in the F-111 fighter-bomber and the FB-111 strategic bomber variants. The F-111 matured as a platform offering exceptional capabilities.

To match the B-58 supersonic bomber, the Soviets unveiled the Tu-22 "Blinder" in 1961. This possessed a somewhat unusual appearance as its two engines were located above the tailplane, one on each side of the vertical tail surfaces. The Tu-22, which came as a considerable shock to the West, was capable of Mach 1.5 but was considered deficient in range by the Soviets. Next came a very formidable warplane, the Tu-22M "Backfire" variable-geometry strategic bomber. Capable of Mach 2.3 at high altitude, the "Backfire" can carry large free-fall nuclear weapons or a pair of stand-off missiles.

The cost of bomber and fighter development continued to escalate, putting a major (ultimately fatal) strain on the Soviet Union's finances and causing enormous conflict within domestic American politics. In the 1970s, the Rockwell Corporation developed the B-1 variable-geometry bomber. It offered excellent capabilities, yet steadily improving Soviet surface-to-air missiles made deep-penetration bombers less attractive compared to missiles. The B-1 was therefore canceled by President Carter in its high-supersonic B-1A form, only to be re-instated by President Reagan as the B-1B Lancer with more modest supersonic capability and optimization for a low-level role. The cost per plane approached $500 million.

The concept of the light bomber has declined in importance since 1945, principally because attack fighters can pack almost as great a punch and are considerably cheaper to build and operate. There have, however, been two classic examples of the light bomber in the form of the English Electric Canberra from the United Kingdom and the Ilyushin Il-28 "Beagle" from the U.S.S.R. The Canberra was conceived in 1945 and first flown in 1949, and then entered service with great distinction in many air forces, including that of the United States. Extremely versatile and agile for a twin-engined warplane, the Canberra could outfly most of the fighters current in its heyday and established a number of records. The Il-28 flew two years before the British bomber, and despite its obsolescence is still flown by a few countries within the former Soviet sphere of influence.

The only other country to have produced advanced combat aircraft is Sweden, whose policy of strongly armed neutrality paved the way for the indigenous design and procurement of the highly original and very interesting Saab 35 Draken (dragon) double-delta and Saab 37 Viggen (thunderbolt) canard multirole aircraft, both capable of performance in the region of Mach 2. The success of these two Swedish aircraft, together with that of predecessors such as the Saab 29 "Tunnen" (barrel) and Saab 32 Lansen (lance) should have been an object lesson for the West: Once a decision had been reached on the requirement, no effort was spared in the creation of the right machine to meet the requirement.

THE DOMINANCE OF THE SUPERPOWERS

The vast cost of advanced aircraft programs meant that the only aircraft produced by other nations have been of limited performance. Even the richer European countries reached the stage in the mid-1960s at which collaboration became financially as well as politically attractive. Excellent examples of the trend have been the SEPECAT Jaguar strike, attack, and reconnaissance fighter built by the United Kingdom and France, the Panavia Tornado variable-geometry multirole warplane built by the United Kingdom, Germany and Italy,

The Panavia Tornado was developed in concert by Germany, Italy, and the United Kingdom to provide their air forces with a medium-range nuclear strike and conventional attack interdictor with STOL capability to operate from very short lengths of runway. Key elements of the two-seat design were powerful yet compact afterburning turbofan engines with thrust reversers, a fly-by-wire control system, a variable-geometry wing fitted with extensive high-lift devices, and advanced electronics including a very capable nav/attack system and terrain-following radar to provide a blind first-pass attack facility after penetration of defended airspace at very low level under the enemy's radar coverage.

Created by General Dynamics, now part of Lockheed Martin, the F-16 resulted from a U.S. Air Force initiative to produce a highly agile air combat fighter that was lighter and cheaper than types currently in service, such as the McDonnell Douglas F-4 Phantom II, but not inferior in overall capability. The design of the single-engine and single-seat F-16 sacrificed a small measure of outright per-formance, but more than balanced this in its affordability and excellent air com-bat capabilities. Since its entry into service in 1980, the F-16 has matured as a phenomenally successful multirole fighter that has not been shot down in air combat and has also secured large export as well as domestic orders.

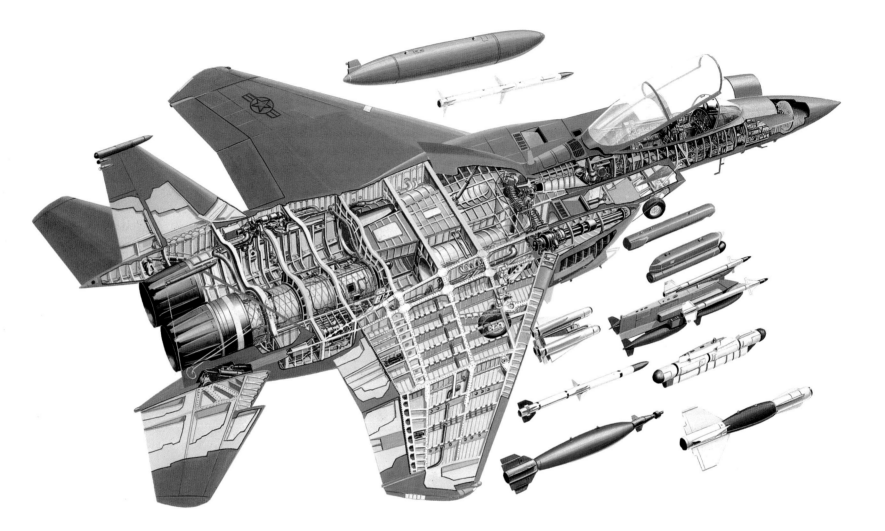

The U.S. Air Force and McDonnell Douglas schemed the F-15 Eagle to succeed the company's F-4 Phantom II as an advanced tactical fighter optimized for the air-superiority role. The F-15 entered service in 1974 and has been produced in significant numbers for the export and domestic markets in both single-seat and combat-capable two-seat forms. The type was upgraded in its later variants with an improved attack capability, and reached its apogee in American service in the two-seat F-15E variant, depicted here, for the dual attack and air-superiority roles.

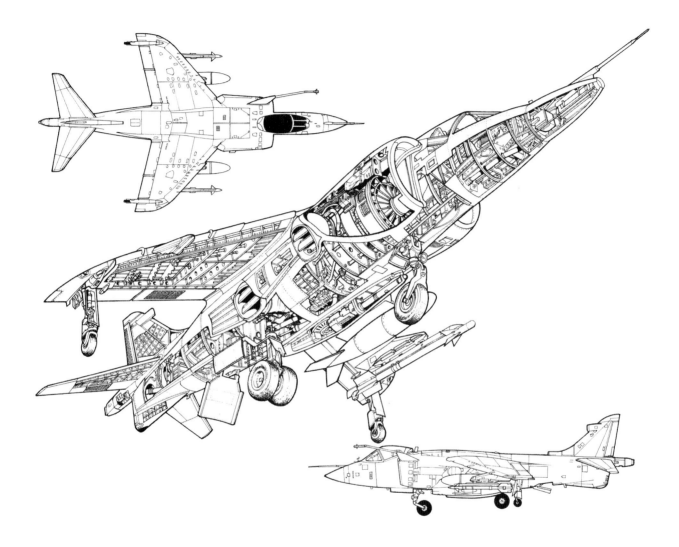

The Harrier was designed by Hawker Siddeley (later part of British Aerospace) on the basis of its Kestrel service test and P.1127 technology demonstration aircraft. As such the Harrier close-support and reconnaissance airplane was the world's first operational warplane with VTOL capability. This was provided by vectoring of the thrust from the Pegasus turbofan engine (cold gas from the compressor for the two forward nozzles and hot exhaust from the jetpipe for the two rear nozzles) to allow the Harrier to operate from any cleared space large enough to accommodate it. The U.S. Marine Corps took a version as the AV-8A. The cutaway illustration reveals the basic land-based Harrier with a laser rangefinder and marked target seeker in the nose. The two line illustrations show the carrierborne Sea Harrier multirole fighter with radar in the nose and a cockpit set higher under a canopy offering better all-round fields of vision.

and the Dassault/Dornier Alpha Jet light attack/trainer airplane built by France and Germany. The Hawker Siddeley (then BAe and now BAE Systems) Harrier vertical takeoff and landing warplane, with its radical arrangement of vectoring jetpipes to deflect the engine's thrust, was possibly the last major type built wholly in the United Kingdom. Collaborative design and manufacturing programs have become increasingly the norm.

During the first half of the 1980s the United Kingdom was actively seeking partners for the collaborative development of the Agile Combat Aircraft technology demonstrator as a vital step along the road to a new European warplane with help from West German and French companies; this effort finally matured as the Eurofighter 2000, now known as the Typhoon.

Today's most current military jets, such as the General Dynamics (now Lockheed Martin) F-16 Fighting Falcon and the McDonnell Douglas (now Boeing) F-15 Eagle for the USAF and the F/A-18 Hornet for the U.S. Navy use computerized avionics for phenomenal control, flight, and weapons accuracy and reliability. They are not necessarily faster than the planes of 10 years ago—indeed, jet fighters have long since exceeded the speed at which dogfights or long, straight bombing runs are practical. Instead, electronics and software have made them ultraresponsive to the pilot's wishes. Yet for all that engines, designs, and technology have accelerated in quality, the value of the pilot has stood out ever more sharply. Great pilots win air wars, not great planes.

ROTARY-WING FLIGHT FROM LEONARDO TO SIKORSKY

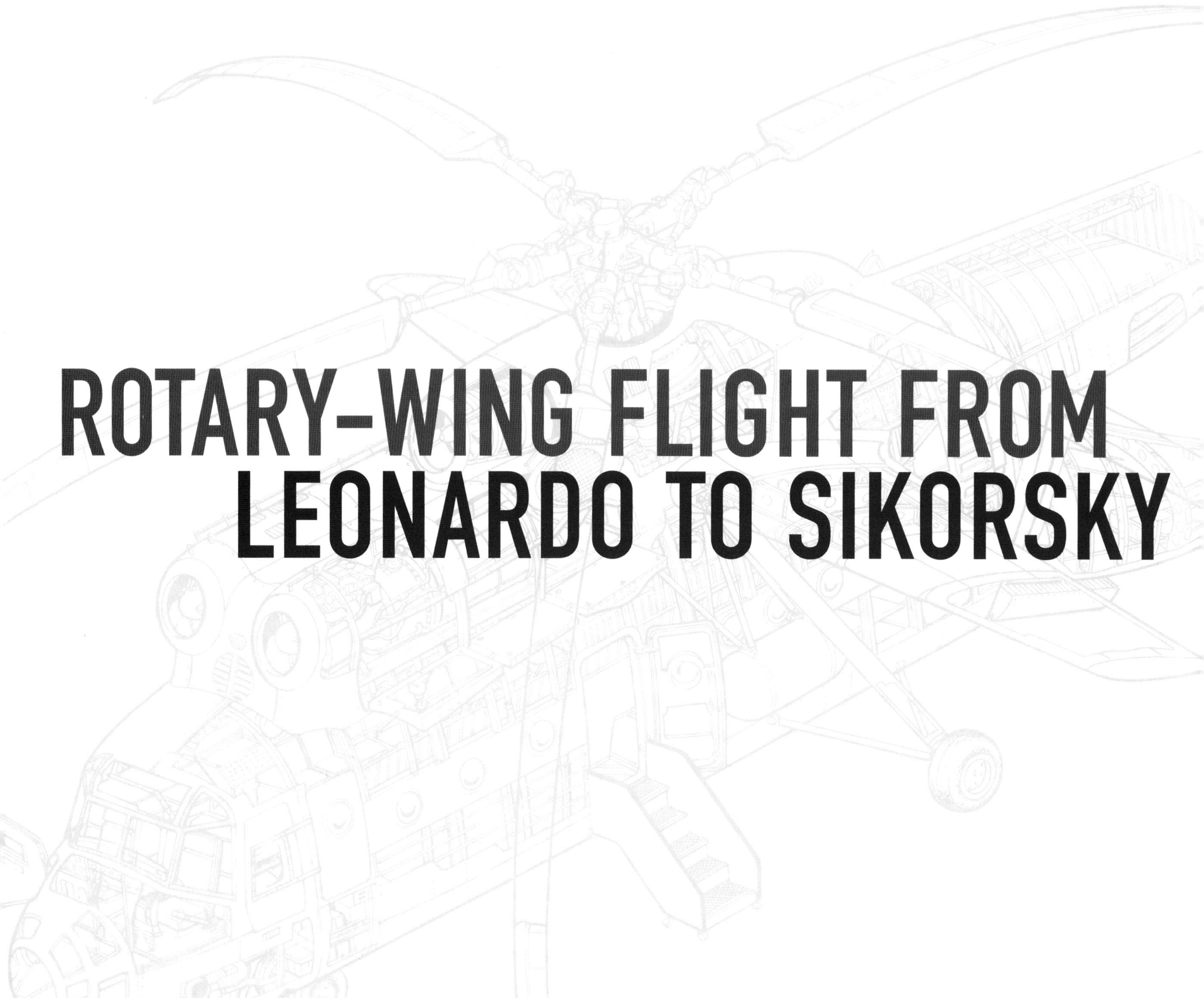

FACING PAGE One of the principal ways of reducing the overall length and weight of a helicopter is the omission of the tail rotor conventionally used to provide torque reaction, but this requires the use of two main rotors rotating in opposite directions. The leading exponent of this concept has been Charles Kaman, whose "take" on the twin-rotor notion was based on a side-by-side pair of rotors whose axes were angled out from each other and whose blades were indexed at ninety degrees to each other to allow safe intermeshing of the two rotor discs. Kaman's first helicopter to receive civil certification, in 1949, was the K-190 that is seen here in crop-dusting form.

A helicopter toy is the first flying machine for which definite evidence survives. It resembled a small windmill with a horizontal four-blade rotor that lifted it into the air when its spindle was rotated by a drawstring. An image dates from about A.D. 1325. In about 1500 Leonardo da Vinci, despite a complete lack of knowledge of aerodynamic and planing lift, designed a helicopter. His drawing reveals a machine that could possibly have risen into the air if built in model form, but the concept was eccentric. Leonardo's design was an airscrew in the literal sense of the word: a helical wing whose rotation would have caused it to "screw" itself up into the air. Realizing that landing might be painful, he also designed wooden shock absorbers that attached to the pilot's legs. Leonardo's and later designs might have been made to work in model form, but would have been completely impractical as full-size machines. Their designers totally ignored the problems of control, especially the torque reaction of the rotor's movement. It is a matter purely of speculation whether Leonardo ever built his machinery, or experimented with it; no accounts survive that provide any evidence.

WRESTLING WITH TORQUE

The helicopter, or rotary-wing airplane, like the fixed-wing airplane, is based on the concept of aerodynamic lift. A conventional airplane is driven forward so that air circulates over and under its wing, generating lift. The helicopter relies on the turning of a rotor to create the flow of air past the rotor blades to create lift.

The notion of the helicopter, especially its ability to take off and land vertically, fascinated men in the centuries after Leonardo's death. This led to the creation of extraordinary and sometimes technically interesting models, but all pioneers lacked two essentials: a true understanding of lift and an engine of adequate power/weight ratio. Sir George Cayley drew up plans for a helicopter, and in 1842 W. H. Phillips produced a fascinating steam-powered model.

It was the invention of the light gasoline engine toward the end of the nineteenth century that allowed rotary-wing flight to progress from models toward full-sized machines. Yet a basic problem of helicopter flight remained: the control of torque reaction to the spinning rotor. As the fuselage-mounted engine powers the rotor's main shaft, and with it the rotor blades, the fuselage tends, by reaction, to rotate in the opposite direction. Engineers saw several ways of overcoming this problem, such as the use of contra-rotating coaxial rotors, counter-rotating rotors on different shafts, or a small propeller mounted vertically at the rear end of the fuselage. They could even suggest a practical means of controlling the helicopter's forward/backward and lateral direction in level flight by cyclic-pitch control, that is, by changing the pitch angle of each blade consecutively (or cyclically).

However, of all the technical problems facing the would-be designers of the first practical helicopters, the most intractable was cyclic pitch. The nature of the problem was first expounded by G. A. Crocco in 1906. When a helicopter lifts vertically in still air, the speed of the airflow over all the rotor's blades is equal, and so too is the lift generated by each blade. But when the helicopter translates into forward flight, the movement of air over any advancing blade is greater than that over any retreating blade, resulting in greater lift on the side of the advancing blade and a tendency to roll in the direction of the retreating blade. The theoretical solution was as just as easily appreciated as the problem: There had to be an automatic system whereby the pitch of each blade was adjusted consecutively (or cyclically) according to its location through each revolution of the rotor. The problem was solved by inserting a flapping hinge connecting each rotor blade to the rotor head. As the rotor increased its speed and generated more lift, the flapping hinge allowed each blade to rise, thereby decreasing its apparent angle of attack and limiting its lift; as it retreated and fell, the flapping hinge allowed each blade to fall, thereby increasing its apparent angle of attack and increasing its lift. Each half of the rotor thereby equalized its lift with that of the other.

By 1912 two French helicopters had left the ground, although neither could be said to have flown in the proper sense of the word as neither possessed cyclic-pitch control or any other means of adopting a given course in the air. The first of these French machines was built by the Breguet brothers, Louis and Jacques, in association with Professor Charles Richet. Powered by a 50-hp (37.3-kW) Antoinette engine, this Breguet-Richet Gyroplane I first rose into the air at Douai on September 29, 1907. Four men, one at each corner, had to steady the craft with long poles. The French pioneer Paul Cornu built the first manned free-flying helicopter. Powered by a 25-hp (18.6-kW) Antoinette engine, his twin-rotor "flying bicycle" helicopter lifted (but only just lifted) its designer into the air on November 13, 1907.

The Breguet brothers were convinced that they had the the right idea and kept on with their efforts. In 1908 they produced a developed form of their first machine, the Breguet-Richet Gyroplane II. On July 22 and September 18 the machine left the ground

ABOVE The Focke-Wulf Fw 61, which made its initial free flight in June 1936, was the world's first technically successful helicopter. Its reliance on a pair of rotors turning in opposite directions at the tips of long outriggers made this an ungainly machine, but the arrangement overcame the problem of torque reaction with a single main rotor.

BELOW There were many and very varied attempts to turn the autogyro into a commercially attractive as well as fully practical flying machine. As one of the Cierva Autogiro Company's licensees, to which the parent company delivered only rotor assemblies, de Havilland created the C.24, which first flew in September 1931, with fully enclosed two-seat accommodation, fixed tricycle landing gear, and a three-blade rotor at the head of a very neat pylon. The rotor was later replaced by a two-blade unit, but no production followed.

at Douai, and was then modified as the Gyroplane IIbis for exhibition in Paris at the end of the year. Test flights with the Gyroplane IIbis were made in April 1909, but the helicopter was destroyed in its hangar by a storm during the following month. The development of the helicopter then effectively ceased until after World War I.

After 1918, several experimental types managed to rise into the air, but none of them achieved anything more than this. Incidence or pitch control was finally achieved by a Spanish pioneer, the Marquis Raoul Pateras de Pescara, who produced a series of helicopters in Spain and France between 1919 and 1925. A far-sighted man whose machines had clearly overcome the main problem of unequal lift, Pescara failed to recognize the need for torque control. Nonetheless the Pescara helicopters showed what could be anticipated once full control had been achieved.

THE FIRST GYROPLANES

The key figure in the development of practical rotorcraft was another Spaniard, Juan de la Cierva. The type of rotorcraft that Cierva invented (and patented as the Autogiro) was not a helicopter at all. It was a gyroplane or, as it later came to be called, an autogyro. In this type of machine, the lifting rotor is unpowered: Lift is generated by the freely windmilling overhead rotor, and a combination of an engine and conventional propeller drive the machine through the air. Most early autogyros had a tractor engine/propeller combination at the front of the airplane-type fuselage, while most later autogyros have used a pusher engine/propeller combination at the rear of a fuselage that also supports the conventional tail unit by means of a boom extending rearward under the propeller. The autogyro depends on forward motion in the air, without which the rotor will slow and the machine will descend.

Cierva wanted to create a heavier-than-air craft that could not be stalled, as had happened in the fatal crash of his first fixed-wing airplane. Cierva's first three Autogiros, built and tested between 1920 and 1922, failed because of their use of inflexible rotor blades. In 1922, however, Cierva built a model with articulated hinges that permitted the blades to flap vertically. When this system was applied to the C.4 in 1923, it was a success. The real beauty of the system lay in its simplicity: The blades moved automatically until the whole rotating system was in equilibrium.

In 1925 Cierva decided to move to the United Kingdom, where he hoped to find a better market for his Autogiro. His later models were more sophisticated, but remained essentially the same as the C.4, operating entirely automatically under the influence of purely aerodynamic forces. Although its success gave helicopter designers a clear indication of what they should be looking for, the Autogiro system could not be used as it stood. The application of power to the rotor prevented the system from operating automatically. Cierva's Autogiros became quite popular with the public as well as the military. For this he was indebted to the exhibitions and test flights undertaken by his two most important supporters, Harold F. Pitcairn in the United States and Captain Frank Courtney in the United Kingdom.

The Autogiro's primary limitation was its inability to take off vertically or to hover in the air. The second factor did not worry Cierva, but he was determined to achieve vertical takeoff. Cierva had already introduced a system for spinning the rotor before takeoff, thus shortening the ground run. A pitch-changing mechanism was incorporated into Autogiros in the late 1920s to supplement the flapping motion in equalizing lift, and finally a clutch device was added in July 1933. The power from the engine at the front of the fuselage was transferred via a series of shafts back through the fuselage and up to the rotor, giving the Autogiro capacity for a "jump start" some 20 ft (6.1 m) straight into the air. The key to rotor spin-up on the ground was the pitch-control mechanism, which kept the rotor blades at zero incidence, preventing them from generating lift until the moment when the clutch was disengaged and the rotor reverted to its natural performance.

The Autogiro was a startling sight in operation and proved very successful at the technical level, continuing in service well into World War II. The British exploited its ability to stay almost in one spot for the calibration of radar equipment, a function that could not readily have been undertaken by conventional aircraft. After the war the autogyro faded into relative obscurity but was rescued in the 1960s by a wave of enthusiasm for miniature types intended only for sporting use.

The key features of the early Autogiro, as revealed in this image of two Pitcairn machines, was the combination of an unpowered rotor on a pylon over the center of gravity position, an air-cooled radial engine driving a tractor propeller, and, in many cases, an auxiliary wing with upturned tips.

The Germans developed an experimental unpowered kite-autogyro, the Focke-Achgelis Fa 330, for possible use as an observation platform for U-boats. It could be dismantled into small units for stowage, and in operation the U-boat would tow the Fa 330 at the end of a wire, thus giving it the necessary forward speed. From behind and above the parent U-boat, the Fa 330's operator could report targets via a telephone wire attached to the towing cable. This ingenious and workable system was not used operationally, however, since it meant the U-boats had to stay on the surface for dangerously prolonged periods.

The Autogiro's success spurred the development of the helicopter. The most important figures in this final stage were Professor Heinrich Focke (one of the parent figures of the Focke-Wulf company), and the Russian-born Igor Sikorsky. Well known before World War I for his giant four-engined aircraft, Sikorsky had produced flying boats and amphibians in the United States ever since he left the Soviet Union in the wake of its 1917 revolution.

Focke was the first to achieve any success when his Fw 61 experimental helicopter went into production. The Fw 61 recorded its maiden flight a year after the first flight of the Breguet-Dorand Gyroplane Laboratoire: It used coaxial twin rotors to overcome the torque reaction factor. Focke was aided by Gerd Achgelis, with whom he had teamed in 1932. Achgelis had been a Focke-Wulf employee and was a superb aerobatic pilot, a useful background for learning to handle a new type of flying machine.

The prototype of the world's first successful helicopter flew on June 26, 1936. Powered by a 160-hp (119-kW) Bramo (Siemens-Halske) Sh. 14A radial engine, the Fw 61 was lifted and propelled by a pair of counter-rotating rotors. The torque reaction of each rotor canceled that of the other and made the machine directionally stable. The Fw 61 set up some impressive world records for helicopters, including a distance of 143 miles (230 km), speed of 76 mph (122 km/h), altitude of 11,243 ft (3,427 m), and endurance of 1 hour 20 minutes 49 seconds. One of the type's main pilots was the celebrated German, Hanna Reitsch, whose helicopter flights included one inside a sports hall.

The Fw 61 was fully controllable and thereby proved that the helicopter could be a practical flying machine, but this was only a prototype and therefore lacked the power/weight ratio that permitted the carriage of any sort of payload. So the designers decided to refine and lighten their basic concept before producing a production model. Four years passed before the Fa 223 Drache (dragon) was ready for production in 1940 for military service. The manufacturing program was hampered by Allied air attacks and only nine Fa 223 helicopters came off the production line in World War II. Another three were assembled after the war from salvaged parts.

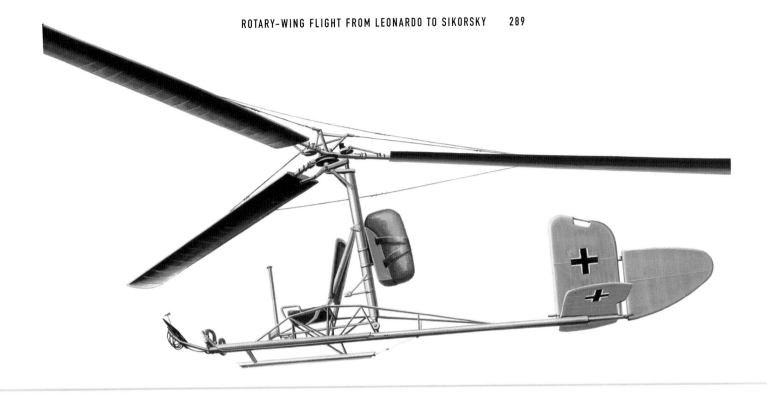

ABOVE The Focke-Achgelis Fa 330 was a German gyro-kite of World War II. The type was designed to be towed behind a surfaced submarine, the pilot's greater altitude giving him a horizon of some 25 miles (40 km) in which to search for targets for the submarine, whose conning tower provided a horizon of only some 5 miles (8 km). In emergencies the pilot jettisoned the rotor, which flew off above the rest of the Fa 330 and drew the pilot's parachute from a pack attached to the rotor mast. Only very limited use was made of the Fa 330.

BELOW The Cornu helicopter was powered by a centrally located 24-hp (18.6 kW) Antoinette engine whose power was translated by belt drives to the fore-and-aft pair of spoked wheels that were the structural cores of the counter-rotating pair of two-blade rotors. In November 1907 this "flying bicycle" became the world's first helicopter to take off vertically and make a free flight while carrying a pilot.

ABOVE With the VS-300 designed by Igor Sikorsky, the single-rotor helicopter finally came of age as a practical flying machine. As such it paved the way for the modern helicopter and reinforced the position of Sikorsky as one of the great pioneers of aviation.

BELOW The Focke-Achgelis Fa 223 was based on the same conceptual thinking as the Fw 61, and saw limited service in World War II.

THE GREAT SIKORSKY

Sikorsky had long been interested in helicopters and other rotorcraft, building two unsuccessful prototypes in 1909 and 1910 even before he left Russia. Yet he did not start the definitive stage of his helicopter work until the 1930s. In 1938, as the engineering manager of the United Aircraft Corporation's Vought-Sikorsky division, he designed the VS-300. Crude in its finish, largely as a result of its uncovered metal-tube fuselage, the VS-300 is the true ancestor of the modern helicopter. With cyclic pitch control as its decisive feature, and powered by a 75-hp (55.9-kW) Lycoming engine, the VS-300 was lifted by a single rotor with a diameter of 28 ft (8.53 m); the reaction to the main rotor's torque was counteracted by a small rotor at the tail.

The VS-300 first flew on September 14, 1939. It made a tethered flight with weights suspended under it for improved stability. It recorded its first free flight on May 13, 1940, as an open-frame fuselage carrying, in addition to the vertical tail rotor, two horizontally rotating tail rotors for improved controllability. In 1940 and 1941 several improvements were incorporated, the cyclic pitch control system was restored, and the configuration of the tail was fixed as a steel-tube pylon rising above the fuselage and carrying a single antitorque rotor. In all of these early forms the VS-300 was underpowered, and in May 1941 Sikorsky improved performance by fitting a 90-hp (67.1-kW) Franklin engine. With this powerplant the VS-300 set a new world helicopter endurance record of 1 hour 32 minutes 26 seconds. Further improvements included the installation of a 150-hp (122-kW) Franklin engine, revised landing gear, and a fully enclosed fuselage, and during 1942 the VS-300 matured as the world's first fully practical single-rotor helicopter.

The most important aspect of the fully developed VS-300 was the cyclic pitch control, perfected by Landgraf and fitted in December 1941. It became the heart of the helicopter in every form. The American Kellett company, which had previously produced autogyros, developed a helicopter with counter-rotating twin rotors, set on angled shafts so that the blades intermeshed, helping to keep the overall "span" down. Friedrich von Doblhoff, an Austrian, made his mark with the first jet-propelled helicopter, the Doblhoff WNF 342. Von Doblhoff introduced the unusual concept of feeding compressed air and fuel into combustion chambers at the tips of the rotor blades, where the vapor mixture was burned to provide thrust. The generation of power at the rotor tips rather than in the fuselage avoided torque problems and made the tail rotor unnecessary. Experimental models with this sort of propulsion have been tested ever since, but despite its clear advantages the type has never really been accepted in a production helicopter, generally as a result of its high fuel consumption.

IGOR SIKORSKY

IGOR SIKORSKY (1889–1972) Igor Ivanovich Sikorsky was born in the Ukrainian city of Kiev in the Russian empire on May 25, 1889. He developed an interest in flight as a boy after he learned of the work of pioneers such as the Wright brothers and Count Ferdinand von Zeppelin. Sikorsky graduated from the Naval College in St. Petersburg, studied engineering at the Kiev Polytechnic Institute and in Paris, and returned to Kiev in 1907. In 1909 Sikorsky went back to France with the intention of learning as much as possible about flight, and once more returned to Kiev, in this instance with a 25-hp (18.6-kW) Anzani engine. This he installed in his first attempt at an airplane, the S-1 helicopter with a pair of coaxial two-blade rotors. It was unsuccessful, as was his S-2 with two three-blade rotors. Sikorsky then turned his attention to fixed-wing flight, and in collaboration with Bylinkin and Iordan designed and built the BIS pusher biplane in April 1910, capable only of short flights.

The S-3 was a slight improvement over the BIS, but could achieve only short nonturning flights. The S-4 was built to order for a Kiev customer but soon crashed. However, the S-5 two-seater was generally successful and proved itself capable of turning under full control: It set Russian records for speed (78 mph, 125 km/h), altitude (1,640 ft, 500 m), and distance (53 miles, 85 km). The S-5a was a twin-float seaplane unrelated to the S-5 but accepted by the Russian navy despite being underpowered. The S-6 was a tractor biplane able to carry two or three passengers, and the S-6a was a revised version of the S-6 with an enclosed rather than open lattice fuselage and the ability to carry four passengers.

The man rightly credited as the father of the "standard" type of helicopter, typified by a single main rotor and a small antitorque rotor at the tail, is Igor Sikorsky.

Sikorsky then became head of the aviation subsidiary of the RBVZ (Russian Baltic Wagon Factory). After a number of new helicopter designs, Sikorsky suffered an engine failure as a result of a blocked carburetor, causing him to switch his attention to multiengined aircraft. The first result of this change was the Ruskii Vitiaz (Russian knight), also called Le Grand, that first flew in March 1913 as the world's largest airplane. The Ruskii Vitiaz was first powered by two 100-hp (74.6-kW) Argus engines, but trials led to the addition of two more engines of the same type, and in this form the airplane carried seven passengers as well as a two-man crew for almost two hours. The fuselage was laid out with an open nose position carrying a searchlight, and a cabin with glazed windows, double doors, a lavatory, camp stools, a sofa, and a table, as well as a railed "promenade deck" above it.

The Bolshevik Revolution of November 1917 persuaded Sikorsky to emigrate, first to France but then to the United States, which he reached in 1919. Unable to find a career in aviation, Sikorsky became a teacher before, in 1923, some students and friends found the capital to establish the Sikorsky Aero Engineering Corporation. The new company's first product was the S-29-A, the letter suffix indicating America, which was a twin-engined all-metal transport that may be seen as a precursor of the modern airliner. There followed a number of other aircraft, of which the most successful was the S-38 twin-engined amphibian flying boat: Pan American Airways used this type to launch its air services to Central and South America. The Sikorsky company later became a subsidiary of the United Aircraft Corporation and continued to concentrate on the flying boat. Yet increasingly Igor Sikorsky's attention became refocused on rotary-wing flight, one of the most problematical kinds of flight and one for which most of the solutions had now been found.

On September 14, 1939, Sikorsky lifted his VS-300 experimental helicopter just a few feet off the ground, and the steadily improving technical success paved the way for the emergence of the helicopter as a major element in Western aviation. These technical developments culminated in the 1943 order for the R-4, which became the world's first helicopter to enter full production. Sikorsky continued to play an important part in the development of the helicopter, and even after his retirement in 1957 continued as an engineering consultant for the company. Sikorsky was at his desk the day before he died on October 26, 1972.

The world's first practical single-rotor helicopter was the Sikorsky VS-300. This is captured by the camera in its intermediate form with its original tail (incorporating a single antitorque rotor on a pylon above the boom) complemented by a pair of outrigger booms each carrying a 6 ft 8 in (2.03 m) rotor turning in the horizontal plane in an attempt to improve lateral control.

LEFT Known colloquially as the Kolibri (hummingbird), the Flettner Fl 282 was potentially the most important and practical helicopter that Germany had under development in World War II. The type had a side-by-side pair of intermeshing rotors driven by a single engine. The Fl 282 proceeded no further than operational trials, however, for the destruction of Germany's aircraft industry and transportation network by Allied bombing severely hindered the plans for large-scale production.

RIGHT Known to the manufacturer as the VS-316A, the Sikorsky R-4 was the definitive development of the VS-300 prototype. The type became the first helicopter to enter full-scale production after it had been accepted for service in 1944, and though of only limited operational value, mainly for the observation and air/sea rescue roles, proved useful for training and for the familiarization of the services with the nature of rotary-wing aircraft.

Once he had resolved the last problems with full cyclic pitch control, Sikorsky forged ahead with a fully developed design, the VS-316A. It was powered by a 165-hp (123-kW) Warner radial engine, the best type of engine for helicopters at this time because of its good power/weight ratio. By the end of World War II the production R-4 was in service with the U.S. Army and U.S. Navy, serving mostly in the Pacific and Burma as an observation platform. Its success was immediately apparent, particularly as a spotter carried on warships.

In 1946 the VS-316A (R-4) was followed by the S-51, which entered service as the R-5. It was the world's first truly practical military helicopter. The new machine could carry up to three passengers in addition to the pilot over a range of more than 250 miles (400 km) at a cruising speed of 85 mph (135 km/h). The R-5 was used for spotting and communications work, and also became celebrated in the Korean War as a rescue type, picking up pilots who had crashed behind enemy lines or into the sea. With its ability to take off and land vertically, the helicopter was also used to ferry seriously wounded soldiers direct from the battlefield areas to hospitals just behind the front, greatly improving their chances of survival.

The Sikorsky S-55 helicopter was the company's first major production type and fully confirmed the fact that the rotary-wing airplane had emerged as a machine offering useful performance and payload. The S-51 was sold on the domestic and export markets in land-based and shipborne variants, and all of the U.S. forces operated the type: To the U.S. Army and Air Force it was the H-19 utility transport, to the U.S. Navy it was the HO4S planeguard and air/sea rescue helicopter, and to the U.S. Marine Corps it was the HRS assault and logistic transport.

Another American pioneer in the field of single-rotor helicopters was the Bell Company. Bell's first production helicopter, derived from the Model 30 prototype that flew in World War II, was the Model 47. On March 8, 1946, this became the world's first helicopter to gain civil certification. Large-scale production had started in 1945, and lasted until the 1980s. The Model 47 proved especially useful in urban areas, because of its small size and because it did not depend upon specially constructed landing sites. New buildings began to feature landing pads on their roofs, and police departments realized that the helicopter, with its slow flying speed and ever-increasing endurance, was ideally suited for traffic surveillance and similar activities. So far as the urban environment is concerned, the helicopter's only major problem is its high noise levels. In the 1950s their smaller engines were relatively quiet and the public was less concerned about the environment than would later be the case. The growing size and therefore the greater weight of helicopters, however, meant the introduction of more powerful and considerably more noisy engines.

Improved control and the introduction of more advanced rotors have allowed the helicopter to carry increasingly heavy payloads and also to undertake a wider variety of tasks. The turboshaft, which has a considerably higher power/weight ratio than the radial piston engine, provided a greater power/weight ratio and improved the helicopter's payload. It also improved fuel economy; the powerplant was smoother-running, with greater reliability, smaller volume, and lighter weight. These last two factors have been particularly important, for they opened the way for the powerplant to be moved from a location inside the fuselage to one above the cabin. This location, closer to the main gearbox and rotor shaft, freed fuselage volume for more payload, and significantly lightened the helicopter's whole dynamic system by removing the need for long transmission shafts connecting any fuselage-mounted engine with the gearbox located at the base of the rotor shaft.

By the 1950s several European companies had entered the arena of helicopter design and manufacture. Bristol, Saunders-Roe, and Westland were early leaders in the United Kingdom. The market leaders in other European nations included Sud-Est (later part of Aérospatiale) in France, Bölkow in Germany, and Agusta in Italy. The Mil design bureau has a virtual stranglehold on the design of land-based helicopters in the U.S.S.R. (now C.I.S.) with some outstanding designs in several categories of medium single-rotor and heavy twin-rotor machines, while the equivalent for naval helicopters has been the Kamov bureau, whose primary capability rests on helicopters of a layout made notably compact, with clear advantages for shipborne deployment, through the use of a coaxial arrangement of two contra-rotating rotors.

The most striking attribute of the helicopter is its versatility, especially after the general introduction of the turboshaft as the standard type of engine for all but the lightest helicopters. Some types of helicopter were built for particular roles, but one of the great advantages of the helicopter is its very great versatility in the tasks it can undertake. While the basic helicopter can be configured for passenger transport on a commercial basis, it can also be adapted for use as an antisubmarine, search-and-rescue or air/sea rescue, and heavy-lift machine. Its versatility offers clear economic advantages. Only in the late 1960s were helicopters streamlined for operations in a hostile environment. The helicopter's success in the Vietnam War combined with new technology and design ideas to foster a growing, but not altogether complete, division between civil and military helicopters.

The U.S.S.R. was the next major country after the United States to produce a helicopter of its own design. The Mil Mi-1 "Hare" entered production in 1948 as a light transport type, but was soon supplanted by the Mi-2 "Hoplite" that was also built in large numbers. A year later Hiller introduced in the United States its Model 12 series of light utility helicopters, of which eventually more than 2,000 were built. Helicopters as small as these represented the only early designs that could not easily be adapted for other uses, as their payloads were too small; the only tasks that they could readily perform were training, observation, and light communications.

VERSATILITY IN MOTION

The Alouette II was the first truly successful French helicopter, and although designed by Sud-Aviation became known as an Aérospatiale product after the merger of Sud- and Nord-Aviation as Aérospatiale. The Alouette II was also the first turboshaft-powered helicopter to enter large-scale production anywhere in the world.

The helicopter really began to come into its own as a genuinely useful machine only during the early 1950s, partly as a result of the celebrated successes of American "choppers" in Korea. New production facilities were built in other countries and numerous helicopter designs appeared in the first half of the decade. Sud-Est, a French nationalized group, produced its first model in 1951. A utility helicopter, the Alouette (lark) proved outstandingly successful and the most versatile helicopter designed in France. Production variants were the Alouette II and enlarged Alouette III, which were each developed in variants with the Turbomeca Artouste and later the Turbomeca Astazou turboshaft engines. The Yakovlev Yak-24 "Horse" appeared in the same year and was the world's largest helicopter at the time. Intended as a military transport, the Yak-24 set a number of world rotorcraft records but was built only in small numbers because of intractable handling problems.

In 1952 Mil produced a large helicopter, the Mi-4, that clearly drew its inspiration from the Sikorsky S-55 of 1949. The American helicopter was one of the most successful helicopters ever brought into production anywhere in the world. It was designated the H-19 by the U.S. Army (with the name Chickasaw) and U.S. Air Force, HO4S by the U.S. Navy, and HRS by the U.S. Marine Corps; Westland produced the type in the United Kingdom as the Whirlwind. The Mi-4, by comparison, was a general-purpose machine,

and by adapting the main features of the S-55, Mil's design team was able to reduce the time that would otherwise have been needed for development.

One year later, Sikorsky responded with the S-56, the world's first twin-engined helicopter. The U.S. Marine Corps used it as an assault transport helicopter; the U.S. Army used it as well. After a year the S-58 general-purpose helicopter appeared, quickly followed by a specialized antisubmarine version. The S-58 was an outstanding design and secured large orders from the U.S. armed forces and from other users.

The first helicopter to gain civil certification anywhere in the world was the Bell Model 47, which was also adopted by large numbers of air arms for the general-purpose, observation, and training roles. The type was known to the U.S. Army and U.S. Air Force as the H-13, as is here represented by one of two H-13J executive transports on the White House lawn with President Dwight D. Eisenhower waiting to embark.

Most of the helicopters built up to the mid-1950s had a cruising speed of just under 100 mph (160 km/h) and a range in the order of 250 miles (400 km). The main differentiating factor in their performance, therefore, had been the load they could carry. This was beginning to increase rapidly in later types, and the next generation of helicopters also saw the start of major improvements in overall performance. The year 1955 saw the introduction of the Kamov Ka-15 "Hen" and Ka-18 "Hog" as the first variants of the world's only genuinely successful coaxial twin-rotor helicopter series. These entered service with the Soviet army and navy, and were also used by Aeroflot, the Soviet airline organization. The performance of these two Kamov helicopters was inferior to that of the Alouette II, but their importance lies in the fact that they paved the way for the Ka-25 "Hormone" shipboard multiple helicopter.

The most important helicopter adopted by the U.S. forces up to that time appeared in 1956. This was a product of the Bell Company, the Model 204 nine-seat utility type entered service as the HU-1 (later UH-1) Iroquois but is best remembered as the "Huey" of the Vietnam War. The HueyCobra established the configuration that has remained essentially unaltered for attack helicopters since its introduction. The fuselage accommodated the copilot/gunner and pilot in tandem with the pilot behind and above the copilot/gunner: The pilot could launch the disposable armament carried on the four hardpoints under the HueyCobra's stub wing, but the primary weapons operator was the copilot/gunner, who also handled the chin-mounted trainable turret with its elevating armament initially of one multibarrel machine gun and one grenade launcher. Quickly developed and simply equipped, the HueyCobra was then evolved into more powerful variants with heavier and more versatile armament aimed with the aid of increasingly sophisticated avionics. The HueyCobra is still in widespread service in its latest AH-1S form. A twin-engined version was developed for use by the U.S. Marine Corps, and the original AH-1J SeaCobra was later succeeded by the upgraded AH-1T Improved SeaCobra and finally by the AH-1W SuperCobra and AH-1Z KingCobra.

The Soviet Mi-6 "Hook" of 1957 brought a new dimension to heavy-lift helicopter capabilities, setting world records with payloads of more than 44,092 lb (20,000 kg). In its time the Mi-6 was also the world's biggest helicopter, and it paved the way for the Mi-10 "Harke" flying crane helicopter of 1960. This later model was intended to carry loads that were heavy and also bulky, and therefore introduced a wide-spread landing-gear arrangement under the slim fuselage so that a load could be brought up under the helicopter and attached to the lifting points.

In 1959, the Kaman SH-2 Seasprite became the world's first truly all-purpose helicopter, with the excellent speed of 155 mph (250 km/h) and a range of 450 miles (724 km). The importance of the Seasprite lies in design features such as its retractable landing gear and watertight fuselage bottom, allowing the machine to sit in the sea, deceiving enemy submarines into thinking it has gone, and making rescue operations easier. With advanced avionics and flying systems, the Seasprite has all-weather capability and can serve as an antimissile defense when fitted with the appropriate electronics. The SH-2 was steadily upgraded in its operational capabilities and is still used in its SH-2F Seasprite and SH-2G Supersprite twin-engined models.

In 1960 the important Sikorsky S-61 emerged in prototype form. It entered service with the U.S. Navy as the SH-3 Sea King with two General Electric T58 turboshaft engines. The Sea King was the world's first all-weather helicopter. It combined submarine-hunting and submarine-killing and was the first helicopter equipped with sonar. It carried depth charges and/or homing torpedoes. The U.S. Coast Guard deploys the HH-3F variant as a patrol and rescue helicopter, while the USAF operated the same basic airframe as the CH-3 for transport missions and the HH-3 Jolly Green Giant for the recovery of aircraft and the rescue of their crews.

In its land-based military role, the S-61 was complemented and then supplanted by the Boeing-Vertol CH-47 Chinook medium-lift helicopter of 1961. The Chinook proved its value in the Vietnam War by moving vehicles and artillery to the weight of 12,000 lb (5,443 kg) into every combat area. The Chinook has stayed in production up to the present, the latest

ABOVE LEFT One of the first and most successful of heavy-lift helicopters, the Mil Mi-6 was designed in the Soviet era and first flew in September 1957. Powered by two potent turboshaft engines, the type has clamshell rear doors to facilitate the loading of bulky freight into the large hold, and there is provision for the addition of a small wing to help offload the large five-blade main rotor in forward flight.

ABOVE RIGHT Not typical of the design thinking of the Kaman company as it had just one main rotor, the H-2 Seasprite has proved very successful and long-lived. The original UH-2 utility series was initially single-engined, but the definitive later variants, in utility and SH-2 LAMPS (Light Airborne Multi-Purpose System)

configurations, switched to a twin-engined powerplant for greater performance and enhanced survivability in overwater flights as the machine can remain airborne on only one engine.

BELOW The CH-47 Chinook helicopter is based on the design thinking of the Vertol (originally Piasecki) company, which was later taken over by Boeing. The Chinook is therefore optimized for the medium/heavy transport task with a voluminous cabin supported on the ground by quadricycle landing gear and in the air by a fore-and-aft pair of rotors powered by two turboshaft engines mounted in nacelles to the sides of the tall pylon carrying the rear rotor.

helicopters of this important type having enormously more power than their predecessors as well as much-enhanced avionics in both the transport and the increasingly important task of delivering and later extracting special forces into all types of geographical and military situations at very low altitude by day and night in any weather.

In 1962 United States finally produced a dedicated heavy-lift helicopter. The Sikorsky S-64 bears a close conceptual resemblance to the Soviet Mi-10 and entered service as the CH-54 Tarhe. In Vietnam it was tested to the limits of its structural strength and versatility. The S-64 was used for naval minesweeping and even for lifting light naval vessels. Europe's only heavy-lift helicopter, the Aérospatiale Super Frelon (Super Hornet), appeared in France in 1962. Sikorsky helped in the development of its three-engined dynamic system and associated rotors. Now obsolescent, the Super Frelon was adopted by several other nations. The Israelis, for example, made good use of the type as a commando carrier. The Super Frelon proved versatile and is currently operated by the French as a land-based heavy antisubmarine helicopter.

GUNSHIPS WITH ROTORS

The Model 209 HueyCobra, the world's first helicopter gunship, marked the division of helicopter design into more role-dedicated types. Although it suffered heavy losses in Vietnam, the HueyCobra was confirmed as a valuable combat type offering much development potential. Its narrow fuselage and turret in the chin position under the nose, where it was remotely controlled by the copilot/gunner, showed clearly that armed helicopters could be used for the close support of ground forces through the use of weapons such as machine guns, cannon, and grenades as well as unguided rockets and, in later variants, guided missiles such as the BGM-71 TOW wire-guided antitank missile. Although other helicopters had been fitted with close-support armament, mainly machine guns firing from the side doors and a number of different light air-to-surface missile and unguided rocket types, it was only in the HueyCobra that the concept matured.

The Hughes Model 369 light utility helicopter, which appeared in 1966, also proved its qualities in Vietnam as the OH-6 Cayuse. It was later adopted by other countries. Part of its success derives from its sleekly streamlined fuselage, low-drag rotor head, simple skid landing gear, and an advanced structural design. The combination of these factors made the OH-6 agile for its size, although not aerobatic. Further development of

the type by Hughes, and then by McDonnell Douglas after it had bought the company, resulted in the Model 500, intended mainly for the civil market but also developed into the Model 500 Defender series with provision for many types of armament. Boeing later bought McDonnell Douglas Helicopters but subsequently sold the organization to a Dutch company for continued existence as MD Helicopters, which maintains production and development of this excellent light helicopter. Some later variants have their antitorque rotor replaced by a system to deflect the engine exhaust gases for the achievement of the same effect.

Perhaps the oddest helicopter of the 1960s was the Mil V-12 "Homer." It never entered production but remains the largest helicopter yet built. The airliner-type fuselage was fitted with a large inversely tapered and strut-braced wing carrying at each tip a complete Mi-6 "Hook" dynamic system (powerplant and main rotor) for the carriage of payloads in the order of 88,182 lb (40,000 kg). The Mi-26 Halo, first flown in 1977, is currently the world's largest production helicopter, with an eight-blade main rotor powered by two turboshaft engines.

The two major recent developments in helicopter design derive from the U.S. helicopter experience in the Vietnam War. First, helicopters became combat machines and therefore needed heavy gun and missile armament. The only armed helicopters before this time had been antisubmarine types, operating from shore bases and warships. Second, the deployment of the helicopter in combat operations over the battlefield had made it apparent that survivability and operational utility required significant improvement in maneuverability and speed.

The helicopter has always been limited in terms of its performance and payload, and one of the more promising attempts to overcome this type of limitation is the combination of rotary- and fixed-wing elements in aircraft such as the Bell/Boeing V-22 Osprey. This is configured as a fixed-wing airplane but has at the tips of its wing a pair of nacelles each carrying a turboshaft engine and a large-diameter "proprotor." With the nacelles swiveled to the vertical position, the proprotors generate enough downward thrust to give the Osprey the ability to take off and land vertically.

To allow for heavier and more diverse armament, helicopters sprouted a variety of stub wings and other protuberances fitted with the hardpoints for the carriage and release of external weapons. The weight and drag of these additions adversely affected performance, and stub wings are now optimized to minimize drag and so degrade performance as little as possible. The increased use of advanced avionics has led to a revision of the basic fuselage shape, which in modern combat helicopters beginning with the HueyCobra resembles a conventional combat airplane.

Designed as the Advanced Aerial Fire-Support System, the Lockheed AH-56 Cheyenne was an example of this trend. Speed was boosted to a maximum of 244 mph (393 km/h) through the adoption of retractable landing gear, a powerful General Electric T64 turboshaft engine, and a novel lift/thrust concept: As the helicopter began forward flight, an increasing proportion of the lift burden was assumed by the large stub wing, allowing power to be diverted from the main rotor to the large pusher propeller located at the extreme tail. Apart from a heavy load of avionics, the AH-56 also carried a formidable array of guns, bombs, guided missiles, and grenade launchers. The model did not enter service, as it was too costly and complex, but its concept was used for the creation of the Advanced Attack Helicopters.

The AH-64 Apache, introduced by Hughes in 1975, exemplifies another inevitable feature of recent choppers: stunning electronics. The AH-64 is smaller, lighter, and less powerful than its predecessor AH-56, but it boasts advanced design, modern avionics, and potent armament. The U.S. Army uses the Apache with the AGM-114 Hellfire missile.

ABOVE The Apache, more formally known as the AH-64 and originally designed by Hughes before this company's helicopter operation was taken over by McDonnell Douglas, which then merged with Boeing under the latter's name, is the U.S. Army's standard heavy attack and antitank helicopter. The Apache is operated by the copilot/gunner and pilot in tandem, and has advanced target-acquisition and fire-control systems in its nose turrets, supplemented in the latest model by radar in a radome above the main rotor. There is a trainable 30-mm cannon under the fuselage, and the four hardpoints under the stub wing typically carry a heavy load of rocket launchers and antitank missiles.

BELOW The Mil Mi-24 was created as a battlefield transport for the Soviet forces, and was then developed in its Mi-24D and later forms with a revised fuselage and stub wings as the counterpart of the Apache in the close-support, attack, and antitank roles with trainable or later fixed guns as well as rocket launchers and air-to-surface missiles on its underwing hardpoints.

The British 10-seat Westland Lynx general-purpose helicopter is one of the new breed of helicopters that can be rolled and looped. Other machines, such as the Sikorsky S-67 Blackhawk designed to meet the AAFSS requirement and then used in the development of the AAH specification, could be even more maneuverable. Although it was the United States that took the early lead in the development of agile and heavily armed combat helicopters, the U.S.S.R. began to whittle away this technical lead with the Mi-24 "Hind-D" gunship version of the Mi-24 "Hind" assault transport helicopter. Though it is large and comparatively unwieldy in the air, the "Hind-D" has the same type of narrow fuselage with a vertically stepped cockpit as the Blackhawk. Among its virtues are good weapon-aiming systems and the ability to carry a heavy load of several weapon types. By the early 1980s the Soviets had evaluated the concept of combat helicopters and begun to develop more specialized purpose-designed types such as the Kamov Ka-50 "Hokum" and Mil Mi-28 "Havoc."

A NEW CIVILIAN INDUSTRY

The ever-growing success of the helicopter for military applications has been mirrored by its flourishing sales on the civil market, especially in the United States, and larger helicopters may in future be built specifically for the civil market. The Soviets pioneered the use of heavy-lift helicopters for tasks such as the support of mining industries in inaccessible regions, such as Siberia.

In whatever other roles the helicopter may be used, it is by far the best vehicle available for search and rescue. Over the years helicopters flying in this type of service, often in appalling weather over land and sea, have saved the lives of many thousands—people snatched from the tide on secluded beaches, sailors rescued in storms or when their vessel has sunk, or the sick or critically injured lifted from road accidents, ships, or the sides of mountains.

It should be noted that the autogyro and helicopter (counting tilt-wing convertiplanes among the latter) are the only aircraft capable of vertical takeoff and landing. Several other concepts have been tried, but the only practical method so far found is the thrust of a turbine engine. Once such a vehicle takes off, however, it can fly conventionally at purely wingborne high speed without the cumbersome drag of even the most advanced rotor systems.

The two most efficient systems of direct lift with jet engines are the so-called vectored thrust of the type pioneered in a British airplane, the Hawker (later Hawker Siddeley and then BAe), and the direct thrust of special engines as used in aircraft such as the West German Dornier Do 31 experimental transport and EWR-Süd VJ 101 experimental combat airplane. In the British system, the exhaust nozzles of the centrally located engine can be swiveled downward so that the exhaust generates direct lift and then gradually turned back to the horizontal so that the exhaust drives the airplane forward into increasingly rapid wingborne flight.

In the German aircraft the system took two forms. The first, employed in the Do 31, requires the airplane to be provided with both vertical-lift and horizontal-thrust engines. The system is feasible rather than genuinely practical. It imposes considerable drag and weight penalties, even if the mechanics of the whole system are simple. The second, evaluated in the VJ 101, was based on the mounting of the whole engine system in pods that can be rotated. Located on the center of gravity, these pods were rotated to point down for takeoff (and later for landing) and are then gradually moved to the horizontal position for forward flight.

The only operational VTOL (Vertical Takeoff and Landing) airplane in the world in the late 1960s and early 1970s was the Harrier. It was based on a vectored-thrust lift/propulsion system that offered the advantages of simplicity and light weight. On the other side of the Iron Curtain, another VTOL type entered service in 1976. Intended as a carrierborne attack airplane, the Yakovlev Yak-38 "Forger" was based on a hybrid fuselage-mounted powerplant.

Arguments can be made for both concepts of reactive lift using jet engines, but the vectored-thrust method clearly offers greater scope for military aircraft since it is comparatively small and light. Should vertical takeoff ever reach civil aviation, a large number of small lightweight engines in fixed downward-facing pods might possibly prove better. Projects for such aircraft have been created for some time, but with high development costs, STOL (Short Takeoff and Landing) aircraft seem more likely. These would allow large aircraft to use smaller airports, make less noise than VTOL aircraft, and cost less. Two examples in prototype are the Boeing YC-14 and McDonnell Douglas YC-15.

A brave British attempt to create a convertible helicopter was the Fairey/Westland Rotodyne, which first flew in November 1957. This was laid out as a fixed-wing airplane with retractable landing gear and a fuselage that could carry forty passengers as well as the crew of three. Power was provided by two Napier Eland turboprop engines in nacelles on the leading edge of the short-span wing: For vertical takeoff and landing the entire power of these engines was directed to the four-blade rotor on a tall pylon over the fuselage, and the Rotodyne then translated into forward, wingborne flight as the power was gradually transferred to the propellers.

ABOVE The key to the capabilities of the Harrier series of warplanes for VTOL and STOL is the Rolls-Royce (originally Bristol Siddeley) Pegasus turbofan engine. As seen in this cutaway illustration of an AV-8B Harrier II, cold air from the fan and hot gases from the core are exhausted via the front and rear pairs of nozzles respectively to provide four-poster thrust anywhere between slightly ahead of downward and straight to the rear.

BELOW An approach to vertical takeoff and landing altogether different from that used in the rotary-wing airplane was represented by the Ryan X-13 Vertijet. Seen here at a demonstration in Washington, D.C., the Vertijet was basically a conventional delta-winged airplane with no real landing gear, as it was designed to operate from a stand, to which it was attached by a hook under the nose. For operations the stand was elevated to the vertical position, and the thrust of its Rolls-Royce Avon turbojet then allowed the Vertijet to climb straight from the stand before tilting over into wingborne flight. The process was reversed when the pilot wanted to hook onto the stand once more. Control of the Vertijet in vertical mode was effected by deflection of the engine's exhaust.

Beginning in the late 1970s, a flood of new helicopter models hit the market. These included the Bell Model 212 (Twin Two-Twelve), Model 214, and Model 222, the Boeing-Vertol 234 civil version of the CH-47 Chinook twin-rotor military transport, the Sikorsky S-70 civil version of the UH-60 Black Hawk helicopter, and the Sikorsky S-76 Spirit, as well as two French types, the Aérospatiale Puma and the Super Puma. The keynote of these machines is greater reliability at the maintenance and operational levels in combination with better capability for all-weather operations thanks to upgraded avionics and systems designed to prevent the accretion of ice on the rotor blades. Further improvements introduced in the last 20 years are the increased use of composite materials to reduce structure weight and thus make possible greater payload or range. A new generation of turboshaft engines offers improved power/weight ratios, lower specific fuel consumption, and more time between overhauls.

For decades, science-fiction writers have described a future in which urban dwellers hop into a vehicle, take off vertically as if pulling out of their driveways, and then zip forward as if in a lightweight, high-speed airplane. More likely, however, is a less glamorous future in which small airfields dot suburban landscapes, and all sizes of planes take off and land on short runways. Evolution, not revolution, is a very safe bet.

The Bell Model 206 JetRanger is a utility light helicopter developed through a succession of variants. The type was originally created as the OH-4 to meet a U.S. Army requirement for a light observation helicopter. It initially lost out to the Hughes OH-6, but then received large orders as the H-58 Kiowa for the observation role. H-57 SeaRanger for naval helicopter training. and H-67 Creek for army helicopter training.

THE MODERN AGE

FACING PAGE The upper end of the U.S. Air Force's fighter capability is to be provided from about 2006 by the F-22 Raptor, developed and produced jointly by Lockheed Martin and Boeing. The Raptor can cruise supersonically without the use of fuel-expensive afterburning, is highly agile through the combination of powerful control surfaces and vectoring of the two turbofan engines' exhausts, and has a very advanced system to "fuse" the data from a variety of sensors to provide the pilot with an unrivaled but comprehensive, easily assimilated, almost intuitive awareness of his overall tactical situation.

The future of powered flight will be a paradoxical mix of extremes. An explosion of private planes and amateur enthusiasts at one end and hybrid cutting-edge technologies at the other. Military planes will undoubtedly continue to improve speeds to unheard-of levels. It is the vast middle ground of commercial aviation that has suffered the most of late and may continue to struggle for footing.

World War II marked a turning point in history for civil flying as much as military aviation. The civil aviation industry had come virtually to a halt in Europe, but had continued to develop, at a reduced rate, within in the United States. In the period of reconstruction that followed the war, the European nations remained sure, as they had been before the war, that airlines could operate successfully only within a framework of government support and financial assistance. The belief that civil aviation was by its nature uneconomical had a decidedly adverse effort on the development of light and general aviation, and also on the initial development of commercial aviation in Europe. Also, the prewar airliners and converted aircraft struggled to compete with trains for speed on short routes, and the latter offered greater comfort.

Most airlines were happy to progress slowly under the financial umbrella provided by their governments. It was hard for airlines to get the right aircraft at the correct time. Above all, their controlling governments wanted economy, and no large investments could be made. This false economy was combined with bad judgment about the types of aircraft that should be developed and built. Germany had lost its industrial base, Italy was short of resources, and France faced great problems of reconstruction before it could turn to civil air transport. This meant that only the United Kingdom was in any sort of condition to start large-scale airliner projects.

Yet even the United Kingdom had to start virtually from nothing. Several interesting projects incorporating the very latest technology had been considered in the last few months of peace only to be abandoned during the war. Based on advanced engine and airframe technologies, Short and Fairey projects for long-range transports with a four-engined powerplant were ignored by the Brabazon Committee, which had been set up in 1943 to examine the needs of British civil aviation at the end of the hostilities. The Brabazon Committee faced a very difficult task. During the war the most important requirement for the British aircraft industry had been the design, development, and mass production of warplanes, and for this reason the development of transport aircraft ceased, even for military purposes. Britain relied on converted aircraft such as obsolescent bombers and then, as the emergency between 1939 and 1941 eased, on American sources.

Even so, it is difficult to see how the Brabazon Committee arrived at its conclusions. The aircraft that the committee decided were essential, and therefore ordered into design and preliminary development, were technically advanced but wholly inadequate for the tasks ultimately required of them. The committee ordered low- and medium-capacity airliners when it should have demanded medium- and high-capacity aircraft.

The Americans displayed a considerably more realistic approach that was greatly aided by their experience in World War II, when they had ferried troops over long distances, from the United States to North Africa via the South Atlantic crossing between Brazil and West Africa. They had also airlifted supplies from India to China over the eastern Himalayas. The Americans also judged the size and demands of the market five years into the future with a high degree of accuracy. Airlines such as Pan American, Trans World Airlines, National Airlines, and American Airlines knew exactly what aircraft they would need. For-profit competitors, as a group, proved to be far more efficient than government-run monopolies.

New British planes were notable failures. The huge Bristol Brabazon was intended for the low-capacity transatlantic route but canceled after eight years of development before it entered production. The Short Sandringham flying boat failed to find a large market, and the beautiful Saunders-Roe Princess flying boat was also canceled before it entered service. The Americans, on the other hand, were creating and producing several comfortable, high-performance transport aircraft matched to the steadily growing number of continental and intercontinental routes. The railways soon lost a large proportion of their long-distance passengers and freight.

What British airlines did not appreciate was the fact that the airliner should no longer operate at medium altitude and short range for a small number of high-paying passengers. The future lay in high-altitude, long-range, high-capacity flights for middle-class passengers.

On flights across the United States it was not necessary to land every 500 miles (805 km) or so, with the passengers disembarking for an hour while the airliner was refueled. Nonstop service proved a big drawing card. There was also every possibility of regular, safe flights across the Atlantic. High-altitude flight was cheaper *and* less turbulent.

In the late 1940s BOAC introduced the Avro Tudor, ordered by the Brabazon Committee: It compared unfavorably to its American rivals. In 1947 BEA received the first of its twin-engined Vickers Viking short/medium-haul airliners, which proved popular and successful in operation, although even they could not match contemporary American airliners in economy and performance.

Worthy as the DC-2 was, Douglas felt that the basic concept could be improved significantly and therefore created the DC-3, seen here at La Guardia Airport, New York. The DC-3 was the airliner that can rightly be said to have "made" the American airline industry, and is one of the great classics of aviation history. The DC-3 was built as such in good numbers before World War II, which then saw the type's production in vast numbers for service as the C-47 Skytrain with the U.S. Army Air Forces, the R4D with the U.S. Navy and Marine Corps, and the Dakota with the air forces of the British Commonwealth. War-surplus aircraft then allowed the development of airline operations in many parts of the world, and the type is still in limited service.

By now there were more than 200 airlines in the world and nearly 1,000 major airports. There were at first many small airlines operating in remoter areas, but by the late 1940s the "established" airlines led a consolidation. Small private operators, especially those using the DC-3, were left with the growing freight market in the world's more inhospitable and inaccessible regions.

The American dominance of the air transport market was nearly total. Their airlines had two excellent four-engined airliners for longer-range routes and had in prospect a replacement for the DC-3 for medium-range routes. The two four-engined airliners were the strangely elegant and indeed beautiful Lockheed Constellation and the more workaday but no less successful Douglas DC-4. A comparison of these two airliners with the best comparable British aircraft of the time, the York, reveals the magnitude of the American technical lead. The DC-4 could carry up to 58 passengers at 245 mph (395 km/h) for almost 2,000 miles (3,220 km), and the Constellation could carry up to 100 passengers at 330 mph (530 km/h) for more than 2,400 miles (3,860 km), but while the York was able to reach almost 300 mph (485 km/h) and possessed a range of 2,700 miles (4,345 km), it could carry only 24 passengers.

The British airliner also provided considerably less comfortable accommodation, and another factor that has to be borne in mind is that while the York was the last stage in an evolutionary design process and could be improved no further without very extensive design, the two American airliners were near the beginning of their evolutionary lives. Development of the Constellation continued up to 1958, when it was still a marginally competitive design at a time when the first American-designed jet airliner was on the verge of entering service. The Douglas airliner, too, proved durable, and the same basic layout was kept in subsequent Douglas types, which were in essence enlarged DC-4 aircraft with full cabin pressurization, more powerful engines, and improved performance in terms of speed, range, and cruising altitude. Finally, both American airliners had tricycle landing gear of the type that kept the fuselage level on the ground, while the York had tailwheel landing gear.

The Convair CV-240 was inspired by a request from American Airlines for a successor to the DC-3 and appeared in 1947. The CV-240 can be regarded as a postwar development of the DC-3's basic concept with the latest technical developments, and was capable of considerable development. From the CV-240 evolved the CV-340 and CV-440, of which useful numbers were still in service into the 1990s in their original piston-engined and later converted turboprop-powered forms. The CV-240 and its successors

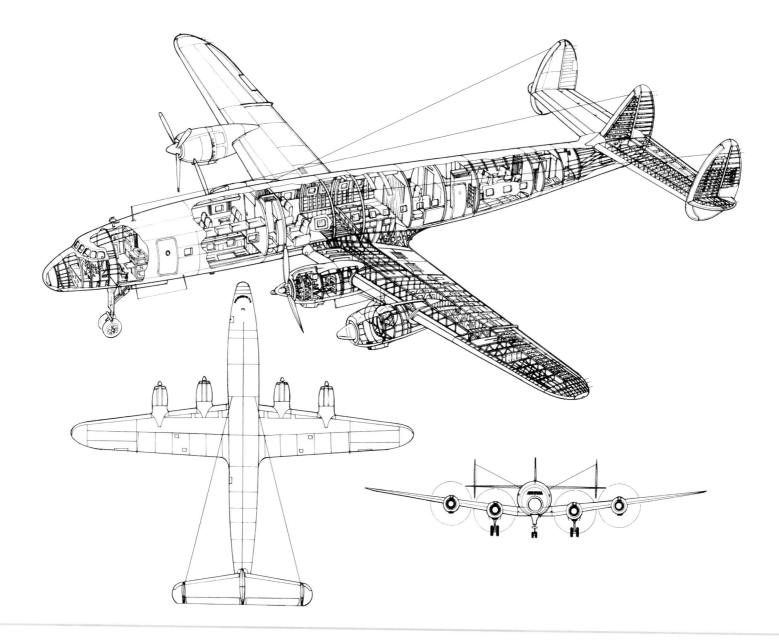

The last years of peace before the United States' entry into World War II were devoted, so far as the U.S. airline industry was concerned, to its expansion using mainly the DC-3 twin-engined airliner, and the possibility of longer-range services with four-engined airliners that would offer greater passenger capacity in pressurized accommodation, allowing the airliner to cruise above the worst weather conditions. Though Boeing led the way with the Model 307 Stratoliner, the war intervened, and after the end of hostilities it was Douglas and Lockheed that took the lead. This is Lockheed's Constellation, which was developed into ever more capable Super Constellation and Starliner versions in competition with the Douglas airliners of the same period.

achieved success as a result of careful and forward-looking design. High-lift devices kept wing area to a minimum, ensuring high speed but providing good handling and safety at low speed for takeoff and landing; tricycle landing gear improved ground handling as well as passenger accessibility on the ground; cabin pressurization enhanced passenger comfort; and the two excellent Pratt & Whitney Twin Wasp radial engines had a basic form of jet propulsion from the residual thrust of the exhaust gases to boost performance.

In 1948 Douglas unveiled its DC-6. An improved DC-4 capable of carrying some 70 passengers at 280 mph (450 km/h) over transcontinental and intercontinental ranges, the standard DC-6 was soon replaced by the larger DC-6B, itself later superseded by the definitive DC-7 as the classic model of the Douglas long-range airliner family. In the first half of the 1950s this Douglas airliner family represented the most successful commercial aircraft in the world.

Aircraft such as those of the CV, DC, and Constellation series confirmed the total professionalism of the U.S. aviation business, which was also notable for the success of its airlines in ordering just the right number of the right aircraft at just the right time to satisfy the growth of the market. Some people may have argued that the romance had gone out of flying, but passengers were more than happy, so the combination of speed, comfort, and reliability offered by the airlines in the early 1950s meant that aircraft became dominant for long-range American transport.

The United Kingdom could not hope to match the volume of American air travel or the civil aircraft production capacity of the United States, but by the late 1940s British aircraft were beginning to equal and in some respects to excel their American rivals in performance. Among the civil types introduced in 1949 were the four-engined Handley Page Hermes in its fully developed form, the elegant twin-engined Airspeed Ambassador high-wing design for BEA's European routes, the four-turboprop Vickers Viscount medium-range airliner, and the four-turbojet de Havilland D.H.106 Comet.

The Hermes and Ambassador were the equals of anything the Americans were flying, but the Viscount and Comet were far more advanced than anything available from American manufacturers. The Viscount was basically conventional in appearance, but its most striking and technically important feature was its use of a turboprop powerplant for an unrivaled combination of speed and range for a given fuel load. The selected engine was the Rolls-Royce Dart, which was considerably quieter and smoother-running than any piston engine of the same power and, being smaller and lighter, also produced less drag and simplified the problems of wing design.

ABOVE Douglas rivaled the Constellation series with its DC-4, which first appeared in military garb as the C-54. The basic type was then developed after World War II in other military forms, and also in parallel civil forms as the DC-6 and DC-7. It can be argued that the Starliner and DC-7 marked the high point in the development of the piston-engined airliner for long-range transport.

BELOW Even as the Americans were pressing the development of the ultimate piston-engined airliners, the British decided that turbine power offered greater possibilities for the future. An early result of this process was the Vickers Viscount, a short/medium-range airliner powered by four notably slim Rolls-Royce Dart turboprop engines.

Air transport moved fully into the modern age with the arrival of the de Havilland D.H.106 Comet. This was conceived shortly after World War II as a medium-range type with a powerplant of four turbojet engines located in the wing roots. The result was a radical transformation of civil transport performance. G-ALYP was the first production example of the Comet 1 initial model, and was one of the machines whose crashes led to the type's grounding and structural revision.

The most important airplane of 1949, however, was undoubtedly the Comet, which was the world's first turbojet-powered airliner. Compared with the piston-engined airliners of the period, with their straight wings carrying massive engines and large propellers, the Comet was incredibly sleek as a result of its beautifully streamlined nose with an unstepped cockpit, modestly swept wing, tricycle landing gear, and four turbojet engines installed in a low-drag installation in the wing roots. The only feature to mar the Comet's looks was the relatively short fuselage, and this was a result of the type's origins as a mailplane ordered by the Brabazon Committee. This meant that the passenger accommodation was limited to just 36 passengers. The prototypes and very first production aircraft were lifted to a more-than-ample performance by de Havilland Ghost centrifugal-flow turbojet engines, but later Comet aircraft switched to Rolls-Royce Avon axial-flow turbojet engines, which allowed a longer and more capacious fuselage to be combined with the existing high-lift wing.

The implications of the Viscount and Comet for the long-term development of air transport were not lost on the Americans, who nonetheless appreciated from the beginning that British production could never hope to take full advantage of this technical lead to rival the Americans in the tempo of deliveries to airlines. At a time when most American airliners flew at less than 300 mph (483 km/h) but carried up to 100 passengers, the Comet traveled at nearly 500 mph (805 km/h) although its considerably smaller payload meant that the type was attractive only for long routes used by small numbers of passengers. Even so, American manufacturers were sufficiently worried by the British turbine-powered transports to launch a public relations campaign designed to persuade airlines that American manufacturers would soon be in a position to offer turboprop-powered aircraft only marginally slower than the Comet and would then move forward to a superior turbojet-powered airliner offering considerably greater capabilities than the Comet in terms of payload and speed. This campaign combined with an intrinsic caution on the part of the major airlines and successfully kept orders for the Comet down to limited numbers.

By 1951 BOAC was training crews for the new airliner, and some of the proving flights were so impressive that several other operators decided that they must have the Comet for their prestige services or be left behind in a market in which passengers had now expressed a clear preference for high speed and a more modest level of comfort over modest speed and a higher level of comfort. In May 1952 the Comet began commercial flights to South Africa and the type's future looked assured, especially as the model with Avon engines was now in production and the order book was swelling. Passenger reports of the Comet's quiet and smooth flight helped reinforce the statistical evidence of the Comet's excellence.

Then disaster struck: In 1954 two of the first production aircraft disappeared over the Mediterranean after taking off from Rome. Public anxiety was particularly intense because of the radical nature of the new airliner's design and powerplant. Wreckage was eventually brought up from the bottom of the sea, and the cause of the problem was diagnosed as metal fatigue around the passenger cabin's square-cut window apertures. A cure was swiftly devised in the form of reinforcement panels around each aperture. So great was the psychological shock, however, that this simple solution was not adopted, and the whole Comet program was fatally delayed for the development of a new fuselage with rounded windows. The Comet's advantage over American rivals had been lost by the time the revised Comet 4 entered service in 1958, to be operated by BOAC on the North Atlantic route, which was really too long for effective service by an airliner originally intended for the British routes to Africa and the Far East.

Only one month after the Comet 4 had entered full-revenue service, the death knell for the type on prestige high-density, high-speed routes such as that across the North Atlantic was sounded by the introduction of the Boeing Model 707 turbojet-powered airliner. Bearing a distinct family likeness to the earlier B-47 Stratojet and B-52 Stratofortress turbojet-powered bombers, the Model 707 was far superior to the Comet as

The Americans were slower off the mark than the British in the creation of turbojet-powered airliners, but this proved an advantage as their first such type, the Boeing Model 707, was larger and more advanced than the Comet, and as a result secured altogether better sales success.

it was a conceptually more advanced airliner offering higher speed, greater payload, longer range, and more development potential.

Shortly after this, there appeared a second American turbojet-powered airliner, the DC-8, that had been rushed through design and development to provide Douglas with a competitor to the Boeing airliner. Produced in large numbers at a low unit cost in large and very efficient factories, the Model 707 and DC-8 immediately revealed the obsolescence of the Comet and soon outsold the pioneering British airliner by a very considerable margin.

The main obstacle to the success of the new American airliners was size and weight greater than those of their predecessors. This translated into the need for longer and stronger runways at airports that also had to improve and enlarge their passenger- and baggage-handling facilities for the new airliners' greater passenger capacities. This raised financial problems for many airports, but the superiority of the new airliners and the growing volume of traffic they made possible meant that the required improvements were ultimately profitable. Very soon all the major airports could handle the Model 707 and DC-8, accompanied by very much smaller numbers of the rival Convair CV-880 and CV-990, and piston-engined airliners soon disappeared from the prestigious long-range routes, on which their lack of speed and payload made them hopelessly inefficient in financial terms relative to the turbojet-powered types.

The British government had convinced itself that the future for long-haul services lay with large turboprop-powered machines such as the Bristol Britannia, but had to rethink its attitude from 1957, when BOAC suddenly became worried about its technical inferiority on the prestigious North Atlantic route. The result was the Vickers VC10, in many respects an outstanding airplane. Sure that there was a market for passengers wanting to fly between the smaller airports unwilling or unable to expand their facilities to the levels required for the Model 707 and DC-8, BOAC specified runway requirements considerably shorter than

FACING PAGE The large-scale production of modern airliners, such as the Boeing Model 747 seen here, is a highly technical matter that permits the extensive use of automation but also needs a highly motivated and skilled work force. Like the DC-3, the Model 747 falls into the category of a classic airliner, for this pioneering wide-body airplane was the transport that allowed the blossoming of the long-range mass transportation market pioneered by earlier types, including the Boeing Model 707 and Douglas DC-8.

those of the U.S. aircraft. As a result Vickers chose to base its design on a large wing, un-cluttered by engines, as a means of increasing lift and reducing takeoff/landing speed: The American airliners had comparatively small wings with the engines in four nacelles pylon-mounted below and ahead of the leading edges, but the VC10 had its four engines in pairs of nacelles on each side of the rear fuselage, with the tailplane mounted on top of the vertical tail to keep it well clear of the engine exhausts. The VC10 met BOAC's specification without difficulty, but the requirement itself had been based on the erroneous assumption that most airports would be reluctant or unable to extend their runways and terminals to the standards required for the American airliners. When they did, allowing the American turbojet-powered transports to operate virtually everywhere in the world, the VC10 proved a commercial failure: Its large wing increased drag slightly, making the type relatively uneconomical.

This left the market open to the Americans, who built the Model 707 and DC-8 in large numbers in variants matched to the needs of airlines wanting different passenger capacities, greater or lesser range, the ability to fly to and from "hot-and-high" airports, and internal layouts such as passenger, freight, quick-change passenger/freight, and mixed passenger/freight. The original models carried 175 passengers at 570 mph (917 km/h) for 3,075 miles (4,950 km), while later models were able to transport 190 passengers at 607 mph (977 km/h) for 6,160 miles (9,915 km) with minimal alterations to the airframe except the lengthening of the fuselage.

The modest enhancement of payload but major improvement in performance was made possible by engine technology developments between 1955 and 1970. Powered by the excellent Pratt & Whitney JT3 turbojet, the civil counterpart of the J57 military unit, the first Model 707 and DC-8 variants could call on only 12,500 lb st (55.60 kN) from each engine, but later variants were powered by the same basic engine's JT3D turbofan development at a rating in the order of 18,000 lb st (80.07 kN).

In the turbofan, the turbine driven by the hot gases streaming back from combustion chambers drive not only the compressor at the front of the engine but also a fan stage located ahead of the compressor. Larger in diameter than the engine itself, this fan produces great thrust and also smoothes out the airflow at the jetpipe end of the engine, increasing efficiency and reducing the noise level by a very considerable margin. This last was significant in itself to a world becoming ever more concerned about the need to cut noise pollution, but more directly to airlines for the economic advantage of getting up to 50 percent more thrust out of their engines for only a marginal increase in fuel consumption, which translated into much-enhanced range for a given weight of increasingly expensive fuel.

The high-bypass-ratio turbofan, in which a larger proportion of the air passing through the fan stage goes around the engine instead of entering the compressor stage and then the combustion chambers, has become the dominant type of jet engine for civil aviation, and has also made a great impression on the military market. Continued development of the turbofan showed that major improvements were still possible. Thus the turbofan engines of the 1980s were not only more efficient than their predecessors, but also considerably quieter. This process has continued into the first part of the twenty-first century, and the operators of older airliners have been compelled to "hushkit" their aircraft to comply with increasingly stringent noise-reduction regulations.

The turbofan's advent helped to crystallize differing types of airliners emerging to meet the demands of a growing market. In the 1950s, for example, there were two basic types of airliner, the short/medium- and long-range types. The great majority of passengers traveled only short/medium distances, for which turboprop-powered machines such as the Viscount, Vickers Vanguard development of the Viscount, Fokker F.27 Friendship, Lockheed Electra, and Handley Page Herald were ideally suited. Routes of under 1,000 miles (1,610 km) did not require the high speeds at which the turbojet is economical, but for long-range routes the turbojet offered major advantages.

Toward the end of the 1950s, the need for an airliner intermediate between the short/medium- and long-range types became apparent, and the French SNCASO group, more commonly known just as Sud-Ouest and later a component of Aérospatiale, brought France into the international marketplace with its classic Caravelle: a forward fuselage based on that of the Comet was married to a new and very efficient wing and a rear fuselage carrying two Rolls-Royce Avon turbojet engines in lateral nacelles, the first time such an installation had been used on an airliner. After a slow start, the Caravelle proved successful not only in itself but also as an influence on later designs.

The design teams of the 1960s felt that the turbofan was best suited for long-range airliners. Then the turbofan's increasing efficiency and the development of smaller engines combined to make the turbofan relevant to all airliner types during the early 1980s, and as a consequence the turbojet has all but disappeared from airline service. Over much the same period the turboprop, which many considered obsolete on all but the smallest transports from the mid-1960s, was turned into a highly competitive type, especially when driving an advanced propeller controlled by means of a computerized control system of the type now standard on turbine-powered aircraft. The turboprop never faded entirely from the airliner scene, and from the early 1980s the type has undergone a considerable renaissance for airliners such as the ATR 42 and 72, de Havilland Canada (now Bombardier) DHC-7 Dash 7 and DHC-8 Dash 8, EMBRAER EMB-110 Bandeirante and EMB-120 Brasilia, Fokker 50, Saab 340 and 2000, and Shorts 330 and 360. Small airliners of this type, now generally called regional airliners, can carry up to 50 passengers over a maximum-payload range of up to 1,000 miles (1,610 km) at a cruising speed of 310 mph (500 km/h) or more at a low specific fuel consumption.

The Soviet Ilyushin and Yakovlev design bureaus had built small turbojet-powered airliners before the dominance of the Tupolev design bureau in large aircraft extended itself to the airliner field in the 1950s. The first modern Soviet airliner was the Tu-104, which was clearly derived from the Tu-16 "Badger" bomber but was nonetheless admirably suited to Soviet operating practices. The Tu 104 set a pattern for another bomber-derived Soviet transport, namely the Tu-114, based on the Tu-95 "Bear." Since then, however, Soviet designers have tended to follow the lead set by the West, saving time and effort by taking successful ideas for their own use but failing to create anything that breaks new technical or aerodynamic ground. Later Tupolev types include the Tu-110 four-engined development of the twin-engined Tu-104; the Tu-124 scaled-down version of the Tu-104; the Tu-134, again based on the Tu-104 but with its two engines moved to pods at the rear of the fuselage in the manner of the Caravelle; the Tu-144 supersonic airliner with its ogival wing; and the Tu-154, which is in essence an enlarged Tu-134 with three of everything of which the earlier airplane had only two: three engines, three pairs of wheels on its main-landing-gear legs, triple-slotted flaps, and so on.

Tupolev's main rival in civil aircraft design was the Ilyushin bureau, which was responsible for machines such as the four-turboprop Il-18 long-range airliner; the four-turbofan Il-62, conceptually akin to the VC10; the four-turbofan Il-86 wide-body airliner with its engines in under-wing nacelles in the Boeing and Douglas fashion; and the four-turbofan Il-96, derived conceptually from the Il-86 but introducing a number of advanced features such as tip-mounted winglets, composite materials, and a "glass" cockpit with many instruments replaced by six multifunction displays.

Several other types were developed in the U.S.S.R., with designs by Antonov proving the most successful in the heavy-lift capacity for both military and civilian use. Given that it was a large but relatively underdeveloped country with huge natural resources in many of its poorly accessed remoter areas, the U.S.S.R. inevitably became a major exponent of heavy-lift aircraft for civilian use. The Western nations, with well-developed rail

The airplane that defined the type of tactical transport that would become standard from the mid-1950s was Lockheed's Hercules, known to the U.S. military services as the C-130. The Hercules was created to move modest loads of men and equipment into and out of small, poorly prepared airfields close behind the front line, and was therefore based on straight flying surfaces and Allison T56 turboprop engines driving three- but later four-bladed propellers. The wing was located high on the fuselage to keep the propeller blades well clear of the runway's surface, and the fuselage itself was optimized for payload by being of large and constant diameter over much of its length. Access to the hold inside this fuselage was provided by side doors and, more important, a ramp/door arrangement under the upswept tail unit. This arrangement could be opened in flight for the paradropping of men and equipment, and also allowed freight to be loaded straight into and out of the hold, whose floor was at truck-bed height to facilitate this process. The final element in the design thinking was the location of the main landing-gear units in blister fairings on the lower corners of the fuselage, an arrangement that reduced weight by keeping the legs as short as possible and avoided any volume-consuming intrusion into the hold. The Hercules is still in production and continued development with more advanced engines, propellers, and avionics.

networks, have a greater need for freight aircraft, a demand that can be met largely by the conversion of airliners or the construction of freight-dedicated variants of standard airliners. Few alterations need normally be made beyond strengthening the fuselage floor and fitting larger doors so that bulky items can be loaded. A few such aircraft, such as the Canadair CL-44 version of the Britannia, have been built with a hinged rear fuselage to ease the loading of long, wide loads.

After World War II, which proved the general utility of transport aircraft, there has been steady growth in the use of large transport aircraft. In recent years the U.S. Air Force's two main heavy-transport aircraft have been the Lockheed C-141 StarLifter and Lockheed C-5 Galaxy, the latter the world's largest airplane at the time of its introduction. These two long-range transports were complemented in the early 1980s by a modest number of KC-10 Extender dual-role tanker/transport aircraft derived from the DC-10 airliner, and from the mid-1990s were being joined by another advanced military transport, the McDonnell Douglas (now Boeing) C-17A Globemaster III. Both the United Kingdom and France developed large transports, but these were phased out of service by 1980.

However, there can be no doubt that the most remarkable and versatile transport since 1945 has been the four-turboprop Lockheed C-130 Hercules tactical airlifter. This has been adopted by a large number of air forces as well as a smaller number of civil operators, and though it entered service in the first half of the 1950s is still in large-scale production and continuing development in the early part of the twenty-first century. The Hercules has excellent STOL characteristics and possesses the capability for operations to and from rough airstrips.

As pioneered in the Hercules and two Soviet military transports from Antonov, namely the twin-turboprop An-8 "Camp" and four-turboprop An-12 "Cub," modern dedicated transport aircraft feature an upswept rear fuselage and tail unit so that the lower rear section of the fuselage can be hinged down as an access ramp to the uncluttered interior of the airplane. Such a system allows such items as artillery, light tanks, missiles, and large trucks to be loaded easily, and also permits very heavy loads to be dropped by parachute straight from the fuselage. Other features of such aircraft are multiwheel tricycle landing gear whose main units retract into external blisters that leave the fuselage free for payload, short landing-gear legs so that the floor of the hold is at truckbed height to facilitate loading and unloading of the freight, and a high-set wing so that the propellers driven by the wing-mounted engines have plenty of ground clearance during operations into and out of semiprepared or even unprepared airstrips.

This head-on view of a C-130J, the latest version of the Hercules with updated avionics and Rolls-Royce North America (Allison) AE2100 turboprop engines driving six-blade propellers, emphasizes some of the type's tactical features, including good fields of vision from a flight deck right up in the nose, short but well-spaced main landing-gear units, and good clearance under the propellers.

SHORT- AND MEDIUM-RANGE CRAFT

The almost explosive growth in civil passenger traffic during the 1960s, within the context of a mass market made possible by the creation of high-capacity aircraft of low operating cost, made inevitable the creation of a new generation of short- and medium-range aircraft. First into the market was the United Kingdom. For medium-capacity operations over medium-range routes, de Havilland (already part of the Hawker Siddeley conglomerate and soon to be absorbed fully into it) produced the three-turbofan Trident, which was later stretched to accommodate twice as many passengers as the first models and secured an enviable reputation on the longer European routes. The Trident was initially sized to a wholly inadequate passenger capacity demanded by BEA and never secured the commercial success it might have enjoyed if the first model had offered more passenger seats.

Boeing responded with the three-turbofan Model 727 medium-range transport in 1961. For the first time Boeing adopted the rear-engined formula, a tall T-tail to keep the elevators well above the engine exhausts, and full independence from ground services through the incorporation of a ventral airstair door and an auxiliary power unit. The company's vast production capacity soon saw the American airliner overtake its rival in sales, and although produced in only a few variants, the Model 727 went on to become the world's best-selling airliner, overtaken in numbers only in the late 1980s by another Boeing transport, the Model 737.

The British gained a greater lead with their new short-range airliner, the twin-turbofan One-Eleven built by the British Aircraft Corporation, formed in 1961 by the amalgamation of the Vickers, Bristol, and English Electric companies, later joined by Hunting. The One-Eleven first flew in 1963 and immediately won domestic and export orders, soon proving itself popular with passengers and operators as it was both reliable and economical. Some 230 such aircraft were delivered from the British production line by the end of the 1970s, when the production rights were sold to Romania for the construction of a comparatively small number of additional aircraft.

Oddly enough, the Americans were slow to respond to the One-Eleven, but the Douglas DC-9, which appeared in 1965, soon overtook the One-Eleven and remained in production, in much-developed McDonnell Douglas and Boeing forms, into the first decade of the twenty-first century. Boeing was even later into the field with its Model 737, another twin-turbofan transport. The Model 737 reverted to the traditional Boeing concept of engines under the wing, although the nacelles for the two turbofan engines are attached directly to the underside of the wings without a pylon. The Model 737 first flew in 1967, and has since that time been developed in a number of steadily more impressive variants that remain in production, and indeed in major development, right up to the present. The Model 737 has the extraordinary record of having secured more sales than any other airliner in history.

Two other twin-turbofan contenders in the short-range category were the successful Fokker F.28 Fellowship of the Netherlands and the generally unsuccessful VFW-Fokker 614 from Germany. The former has the look of a smaller One-Eleven and was

Boeing created its three-engined Model 727 as a medium-range type that would partner the four-engined Model 707 long-range airliner and the later two-engined Model 737 short-range airliner in giving the company the ability to offer the civil market types that could be operated in all major aspects of the air transport field.

ABOVE Although the Sukhoi design bureau is best known as the creator of some of the U.S.S.R.'s most capable tactical warplanes, both interceptor and attack aircraft, it was only in later years that the organization started to create warplanes of more general utility, starting with the excellent Su-27. The organization's most advanced airplane at the beginning of the twenty-first century is the Su-47 experimental fifth-generation fighter, previously known as the S-37 Berkut (golden eagle). The Su-47 was completed before 1996 (prototype only) as a demonstrator of advanced technologies including a rear-mounted and forward-swept wing, thrust vectoring, high maneuverability, and low radar cross-section.

later upgraded as the Fokker 100 counterpart of the Fokker 50 modernized version of the twin-turboprop F.27. The latter had its two engines in nacelles on pylons above rather than below the wing to allow the use of very short landing-gear legs, in the process saving weight as well as easing the task of providing access to the cabin on airfields lacking ground-support facilities.

A Japanese design, the twin-turboprop YS-11 built by NAMC (Nihon Airplane Manufacturing Company) also did moderately well in the short-range market, as did the British twin-turboprop transport from which its design was clearly derived, the Hawker Siddeley 748 designed by Avro, another component of the Hawker Siddeley conglomerate. The 748 was later upgraded as the ATP.

THE JET SET

The late 1960s witnessed the development of a new market as businessmen and other small parties needed to get around the world ever more frequently at their own rather than at the airlines' convenience. The aircraft designed to meet this need is the "bizjet" or executive jet, although it should be noted that there are a few turboprop-powered types. The "bizjet" has much the same performance as the big civilian airliners in terms of speed and range, and while originally designed for 10 or fewer passengers has in more recent years developed into corporate jets with accommodation for up to 20 passengers. Larger companies with international interests tend to keep one or more of these jets for high-speed travel by their executives, and charter companies with a few such aircraft have sprung up all over the world to cater to the needs of smaller companies. Fitted out as comfortable flying boardrooms or offices, executive jets have become part of the businessman's life.

Most of the market in the pure-jet end of the range was captured initially by the 1963 Gates Learjet (later Learjet) 24, an extremely impressive airplane with twin turbojet engines podded at the rear of the fuselage, in the manner most commonly accepted in executive jets, and the 1966 Grumman American (later Gulfstream Aerospace) Gulfstream, another clean design with its two turbofan engines podded on the sides of the rear fuselage. Both of these types proved to be just the beginning of a long line of related developments offering greater payload, higher speed, and in their later turbofan-engined variants, considerably greater range. A later but extremely successful contender in the American "bizjet" market has been Cessna, with a series of impressive rear-engined aircraft marketed under the name Citation.

For shorter-range and lower-speed operations in the United States and also for export to less-developed countries, there are the Beech Queen Air and King Air, and a number of other models that can be finished to the customer's own specifications. With the exception of the Queen Air, which has piston engines, these Beech models are powered by turboprop engines. Several of the twin-engined cabin monoplanes built by Cessna and Piper can also be delivered as executive aircraft.

The only "bizjet" of British origin was the de Havilland (Hawker Siddeley) 125, which was also adopted by the RAF as a liaison machine and navigational trainer. The first prototype of this twin-engined "bizjet" flew in August 1962, and by March 1975 no fewer than 336 examples had been sold, including 183 in North America. Continued production and development were undertaken by British Aerospace, created by a merger of Hawker Siddeley and BAC, and in the early 1990s the brand was sold to Raytheon. The French equivalent of the HS 125 is the basic Dassault Mystère/Falcon series. Based on the same airframe, the aircraft of this versatile twin-jet family can be finished as executive jets, small transports, and light freighters. Like the HS 125, the Dassault "bizjet" series has sold well in North America, which has also proved to be a major market for Dassault's larger and longer-ranged corporate transports, the Mystère/Falcon 50 and 900. A later contender in the "bizjet" market was Canada, where Canadair (now like de Havilland Canada part of the very successful Bombardier group) developed the Challenger series that in turn paved the way for a regional airliner.

The period since World War II has also seen a boom in light aviation. The groundwork for this expansion had been laid before the war, especially in the United States, with the appearance of a number of single-engined monoplanes of the high-wing layout with their wings braced to the fuselage by struts. In general powered by small radial or horizontally opposed engines, these light aircraft were highly attractive not just for themselves but also for the fact that they were cheap to buy and run. This allowed an ever-growing number of aviation enthusiasts to take to the air in a way that had been impossible in the late 1920s and early 1930s. Most machines were capable of carrying two or four people and their luggage, and many enthusiasts used their aircraft for travel purposes, but the most important stimulus for light aviation remained the joy of flight for its own sake.

The lightplane of the prewar type reached its peak in World War II, when several classic types were adapted into reliable liaison and observation machines, and also as casualty-evacuation aircraft. After World War II light aviation not only returned in its prewar form but also expanded with considerable speed to include aerobatic flying, gliding, sport parachuting, and in the 1970s the exciting new sport of hang-gliding. Although gliding had enjoyed modest popularity before World War II, it was only after this war's end that gliding matured as a major sport. Gliders are now built in very large numbers in several nations, and the sport has attained great popularity in a large number of nations around the world. Modern gliders are elegant and sleek pure flying machines based on advanced aerodynamic thinking and the latest structural technology. In terms of functional beauty, the glider is without doubt the ultimate flying machine, and skilled pilots can extract the most remarkable performance out of these aerodynamically "pure" types.

One aspect of civil aviation that did not instantly return in a more advanced and larger way after World War II is that embraced by the concepts of the air race and aerial circus, so much a feature of civil aviation in the 1920s and 1930s. Europe still sees a few rather small and insignificant air races, giving the participants great satisfaction but in no way pushing the boundaries, but in the United States air racing later began to regain some of its prewar importance. Extremely popular, this type of air racing is the preserve either of rich individuals heading highly dedicated teams to modify and manage World War II fighters such as the North American Mustang, Grumman Bearcat, and Hawker Sea Fury, or of a growing number of enthusiasts flying small, specially designed racing aircraft in categories that restrict size, weight, and engine power.

Powered lightplanes have been manufactured in a huge assortment of types and sizes since World War II, but about three-quarters of all the airframes, and almost all engines, are manufactured in the United States. Some of the great prewar names, such as Piper, Cessna, and Beech, emerged from the war with considerable production capacity as a result of their wartime manufacture of utility and training aircraft and were therefore in a position to exploit this capacity to satisfy the demands of a large market happy in the short term to use war-surplus machines but also waiting for the new generation of lightplanes. Since that time the American giants have enjoyed an almost unchallenged supe-riority against which their European rivals failed to snatch more than a toehold.

The lightplane market grew steadily into the early part of the 1980s, but the increasing sophistication and cost of the aircraft produced by the larger companies led to a certain disenchantment on the part of lightplane enthusiasts. During the middle of that decade the rising cost of such lightplanes coincided with mounting financial demands as a result of product-liability cases to cause what came close to being the virtual death of the American lightplane industry. Beech, Cessna, and Piper all trimmed the extent of their product lines and the number of aircraft they manufactured each year, and this meant survival even though sales were much reduced. Little altered, though, was the fact that the aircraft of the primary lightplane manufacturers were in general not lightplanes or enthusiasts' flying machines, but rather small airliners or aerial family saloons. This paved the way for a split in the market, with the large companies continuing as before, but an ever-increasing number of small companies offering low-cost but interesting air-craft and even amateurs entering the market with small aircraft of the "experimental" type. These latter can normally be built from plans or even kits of parts, using simple materials and tools, by anyone with a modicum of basic skill, and have recreated "seat of the pants" flying.

The Americans have been less active in the area of civilian transport aircraft, which are used mainly for moving awkward loads to inaccessible spots. The British have excelled in this field, with aircraft such as the Shorts Skyvan and Britten-Norman Islander, together with the Islander's three-engined derivative, the Trislander. Careful design has meant that such aircraft can also be used as aerial buses for short hops, and all such types rely very heavily on rough-field and STOL techniques, allowing steep approaches into small fields. Perhaps the airplane with the most impressive such per-formance is a Swiss offering, the Pilatus Porter, which can operate with enormous agility from the slopes of mountains.

The light STOL types became increasingly popular with civilian operators in the 1970s. Current types rely for the most part on horizontally opposed air-cooled piston en-gines, designed by American companies such as Continental and Lycoming, and offer an unrivaled combination of power, lightness, economy, and reliability. A generation of turbo-prop engines, developing between 250 and 500 hp (186 and 373 kW), entered service during the late 1970s. Engines of this type have since come into their own as the main rival to the horizontally opposed piston engine as they offer a high power/weight ratio, run on more easily available fuel, are very reliable, and do not need major services quite as often.

THE BIG CARRIERS IN CRISIS

Developments in the field of advanced passenger aircraft were checked by the financial slump that followed the Arab-Israeli war of October 1973. Fuel prices started to climb rapidly. The growth rate of passenger traffic, which had been increasing quickly ever since the end of World War II, suddenly slowed and in some cases even went into reverse. Airlines were hard pressed to make ends meet with the aircraft they already had. As a result the airlines temporarily abandoned their plans to order the new and considerably larger machines that were becoming available.

American manufacturers were used to enjoying the largest proportion of the world airliner market and were now caught in a very difficult situation. They had expanded in the 1960s on the assumption that the market would continue to grow at the previous rate and were concerned not to be caught without new aircraft available. Then they faced the prospect of a slump hitting them before they could sell enough machines to recoup their development and production costs.

A case in point was Boeing. With the technology it had developed while producing and planning large aircraft for the U.S. Air Force, Boeing was ready in 1965 to start work on a new airliner capable of carrying a very large number of passengers over very long routes. The huge Model 747 first flew in February 1969, and Boeing had already been so certain of success that it had thought it unnecessary to produce a prototype, so the development tests and certification trials were undertaken with the first production airplane.

The Model 747 was inevitably dubbed the "jumbo jet" and can carry a maximum of 500 passengers in a high-density seating layout, although a more typical load is 385. The airliner's maximum speed is 610 mph (980 km/h), and its range is 6,200 miles (10,000 km). In its initial form, the Model 747 was powered by four Pratt & Whitney JT9D turbofan engines each capable of developing 43,500 lb st (193.50 kN), though the type was later developed in variants with still more powerful engines produced by General Electric and Rolls-Royce as well as Pratt & Whitney. From a distance the Model 747 seems quite ordinary, and it is only closer proximity that reveals the huge size of the airplane, which in its initial Model 747-100 form is 231 ft 4 in (70.51 m) long and 63 ft 5 in (19.33 m) high with a wing spanning 195 ft 8 in (59.64 m). Although the Model 747 is expensive, it is economical in service, and most of the larger airlines have found it ideal for their long routes. To suit the requirements of airlines operating under particular circumstances, Boeing has also produced the "jumbo jet" in a number of variants suiting the airplane to shorter "fat" routes demanding maximum payload capacity over modest ranges, and longer "thin" routes calling for more modest payload over long ranges; there are also mixed passenger/freight and all-freight variants.

The Model 747 gained rapid success, for this pioneering "wide-body" airliner proved beyond doubt that the era of mass air transport had arrived despite the considerable runway and terminal facility demands it placed on airports. The swift increase in the Model 747's order book made it clear to manufacturers and airlines that the more passengers were carried in a single airframe, the greater would be the profits. As a result, companies all over the world considered the development of wide-bodied aircraft in an effort to cash in on the mass transport boom.

In the United States Lockheed during 1969 and 1970 developed the TriStar, with three Rolls-Royce RB211 turbofan engines, each developing 42,000 lb st (186.83 kN), installed as two in nacelles pylon-mounted under the wing's leading edges and one in the tail. The TriStar provided carriage for up to 400 passengers over a range of 4,500 miles (7,240 km). Created by the 1967 amalgamation of the flourishing McDonnell and problem-hit Douglas companies, McDonnell Douglas felt that it too had to compete, and created the DC-10. This had a powerplant configuration akin to that of the TriStar, and the engines were a trio of General Electric or Pratt & Whitney turbofan units each generating 45,000 lb st (200.17 kN). Accommodation and performance were comparable with those of the TriStar.

Europe also planned the creation of wide-body airliners. However, the cost of developing such types was so high that France and Germany decided to collaborate, with the United Kingdom's Hawker Siddeley building the wings as a private venture and smaller elements of the program entrusted to CASA in Spain and Fokker in the Netherlands. Power for the A300, which was the first product of the new Airbus Industrie, was provided by two General Electric CF6 turbofan engines each rated at 51,000 lb st (226.86 kN). By the standards of twin-engined airliners, the A300 carries a considerable number of passengers, up to a maximum of 375 but generally 267, and entered service in 1974 as a short/medium-range type.

As implied by their name, the most notable feature of wide-bodied aircraft is the width of the fuselage. This allows the passengers to be seated in long transverse rows divided by two longitudinal aisles separating the seats into groups and giving easy access to the aircraft exits and facilities. Also notable is the use of the new generation of very high-powered turbofan engines built by General Electric, Pratt & Whitney, and Rolls-Royce, and using many advanced structural techniques and materials.

With the resurgence of air travel by holidaymakers and other mass travelers, these wide-bodied aircraft soon became the norm for high-density routes where speed is not absolutely necessary. Keeping drag down to acceptable limits in aircraft with very large-diameter fuselages was inevitably difficult and called for the utmost skill on the part of designers. Newly developed high-lift devices were of great use, for in the sophisticated forms

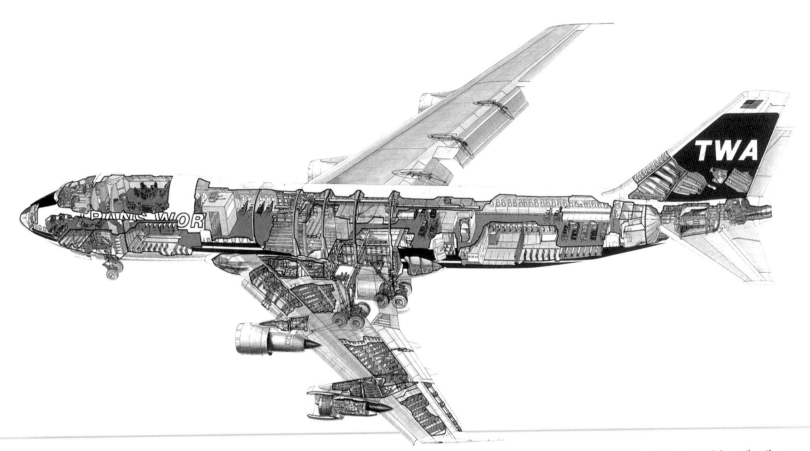

ABOVE Boeing extended its range of civil aircraft with the classic Model 747 high-capacity airliner, offering exceptional range and passenger capacity through the use of a large airframe powered by turbofan engines and including a fuselage wide enough to provide accommodation with two aisles rather than the single aisle that had been standard up to this time.

BELOW Boeing Model 747 over Washington state.

used on the wide-bodied aircraft and new military aircraft such devices permitted the wings to be cut down to a minimum span and area but still provide more than adequate slow-speed landing and takeoff characteristics.

With aircraft such as these, commercial aviation had reached what was at the time thought to be the highest subsonic speeds practical without very expensive airframes and unacceptably high fuel consumption, for which slightly reduced journey times would not compensate.

In this capacity it is worth noting the importance to this American attempt of a research program that had ramifications across much of U.S. aviation in the 1950s and 1960s. The nature of flight and aircraft had meant that there had been a strong analytical and investigative element within aviation from its earliest practical times. Great names from the earlier period of aviation included the Royal Aircraft Establishment in the United Kingdom, the Deutsche Versuchsansalt für Luft- und Raumfahrt in Germany, and the National Advisory Committee for Aeronautics in the United States. This last had been chartered by Congress in 1915 and began work in 1917, and in 1958 became the National Aeronautics and Space Administration in recognition of the increasing importance of space operations.

During the 1920s the U.S. government funded through NACA a program of systematic aerodynamic research, which led to major advances in aircraft performance through the development of advanced structures, airfoil enhancement, and a whole range of features applicable to tasks such as drag reduction and engine cooling. Since 1958 NASA, which is headquartered in Washington, D.C., has undertaken research into and the development of the science and technology for the creation of the vehicles and equipment needed for flight and exploration both inside and outside the atmosphere of the Earth.

The development of NACA into NASA was spurred largely by the USSR's 1957 launch of the world's first spacecraft, the Sputnik vehicle. The development of NASA into its current form was already well advanced by the early 1960s, when President John F. Kennedy established the American goal of putting a man on the Moon by the end of that decade. This paved the way for the Apollo manned spacecraft program, and as a result the American astronaut Neil Armstrong became the first man to set foot on Earth's moon in 1969. Unmanned programs such as the later Viking, Mariner, Voyager, and Galileo efforts, resulted in the creation of spacecraft to begin the exploration of other bodies in our solar system under the aegis of the NASA organization. NASA also developed many satellites for a host of Earth applications. Typical of these latter has been Landsat, which comprises a number of satellites for the collection of data on natural resources and other Earth features. NASA has also launched communications and weather satellites.

North American's B-70 Valkyrie, seen here in XB-70A prototype form, was designed to provide the Strategic Air Command of the U.S. Air Force with a Mach 3 successor to the subsonic Boeing B-52 Stratofortress. The aerodynamics, structure, and powerplant of the Valkyrie were advanced by the standards of the time, and notable features were the very slender fuselage, the canard foreplanes just to the rear of the flight deck, and the large delta wing whose outer portions hinged down in high-speed flight for improved stability. The development of this beautiful airplane was then canceled in the mid-1960s as increasingly irrelevant in the face of the Soviets' development of surface-to-air missiles and interceptors able to decimate high-flying aircraft such as this bomber.

Although space matters currently dominate NASA's work, the organization was notable in a slightly earlier period of its incarnation for pioneering work in flight inside and on the edges of the Earth's envelope of air. One of the most important was the Research Airplane Program, which was undertaken jointly by NASA and the American military services. The RAP was first planned in the later part of World War II to build and fly a series of advanced research aircraft for the examination of all aspects of flight into regimes as yet unexplored. The first practical result of this effort was the approach to and then past the "sound barrier," otherwise the transonic and low supersonic flight regimes. Supersonic flight was first achieved in 1947, and extensions of the RAP program then yielded significant increases in man's knowledge of winged flight up to speeds of 4,500 mph (7,240 km/h) or more and altitudes of 350,000 ft (106,680 m) or more.

In general, the aircraft of the RAP effort were of two categories. First were those for exploration into the realms of higher speeds and altitudes, as exemplified by the Bell X-1 and X-2, the Douglas D-558, and North American X-15. Second were those created for investigation of different layouts on handling and performance, as exemplified by the Douglas X-3, Northrop X-4, Bell X-5, North American XB-70, and Martin Marietta lifting bodies including the X-24. The RAP effort made enormous contributions to the development of high-speed flight in terms of valuable data about aircraft characteristics that had not previously been examined, the correlation of the transonic/supersonic characteristics suggested by wind tunnel and other analytical processes with the real nature of full-size aircraft, and the generation of practical experience of a less quantifiable but nonetheless vital significance in the building of confidence toward the realization of supersonic flight as a safe and fully controlled matter of everyday aviation.

This last was of signal importance when the United States began to consider the development of an SST, or Supersonic Transport, for civil use.

By the mid-1950s design teams in France, the United Kingdom, and the United States were considering SSTs (supersonic transports). French and British teams concentrated on designs offering a cruising speed of Mach 2.2 so that there would be no need for special and therefore expensive alloys to cope with the high temperatures generated by high-speed flight. American teams proposed a Mach 3 airplane making extensive use of new temperature-resistant alloys and metals such as titanium. The American program was canceled in 1970.

Political and economic factors then decided the French and British governments that a collaborative project was the best course. The agreement between France and the

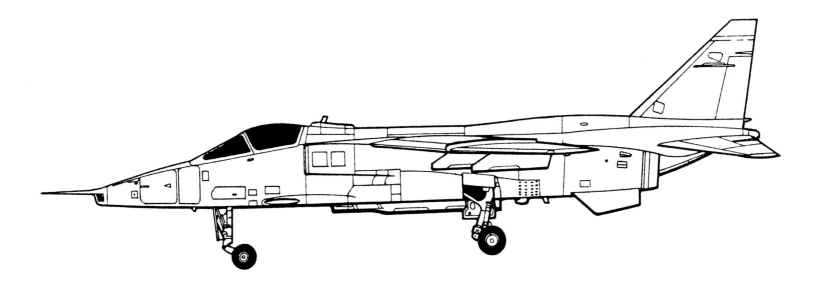

ABOVE The growing cost of designing, developing, and manufacturing modern aircraft was reflected in Europe by the introduction of collaborative programs. The first of these to reach fruition was the SEPECAT Jaguar, which was created as an Anglo-French supersonic type in variants optimized for the attack and advanced training roles.

BELOW Another major Anglo-French collaborative program led to the BAe/Aérospatiale Concorde, which is today's only supersonic transport airplane since the demise of its unsuccessful Soviet counterpart, the Tupolev Tu-144.

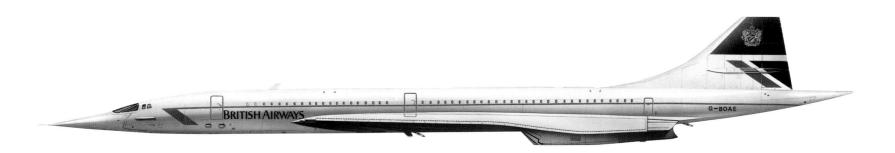

United Kingdom was signed in 1962, and by 1963 the designers of this first major international aerospace venture had settled on the basic design of a Mach 2.2 airliner with 130 seats and the range to operate on the air routes across the Atlantic. The development of the airplane, which eventually became the BAe/Aérospatiale Concorde, was technically successful, the first prototype flew in 1969, and the Concorde entered service with Air France and British Airways simultaneously in January 1976. The future of the Concorde remained uncertain a year later. Political and environmental concerns had prevented the Concorde from operating on the primary route for which it had been conceived, namely that between New York and Paris or London. In the long run, though, the Concorde entered full and operationally profitable service on the Atlantic routes, though the project as a whole was a commercial failure as only a very small number of the aircraft were built for service that in fact yielded operating profits.

Not to be outdone, the U.S.S.R. also created an SST, the Tupolev Tu-144, which was remarkably similar to the Concorde. There were serious problems with this Soviet type, and considerable structural revision was required before the type could be considered for service. Progress was further hampered, moreover, by the unaccountable crash of a prototype during the 1973 Paris Air Show. During the late 1970s and very early 1980s the Tu-144 saw limited freight and passenger service within the U.S.S.R., but was withdrawn from service in the light of technical problems.

During the early part of the 1980s the airline business underwent a traumatic period of economic adjustment as the major operators began to come to grips with the financial realities of virtually no seat-mile growth at a time of much-enhanced fuel costs and capital outlay on new aircraft. Yet better times for the airlines were imminent, with a resurgence of confidence in the desirability of air transport, a fall in the price of fuel, and the emergence of aircraft that were either entirely new or much-developed forms of the best machines from the current generation.

Through the 1970s and into the early 1980s the world of aviation moved somewhat unsteadily past an important turning point possibly as significant as any in its short but momentous history. This point had two major interconnected causes: the world recession of the period and the enormously increased cost of all aviation fuels. Both these factors directly affected the development of aviation in general and civil aviation in particular. Four important families of wide-bodied civil transport aircraft entered service in the 1970s to cater for the steady growth in passenger demand and at first secured great success. Then the combination of recession and greater airline costs, passed on to the passenger in the form of higher prices, severely curtailed this growth during the early 1980s and in turn jeopardized the future of many airlines and the several aircraft manufacturers who depended for their economic stability on the twin factors of growth and a consistent purchasing policy by the airlines.

Such has been the cost of engine development from the 1980s that all major engine manufacturers plan their engines in families that can be matched to several aircraft in service or under development. In this way costs can be kept in check, but engines are still the single most expensive item in any major aircraft. The three Western companies that dominate the market for civil and military turbofans in the West are General Electric and Pratt & Whitney in the United States, and Rolls-Royce in the United Kingdom. During the late 1980s and early 1990s, however, a slight supplement to the efforts of these major players was created by the growing involvement of engine manufacturers from France, Germany, and Japan, often in alliance with one or more of the major companies for the design, development, and production of engines matched to a niche in the airliner market requiring engines of less power than those developed by the large companies.

The progress of the late 1980s was maintained through the further development of engines along this course, with further improvements in all aspects of "conventional" engine technology to reduce specific fuel consumption and increase the ease with which engines can be maintained. This latter can be achieved in part by the improved manufacture of key components such as compressor blades, using advanced industrial processes to ensure high accuracy and unflawed basic materials (including single crystals, carbon fiber, graphite, boron, and ceramics, all of which are becoming increasingly common in the latest generations of aircraft). It can also be achieved in part by the greater use of modules in the basic construction of the engine: Thus a suspect or time-expired module, such as a complete compressor, can be removed simply and quickly as a unit and replaced by a similar unit while the original is repaired, overhauled, or merely examined. The use of modular construction on a larger scale also opens the way to increased accuracy, so that high-speed rotating assemblies such as compressor stages can be balanced after construction and then placed into the engine without the need for the entire unit to be rebalanced. This saves time and money directly and also benefits the operator's economics by reducing the required quantity of spares and servicing equipment.

Another aspect of powerplant development that became increasingly important in the 1980s and the 1990s was the computerized control of the engine by means of a FADECS (Full-Authority Digital Engine Control System). This small software-controlled "black box"

system is designed to operate the engines at maximum safety and economy levels. Inputs from the crew, air data sensors, flight-management system, and the engines themselves are all assessed continuously by the computer to provide optimum and constantly updated control settings for the engines given all the ambient conditions, and to monitor the performance of the engines with information displayed to the crew only when the data necessary for a decision are not instantly derivable from the computer's programming. FADECS has been found to offer very significant improvements in overall engine management and hence in fuel economy, and despite their cost such systems became standard in almost all civil and military aircraft from the late 1980s.

The two factors that most affect the operating economics of modern aircraft are engine performance and basic aerodynamic design, but too high a structure weight is also a major factor, especially in range. Whereas military aircraft are generally designed to the safe-life concept, in which components are proved by testing to have a statistically established life expectancy before failure, civil aircraft conform to the fail-safe design principle in which the system can withstand any failure, usually by the provision of redundant components, systems, or even structures. A fail-safe design is inevitably safer than a safe-life design, but generally suffers from a higher structure weight: Superfluous weight in the airplane's structure or systems is necessarily translated as reduced payload and/or fuel, which in turn means degraded operating economics. It is very important for the design team, therefore, to trim the weight of the airframe to the minimum consonant with the fail-safe design philosophy. By the 1970s this philosophy was very well-developed, but of course there is also a downside to the concept.

For a given maximum takeoff weight, it is possible to calculate a fail-safe structure of optimum weight. If the design team fixes this weight at the proposed maximum for the initial model, however, it makes it difficult to increase the maximum weight of later models, and, conversely, allowance for growth in the future can saddle the initial model with

The Lockheed SR-71 Mach 3 reconnaissance airplane was generally known as the "Blackbird" for its very dark blue/black finish, and the layout of its pilot's cockpit reveals the state of the art in terms of instrumentation when the type was designed in the late 1950s and early 1960s. Compared with a modern cockpit, which has only a relatively small number of digital displays, keyboards, and multirole switches, that of the SR-71 was crammed with analog instruments, gyroscopic indicators, and single-purpose switches. Yet the SR-71 remains the fastest conventional airplane yet built.

too heavy an airframe. Thus design teams are forced to juggle with the ratio between these two factors to reach a sensible solution.

Then there came the concept of active controls, opening up the possibility of considerably higher weights without the need for a significantly strengthened structure, especially in the wing roots where alterations are always expensive in terms of money and weight. The problem with increased weight, so far as this particular application is concerned, is that it increases the bending moment on the wing, and in the process adversely affects the structural problems resulting from transient but nonetheless highly significant gust and maneuvering loads. For economic and safety reasons it is not desirable to fall back on alternatives such as lower speeds and reduced maneuvering parameters to limit "g" loads, so the idea of active flight controls for dealing with the increased bending loads associated with higher weights was particularly attractive. So far only Lockheed has used such a system, in the case of the L-1011-500 model of its TriStar transport, intended to carry smaller numbers of passengers over longer routes than earlier versions of the TriStar. The reduction of induced drag made it desirable to increase span by some 9 ft (2.74 m), with great benefits to range performance, but then only the introduction of active controls on the wings could prevent unacceptably high bending moments with the original root structure.

The L-1101-500 was accordingly manufactured with three sets of sensors to measure vertical acceleration, and the resulting data were processed by the onboard automatic flight-control system computer to control the ailerons. In short, the sensors tell the computer the moment a gust strikes the airplane in such a way as to cause an upward bend in the wings, whereupon the computer instructs the outboard ailerons to move symmetrically upward, thereby canceling the upward bending movement initiated by the gust. The system thus negates the aerodynamic feature of the wing's higher aspect ratio, which tends to move the lift distribution outward from the roots and thus increase bending moment, by artificially shifting the lift distribution inboard at critical times. The net effect of this theoretically simple but practically fairly complicated feature is greater aerodynamic efficiency and less drag, with a resultant decrease of 3 percent in fuel consumption. This may seem an insignificant saving, but it was equivalent to just under 950 U.S. gal (791 Imp gal, 3,596 liters) in the case of the L-1101-500's maximum fuel capacity of 31,642 U.S. gal (26,348 Imp gal, 119,778 liters), and over a period represented a very useful fuel saving.

During 1982 Lockheed decided to drop out of the airliner manufacturing business once it had completed its current orders for the TriStar in 1985, so there seems little im-

In the first part of the twenty-first century much is expected in military terms from the UAV (Unmanned Air Vehicle), which can range in size from hand-launched minivehicles for reconnaissance in a possible urban battlefield to large aircraft carrying substantial sensor payloads over very long ranges and/or endurances for operational and strategic reconnaissance. Further development of the concept, already trialled by combat UAVs armed with air-to-surface weapons, including missiles, is being directed toward the creation of UCAVs (Unmanned or Uninhabited Combat Air Vehicles) able to undertake the complete air warfare role specified for the type. The United States' primary long-range UAV in the early 2000s is the Northrop Grumman RQ-4 Global Hawk, the only survivor of a major UAV development effort that also included the type illustrated here, the Lockheed-Martin/Boeing Dark Star.

mediate chance for active tail controls to be introduced as had been hoped. An active tailplane, for example, would have permitted smaller control area, allowing the slab tailplane to be reduced in size with a saving in weight of 1,680 lb (762 kg) and a further 3 percent cut in fuel consumption. During the later 1990s there was a resurgence of interest in the active control concept as a means of trimming structure weight and reducing drag.

Sensors and the computer within the control loop are the keys to active control, and these two factors have become increasingly dominant in aviation. They constitute the core of the AFCS (Automatic Flight-Control System) that manages the operation of most modern airliners, providing the flight-management capability that optimizes the flight profile. This yields significant operating economies and also reduces the flight crew's workload by undertaking navigational routines as well as monitoring systems such as the powerplant, flight controls and high-lift devices, communications, and environmental control system. This factor has allowed the standard flight crew of even a long-range airliner to be reduced to a mere two pilots in most aircraft. Airliners of the previous generation required a flight crew of four or five: two pilots, a flight engineer, a navigator and, in some cases, a radio operator. This reduction in manning is obviously attractive to airlines and has longer-term implications in permitting the reduction of the size of the flight deck and any crew rest station, with advantages in reduced structure weight and cost.

Coordinating the capabilities of an autopilot, INS (Inertial Navigation System) or other advanced navigation system such as GPS (Global Positioning System), and meteorological system into one computer-controlled package, the AFCS allows the flight crew to concentrate its efforts on decision-making and vital-level monitoring functions without detriment to safety. At a considerable increase in capital cost, therefore, the new breed of airliner reduces the operator's running costs by reducing fuel consumption, cutting crew training and salary requirements, and easing maintenance. The AFCS is a remarkably versatile system, and allied to it individually or collectively are several other computer-directed systems, such as the CSAS (Command and Stability Augmentation System), the INS, which measures the airplane's three-dimensional accelerations and integrates these in time to determine the position of the airplane relative to the predetermined starting point, and VOR (VHF Omni-Range), which is a ground-located navigation aid usable only when the airplane is flying along predetermined airways. Other important systems increasingly important in civil and, to a lesser extent, military operations, are ground- and aircraft-proximity warning systems and a wind-shear detection system.

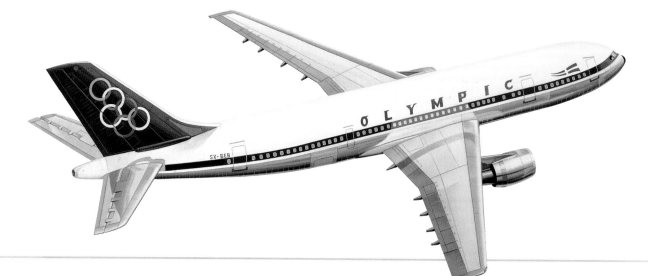

ABOVE Further expansion of international collaboration saw the establishment of Airbus as a European organization to rival Boeing. The first Airbus type to reach service was the A300 airliner.

BELOW Based on the Boeing Model 747-200B airliner, the E-4 was schemed in the early 1970s as replacement for the Boeing EC-135 series in the U.S. Air Force's airborne national-command-post role providing the national command authority (the U.S. president accompanied by his senior civil and military leaders) with a communications center capable of surviving a nuclear exchange through its combination of shielding against nuclear thermal and electromagnetic pulse effects and its ability to orbit clear of primary targets. This airplane made its maiden flight on June 13, 1973, and the three aircraft entered service in 1974–75 as E-4A National Emergency Airborne Command Posts with equipment stripped from Boeing EC-135J machines and updated by E-Systems. Delivered in December 1979, the fourth airplane was completed to the more advanced E-4B standard with a large

blister on the upper rear of the upper deck for a super-high-frequency satellite communication system as well as a Collins LF/VLF communication system using a trailing wire aerial 42,240 ft (12,875 m) long. The three E-4A machines were then upgraded to the same standard with an extremely wide-ranging assortment of voice, teletype, and data communication links. The upper deck is occupied by the flight deck and the rest area for the flight crews, the five compartments of the main deck are allocated, from front to rear, as a flight crew section, the National Command Authority section basically equivalent to the White House's situation room, a conference section, a battle staff section, and C3I planning section. The lower deck is reserved for equipment, maintenance, and the operator's station for the trailing antenna. The shifting nature of world events is reflected in the fact that the E-4 aircraft were initially known as AABNCP (Advanced Airborne National Command Post) machines but then became NEACP (National Emergency Airborne Command Post) or "Kneecap" aircraft before reaching their current appellation of NAOC (National Airborne Operations Center) machines.

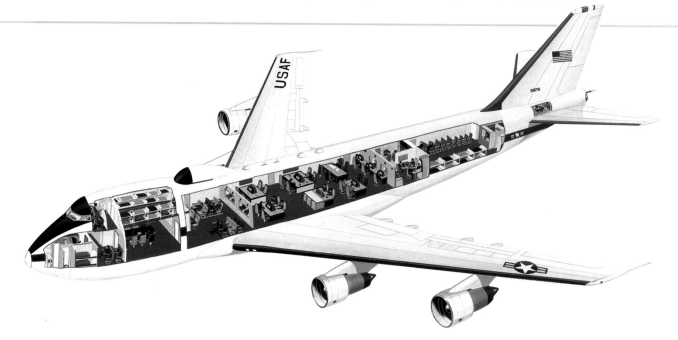

The commercial aircraft of the newer generation, including such Airbus types as the A310, A320, A330, and A340 series, Boeing types such as the Model 757, Model 767, and Model 777 series, and the Boeing MD-11 upgraded version of the DC-10, each have a flight deck layout based on a small number of keyboard-controlled multifunction displays of the CRT (Cathode Ray Tube), LED (Light-Emitting Diode), or liquid-crystal types replacing most of the earlier airliners' great banks of dials, gauges, and switches. On these displays, generally of the full-color type, the flight crew can call up any information they need. At the same time the AFCS can override the standard information shown on the screens to warn the crew of anything beyond the capabilities of the computer and therefore demanding a human decision. These visual warnings are generally accompanied by some type of aural warning to ensure that the flight crew take immediate notice of information required for their rapid arrival at a decision that may have safety implications.

The upper end of the commercial aircraft market seems to be capable of supporting only the two current giants, namely Airbus Industrie and Boeing. It became clear during the 1980s how Airbus has come to challenge Boeing for domination of the market for wide-body airliners currently dominated by products such as the Model 737, Model 747, and Model 767. To maintain this challenge Airbus had to expand its product range so that it could compete with Boeing across the whole spectrum of the civil market, and this

Announced in 1978, along with the Model 757 whose basic configuration it shares, Boeing's Model 767 was schemed as a "wide-body" type for the medium- and long-range tasks. The Models 757 and 767, along with the related Model 777 "wide-body" type for the long-range role, have sold very well to airlines all over the world.

process has continued into the early 2000s. It is likely that the only two major manufacturers of large civil transports in the foreseeable future will be Airbus and Boeing, which both concentrate on advanced-technology aircraft for the mid and upper portions of the market spectrum for passenger and freight aircraft. It is worth noting, however, that while there appeared to be little demand for the "jumbo" size of airliner, with seating for some 500 passengers, during the first half of the 1980s, Boeing kept its Model 747 in production and thereby gained considerable benefit when the market for high-capacity transports revived later in the decade. Boeing has also devoted considerable effort to the continued development of the Model 747, which has profited from the introduction of improvements and updated models in terms of increased orders.

The resurgence of airline demand for high-capacity transports also persuaded Airbus to enter this commercially dangerous but potentially lucrative market with the A330 and A340 half-brothers. Both aircraft can carry up to 440 passengers, although 375 is more typical, and are aimed at the medium/long- and long-range markets respectively. The two types share an essentially similar airframe, but whereas the A330-300 is powered by two General Electric CF6-80E turbofan engines each rated at 67,500 lb st (300.25 kN) but replaceable by similarly rated Pratt & Whitney PW4000 or Rolls-Royce Trent turbofan units for the delivery of a typical payload over a range of 5,445 miles (8,765 km), the A340-300 baseline model is powered by four CFM International (General Electric/SNECMA) CFM56-5C turbofan engines each rated at 32,500 lb st (144.57 kN) for the delivery of a typical payload over a range of 7,600 miles (12,225 km). The aircraft entered service in January 1994 and March 1993 respectively, and are offered in a number of variants with different engines, weights, fuel capacities, and seating layouts.

At a lower capacity level, several medium-capacity airliners of the 1960s and 1970s were still in production during the 1980s, but again the two dominant players have become Airbus and Boeing, the former offering the wide-body A310 as a short/medium-range transport for a maximum of 255 passengers, and the latter bracketing the target market the narrow-body Model 757 as a short/medium-range transport for a maximum of 223 passengers and the wide-body Model 767 as a medium-range transport with seating for a maximum of 289 passengers. A passenger capacity of about 250 was typical of the requirement of airlines from the late 1980s, and apart from their narrow- and wide-body fuselages, all three aircraft adhere to the same basic design concept with a low-set wing characterized by moderate sweep and extensive high-lift devices, a swept tail unit with a low-set tailplane, and two turbofan engines in nacelles pylon-mounted below and ahead of the wing's leading edges.

A lightplane that began its life before World War II, then saw service in that conflict as a liaison and observation type, was the Piper J-3 Cub. This was of the classic fabric-covered lightplane configuration for the time, with a high-set strut-braced wing, fixed tailwheel landing gear, a flat-four engine, and tandem accommodation in a simply equipped cockpit. Development of the basic concept embodied in this type then led to the lightplane seen here, the PA-18 Super Cub.

The first part of the 1980s was marked by considerable enthusiasm among airlines and manufacturers for smaller-capacity airliners. It was widely accepted that growing demand for seats on the world's short/medium-range routes required new 150-passenger airliners based on the latest technology and designed to replace older airliners such as the three-engined Model 727, two-engined Model 737, and two-engined DC-9. All three of these older types were still ordered in useful numbers into the early 1980s, but the Model 727 program ended in 1983. The two twin-engined designs remained in full-scale production, and moreover in continued development, but gradually the Model 737 eclipsed the DC-9 to become the best-selling airliner of all time in succession to the Model 727. The fortunes of the DC-9 and its upgraded derivatives of the MD-80 and MD-90 series waned. Production of the last variant, known as the Model 717 since McDonnell Douglas's merger into Boeing following an announcement in December 1996, is to end in the early part of the twenty-first century. The position of the Model 737 is unrivaled and indeed is likely to remain so as Boeing develops new variants with longer fuselages, more modern engines, and more advanced features such as a "glass" flight deck.

Given the availability of the DC-9 and Model 737 as still-capable machines meeting current and expected requirements in well-proved airframes, therefore, most airlines were content not to take the risk of ordering a new airplane before it had flown, while the airframe and engine manufacturers were unwilling to commit scarce capital to projects that had attracted no genuine customer commitment.

At the low-capacity end of the airliner market, the 1980s saw moderately healthy sales continue for small airliners, the market being boosted by the deregulation of the U.S. air transport industry, which made it possible for many small airlines to spring up either as feeders for the main operators or to service the requirements of smaller communities wanting air links to major cities. A smaller version of this tendency extended itself to other parts of the world during the late 1980s and early 1990s and created the situation in which well-established machines such as the F.27 Friendship and F.28 Fellowship could flourish. Such was the continued success of its two types during the 1980s, indeed, that Fokker developed updated versions as the Fokker 50 and Fokker 100 respectively, and although the airline industry's downturn in the early 1990s adversely affected sales, both types sold moderately well and were being developed into slightly more capacious variants to cater for the enlargement of this segment of the air transport market. But in 1997 Fokker went into bankruptcy.

Still further down the passenger capacity ladder, the 1980s saw a small but significant boom in commuter airliners, and here there was and indeed continues to be a growing number of new aircraft. The three most ambitious contenders in this increasingly strongly contested market were the Aeritalia/Aérospatiale ATR 42 and higher-capacity ATR 72, the Saab-Fairchild SF-240, changed to Saab 340 in 1987 following Fairchild's 1985 withdrawal from the program, and the de Havilland Canada DHC-8 Dash 8. This is a market niche in which the superiority of the turboprop was at first unchallenged, providing major opportunities for companies such as Allison (now Rolls-Royce North America), Garrett AiResearch (now Honeywell), and Pratt & Whitney Canada.

Boeing launched the development of its Model 777 twin-jet airliner to provide itself with a rival to the Airbus A330 and A340 series, and also the McDonnell Douglas MD-11 updated version of the DC-10. The first Model 777 flew in June 1994, and entered service twelve months later. The type can be configured for the carriage of between 300 and 550 passengers depending on the number of classes and the seat pitches selected, and the company had received orders for almost 580 of this advanced type by the fall of 2001.

Yet there were clear signs of uncertainty in the third-level/commuter market evident from the mid-1980s, persuading many manufacturers that the time was past for any but the most modest level of risk-taking. Even so, there was a steady if unspectacular place for the cheapest commuterliners such as the Shorts 360, de Havilland Canada DHC-7 Dash 7, Let L-410 Turbolet, Dornier Do 228, CASA C-212 Aviocar and various offerings (notably the EMB-110 Bandeirante and EMB-120 Brasilia) of the Brazilian EMBRAER concern, whose inroads into the American market caused much concern to the troubled Swearingen firm, taken over by Fairchild in 1981. The American company overcame its problems, and during the early 1990s its Metro series began to enjoy a revival of fortune.

The longer-term future of the commuterliner now seems assured by the steady expansion of the market, whose upper level has moved into the regional transport niche, often with turbofan-powered aircraft offering attractive combinations of higher performance and greater passenger capacity than turboprop-powered pure commuterliners. Typical of this new breed are the turbofan-powered EMBRAER RJ-145 and its family of variants as well as the Canadair Regional Jet development of the CL-601 Challenger corporate transport, and turboprop-powered aircraft such as the Dornier Do 328 (later taken over by Fairchild and further developed in variants with the original two turboprops replaced by two turbofans), Airtech CN-325, Saab 2000 development of the Saab 340, and British Aerospace ATP development of the BAe 748.

DANGEROUS TOYS

Running in parallel with these and other developments in the sphere of commercial aviation between the 1950s and the end of the twentieth century was a stream of progress in military aviation. During the 1950s there were strong suggestions that the advent of the computer and advanced sensors might make the manned airplane a thing of the past, especially in military service. It was postulated that the removal of the pilot, together with all the systems that were required for his life support and to provide him with control of the airplane, would open the way for a major decrease in fuselage cross-section, in turn creating the opening for other enhancements such as reduced structure weight, less powerful engines without sacrifice of performance, and smaller fuel tanks without sacrifice of range. Such aircraft would be cheaper to build and maintain, allowing the procurement of more aircraft and reducing unit cost considerably, thus permitting further purchases. The absence of a pilot would make it feasible to increase the permissible "g" loadings so that the aircraft could be thrown about the sky in much tighter maneuvers.

Events soon proved that such expectations were more than half a century premature, and it seems clear that even if the state of the avionics art had permitted the creation of such aircraft, they would not have been built on a production basis except in missile form: For example, the cruise missile is essentially an unmanned airplane and has been a major element of the U.S. strategic nuclear deterrent since the late 1980s. The reason is simple: In civil aircraft the presence of a flight crew was and indeed remains essential for psychological purposes, as few passengers would permit themselves to be flown by an unmanned system, and in military aircraft the presence of an onboard pilot until very recently offered an unrivaled decision-making capability that may never be matched by a computer unless true artificial intelligence can be created. Only in this event would it be possible to do away entirely with manned military aircraft, for there will always be situations in which lack of concrete data will call for the flexible responses of human judgment, or even the use of intuition.

In the first part of the twenty-first century, though, technical developments have again resurrected the concept of the UCAV (Unmanned Combat Air Vehicle). In the later part of the twentieth century the creation of ever more sophisticated computers and satellite-relayed communications opened the way for the creation of UAVs (Unmanned Air Vehicles) for reconnaissance in conditions in which it would be foolhardy to risk a manned airplane or in which the low observability of the unmanned machine offers special advantages. For example, the General Atomics RQ-1 Predator is a small piston-engined machine designed for the completion of medium-altitude tactical reconnaissance missions over the battlefield with optronic, infrared, or synthetic-aperture radar sensors, while the Northrop Grumman RQ-4 Global Hawk is a larger turbofan-powered machine intended for long-range and/or long-endurance high-altitude operational and strategic reconnaissance missions with more advanced sensors of the same basic types as those carried by the Predator. UAVs of these types have an onboard guidance package that can be programmed to control a specific mission from takeoff to return via a variable number of waypoints, but can be taken over in flight from a ground station should the situation demand.

Both of these UAVs proved very useful in American-led campaigns from the last years of the twentieth century, most notably the campaign that started in 2001 to find and destroy terrorist organizations based in Afghanistan. The Predator was also operated in an interim combat form with air-to-surface guided missiles and proved successful. The concept is now being take a step further toward the UCAV, with the United States and other countries actively planning or developing the UCAV concept specifically for the combat role.

Even so, the manned airplane is here for the foreseeable future. The flexibility offered by humans is nowhere better attested to than in the control of the strategic nuclear deterrents of the two superpowers up to the time of the U.S.S.R.'s collapse in 1989. The United States and U.S.S.R. each had large numbers of surface- and submarine-launched ballistic missiles but felt the need to retain comparatively small but nonetheless significant manned bomber forces that could be retargeted after "launch," be recalled, undertake a variety of approaches to the target, and fly other missions with the aid of additional or different equipment.

The Soviets' most important such assets, which are still operated by some of the U.S.S.R.'s successor states in the Commonwealth of Independent States such as Russia and the Ukraine, are the Tupolev Tu-22M "Backfire" and the Tu-160 "Blackjack" variable-geometry bombers. Of these the first is a radical development of the disappointing Tu-22 "Blinder" fixed-wing bomber, while the latter bears a strong conceptual affinity to the Rockwell B-1 Lancer, the American type designed as successor to the Boeing B-52 Stratofortress, even though it is larger than the American machine. Although designed for long-range subsonic missions carrying free-fall nuclear weapons, in its last B-52G and B-52H variants the Stratofortress was revised for the low-level penetration of Soviet airspace with two North American AGM-28 Hound Dog air-to-surface supersonic cruise missiles. The Hound Dogs were later replaced by 12 or more examples of the Boeing AGM-86 air-to-surface subsonic cruise missile offering far higher penetration capability than the AGM-28 as a result of its very accurate guidance and relative invulnerability to interception as a result of its very low-level cruise altitude and "stealthy" design. The B-1A was created for high supersonic performance at high altitude, but the growing sophistication of Soviet air defense systems led to the type's cancellation, though it was later reinstated as the B-1B with lower overall performance but superior capabilities in the lower-level penetration role with a large complement of cruise missiles and/or free-fall nuclear weapons. In financial terms it is hard to see how the B-1B could be justified as genuinely cost-effective in its primary role, but in strategic and political terms there can be no doubt that the type still provides the United States with important capabilities in the power-projection role that demands extreme operational flexibility right up to the moment of weapon release with nuclear and/or conventional bombs.

The B-1B is an exceptional illustration, for the cost and complexity of a dedicated single-role airplane have made such types rare in modern air forces, in which single-role aircraft are generally dedicated reconnaissance aircraft as exemplified by the Lockheed SR-71 "Blackbird" and U-2R/S in American service, or the Myasishchyev M-17/55 "Mystic" planned for Russian service from the mid-1990s, or aircraft dedicated to control as exemplified by the Boeing E-3A Sentry developed from the Model 707 transport and by the Beriev (Ilyushin) A-50 "Mainstay" developed from the Il-76 "Candid" transport. These extremely costly aircraft have good survival chances as they are not intended for operations in the combat zone.

Thrust vectoring and the combination of powerful canard surfaces ahead of the center of gravity and ailerons and slab elevators behind it give the F-15SMTD very considerable agility and also the ability to reach and maintain very high angles of attack.

ABOVE The world's first "stealth warplane" to enter service was the Lockheed F-117 Night Hawk, which first flew in June 1981. The "stealthiness" of this pioneering warplane is based on its configuration, materials, buried powerplant, nonemitting sensors, and internal weapons carriage.

BELOW The shaping of the Lockheed F-117's forward surfaces and the structures supporting them was conceived to trap incoming electromagnetic radiation and, when this was impossible, attenuate it and allow its reflection only in directions away from the original emitter.

The SR-71 was a genuinely remarkable airplane, and remains the holder of the world absolute speed and altitude records. The airplane was planned as the launch platform for supersonic reconnaissance drones, developed into the YF-12A experimental interceptor, and then turned into the SR-71 strategic reconnaissance platform. The "Blackbird" was a massive delta-wing machine with the fuselage contours faired laterally into a lifting shape and was powered by two afterburning bleed-turbojets running on special low-volatility fuel. Prodigiously expensive to build and to maintain, the SR-71 provided the U.S. command structure with a mass of reconnaissance information after Mach 3-plus flights at very high altitudes.

For the control of its armed forces, the United States deploys two types modified from civil airliners. As noted above, the Boeing E-3 Sentry is an adaptation of the Boeing 707 with a large rotodome above the fuselage containing the antenna for the very capable long-range surveillance radar. Flying long-endurance patrols at high altitude, the E-3 can watch all air activity within a radius of 250 miles (402 km) at whatever altitude, while an onboard tactical team uses computers to assess data from this radar and other sources (provided by secure data link) and then controls friendly forces to tackle the threats revealed. The United States planned a fleet of 40 Sentry aircraft, but in fact ordered just 34, while later purchasers were NATO with 18, Saudi Arabia with five, France with four, and the United Kingdom with seven. The U.S.S.R.'s first such airplane was the considerably less sophisticated Tupolev Tu-126 "Moss," but from the early 1990s this was replaced by the A-50 "Mainstay" derivative of the Il-76 "Candid" transport mentioned above. These AWACS (Airborne Warning and Control System) aircraft are marvelously complex yet efficient adjuncts to the tactical control of air power: They are really airborne command posts, generating data for themselves but also receiving input from other aircraft, satellites, and surface forces. In fact, each airplane is capable of controlling the entire range of air activities in a complete theater of war.

For national command capability there is the Boeing E-4, based on the Model 747 airliner, and though six such aircraft were originally planned, the final total is just four. These are the most expensive single aircraft yet built, but provide the United States with the means of controlling the entire national war effort from a single airborne, and therefore relatively invulnerable, airplane. Designated the ABNCP (Airborne National Command Post), the E-4 is crammed with computers and communications gear, making each airplane a U.S. "war emergency capital."

Despite its designation in the F-for-Fighter category, the Lockheed F-117 Night Hawk is an attack rather than a fighter warplane, and is one of the most important warplanes in the U.S. Air Force's inventory in the first part of the twenty-first century. The F-117 has firmly subsonic performance, and was designed to deliver attacks of pinpoint accuracy on key targets using precision-guided munitions. To do this the F-117 uses its "stealthiness" or low observability to reach its target area without being detected by the enemy's defenses. The keys to this stealthiness are the airplane's structure and design: Shrouded engines emit little noise or heat, while the airframe either traps electromagnetic radiation or reflects it away from the emitter so that no radar "echo" is created.

The control of tactical air operations has also become increasingly important, and the world's most successful exponent of this art is the Grumman (now Northrop Grumman) E-2 Hawkeye, which was developed for carrierborne use by the U.S. Navy and has proved itself very successful. The E-2 is still in production and development during the early part of the twenty-first century for the U.S. Navy, and other operators of this highly effective yet affordable "force multiplier" platform include Egypt, France, Israel, Japan, Singapore, and Taiwan.

Although very expensive to buy and operate, aircraft of this type can make the use of combat aircraft much more efficient, hence their description as "force multipliers." It is probable, therefore, that AWACS if not ABNCP aircraft are likely to feature strongly in the plans of the major air forces.

The other side of the AWACS coin, however, is the fact that if it is important to make full use of one's own "force multiplier" aircraft, it is just as vital to prevent an enemy from making full use of his own "force multipliers." Thus the role of ECM (Electronic Counter-Measures) aircraft, in the form of either dedicated aircraft or otherwise standard warplanes fitted with the required internal and/or external equipment, will be further extended. It was over Vietnam from the late 1960s that the U.S. Air Force pioneered the modern use of such electronic warfare aircraft, and since then they have proved themselves invaluable in promoting the success and survivability of combat aircraft, jamming the radar of enemy ground and air missiles and hampering the use of early warning systems.

As with AWACS aircraft, the electronics for such machines are very costly and make the purchase of such aircraft a subject for major consideration. Such is the pace of electronic development, moreover, that ECCM (Electronic Counter-Counter-Measures) are soon developed for the ECM equipment, and ECM equipment requires constant updating to keep abreast of enemy advances in radar and other electronic technologies. Yet the overall importance of such EW (Electronic Warfare) equipment was amply confirmed during the 1973 Arab-Israeli war, in which only the arrival of ECM equipment from the United States saved the Israeli air force from an even heavier mauling by Soviet-made missiles.

The deployment of EW aircraft thus increased considerably during the 1980s, largely in the United States. Few other countries can afford to purchase single-role aircraft with the extraordinary capabilities of the USAF's now-retired General Dynamics EF-111 Raven and the U.S. Navy's Grumman EA-6 Prowler all-weather types. The Prowler is useful at the strategic, operational, and tactical levels, and while it has internal equip-

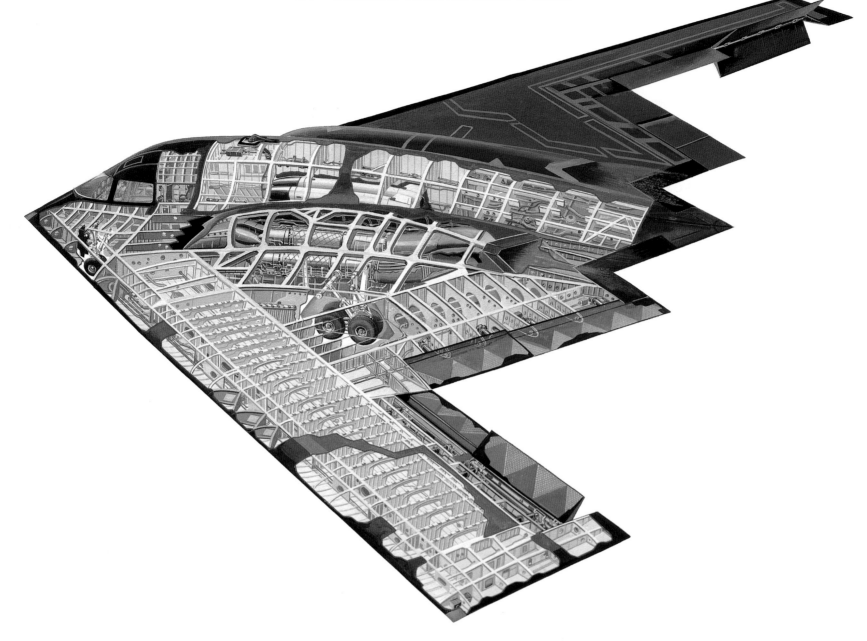

Northrop Grumman's B-2 Spirit strategic heavy bomber was designed, like the F-117, to reach and attack its target by "stealthy" means rather than through brute performance. As the bomber's clean shapings and other features reveal, however, the attainment of the required low-observability features was achieved by means different from those employed in the F-117 attack warplane.

ment for the reception and analysis of the enemy's electromagnetic signals, it relies on ECM equipment in self-powered pods located on external hardpoints. There is little doubt, however, that the increased survivability of combat aircraft carrying ECM pods more than offsets the reduction in their theoretical warloads. ECM pods are standard on the combat aircraft of all air forces with any claim to modernity of equipment.

Both the United States and, before its 1989 dissolution into the C.I.S., the U.S.S.R. introduced new combat aircraft over the last few years, as have the western European countries. The most important of these in the 1980s were the Fairchild Republic A-10 Thunderbolt II antitank airplane, General Dynamics F-16 Fighting Falcon air-combat and multirole fighter, Grumman F-14 Tomcat carrierborne multirole fighter with a variable-geometry wing platform, McDonnell Douglas F-15 Eagle air-superiority fighter, and McDonnell Douglas F/A-18 Hornet carrierborne dual-role fighter/attack airplane for the United States; the Mikoyan-Gurevich MiG-23 "Flogger" variable-geometry tactical fighter, MiG-27 "Flogger" attack fighter derivative of the MiG-23, Sukhoi Su-24 "Fencer" variable-geometry strike and attack airplane, and Su-25 "Frogfoot" close-support and antitank airplane for the Warsaw Pact forces; the Dassault Mirage F1 and Mirage 2000 multirole fighters for France; and the variable-geometry Panavia Tornado multirole combat airplane for Germany, Italy and the United Kingdom.

The United States and United Kingdom are collaborating on a supersonic STOL combat airplane. After the evaluation of the Boeing X-32 and Lockheed Martin X-35 prototypes, the United States selected the latter as the basis of the F-35 Joint Strike Fighter. This is to be produced initially in three basic forms as CTOL (Conventional Takeoff and Landing) and STOL (Short Takeoff and Landing) warplanes with a smaller wing, and a carrierborne type with a larger wing. The core of the X-35's unique capabilities is the lift fan buried in the airframe and shaft-driven by the Pratt & Whitney F119 turbofan engine. The only other contender in this major but wholly underestimated field was the U.S.S.R., where the pioneering

With its very clean basic airframe and light weight, the F-16 Fighting Falcon is given sparkling performance by its single turbofan engine. This latter can be either a General Electric F110 or Pratt & Whitney F100 unit. While the Fighting Falcon does not possess phenomenal speed capability, it is notably fast in terms of acceleration and climb rate.

Yakovlev Yak-38 "Forger" VTOL carrierborne attack airplane was to have been replaced by the supersonic Yak-141 "Freehand," whose development was canceled for a number of technical as well as economic problems.

The performance plateau reached with current military aircraft results from reliance on aluminum alloys as the primary structural medium, and this precludes sustained speeds in excess of Mach 2.25. Titanium alloy is used in special cases where heat is likely to be extreme, but the cost of creating and working this alloy prohibits its use on a

Lockheed Martin's X-35 demonstrator for the JSF (Joint Strike Fighter) competition beat Boeing's X-32 contender to be ordered as the F-35. Intended primarily for service with the U.S. Air Force in a conventional takeoff and landing version and by the U.S. Navy in a vertical takeoff and landing version (illustrated) with a lift fan behind the cockpit and a thrust-vectoring nozzle at the tail, the F-35 has attracted very considerable international interest and collaboration, and could become the heart of the single most important military airplane program of the first part of the twenty-first century.

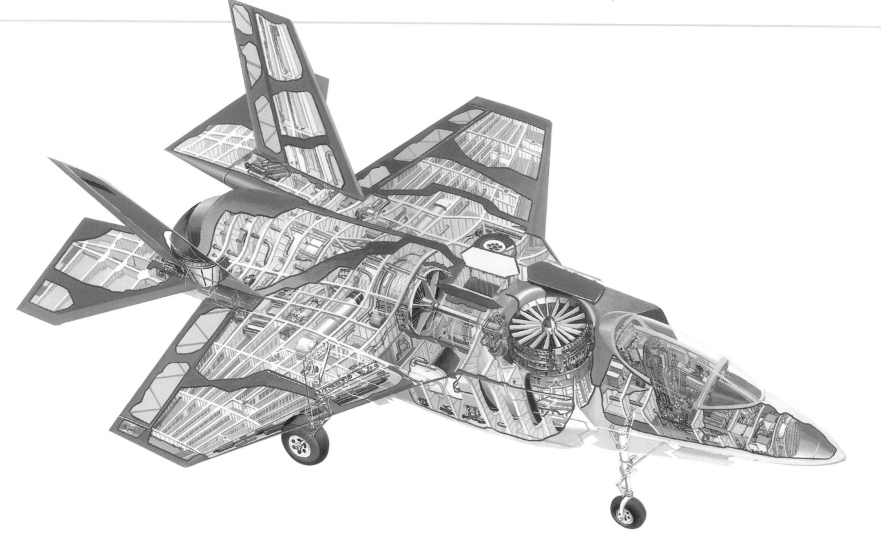

large scale. Composite materials of various kinds became commoner during the 1980s, but again their costs are high and their applications were at first limited and specialized. Later in the decade continued development of aeronautical materials made it practical to use composite materials on a larger scale for load-carrying structures, and advanced alloys of lithium and aluminum came to see more regular employment. The gradual acceptance of these high-technology materials did not indicate any desire for higher performance, however, but rather the desire to reduce weight without any sacrifice of strength and to simplify the production and maintenance of complex structures not readily buildable in conventional materials.

The C.I.S. is still actively involved in the development of advanced combat aircraft such as the Sukhoi Su-47 Berkut, but is troubled by financial difficulties and is not likely, at least in the short term, to reemerge as a realistic successor to the U.S.S.R. in terms of military power. Russia inherited the bulk of the U.S.S.R.'s military machine, with lesser portions going to the Ukraine and the other ex-Soviet republics that now constitute the Commonwealth of Independent States, and is hard pressed to maintain its current strength without investing heavily in advanced weapons for a future that is unlikely to see any real military threat to the C.I.S. or its components.

It was the threat seen in the ambitions of the U.S.S.R. that spurred the development of other modern weapons for the countries of the Western bloc. So far as aircraft are concerned, these range from light multirole tactical fighters such as the Italian-originated but now Italo-Brazilian AMX International AMX to advanced tactical combat aircraft such as the Dassault Rafale (squall) for the French air force and naval air arm, and the Eurofighter Typhoon for the British, German, Italian, and Spanish air forces. The AMX has entered service, and the Rafale and Typhoon are due to enter service at the beginning of the next century, although the reduced level of the threat for which they were designed has already seen the trimming back of certain of the programs' most advanced elements and a scaling down of both the urgency and planned numbers of the two types. It is worth noting that the Rafale and Typhoon, together with the Saab JAS 39 Gripen (griffon) already in service with the Swedish air force, are of the "modern" configuration with canard foreplanes and an aft-mounted delta wing controlled via a "fly-by-wire" system for extreme agility and the capability to fly at very high angles of attack. This last has been shown to offer superior combat capabilities and is a notable feature of the MiG-29 and Su-27. All three Western types are inherently "stealthy," have advanced powerplants offering a very high power/weight ratio in afterburner, and have electronics based on a

digital databus system for the maximum exploitation of active and passive sensors, advanced computers, and the very latest in disposable weapons. These are all features of the combat aircraft currently being delivered or under development for service in the next century.

Currently the most advanced single-role warplane under development for the U.S. Air Force is the F-22 Raptor, created by Lockheed Martin and Boeing as an air-supremacy fighter scheduled for service from 2005. This twin-turbofan fighter is notably "stealthy" as a result of its materials, shape, and internal weapons carriage, has very advanced electronics including a system to "fuse" the data from different sensors to give the pilot an extremely comprehensive picture of the situation around his airplane, and is capable of cruising at supersonic speed without the use of afterburning.

The upper speed and ceiling limits reached in the mid-1970s are likely to remain unchallenged for some time, for there appears to be no pressing need for significant improvements. Instead greater emphasis has been placed on increasing utility within the current performance limits, and thus in making the new generation of aircraft more cost-effective. Only in range is improvement both desirable and likely, and this applies both to military and to civil machines. The ultimate in range performance, it should be noted, was secured by neither a military nor a commercial airplane, but by an extraordinary record-breaker in the mold of the private-enterprise machines of the 1920s and 1930s. Designed by Burt Rutan and flown by Dick Rutan and Jeanna Yeager, the Rutan *Voyager* was powered by two piston engines and attained a nonstop distance of 24,986.67 miles (40,212.1 km) as it flew round the Earth in nine days on December 14–23, 1986.

Commercial aircraft are unlikely to change radically, although "fly-by-wire" control systems have become increasingly common and there will probably be a sharp increase in the numbers and perhaps the types of STOL "taxi" aircraft and medium-

FACING PAGE The rival to the F-16 in the U.S. Air Force's Air Combat Fighter competition was the twin-engined Northrop F-17, which was then developed by McDonnell with Northrop assistance as the F/A-18 Hornet carrierborne fighter and attack warplane, replacing both the McDonnell Douglas F-4 Phantom II fighter and the Vought A-7 Corsair II medium attack warplane. The original Hornet was produced in F/A-18A and F/A-18C single-seat and F/A-18B and F/A-18D combat-capable twin-seat forms, but these are being replaced by the F/A-18E single-seat (illustrated) and F/A-18F twin-seat variants of the enlarged, more powerfully engined and electronically more sophisticated Super Hornet with significantly enhanced operational capabilities.

capacity airliners intended for short-range routes. The real future of civil aircraft, how-ever, lies with improvements in operating economy through the development of structurally and aerodynamically advanced wings (based on airfoils of supercritical sec-tion and carrying tip-mounted winglets for more economical high-speed cruise capability), high-lift devices, and control surfaces used in conjunction with "fly-by-wire" control sys-tems and electronic flight-management systems. This will make it much easier to keep down the size of airports and enable aircraft to be operated with less power. This second factor is of growing importance from both the economic and the public relations points of

The Lockheed Martin/Boeing F-22 Raptor is the very advanced warplane which the U.S. Air Force has ordered as its air-dominance fighter of the foreseeable future, in succession to the McDonnell Douglas (now Boeing) F-15 Eagle.

view. People all around the world are increasingly disturbed by aircraft noise, especially during takeoff and landing at municipal airports. More efficient wings will enable lower power settings to be used, thus reducing noise. The airline operators will be further aided by the development of much quieter engines, which was well under way in the 1980s, and the aircraft will also have greater range, for lower power requirements give the added bonus of increased distance for a given quantity of fuel.

Supersonic commercial flight on a widespread basis is unlikely within the foreseeable future. A supersonic cruising regime would be especially useful for long routes, where the reduction in journey times can be considerable, but environmental objections currently make the development of new-generation SSTs highly unlikely. The United States is devoting considerable resources to the investigation of ways to reduce sonic "boom" for civil as well as military aircraft, and it is possible that the design and development of supersonic "bizjets" may start before 2010. Boeing is the manufacturer of commercial aircraft pushing hardest to increase the speed of commercial transports from the high subsonic into the genuinely transonic range with its Sonic Cruiser concept. On the other hand, Airbus has decided that payload rather than speed will be the decisive factor for the next generation of airliners, and has therefore pinned its future to the A380 maxi transport with about the same performance as the current generation of airliners, but provision for up to 800 passengers.

The type that the F-22 beat in the ATF (Advanced Tactical Fighter) competition for selection as the U.S. Air Force's air-dominance fighter was the Northrop/McDonnell Douglas F-23.

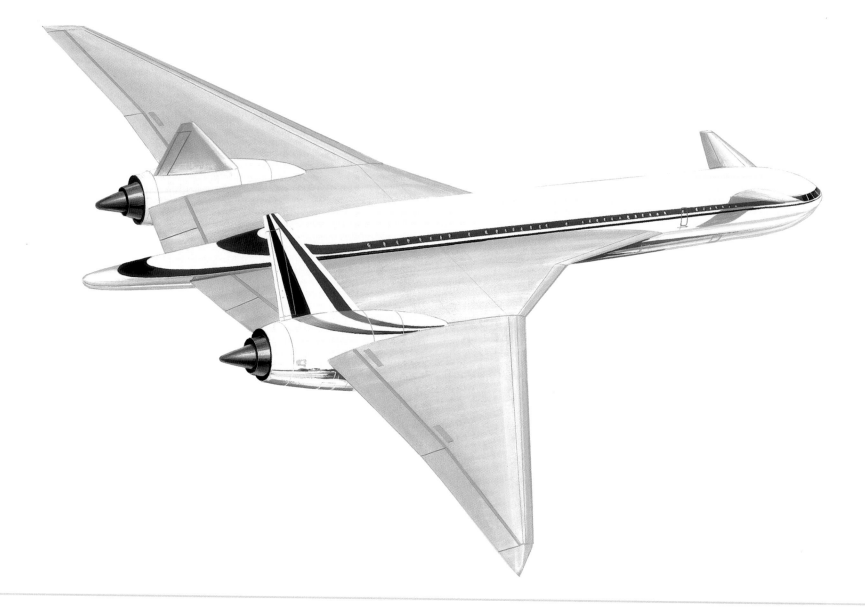

Part of Boeing's strategic thinking for its future in the commercial aircraft manufacturing market is based on its planned Sonic Cruiser, seen here in the form of design thinking in the first part of the twenty-first century. This twin-engined type is planned to cruise at a speed only marginally below Mach 1, and therefore somewhat higher than the current generation of airliners, and is based on an airframe with a rear-mounted wing and canard forward surfaces as well as a structure making very extensive use of advanced materials such as composites and/or advanced aluminum/lithium alloys.

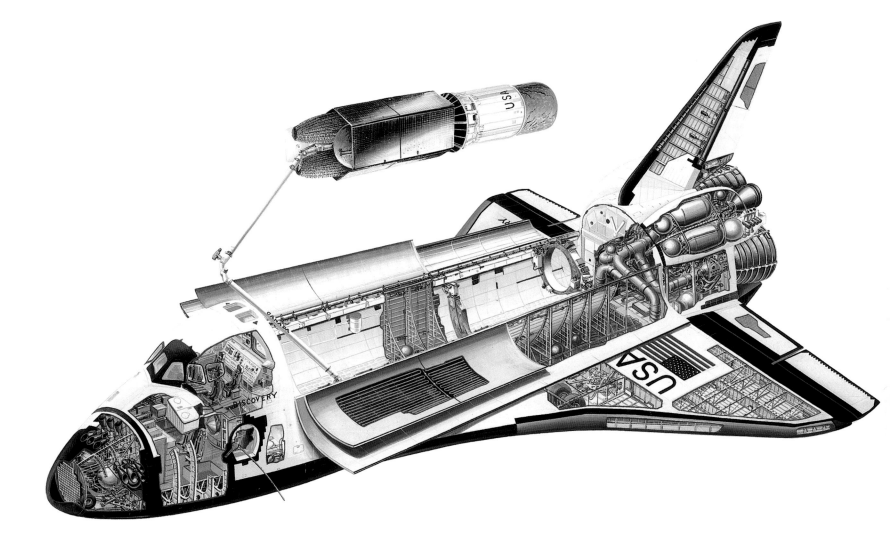

Designed and built by Rockwell before its absorption into Boeing, the "Space Shuttle Orbiter" is currently the world's most significant interface between the Earth and space. The Orbiter is launched on the power of its own immensely powerful rocket motors, drawing its liquid fuel and oxidant from a vast jettison-able tank, supplemented by two potent solid-rocket boosters that are also jettisoned after their fuel has been consumed.

THE FINAL FRONTIER

Aviation so far has been concerned almost exclusively with flight within the earth's atmosphere. The years to come, however, will see the first operations by aircraft designed to work equally well in space. The origin of such machines can be traced back to the Bell X-1 experimental airplane built by the Americans just after the end of World War II. Launched from a parent airplane and landing on a small landing-gear arrangement, the rocket-powered X-1 was the first airplane in the world officially to break through the "sound barrier," reaching 670 mph (1,078 km/h) at 42,000 ft (12,800 m) on October 14, 1947. At the height it was flying, the X-1 had touched Mach 1.015.

The X-series aircraft achieved successively higher speeds and altitudes until the North American X-15 reached the limits of "atmospheric" flight in the 1960s, touching 4,534 mph (7,297 km/h) or Mach 6.72 and climbing to an altitude of 350,000 ft (106,700 m) toward the end of the decade. While the X-1 had been dropped by a B-29 at 30,000 ft (9,145 m), the much larger and very considerably heavier X-15 had to be launched by a B-52 at an altitude of 35,000 ft (10,670 m) before igniting its rocket engine and climbing into the upper reaches of the atmosphere. Reaction "puffer jets" were installed at the tips of the wing, nose, and tail of these aircraft to provide control as conventional flying controls were useless in the incredibly rarefied air of these altitudes.

The aircraft of the X-series were used for research into very high speeds and very high altitudes but also helped considerably in the design of supersonic aircraft for military use. Still more important was their role in pioneering the equipment needed for space flight, such as vacuum seals, pressure suits, null-g devices, and heat-ablative shields. And they are the forerunners of machines that can operate both in space and in the air: The first of these Rockwell "Space Shuttle" air-spaceplanes came into service during 1981.

Launched on the power of its own three liquid-propellant rocket motors (fed during the initial burn period from a vast external tank) plus a pair of strap-on solid-propellant rocket boosters, the Shuttle has proved itself capable of lifting loads of significant weight and volume into space in its capacious hold, and then of returning for a conventional landing, refurbishment, and eventual relaunch for another mission. The use of the Shuttle has altered the economics of the space effort to a great extent, and opens up the very real possibility first of the construction of genuine space stations, and second of the further manned exploration of our solar system. Costs are still enormously high, and hopes of cooperation between West and East for the joint development of Shuttle technology foundered initially on the obdurate nationalist policies of the United States and the U.S.S.R. The U.S.S.R. developed its own reusable Shuttle vehicle in its dying days, but this was never launched into space. Since the demise of the U.S.S.R., the United States and Russia have started to collaborate more effectively in several areas of space research, including the permanently manned ISS (International Space Station), but the effort is bedeviled by both parties' lack of funding.

Even so, such air-spaceplanes form an effective bridge between air and space technologies, and as such point the way to the exploitation of space for industrial and medical purposes, leading eventually to the outward move of mankind toward the other planets of our solar system.

THE SPACE PROGRAM

With the beginning of the Soviet and American space programs, aviation in the broadest sense of the word began to extend its reach outside the shell of air that surrounds the Earth and reach out toward the Moon, the planets of our solar system, and ultimately the stars. Three of the key figures in the early stages of the American space program are seen here, and from left to right were Major Virgil Ivan Grissom, U.S. Air Force, Lieutenant Colonel John Herschell Glenn, Jr., U.S. Marine Corps, and Commander Alan Bartlett Shepard, Jr., U.S. Navy.

Key figures in the American space program's early days, as the sights of the world lifted from flight through the air to space orbits around the Earth, were "Gus" Grissom, John Glenn, and Alan Shepard (left to right).

"GUS" GRISSOM was born on April 3, 1926, in Mitchell, Indiana, and became the second American astronaut to travel in space before becoming the command pilot of the ill-fated Apollo 1 crew: Grisson and the other two members of this crew, Edward H. White and Roger B. Chaffee, became the first fatalities of the American space program on February 21, 1967, when a flash fire erupted in the capsule during a simulated launch of Apollo 1. Grissom had been commissioned into the U.S. Air Force during 1951, flew 100 missions in the Korean War, and was a test pilot and instructor up to 1959, when he became one of the first seven men selected in 1959 for astronaut training for Project Mercury. On July 21, 1961, Grissom became the third man to enter space, after Major Yuri Gagarin of the U.S.S.R. and Alan Shepard, and on March 23, 1965, the first man to return to space, in this instance as the command pilot in company with Lieutenant Commander John W. Young of the Gemini 3 mission that completed three Earth orbits.

GLENN was born on July 18, 1921, in Cambridge, Ohio, and in 1962 became the first American to orbit the Earth. Glenn had joined the U.S. Marine Corps in 1943 and flew 59 and 90 missions in World War II and the Korean War respectively before becoming a test pilot in 1954 and later securing selection as one of the seven Project Mercury astronaut trainees. Glenn was the reserve for Shepard and Grissom, who made the first two American suborbital space flights, and was then chosen for the Friendship 7 initial orbital (in fact three orbits) flight on February 20, 1962. Glenn retired in 1964 to enter the commercial world and politics, in 1974 becoming one of Ohio's two senators and serving four terms. In 1998 Glenn returned to space once more as a payload specialist aboard the STS-95 Space Shuttle mission, in the process becoming the oldest human to have entered space.

SHEPARD was born on November 18, 1923, in East Derry, New Hampshire, and is celebrated as the first American to enter space. Shepard graduated from the U.S. Naval Academy, Annapolis, Maryland, during 1944 and served in the Pacific in the closing stages of World War II. After the war Shepard became a naval test pilot and was one of the seven Project Mercury astronaut trainees. On May 5, 1961, Shepard achieved a 15-minute suborbital flight in the Freedom 7 spacecraft just 23 days after Gagarin had become the first man to orbit the Earth. Shepard commanded the Apollo 14 mission of 1971 with Stuart A. Roosa and Edgar D. Mitchell, and made the first landing in the Moon's highlands. Shepard led NASA's astronaut office between 1963 and 1969 and then between 1971 and 1974, when he retired to enter the world of business. Shepard died in Monterey, California, on July 21, 1998.

ILLUSTRATION ACKNOWLEDGMENTS AND CREDITS

The authors and the publisher would like to thank World of Wings, Inc. for assistance at every stage of this project, from conception to publication. They also wish to thank Caroline Sheen of the Smithsonian Institution for invaluable assistance in identifying and locating photographs for the book.

PROLOGUE

PAGE 3, The Jack Harris Collection

PAGE 4, National Air and Space Museum, © 2002 Smithsonian Institution (SI Neg. No. 95-8815)

PAGE 10, National Air and Space Museum, © 2002 Smithsonian Institution (SI Neg. No. A-30908-A)

PAGE 19, National Air and Space Museum, © 2002 Smithsonian Institution (SI Neg. No. A-31291-B)

PAGE 20, Wright Collection, Library of Congress

PAGE 22, National Air and Space Museum, © 2002 Smithsonian Institution (SI Neg. No. 85-10844)

PAGE 23, The Jack Harris Collection

CHAPTER 1

PAGE 25, National Air and Space Museum, © 2002 Smithsonian Institution (SI Neg. No. 89-1182)

PAGE 26, National Air and Space Museum, © 2002 Smithsonian Institution (SI Neg. No. A-30063)

PAGE 27, National Air and Space Museum, © 2002 Smithsonian Institution (SI Neg. No. A-18870)

PAGE 31, National Air and Space Museum, © 2002 Smithsonian Institution (SI Neg. No. 98-15048)

PAGE 35, National Air and Space Museum, © 2002 Smithsonian Institution (SI Neg. No. 87-6027)

PAGE 38, National Air and Space Museum, © 2002 Smithsonian Institution (SI Neg. No. 87-6027)

PAGE 39, National Air and Space Museum, © 2002 Smithsonian Institution (SI Neg. No. A-3426)

PAGE 40, National Air and Space Museum, © 2002 Smithsonian Institution (SI Neg. No. 85-18299)

PAGE 42, National Air and Space Museum, © 2002 Smithsonian Institution (SI Neg. No. 80-12296)

PAGE 46, National Air and Space Museum, © 2002 Smithsonian Institution (SI Neg. No. A-4401)

PAGE 47, National Air and Space Museum, © 2002 Smithsonian Institution (SI Neg. No. 95-2260)

PAGE 48, National Air and Space Museum, © 2002 Smithsonian Institution (SI Neg. No. 85-18299)

PAGE 53, National Air and Space Museum, © 2002 Smithsonian Institution (SI Neg. No. 89-21552)

PAGE 54, National Air and Space Museum, © 2002 Smithsonian Institution (SI Neg. No. A-3847OD)

PAGE 59, National Air and Space Museum, © 2002 Smithsonian Institution (SI Neg. No. A-1017)

PAGE 61, National Air and Space Museum, © 2002 Smithsonian Institution (SI Neg. No. 75-6157)

PAGE 62, The Jack Harris Collection

PAGE 63 (TOP), National Air and Space Museum, © 2002 Smithsonian Institution (SI Neg. No. 85-19411)

PAGE 63 (BOTTOM), The Jack Harris Collection

PAGE 65, The Jack Harris Collection

PAGE 71, National Air and Space Museum, © 2002 Smithsonian Institution (SI Neg. No. 73-6714)

PAGE 72, National Air and Space Museum, © 2002 Smithsonian Institution (SI Neg. No. A-3853)

PAGE 76, National Air and Space Museum, © 2002 Smithsonian Institution (SI Neg. No. A-47017B)

CHAPTER 2

OPENER RECTO, The Jack Harris Collection

PAGE 100, National Air and Space Museum, © 2002 Smithsonian Institution (SI Neg. No. 15-4801)

PAGE 101, National Air and Space Museum, © 2002 Smithsonian Institution (SI Neg. No. 96-15006)

PAGE 104, National Air and Space Museum, © 2002 Smithsonian Institution (SI Neg. No. 75-7024)

PAGE 106, National Air and Space Museum, © 2002 Smithsonian Institution (SI Neg. No. 76-6103)

PAGE 113, National Air and Space Museum, © 2002 Smithsonian Institution (SI Neg. No. 91-7033)

PAGE 123, National Air and Space Museum, © 2002 Smithsonian Institution (SI Neg. No. 95-2267)

PAGE 125, National Air and Space Museum, © 2002 Smithsonian Institution (SI Neg. No. 86-5015)

PAGE 127, National Air and Space Museum, © 2002 Smithsonian Institution (SI Neg. No. 75-14898)

PAGE 134, National Air and Space Museum, © 2002 Smithsonian Institution (SI Neg. No. 92-3118)

PAGE 135, National Air and Space Museum, © 2002 Smithsonian Institution (SI Neg. No. 86-13506)

PAGE 139, National Air and Space Museum, © 2002 Smithsonian Institution (SI Neg. No. 80-9016)

PAGE 142, National Air and Space Museum, © 2002 Smithsonian Institution (SI Neg. No. A45905C)

PAGE 147 (BOTTOM), National Air and Space Museum, © 2002 Smithsonian Institution (SI Neg. No. 80-19986)

CHAPTER 3

PAGE 151, United States Air Force; Lockheed Martin Corporation

PAGE 162, National Air and Space Museum, © 2002 Smithsonian Institution (SI Neg. No. 95-8815)

PAGE 164, The Lockheed Martin Corporation

PAGE 169, National Air and Space Museum, © 2002 Smithsonian Institution (SI Neg. No. 97-17489)

PAGE 180, National Air and Space Museum, © 2002 Smithsonian Institution (SI Neg. No. 86-11439)

PAGE 200, National Air and Space Museum, © 2002 Smithsonian Institution (SI Neg. No. 2001-1300)

PAGE 216 (BOTTOM), The National Archives

PAGE 223, The Lockheed Martin Corporation

PAGE 228 (BOTTOM), Photo by Eric Long/National Air and Space Museum, © 2002 Smithsonian Institution

CHAPTER 4

PAGE 207, United States Air Force

PAGE 231, Lockheed Martin Corporation

PAGE 242, National Air and Space Museum, © 2002 Smithsonian Institution (SI Neg. No. 34-605AC)

PAGE 251, National Air and Space Museum, © 2002 Smithsonian Institution (SI Neg. No. 98-15050)

PAGE 252, The National Archives

PAGE 260, The Boeing Company

PAGE 265, The Boeing Company

PAGE 266, National Air and Space Museum, © 2002 Smithsonian Institution (SI Neg. No. 87-13093)

CHAPTER 5

PAGE 281, National Air and Space Museum, © 2002 Smithsonian Institution (SI Neg. No. 90-13804)

PAGE 287, National Air and Space Museum, © 2002 Smithsonian Institution (SI Neg. No. A-1751)

PAGE 292, Sikorsky Aircraft Corp.

PAGE 294, United Technologies Archives

PAGE 299, AP/Wide World Photos

PAGE 303, United States Navy

PAGE 304, Vernon Pugh, United States Navy

PAGE 307, Westland Helicopter Limited

PAGE 308 (BOTTOM), National Air and Space Museum, © 2002 Smithsonian Institution (SI Neg. No. 85-089)

CHAPTER 6

PAGE 311, Photo by Eric Schulzinger, Lockheed Martin Corporation

PAGE 314, American Airlines C.R. Smith Museum

PAGE 323, The Boeing Company

PAGE 327, Lockheed Martin Corporation

PAGE 329, Photo by Eric Schulzinger, Lockheed Martin Corporation

PAGE 339 (TOP), The Boeing Company

PAGE 339 (BOTTOM), The Boeing Company

PAGE 346, Photo by Eric Long/National Air and Space Museum, © 2002 Smithsonian Institution

PAGE 348, Lockheed Martin Corporation

PAGE 353, © 2002 Russell Munson

PAGE 355, The Boeing Company

PAGE 359, NASA Dryden Research Center

PAGE 360 (TOP), United States Air Force

PAGE 360 (BOTTOM), Photo by Denny Lombard, Lockheed Martin Corporation

PAGE 365, A. Roels—Belgian Air Force

PAGE 368, Photo by Ron Bookout, The Boeing Company

PAGE 371, Lockheed Martin Corporation

PAGE 376, National Air and Space Museum, © 2002 Smithsonian Institution (SI Neg. No.7B-21347)

INDEX